C000000861

Sermons on the Sacraments (Wholesome and Catholic Doctrine Concerning the Seven Sacraments of Christ's Church). Repr. in Modern Spelling. With a Preface and Biogr. Notice by T.E. Bridgett
by Thomas Watson (Bp. of Lincoln.)

The arms of Bishop Watson, here impaled with those of Lincoln, seem to contain an allusion to our Lord's words: Be ye wise as serpents, and simple as doves (Matt. x. 16).

SERMONS

ON

THE SACRAMENTS.

BY THOMAS WATSON,

MASTER OF ST JOHN'S COLLEGE, CAMBRIDGE,
DEAN OF DURHAM, AND THE LAST CATHOLIC BISHOP OF LINCOLN.

First Printed in 1558, and now Reprinted in Modern Spelling.

WITH A PREFACE AND BIOGRAPHICAL NOTICE
OF THE AUTHOR

BY THE REV. T. E. BRIDGETT,

OF THE CONGREGATION OF THE MOST HOLY REDEEMER.

PERMISSU SUPERIORUM.

London:
BURNS AND OATES,
PORTMAN STREET AND PATERNOSTER ROW
1876.

PRINTED BY BALLANTYNE, HANSON AND CO.
EDINBURGH AND LONDON.

[Original Title Page.]

WHOLESOME AND CATHOLIC DOCTRINE

CONCERNING THE

SEVEN SACRAMENTS OF CHRIST'S CHURCH,

Expedient to be Known of all Men,

SET FORTH IN MANNER OF

𝔖𝔥𝔬𝔯𝔱 𝔖𝔢𝔯𝔪𝔬𝔫𝔰 𝔱𝔬 𝔟𝔢 𝔪𝔞𝔡𝔢 𝔱𝔬 𝔱𝔥𝔢 𝔓𝔢𝔬𝔭𝔩𝔢.

BY

THE REVEREND FATHER IN GOD,

T H O M A S   B I S H O P   O F   L I N C O L N.

Anno 1558, Mense Februarii.

[COLOPHON.]

Imprinted at London, by ROBERT CALY, within the
precinct of Christ's Hospital, The X of
February 1558.

PREFACE.

HERE is a volume of sermons, printed more than three centuries ago in black letter type and uncouth spelling, and the existence of which is only known to a few antiquarians. Why, it will be asked, have I reprinted it in modern guise and sought to rescue it from oblivion? I have done so for its own sake, and for the sake of its author. It is a book that deserves not to perish, and which would not have been forgotten, as it is, but for the misfortune of the time at which it appeared. It was printed in the last year of Queen Mary, and the change of religion under Elizabeth made it almost impossible to be procured, and perilous to be preserved.* The number of English Catholic books is not so great that we can afford to lose one so excellent as this.

But even had it less intrinsic value, it is the memorial of

---

* Mr Arber, in his Transcript of the Registers of the Stationers' Company (1875), has printed from MS. in the British Museum a letter of Bishop Grindal to Sir W. Cecil, relating a search that he had had made in the house of John Stow, the chronicler, for unlawful books. He is accused of being "a great fautor of Papistry" because, *inter alia*, this and another volume of Watson's Sermons were found in his possession. —Vol. i. p. 394.

a great man, little known indeed, because through the iniquity of the times he lacked a biographer. I am confident that any one who will read the following memoir, imperfect as it is, will acknowledge that I have not been indulging an antiquarian fancy, but merely paying, as far as I could, a debt of justice long due, in trying to revive the memory of the last Catholic Bishop of Lincoln.

I have mentioned in the " Life of Dr Watson " the occasion of his composing this volume of sermons, but I will here enter on some further explanations.

Printed sermons are of two sorts. They are either intended to preserve the memory of a discourse which the author has already made, or they are written that they may be preached by others. The sermons on the sacraments now republished belong to this latter class. Their place in Catholic literature will be better understood if I draw up a list of the sermons that had been previously published in England, after the invention of printing. It will not be very long.

The sermons by John Myrc, called the " Liber Festivalis," were printed by Caxton in 1483, and were frequently reprinted by Wynkyn de Worde, Pynson, and others.

Fisher, Bishop of Rochester, before Henry began his schism, had preached against the heresies of Luther, and funeral sermons at the death of Henry VII., and of the Lady Margaret, Countess of Richmond and mother of Henry VII. These sermons were printed by Wynkyn de Worde, and the first also by Berthelet.

Cuthbert Tunstal published the sermon which he preached in 1518, in praise of marriage, at the espousals of Mary, daughter of Henry VIII. with Francis I. (Pynson); and another when he was Bishop of Durham in 1539 (published by Berthelet).

John Longland, Bishop of Lincoln, published in 1531 three sermons preached at Westminster : one against Luther, one when the Legates a Latere began their visitation, and a third at the foundation of Westminster College. These were printed by Pynson. Petit in 1538 printed a fourth sermon preached by the same prelate at Greenwich.

Latimer's first printed sermon seems to have appeared in 1537, and in due time several others. The first book of Protestant Homilies was printed in 1547 by Grafton.

Other Protestant sermons by Hooper, Leaver, and Ponet, were printed in the reign of Edward VI. The only other Catholic sermons with which I am acquainted are :—

Three godly and notable sermons of the most honorable and blessed sacrament of the altar, by William Peryn, (printed in 1546 both by Hill and by Herforde).

Five Homilies by Leonard Pollard, Prebendary of Worcester, printed by Jugge in 1556. These were corrected and edited by Bonner. Bonner's Homilies, printed by Cawood in 1555. Sermons preached at S. Paul's Cross, by Brookes in 1554, by Hugh Glasier in 1555, by John Harpsfield in 1556. (Printed by Robert Caley.)

A Sermon by Feckenham, Abbot of Westminster, on the death of Joan, Queen of Spain, in 1555, and two Homilies by the same preacher on the first, second, and third Articles of the Creed (Caley).

Sermons by Roger Edgeworth, Canon of Salisbury,

printed in 1557. These are on the seven gifts of the Holy Ghost, on the articles of Christian faith, on ceremonies, and of man's law, and an exposition of the first Epistle of S. Peter (printed by Caley).

Lastly, Two Sermons on the Real Presence, by Dr Watson, preached before Queen Mary in 1554.

It will be seen from this list how very scanty was the help afforded to a priest, at the beginning of Mary's reign, anxious to announce the Word of God to his people. He had neither discourses prepared for his use, nor models to direct him in composing. Most of the sermons of the above list were too ambitious for his flights, they were preached by great dignitaries of the Church on solemn occasions. Old John Myrc's "Liber Festivalis" was out of date. Not only was its English antiquated, but it was unsuited to a people whose minds were agitated by theological discussions, and prejudiced by the sarcasms and invectives of the Reformers.

On the other hand, the Catholic clergy were not yet well prepared for instructing and exhorting the people by their own efforts and from their own stock of learning. More than twenty years had passed since the schism. Theological studies had been thrown into utter confusion in the universities. The controversies that raged, while they tended to produce a few great champions of the Faith, such as Watson, only perplexed ordinary minds, or disgusted them, and turned them from the study of truth. Many priests simply floated with the stream, and were carried round in its eddies at the bidding of men in power. When Cardinal Pole, therefore, assembled a Council to remedy all these evils, its attention was at once directed to the subject of preaching, and the instruction of the people. Among other measures taken, one was that homilies should be prepared, to be used by rectors or vicars unable to compose instructions themselves.* The " Institution of a Christian Man," which had been composed in the time of Henry VIII., was brought up for examination. It was divided into three parts, and some of the Lower House of Convocation were chosen to make homilies from it. This was in December 1555. They also ordered a translation of the New Testament to be prepared, and a treatise on the seven sacraments.

The Council was prorogued from time to time, and never reassembled. But in the Convocation of January–March, 1558, the subject was again treated.† It was ordered that four books of sermons should be made :—

1st. On the eucharist, on penance, confession, and the other sacraments ; on free will, justification and good works ; on the Church, and its authority, unity, and ministers.

2d. On the articles of the faith, the Lord's Prayer, angelic salutation, decalogue and sacraments.

3d. Sermons for the Sundays of the year and for saints' days.

---

* Ubi defuerint concionandi periti rectores aut vicarii, homilias ex hujus synodi mandato conscriptas, dominicis et aliis festis diebus legere tenebuntur.—"Wilkins' Concilia," vol. iv. p. 123.

The decrees of the Synod are also given in English in Phillips' Life of Cardinal Pole, vol. ii. p. 126-128.

† Wilkins, vol. iv. p. 156.

4th. On ceremonies; on virtues and vices, and on the last judgment.

The death of Mary prevented the full carrying out of these measures. Yet something was done. Bonner's Book of Homilies was published. But as no one was more capable of supplying the want, so no one more zealously undertook to do so than Dr Watson. Hence the present manual of Catholic Doctrine on the Sacraments.

Being intended for general preaching, or rather, public reading, these sermons are, of course, unimpassioned and colourless. We cannot judge from them of Bishop Watson's own style of preaching. We cannot gather from them, as from the sermons of Latimer and Leaver, pictures of the manners and passions of the times. They scarcely even reflect Watson's personal character, except by the very absence of invective, and the simple dignity which distinguishes them. As specimens of old English before the great Elizabethan era they will be interesting to students of our language, especially as being the work of one of the best classical scholars of the day.

With regard to their doctrine it must be remembered that they were published before the conclusion of the Council of Trent. The 7th Session of that Council, held in 1547, had passed decrees on the Sacraments in general, on Baptism, and on Confirmation. Decrees on the Holy Eucharist had been made in the 13th Session in 1551, but those on the Holy Sacrifice of the Mass were not drawn up until after these sermons had been published, viz., in 1562, in the 22d Session. In the 14th Session, held in 1551, the Catholic doctrine on Penance and Extreme Unction was defined; but the labours of the Council had been suspended in 1552, and were not renewed until 1562, when Watson was in the Tower. Although the Bull of Confirmation was not published until the conclusion of the Council, yet the decrees of each session had received the approval of the Sovereign Pontiff through his legates, and were promulgated at once to the world,* and became the guide of Provincial Synods, as well as of theologians. In all his sermons, therefore, except those on the Mass, on Order, and on Marriage, Watson had before him the luminous teaching of this great Council. He, however, only once quotes or alludes to it, doubtless because it was not then terminated, nor its decrees solemnly confirmed.

His sermons are eminently patristic. I have counted more than four hundred marginal references to the Fathers and ecclesiastical writers; and I may say that they are in great measure woven out of Scripture and the Fathers. I have not reprinted these references, because those who would wish to study the Fathers can use the indications given in the Roman Catechism, or in the popular manuals of theology.

---

* Though I do not find this stated explicitly, it is quite certain from many things mentioned by Pallavicino. See, *e.g.* Istoria del Concilio di Trento, Lib. vi. cap. 7 n. 6; Lib. viii. cap. 16 n. 4, and n. 13; Lib. ix. cap. 12 n. 5. Above all, Lib. x. cap. 9, n. 2, where the legate declares that the decrees already made have been received in all countries and are irrevocable, though in another place (Lib. xi. cap. 1, n. 3) he desires for them the confirmation of the Pope. Provincial Councils conformed their language to these decrees, Lib. xi. cap. 4, n. 5.

I have exactly reproduced the original, with the exception of the spelling. No educated reader will find much difficulty in the old idiom. The sentences, indeed, are rather long, like those of a legal document, yet they are simple in construction, and when read aloud, they can be broken up by a skilful reader without the addition of a word.

I have compared the scriptural quotations with the versions of Tindal and others, and find no resemblance whatever. Watson has made his own translation.

I have added a few short theological notes only, for the doctrine throughout these sermons is both clearly stated and perfectly Catholic. As they certainly embody the traditional teaching of the English Church before the Council of Trent, they are an additional proof that Catholics of the present day are faithful to the inheritance of their forefathers.

The volume of which the present is a reprint is a small quarto, printed in Gothic or black letter. There are two or three editions according to Herbert.* One is dated the 7th June 1558, another the 10th of February 1558. As this represents February 1559, according to the new style, it is a later edition than the other; and this I have used, though there is no variation between the editions, except in an error of pagination, and the placing of the table of contents; and the "compartment" or architectural framework surrounding the title.

The printer was Robert Caley, "the chief Roman Catholic

* See "Typographical Antiquities," edited by Dibdin after Ames and Herbert. Herbert's note, vol. iv. pp. 463, 464.

theological printer in Queen Mary's reign," according to Mr Arber. The colophon of the book tells us that it was "imprinted within the precinct of Christ's Hospital." Robert and Henry Caley had a patent for printing this book for seven years, dated 30th April the 4th–5th of Philip and Mary. It seems to have been eagerly bought up, as two or three editions were exhausted in the few months during which it could be sold. Five months after its publication Mary died, and before it had been published a year its author had been cast into prison and deprived of his bishopric ; and the establishment of Protestantism not only prevented its further sale, but caused the destruction of most of the copies already sold. It has, therefore, become very scarce. Let me express a hope that if this attempt to revive an almost forgotten book should not be unsuccessful, some one may reproduce the homilies of Bonner or of Edgeworth, or some of the numerous Catholic sermons printed during the reign of James II.

T. E. BRIDGETT.

BISHOP ETON,
LIVERPOOL.

CONTENTS.

———◆———

b

BIOGRAPHICAL NOTICE

OF

THOMAS WATSON, BISHOP OF LINCOLN.

———◆———

CHAPTER I.—IN THE REIGN OF HENRY VIII.

IT was the misfortune of Thomas Watson, the subject of this biographical notice, to have lived in the reigns of Henry VIII., Edward, Mary, and Elizabeth. It was his happiness to have learnt wisdom by experience, and to have expiated by his long sufferings for the Catholic faith, the schism, if not heresy, of his early years.

There exists of him no contemporary biography,* and we can only glean the facts of his life from incidental notices in the documents of the time, and can do little more than conjecture his character from the part he played in its varied drama. Yet his heroic constancy during a quarter of a century of imprisonments, and his having been the last of the old Catholic hierarchy who died in England, entitle him to our love and reverence, and make us regret the scantiness of our information.

The precise date of his birth is not known. In the records of the trial of Gardiner, which took place in June 1550, and in

---

* Dodd has only a few lines. Pitts has a page or two of little value. Godwin, Burnet, Strype, and the rest have scanty notices, and those often incorrect. Baker has given the principal facts of his life in his " History of the College of St John the Evangelist, Cambridge," Part I. pp. 137–40 (ed. Mayor, 1869), and Cooper has added a few more details, and given a copious list of references, in his " Athenæ Cantabrigienses." These I have consulted, as well as other contemporary works. A patient search made among the State papers by a friend has enabled me to add other particulars, and to correct some unimportant errors into which Cooper had fallen.

which Watson appeared as a witness, he is stated in one place to be then " of the age of 33 or thereabouts," and in another to be " 34 or 35 years old."[*] We may therefore conclude that he was born about the year 1516. He was of the diocese of Durham, and is said to belong to the family of the Barons of Rockingham. Nothing is known of his early life ; but as he took his degree of B.A. at Cambridge in the year 1533–34, at the age of 17, he must have been sent at an early age to that university.

The College of St John the Evangelist, in which he studied, and of which he was elected a fellow immediately after taking his degree, though but recently founded, then and for some years after was famous for the group of scholars it contained, and for the lead it took in the revival of letters.

Its foundress was the famous Lady Margaret, Countess of Richmond and Derby,[†] and mother of Henry VII. ; but as she died before her pious intentions were realised, the college really owes its existence to the zeal and labours of her confessor, John Fisher, Bishop of Rochester, afterwards Cardinal and martyr.

The college had been opened in 1516, and in a decree of Archbishop Warham for its further endowment in 1519 it is said that he gladly co-operates in the work, " considering what great advantages, both private and public, both spiritual and temporal, daily accrue to the Christian faith from the study of letters. For by means of them the salvation of souls is promoted, rising controversies are settled, peace and tranquillity procured," &c.

At that very moment, however, a controversy was arising in Germany, from the teaching of Luther, which was to frustrate the pious hopes of Warham, of Fisher, and the Lady Margaret, by unsettling the minds of those whom their liberality was educating. Before half a century had passed from its foundation the College of St John's was so entirely transformed, that the doctrine of the Supremacy of the Holy See, for which Fisher laid down his life, was forbidden to be taught within its walls,

---

[*] Foxe, Acts and Monuments, vol. vi. pp. 151, 205 (ed. Catley).
[†] See Cooper's Memoir of Lady Margaret, edited by Mr Mayor (1874). Both as a Catholic and as an alumnus of St John's College, I would express my gratitude to the author and the editor for the noble monument which their patient research has erected to this holy lady.

and the Holy Sacrifice, which Lady Margaret loved more than life, was banished from its desecrated chapel, and impiously repudiated by all its members. The life of Watson will show that in his case, at least, the labours of the founders were not in vain.

When Watson entered St John's, and for the first three years of his residence as a fellow, the college was governed by Dr Nicholas Metcalf, who had been chaplain to Fisher, and was master from 1518 to 1537.

His character has been thus sketched by Roger Ascham, the tutor of the Princess Elizabeth, and a contemporary of Watson's :—

"Dr Nicholas Metcalf, that honourable father," he writes, "was Master of St John's College when I came thither—a father to every one in the college. There was none so poor, if he had either will to goodness, or wit to learning, that could lack, being there, or should depart from thence for any need. I am certain myself that money many times was brought into young men's rooms by strangers that they knew not. In which doing this worthy Nicholas followed the steps of good old St Nicholas, that learned Bishop. He was a Papist, indeed ; but would to God, among all us Protestants, I might once see but one that would win like praise, in doing like good, for the advancement of learning and virtue. And yet, though he were a Papist, if any young man, given to new learning (as they termed it) went beyond his fellows in wit, labour, and towardness, even the same neither lacked open praise to encourage him, nor private exhibition to maintain him, as worthy Sir J. Cheke, if he were alive, would bear good witness, and so can many more." *

Watson was one of those who profited most by the care of this worthy man. He had good talents and a great love of study, so that with the helps he found in his college he became eminent as a classical scholar.

The reader need scarcely be reminded of the struggle that was then going on in England between the old scholastic form of learning and the zeal for polite literature, which we call the Renaissance. Fisher was both a good scholar and an ardent promoter of classical studies, and his influence had drawn many young men of talent to the new foundation.

* Ascham's Works, p. 315.

Sir John Cheke, the famous Greek lecturer, was elected fellow of St John's in 1529, about the time Watson came into
residence, and the youth had the advantage of his public lectures and private instructions.   Among his contemporaries and
fellow-collegians I may mention the names of Roger Ascham,
George Day, afterwards Bishop of Chichester; John Christopherson, afterwards Master of Trinity and Bishop of Chichester ; William Bill, who died in 1560 holding the threefold
dignities of Master of Trinity, Provost of Eton, and Dean of
Westminster ; William Cecil, afterwards the famous Lord
Burghley ; James Pilkinton, afterwards Bishop of Durham ;
Robert Horne, afterwards Bishop of Winchester ; John Seton,
the logician ; Walter Haddon, and Dr Redman, two great
revivers of classical learning.

Roger Ascham writes—

" At Cambridge, in St John's College, in my time, I do
know that, not so much the good statutes, as two gentlemen of
worthy memory, Sir John Cheke and Dr Redman, by their only
example of excellency in learning, of godliness in living, of
diligence in studying, of counsel in exhorting, by good order in
all things, did breed up so many learned men in that one College of St John's, at one time, as I believe the whole University
of Louvain in many years was never able to afford."

In another place he makes honourable mention of Watson—

" Cambridge," he says, " at my first coming thither, but not at
my going away, committed this fault, in reading the precepts
of Aristotle without the example of other authors.   But herein,
in my time, these men of worthy memory, Mr Redman, Mr
Cheke, Mr Smith, Mr Haddon, Mr Watson, put so to their
helping hands, as that university, and all students there, as
long as learning shall last, shall be bound unto them, if that
trade in study be truly followed which those men left behind
them there." *

When Ascham wrote this, in the time of Queen Elizabeth,
Watson was in prison for his faith, and it does the author of
" The Schoolmaster" no little credit that he was not afraid to
declare his esteem and friendship for one now in disgrace, and
who differed from him in religion.   This is not the only passage
in which he is mentioned ; and as we have too little knowledge

* Ascham's Works, p. 314.

of the private and personal life of Watson, I am glad to transcribe the few traits recorded by his fellow-student. Ascham
and Watson were about the same age; both took their degrees
in arts, and were elected fellows of their college at the same
time, and remained together in residence for several years. A
great friendship seems to have sprung up between the young
men, from similarity in literary tastes,* though they were
already taking different courses in matters of religion.

"When Mr Watson," says Ascham, "in St John's College
wrote his excellent tragedy of 'Absolon' Mr Cheke, he, and I
had many pleasant talks together in comparing the precepts of
Aristotle and Horace with the examples of Euripides, Sopho-
cles, and Seneca. Few men in writing of tragedies in our
days have shot at this mark here in England ; more in France,
Germany, and Italy also have written tragedies in our time, of
which not one, I am sure, is able to abide the true touch of
Aristotle's precepts and Euripides' example, save only two,
that ever I saw, Mr Watson's 'Absolon' and Georgius Buch-
anan's 'Jephte.'"†

Ascham also tells us that Watson was so great a purist in
Latin that he would never allow this tragedy to be published,
because he himself considered that there was in one or two
lines some licence in the metre which the best models did not
sanction.

From another passage it appears that the young classics
would have set themselves to mould English verse after the
pattern of Greek and Roman metres, "avoiding barbarous
rhyming," and attending to "quantity" in the syllables. He
gives as a specimen two English hexameter verses of Watson's.‡

But if Watson's university career was happy and brilliant in
a literary point of view, it was far otherwise as regards religion.
While he was still an undergraduate those momentous changes
began which have severed England from Catholic Christendom.

* Ascham writes—"One of the best scholars that ever St John's
College bred, Mr Watson, mine old friend, sometime Bishop of Lincoln."
† Ibid. p. 320.
‡ Mr Cole, in his MS. Notes to Baker (in the British Museum),
wonders at Ascham's praise of such "doggrel." He evidently did not
notice that the lines were hexameters, though even as such they are
only interesting as very early (the earliest?) attempts in that metre.
Among Watson's writings Mr Cooper mentions a translation into
English verse of part of the first book of Homer's Odyssey, now lost.

The minds of several of his fellow-students were infected with the new heresies. The university was agitated by disputes about the divorce between Henry and Katharine, and the marriage with Anne Boleyn. Cranmer had become Archbishop of Canterbury (consecrated 30th March 1533), and men were awaiting an open rupture with the Holy See. In 1534 the schism was consummated, the authority of the Sovereign Pontiff abolished by Act of Parliament, and the royal supremacy substituted. In June 1535, Cardinal Fisher, the venerable founder of St John's,* whom Watson had probably often seen, and whose blessing he may have often received, laid down his life rather than acknowledge that supremacy, and after a few days his example was followed by Sir Thomas More. Surely a thrill of horror must have gone through the hearts of the fellows and students of his college when they heard that the body of the saintly bishop, stripped naked, had been left to lie all day in the gaze of the people on Tower Hill. Yet when the oath of supremacy was exacted from them, terror prevailed and none refused.

To the shame of the university it must be said that in May 1534, a public document had been obtained by the court, signed by the Vice-Chancellor and a great number of the doctors and masters, in which they deny that the Roman Pontiff has by Scripture any greater power or authority in England than any other foreign bishop.† What made this more shameful was the fact that their Chancellor, Fisher, was at that very time in the Tower for his rejection of this heresy. They knew well that their decision was utterly false, and extorted from them by fear. Even if they had forgotten the teaching of all Catholic doctors, they were not ignorant that, only a few years before, the king, in his book against Luther, had proved that (to use his own words) "since the conversion of the world all Churches have been obedient to the See of Rome," and that, "by the unanimous consent of all nations, it is forbidden to change or move the things that have been for a long time immovable;" and that he had declared that Luther was "void of all charity, not only by perishing himself through fury, but much more by endeavouring to draw all others with him into destruction, by

---

* Though he would never allow this title, there is no doubt that it rightfully belongs to him after the Lady Margaret.
† Cooper, Annals of Cambridge, vol. i. p. 367.

striving to dissuade them from their true obedience to the chief bishop."

On the 3d June this same year, 1534, all the scholars of the university took the oath of succession,* which for the clergy included that of the king's supremacy, in St Mary's Church. Cromwell succeeded as Chancellor of the University in the place of Fisher, and in October 1535, made a visitation.

Among his injunctions were the following :—

1. By a writing sealed by the university they were to swear " to obey all statutes made, or to be made, for the extirpation of Papal usurpation."

2. No more lectures were to be read upon any doctors who had commented the " Master of the Sentences," nor after the manner of Scotus.

3. No more lectures were to be given in canon law, nor degrees in canon law to be conferred. †

Contemporary histories tell us how, after this visitation, the scholastics were cast aside, and Scotus especially condemned to the most ignominious uses. ‡

Watson would not thank me were I to try to excuse him for the part he must have taken in these and other schismatical acts. Still it may be remembered that he was but a boy at this period, and that his studies in theology had not begun, and that by these very injunctions he was cut off from the streams of Catholic tradition in his future studies.

Stapleton, a most learned theologian, has made an apology even for men who were older and more learned in ecclesiastical matters than Watson then was. Writing in 1567, he said—

" This matter of the Pope's supremacy and of the Prince's was at the first, even to very learned men, a strange matter, but is now to meanly learned a well-known and beaten matter. Sir Thomas More—whose incomparable virtue and learning all the Christian world hath in high estimation, and who for this quarrel suffered death, for the preservation of the unity of Christ's Church, which was never, nor shall be, preserved but

---

* Cooper, Annals of Cambridge, vol. i. p. 368.

† Ibid. p. 375.

‡ The word dunce is derived from Duns Scotus, but whether it was given to stupid boys out of contempt for the Subtle Doctor, or ironically, I cannot say.

under this one head—as good a man, and as great a clerk, and as blessed a martyr as he was, albeit he ever well thought of this primacy, and that it was at the leastwise instituted by the corps of Christendom for great urgent causes for avoiding of schisms ; yet that this primacy was immediately institute of God (which thing all Catholics now do believe) he did not many years believe. It is the less marvel, therefore, if at the first, for lack of mature and deep consideration, many good and well-learned men otherwise were carried away with the volume of this storm and tempest." *

Whatever may be the value of this apology for bishops and priests, it seems certainly applicable to young men like Watson, who followed the example of priests and bishops.

In the Parliament which assembled 8th June 1536, an Act was passed "for extinguishing the authority of the Bishop of Rome." It required every person, promoted to any degree of learning in any university, to make oath that he from henceforth shall utterly renounce, refuse, relinquish, or forsake the Bishop of Rome, . . . and shall accept, report, and take the King's Majesty to be the only supreme head on earth of the Church of England; . . . and in case any oath hath been made by him to any person in maintenance, defence, or favour of the Bishop of Rome, he reports the same as vain and annihilate. So help him God, all saints, and the holy Evangelists."

This oath must have been taken by Watson when he received his Master's degree, even if he had not taken it before. If, however, he lived in a state of schism for nearly twenty years (*i.e.*, from 1533 to 1553), he expiated his error by more than twenty years' imprisonment in behalf of the supremacy of the Pope and the unity of the Church. But I am anticipating, and must go back to his earlier years.

In due time he must have taken holy orders. He commenced M.A. in 1537, and was for several years Dean of the College and one of its preachers. Dr Metcalf had resigned his mastership in July 1537, and was succeeded by Dr George Day, who governed the college for a year. Both these were staunch Catholics in the rest of their doctrine, however they may have yielded with regard to the supremacy. When Day was elected Provost of King's College in June 1538, he was replaced in

---

* Stapleton's Counterblast to Mr Horn's Blast, pp. 37, 38.

St John's by Dr John Taylor. The career of this man was very singular, and characteristic of the times. Soon after his election to the mastership he had preached a sermon in London in defence of Transubstantiation. This sermon aroused the zeal of a priest and schoolmaster named Lambert, a disciple of Tyndal's, and he presented Taylor with a paper of reasons against his doctrine. For this paper Lambert was tried for heresy, first by Cranmer, and then on appeal by Henry in person, and condemned to the stake. Taylor, who by making known the paper, was one of the causes of Lambert's death, was so touched by his fate or moved by his arguments, that he became a convert to the opinions against which he had preached, and was imprisoned for a short time on suspicion of heresy in 1540. But he seems to have retracted, for he was soon restored to his college. He was, however, involved in continual disputes with the fellows, so that the Bishop of Ely had to interfere in 1543, and the disputes still continuing, he resigned in 1546. In Edward's reign he openly professed heresy, and defended the marriage of the clergy, and was one of the compilers of the Common Prayer-Book. He was rewarded in 1552 with the Bishopric of Lincoln, of which he was deprived in March 1554, and died in the following December.

Watson was one of the appellants to the Bishop of Ely against Taylor's government, but it is not necessary to investigate the nature or the merits of these quarrels, which seem to have regarded the government of the college rather than serious questions of religion.

It was complained in the reign of Edward * that the university had greatly fallen off in numbers and in learning ; and it is admitted that the continual changes in religion both alienated men from theological studies, and deterred many from an ecclesiastical career. On the band of talented young men at St John's the effect seems to have been to make them give themselves almost exclusively to classical studies. In these they met on a neutral ground, and by this means kept up a literary friendship. But it was impossible at that time to avoid taking a side, or engaging in theological disputes, and these seem at last to have made Watson glad to leave the university.

Dr Lingard has truly described the miserable state of things

---

* Latimer's Sermon, April 6, 1549. Leaver's Sermon, December 1550.

from the time of the schism to the end of the reign of Henry—

"The creed of the Church of England depended on the theological caprice of its supreme head. The clergy were divided into two opposite factions, denominated the men of the old and the new learning. The chief of the former was Gardiner, Bishop of Winchester. . . . The latter acknowledged for their leaders Cranmer, Shaxton, Latimer, and Fox. . . . But none of the prelates on either side aspired to the palm of martyrdom. . . . If, on the one hand, Gardiner and his associates, to avoid the royal displeasure, consented to renounce the Papal supremacy, and to subscribe to every successive innovation in the established creed; Cranmer and his friends, on the other, submitted with equal weakness to teach doctrines which they disapproved, to practise a worship which they deemed idolatrous or superstitious, and to consign men to the stake for the open profession of tenets which, there is reason to suspect, they themselves inwardly believed. Henry's infallibility continually oscillated between the two parties." *

The fellows of St John's College were divided in sentiment like the prelates. That Watson openly defended the "old learning," that is the Catholic faith, especially on the sacraments, is certain; for at the accession of Edward he was looked to as one of the champions of that faith against the novelties of Calvin and Zuinglius. But the greater number seem to have taken the other side.

Cheke was disposed to heresy, and by his fame and position as lecturer had much influence on the younger members of the college. Ascham relates how he himself nearly got into trouble by his audacity, and might have lost his fellowship but for the support of Dr Metcalf. Cecil was there from 1535 to 1541, and, while diligently studying Greek and Latin under Sir John Cheke and Sir Thomas Smith, imbibed that spirit of heresy and hypocrisy which made him in later years so great a persecutor of Catholics, and especially of Watson. John Taylor, William Bill, John Redman, Walter Haddon, James Pilkinton, Robert Horne, Thomas Leaver, who were fellows of St John's during Watson's residence, were all infected with heresy, as their subsequent career proves. On the other hand,

---

* History of England, vol. v. ch. ii. p. 100 (ed. 1849).

George Day, who was master in 1537, and became Bishop of Chichester, courageously resisted the innovations under Edward, and suffered deprivation of his bishopric and imprisonment. John Seton, who was some years older than Watson, seems to have been closely united to him in friendship while they resided as fellows, and, subsequently, when they were both chaplains to Bishop Gardiner ; and Seton suffered exile rather than acknowledge the supremacy of Elizabeth.

Another of Watson's friends was Alban Langdale, well known both as a scholar and a theologian, who in Mary's time became Archdeacon of Chichester, and for refusing the oath of supremacy was imprisoned under Elizabeth, and died in exile.

Another fellow of St John's, of about Watson's standing, was John Young, who took the Catholic part in several discussions in Edward's reign, and in that of Mary became Master of Pembroke, Vice-Chancellor of the University, and Regius Professor of Divinity. With Watson he suffered twenty-four years' imprisonment under Elizabeth, and died in Wisbech Castle in 1580 or 1581, probably assisted by Watson in his last moments.

In the year 1540, after the execution of Cromwell, Stephen Gardiner, Bishop of Winchester, was made Chancellor of the University of Cambridge, and became acquainted with the talents of Watson, and in 1545 appointed him his domestic chaplain, at the same time conferring on him the rectory of Wyke Regis, in Dorsetshire. By the erection of the see of Bristol in 1542, Dorsetshire had been taken from the diocese of Salisbury and transferred to the new see, so that Watson was under the jurisdiction of Paul Bush, its first bishop. "The church of Wyke Regis," wrote Mr Hutchins * in 1779, "is a large structure, very ancient, and one of the best in these parts. It is the mother-church of Weymouth." Indeed, Weymouth at that time had only a small chapel-of-ease, dedicated to St Nicholas. The patron was the Bishop of Winchester ; and Watson succeeded to William Meadow, who was also domestic chaplain to Gardiner. Watson certainly held a second benefice in 1550, as appears from the records of Gardiner's trial,† but what it was is not mentioned. He is said

* History of Dorsetshire, vol. i. p. 602.   † Ibid. p. 408.

to have been presented to the vicarage of Buckminster, in Leicestershire, in the diocese of Lincoln, in 1547. He does not seem to have resided in either of these places, at least not before 1550 ; and I have not been able to discover any particular which will help to make him known to us as a parish priest.

From several circumstances it is clear that Gardiner had a great esteem for the learning and judgment of his chaplain. He employed him to negotiate with the Lords of the Council about the famous sermon which he was required by them to preach in the beginning of Edward's reign ; he took his advice as to the matter of the sermon itself, and Watson is said to have greatly assisted Gardiner in the composition of his answer to Cranmer, called " Confutatio Cavillationum." A few words about Gardiner and his troubles will be necessary in order to understand the movements of Watson in Edward's reign, though a full account would belong more properly to a biography of Gardiner than of Watson.

CHAPTER II.—IN THE REIGN OF EDWARD VI.

THE Protestant party who gathered round the deathbed of Henry both hated and feared Gardiner, and at once began a series of vexations and persecutions which ended in his imprisonment in the Tower for more than five years. The first pretext found against him was that he had written some warm letters to the Lord Protector Somerset, and to the Archbishop Cranmer, against the introduction of changes during Edward's minority. In consequence, he was summoned before the Council, and required to promise obedience to the royal injunctions which had just been issued. He replied that should he commit any legal offence he would submit to punishment. But as the object of Cranmer and his party was to keep him out of parliament during the ensuing session, he was committed to the Fleet prison without crime or trial.

Watson had accompanied the Bishop to London, to the Council Chamber, and to the Fleet. He was himself committed there soon after.*

* Foxe, vol. vi. p. 151. " Before this deponent was committed to the Fleet." The deponent was Watson.

The cause of Watson's imprisonment seems to have been the complaints laid against him by two preachers named Tonge and Ayre. They had been sent to Winchester to preach by order of the Duke of Somerset, the Lord Protector, and to be instituted canons in that church. The Bishop himself deposes that he received them very kindly and hospitably, and in no way disgraced them.* But they, on the other hand, declared that the Bishop said to the people—" I understand there be new preachers sent down ; but I suppose there is none of my flock so mad as to believe them that they never saw before, neither that doctrine that they never heard before." The same Sunday afternoon Tonge preached, and Ayre on the Tuesday. "And the Sunday after that," so says Ayre, " Watson, the Bishop's chaplain, did preach in the said church, and inveighed against the said Dr Tonge and this deponent, as this deponent heard say ; " for which cause this deponent and the said Dr Tonge did complain to my Lord of Somerset's grace ; and this deponent gathered certain articles touching the misordering of the said Dr Tonge and this deponent by the Bishop and his said chaplain, which articles the said deponent delivered, within these three days, to Master Secretary Cecil.†

No record seems to exist of Watson's committal, and I can only conjecture that he was made a victim to the indignation of the Protector or the Archbishop for the cause I have just mentioned. While in prison, Gardiner indignantly protested against this abuse of power. In a letter to Somerset, he writes—" Men be mortal and deeds revive, and methinketh my Lord of Canterbury doth (not) well to entangle thus your grace with the matter of religion, and to borrow of your authority the Fleet, the Marshalsea, and the King's Bench, with imprisonment in his house, wherewith to cause men to agree to that (which) it pleaseth him to call truth in religion, not stablished by any law of the realm, but contrary to a law. At the least, a law is not yet ; and before a law is made, I have not seen such a kind of imprisonment as I sustain." ‡

Watson was kept in separate confinement, for Gardiner complains—" Here I remain . . . without comfort of any of

---

* See the Bishop's deposition, Foxe, vol. vi. p. 129.
† Ibid. p. 154.   ‡ Ibid. p. 48.

my friends or servants, . . . no chaplain to accompany me in prayer ;" and in another letter, written towards the end of November 1547—"I have remained here seven weeks without speaking to any man saving my physician." *

Mr Cooper says that Watson remained in the Fleet for two or three years, and was still there when he was brought as a witness in Gardiner's trial in 1550. This is a mistake. A general pardon was granted by the king on 6th January 1548, and Watson was liberated as well as Gardiner. The Bishop, however, was ordered to remain in his own house in Southwark on another frivolous charge, and was not allowed to return to Winchester till Lent. Watson was his constant attendant. From his own evidence we learn that he always kept the Bishop's company at table, and waited on him when he went out.† It was, however, another chaplain, William Meadow, a man sixty years old, formerly rector of Wyke Regis, and then master of Holy Cross Hospital, who acted as the Bishop's confessor.‡ He also had been confined in the Fleet at the same time as Watson and the Bishop.§

On their return to Farnham, the parish priest of the place told Watson, who was staying at his house, that the people were much exasperated at the changes that had been introduced in the manner of worship by the visitors sent into the diocese by the Government during the Bishop's absence in London, and he requested Watson to preach to them, and to appease their minds. Watson, however, communicated the matter to the Bishop, and the latter undertook the unwelcome duty himself.

The changes indeed had been great. All images had been removed from the churches, the procession at Candlemas had been forbidden, with a number of other acts and ceremonies, all of which had been solemnly approved by the Archbishop a few years before as " most godly, and to be retained." But these innovations were trifling compared with those that soon followed—first the Mass sung in English, then the abolition of all the guilds ‖ and chauntries, the Communion in both kinds,

---

* Foxe, vol. vi. p. 53.   † Ibid. p. 207.
‡ Deposition of Coppinger, Ibid. p. 192.   § Ibid. p. 202.
‖ I find a Guild of St George in the chapel of St Nicholas, Weymouth, in Watson's parish of Wyke. Probably there were others in the parish

the Book of Common Prayer instead of the Missal and other service-books, the leave of marriage to the clergy, and still more, the repeal of the Statute of the Six Articles, and the consequent leave to preach Lutheran and Calvinistic doctrines. And while preaching was prohibited to all (even to the bishops) who had not a special licence from the king or his visitors; this licence was only given to fanatics of the new opinions. "A set of noisy declaimers," says Mr Froude,* "first to cry reform while reform was in the ascendant, first to fly or apostatise in time of danger, made the circuit of the towns and parishes." I have not been able to discover how far Watson yielded to any of these measures, or by what means he evaded compliance. A few facts only have come down to us of his conduct in this reign, and these I proceed to give.

Gardiner was not long left in peace. He was again summoned to London in June 1548, by the Council, and commanded to preach before the young king at Westminster, and to write out his sermon and submit it to the Protector's revision before preaching. This he absolutely refused. He was then commanded to preach on certain topics and to avoid others, and to this he partly yielded. Watson was present at the Bishop's house in the Clink when William Cecil was sent, on the part of the Protector, to convey his instructions about the sermon, and next day was the Bishop's messenger to Somerset to complain of Cecil's behaviour—a circumstance which Cecil probably did not forget when he had power to revenge himself in the days of Elizabeth. The sermon was preached on St Peter's day. Watson accompanied the Bishop to Westminster, and during the sermon was present among the throng.† The sermon was certainly neither seditious nor dangerous from a Protestant point of view. It inveighed against the supremacy of the Pope; but as it also defended the Real Presence, a point on which Gardiner had been forbidden by Somerset to touch, the Bishop was considered contumacious, and the next day was committed to the Tower.

For two years and a half Gardiner remained in prison without trial, and during the whole of that time his chaplains were forbidden any access to him, except that once when he

church as well as chauntries. See Hutchin's History of Dorsetshire, vol i. pp. 408, 409. * History, vol. v. p. 97.
† Watson's Evidence. Foxe, vol. vi. p. 151–53.

c

was supposed to be dying, and at Easter, his confessor, William Meadow, spent a few hours with him.* Watson seems to have returned to Farnham to await events; for in June 1550, when there was a rumour that the Bishop was about to be released, Watson, with the rest of the household at Farnham, took horse at ten o'clock at night, and riding all night, reached London at seven in the morning in hopes to welcome their master.† They were, however, disappointed. In December 1550 the Bishop was brought to trial, and Watson was summoned to give evidence both for the prosecution and the defence. Foxe has preserved the records of this trial. The Bishop ably defended himself against the various charges; but by a flagrant abuse of power he was condemned (February 1551), deprived of his bishopric, and sent back to the Tower, from which he was only released on the accession of Mary, to be restored to his see and become Chancellor of the kingdom.

Meanwhile the lands and revenues of the diocese of Winchester were divided into eight portions, of which one was given to the Crown, and the other seven to the friends of the Government. The infamous Poynet of Rochester ‡ succeeded Gardiner in the see of Winchester, and received various rectories and other lands for his support. With this man's accession Watson's connection with the diocese terminated. The next time we meet with him is in a theological conference held in December 1551. It is thus related by Strype §—

"About this time Cheke, with some others, was engaged in two disputations, or rather friendly conferences, privately with Feckenham (who was afterwards Dean of St Paul's and Abbot of Westminster), and one or two more of his party, in the great controversy of the Real Presence in the Sacrament. The first was held at Secretary Cecil's house, and the latter at Sir Richard Morison's. The auditors were but six—viz., the Lord Russel, Sir Thomas Wroth, of the Bedchamber; Sir Anthony Cooke, one of the king's instructors; Throgmorton, Chamberlain of the Exchequer; Mr Knokes, and Mr Harrington, with whom were joined the Marquis of Northampton and the Earl of Rutland in the second conference. The disputants

---

* Gardiner's Articles. Foxe, vol. vi. p. 72.   † Ibid. p. 220.
  ‡ For an account of Poynet very different from that given by Burnet and others, see an article in the "Saturday Review," July 18, 1868.
  § Strype's Life of Sir John Cheke, p. 69 (ed. 1821).

were Sir John Cheke, and with him Sir William Cecil, Secretary of State; Horne, Dean of Durham; Whitehead, and Grindal, who were against the Real Presence; Feckenham, Young, and, at the second disputation, Watson, who were for it. Some account of these disputations is still extant in Latin in the MS. library of Bene't College in Cambridge. And to preserve what remainders we can of Cheke's, and likewise to satisfy any that are desirous to look into the Church history of England in those days, I have translated them into English, and exemplified them here; only first premising that I suppose this conference might be occasioned from an appearance of the said Feckenham before Cheke by public order, to be examined by him." Thus far Strype.

I do not think it necessary to transcribe this disputation. It is imperfectly given by Strype as regards Watson's arguments, since he takes the liberty sometimes to abridge after this fashion—" Watson here cavilled much of I know not what spiritual eating, which yet was proper and without any necessity of suffering;" or again, " Watson eluded the argument with I know not what logical distinction;" or, " Watson did endeavour to evade by certain distinctions;" or, " In which place Watson laboured after a wonderful manner;" or, finally, " Watson again gainsaid somewhat, I know not what, and the most part rose up that here might be an end." This is what Strype calls translating into English and exemplifying.

The Conference left the disputants convinced of their own opinions as before. It is chiefly interesting as bringing together, under new circumstances, men like Cheke, Cecil, Young, and Watson, who had studied together, perhaps disputed together, at the same college, and were now finally ranged on different sides in the great political and religious struggle of the age.

Whether Watson, after the deprivation of Gardiner, resided at Wyke Regis or at Buckminster, or what were his movements or his acts during the remainder of this reign, I have not been able to discover.* The only event mentioned is one without time or place, but as it has been supposed to cast a slur on the character of Watson, I cannot pass it over. It is thus narrated by Foxe †—

* No registers exists at Wyke.
† Acts and Monuments, vol. viii. p. 447.

"Moreover, as touching the said Master Rough, this is further to be noted, that he, being in the north country in the days of King Edward the Sixth, was the mean to save Dr Watson's life (who in Queen Mary's time was Bishop of Lincoln) for a sermon that he had made there. The said Watson after that, in the said days of Queen Mary, being with Bonner at the examination of the said Master Rough, to requite the good turn in saving his life, detected him there to be a pernicious heretic, who did more hurt in the north parts than a hundred besides of his opinion. Unto whom Master Rough said again, ' Why, sir, is this the reward I have for saving your life when you preached erroneous doctrine in the days of King Edward the Sixth ? ' "

It is not easy to know what to make of this story. No documents are quoted, and we have to rely for its truth first on the veracity of Foxe, and next on that of Rough, a Scotch monk, who had taken a wife and the office of reformer in England. What is to be understood by "erroneous doctrine"? And what doctrine could have endangered Watson's life in that reign? The only doctrine that was treasonable, and the preaching of which would have subjected its holder to loss of life, was the denial of the king's supremacy. But Watson can scarcely have preached against this, since, in his evidence given in December 1550, he had admitted the first article proposed in Gardiner's trial, which ran as follows— " That the King's Majesty justly and rightfully is, and by the laws of God ought to be, supreme head in earth of the Church of England, and also of Ireland ; and so is by the clergy of this realm in their convocation, and by Act of Parliament, justly, and according to the laws of God, recognised." * More- over, it is not easy to conceive how Rough could have saved Watson's life had he been publicly guilty of treason, or how no record of danger or escape should exist except in this ambiguous boast of Rough. That Watson may have preached in defence of the Real Presence, or spoken against the recent innovations, is likely enough ; but to have done this might have exposed him to fine or imprisonment, not to the penalty of death. We must, therefore, leave this matter in its obscurity. But it would be unfair to accuse Watson of cruelty on such uncertain grounds.

* Foxe, vol. vi. p. 151.

CHAPTER III.—IN THE REIGN OF MARY.

WE must now pass on to the reign of Mary. Edward expired on 6th July 1553. Watson was about 37 years old. He had now learnt by experience what was meant by royal supremacy, and what were the consequences of casting off that of the successor of St Peter. He had always firmly held the Catholic faith except in this particular. He had been conspicuous for his zeal in defending the Real Presence. There is no proof that he ever subscribed to the forty-two articles drawn up by Cranmer, for the king's command to all clergymen to do so was only issued shortly before his death. On the other hand, not only had he seen the communion service substituted for the Holy Sacrifice of the Mass, but the altars removed from the churches, and the churches themselves robbed of their ornaments by Act of Parliament, in virtue of the royal supremacy. His eyes were opened to the divine constitution of the Church, and in future we shall find him, not only defending with Fisher the sacraments against Luther, but ready also like Fisher to lay down his life rather than again renounce his allegiance to the Vicar of Christ.

Mary entered London 31st July, and Watson was so well known for his attachment to the old faith, that three weeks afterwards he was ordered to preach in her presence. The matter is thus related by Stow *—

"The twentieth of August, Doctor Watson,† chaplain to the Bishop of Winchester, preached at Paul's Cross, by the Queen's appointment; and for fear of the like tumult as had been the Sunday last past, certain Lords of the Council repaired to the sermon, as the Lord Treasurer, the Lord Privy Seal, the Earl of Bedford, the Earl of Pembroke, the Lord Wentworth, the Lord Rich, and Sir Henry Gernigam, Captain of the Guard, with two hundred of the guard, which stood about the preacher with halberts. Also the Mayor had warned the companies of the city to be present in their liveries, which was well accepted of the Queen's Council, and the sermon was quietly ended."

---

* Stow's Annals of England, p. 614 (ed. 1615).
† He did not take his Doctor's degree until some months after this, but he was doubtless already thus named by courtesy or popular fame.

Mr Nichols, in his notes to "Machyn's Diary," has given us the matter of this sermon from a letter, written in London August 22, by William Dalby—

"On Sunday last was a sermon at Paul's Cross, made by one Doctor Watson.   There was at his sermon the Marquis of Winchester, the Earl of Bedford, the Earl of Pembroke, the Lord Wentworth, the Lord Rich.   They did sit where my Lord Mayor and the Aldermen were wont to sit, my Lord Mayor [Marquis ?] sitting uppermost.   There was also in the window over the Mayor (*sic*) the old Bishop of London [Bonner, the late Bishop], and divers others.   There was 120 of the guard, that stood round about the Cross with their halberts, to guard the preacher, and to apprehend them that would stir.   His sermon was no more eloquent than edifying —I mean it was neither eloquent or edifying, in my opinion, for he meddled not with the gospel, nor epistle, nor no part of Scripture.   After he had read his theme, he entered into a by-matter, and so spent his time.   Four or five of the chief points of his sermon, that I can remember, I will, as briefly as I can, report unto you, viz., he required the people not to believe the preachers, but that their faith should be firm and sure, because there is such vanities amongst them ; and if any man doubt of his faith, let him go to the Scriptures, and also to the interpreters of the doctors, and interpret it not after their own brain.   He wished the people to have no new faith, nor to build no new temple, but to keep the old faith, and edify the old temple again.   He blamed the people, in a manner, for that heretofore they would have nothing that was man's tradition, and now they be contented to have man's tradition, showing that in the first year of the reign of our Sovereign Lord King Edward VI. there was a law established that in the sacrament there was the body and blood of Christ, not really but spiritually ; and the next year after they established another law, that there was the body of Christ neither spiritually or really.   These two in themselves are contraries, therefore they cannot be both true.   He showed that we should ground our faith upon God's Word, which is Scripture, and Scripture is the Bible, which we have in Hebrew, Greek, and Latin, and now translated into English ; but he doubteth the translation was not true.   Also, he said there hath been in his time that he hath seen twenty catechisms, and every one varying from other in some points; and well, he said, they might be all false, but they could not be all true; and thus persuading the people that they had followed men's tradition, and had gone astray, wishing them to come home again, and re-edify the old temple. Thus, with many other persuasions, he spent the time till eleven of the clock, and ended." [*]

No doubt Watson had hastened to London to welcome Gardiner on his release from his long captivity, which happened on August the 3d; and it was probably by Gardiner's suggestion that he had been chosen to preach this sermon. It was also by Gardiner's authority, as Chancellor of Cambridge, about a month afterwards, on September 25th, he was deputed to proceed to Cambridge to act on his behalf in restoring the old religion, and to make a report on the state of the colleges.

At the same time he was elected Master of St John's College, and admitted, in the person of Christopher Brown, his proxy, by John Young, Vice-Chancellor, then fellow of Trinity College, at his chamber there, Roger Ascham being present as President of St John's, with several other fellows of that society. The instrument of his admission is dated September 28th, 1553.[†]

To understand his position we must glance back upon the state of his college since he had left it.

The Protestant party had succeeded in getting a new code of statutes in 1545 by the authority of Henry VIII., with whom Cheke was in great favour. [‡] Taylor had resigned his mastership at the beginning of the reign of Edward, and had been succeeded by William Bill, recommended for election by the Protector. The fellows, who were enamoured of the new opinions, having now no fear of the terrible penalty which, while Henry lived, attached to all who denied the Real Presence, began openly to profess their heresy. They even went so far as to hold open controversies against the most Holy Sacrament in the chapel. "After they had overthrown the Mass in their disputations," writes Baker, "because the Host was not removed, the pix that hung over the altar was cut down by a private hand, which cost them some apology with the Archbishop

* From the Harl. MS. 353, f. 141, quoted in note to "Machyn's Diary," p. 332.
† Baker's History of St John's, vol. i. p. 137.
‡ Ibid. pp. 118-21.

(Cranmer), to whom Mr Leaver (one of the leaders in these doings) was sent up to excuse the thing." * They had, however, only anticipated by a few weeks the action of the Government. The college chapel, which the martyred Fisher had solemnly consecrated in 1516, and in which he had hoped that the Holy Sacrifice would be daily offered by the fellows of the college, for whose education and maintenance he toiled so much, was now after thirty years to be devoted to the sacrilegious rites against which Fisher had so warmly written. " It is a strange thing," he wrote in 1523,† " that Luther should have the impudence to lay down new laws for the sacraments, as if he thought that men at the present day were so utterly stupid as to be willing to depart from the ancient rites observed by the Church at the bidding of an insignificant friar." But the age in its pride of learning was more spiritually stupid than Fisher believed. Luther's laws, or those of Calvin or of Cranmer, were preferred to those of the saints and doctors, and the Holy Sacrifice was abolished, the vestments sold for profane uses, the liturgical books given to the flames, the altar-stones broken or thrown aside, and the college statutes again reformed " by taking out the venom of Popery and superstition," to use the words of the Protestant historian of the college.‡

At the end of 1551 Bill had been replaced in the mastership by the famous Protestant preacher Thomas Leaver, who continued until the accession of Queen Mary, when he fled into Switzerland to Calvin. It is enough to quote the words of Baker, " that the Reformation nowhere gained more ground, or was more zealously maintained, than it did here under this man's example and the influence of his government." §

It was into such an abode of spiritual desolation that Watson now entered. Twenty-four of the fellows had resigned or been deprived, ‖ and as it was of course impossible to supply their places at once with men equally skilled in ancient literature, Ascham, who despised and hated theology, canon law, and scholastic philosophy, complained grievously of the ignor-

---

* Baker's History of St John's, p. 125.
† Assertionis Lutheranæ Confutatio, fol. lxxv. (ed. 1523).
‡ Baker's History of St John's, vol. i. p. 127.   § Ibid. p. 133.
‖ I am not sure that they were all deprived during Watson's mastership. According to Strype the vacancies were not all made until October 1554. Baker speaks hesitatingly (vol. i. p. 141).

ance of the new fellows and the decline of the literary reputation of the college. Had Watson remained master, he would no doubt have still more effectually promoted his favourite studies than he had done when one of the junior fellows. When he first quitted the college, a copy of Fisher's " Statutes" had been left with him in trust. These he brought back and enforced, and in other ways sought to carry out the intentions of the founder.* But at the end of seven months from his election he resigned his office, probably because he found its duties incompatible with his other appointment as Dean of Durham.

A few words will be necessary to explain this dignity. In 1540 Hugh Whitehead, the last Prior of Durham, surrendered to Henry; and on the 12th May 1541, the king appointed a dean and twelve prebendaries in the place of the monastic society, Whitehead himself being the first dean. He had been succeeded by Robert Horne, one of Watson's contemporaries at St John's. Under him Protestantism had triumphed, especially as the bishop, Cuthbert Tunstall, was imprisoned. The Duke of Northumberland had got bills through Parliament to suppress the bishopric, and divide it into two new ones (viz., Durham and Newcastle), in the hopes, under the new arrangements, to get into his own hands the great possessions of the see, when his plans were defeated by the death of Edward. The Parliament of the 1st of May repealed these Acts.† Although the country was not yet reconciled with the Holy See, the canon law had been restored, and by its provisions married priests were at once removed from their benefices. Among these was the Dean of Durham. The appointment, being in the gift of the Crown, was, probably by Gardiner's recommendation, conferred on Watson, who was of that diocese. His nomination was on the 18th November 1553. In October he had been one of the proctors of the Convocation, and had strenuously maintained the Catholic faith against John Philpot, James Haddon, Richard Cheyney, and other learned Protestants. ‡ His position as Master of St John's exempted him

---

* See Baker, vol. i. 138, 139.

† For the detail of all these changes, see Hutchinson's History of Durham, vol. i. p. 430, and vol. ii. p. 102.

‡ There is an *ex parte* account of the proceedings in this Convocation published by Foxe. It is also published in Philpot's Examinations, &c. (Parker Society).

from residence in any of his benefices,* yet he resigned his
rectory of Wyke on his appointment to the deanery.†   An Act
passed by the first Parliament of Mary enabled her to make
statutes for the cathedrals, and by her appointment Heath of
York, Bonner of London, Tunstall of Durham, Thirlby of Ely,
and William Armistead drew up those of Durham.   By the
11th chapter of these statutes the dean was bound to residence,
without some reasonable excuse, such as attendance on the
king or queen as chaplain, business of the Crown or Church,
attendance on Parliament or Convocation, &c.   He might be
absent a hundred days in the year on private affairs.‡   I am
unable to state the proportions of Watson's residence, or to
give details of his government of the cathedral.§   As his zeal
for the Blessed Sacrament was so great, it would be very
interesting if any records could be discovered of the manner in
which he re-established the Catholic worship, and endeavoured
to bring back something of its ancient splendour to the grand
old abbey, or cathedral as we may now call it.   In December
1554, the decrees of the Cardinal Legate ratified the erection
of dioceses, chapters, and colleges, which had been made by
Henry VIII.

On the third and fifth Fridays of Lent 1554, Watson again
preached before the queen two sermons which he afterwards
published, one on the Real Presence, the other on the sacri-
ficial character of the Mass. || We have a singular testimony
to the reputation of Watson as a preacher in an answer that
was published in the time of Elizabeth to these two sermons
by Robert Crowley, minister of Cripplegate.   He says in his
Introduction—

"Having occasion oftentimes to be in place where such as
are not yet persuaded that the Pope's Church can err, have

* Act of Parliament of 1536.
† Thomas Haywood succeeded in 1553 (Hutchin's Dorsetshire).
‡ The dean's stipend was £40, and 12s. 5d. each day he was pre-
sent in choir or lawfully absent.
§ Surtees unfortunately did not live to write the history of the abbey
and cathedral.
|| Two notable sermons made the 3d and 5th Fridays in Lent last
past before the Queen's Highness, concerning the Real Presence of
Christ's Body and Blood in the B. Sacrament, also the Mass which
is the sacrifice of the New Testament.   London, 4to and 12mo 1554.
Printed by J. Cawood.

been bold to utter their minds freely, affirming that the doctrine which the Protestants teach is erroneous and false, especially concerning the presence of Christ in the Sacrament of His Body and Blood, and the Sacrifice of the Mass : I have perceived that the same have been chiefly persuaded and stayed by these two sermons made by Doctor Watson in the first year of Queen Mary's reign. I have therefore wished that some man of like learning would have published in print an answer to those sermons ; that thereby such as have been deceived by the subtlety thereof, might, by the plain and simple answer, be brought to the knowledge of the truth."

And again, in his address to Dr Watson, he says—

"The estimation that you have in the Pope's Church is such, that whatsoever is known to be of your doing is of that sort thought to be so learnedly done that none can be found amongst us able to answer any part thereof." *

As Watson was in prison when Crowley's book was written, the latter was left to enjoy in peace his imaginary triumph. In April 1554, being still Master of St John's and Dean of Durham, Watson was one of the divines deputed by the University of Cambridge to proceed to Oxford to dispute with Cranmer, Ridley, and Latimer, on which occasion he was incorporated Doctor of Divinity in that university, having already taken his Doctor's degree at Cambridge at the beginning of the year. From the account of these disputes given by Foxe, Watson took no part in the contests with Cranmer or Latimer, and only a slight one in those with Ridley. They all turned on the Real Presence. He was no doubt in London when the Legate, Cardinal Pole, arrived towards the end of November of this year, 1554, and present in Convocation when the clergy were solemnly absolved from all censures and irregularities at the beginning of December.

This seems the place to say something of the volume of sermons to which this biographical notice is an introduction ; for though they were not published until 1558, the causes of his composing them belong to this period.

* A setting open of the subtyle sophistrie of Thomas Watson, etc., written by Robert Crowley, Clearke. Printed by Henry Denham, 1569. Ridley also made annotations on Watson's sermons, which he sent to Bradford. In his letter he calls Watson "a man of acute parts." See Bradford's Writings, vol. ii. p. 207 (Parker Society).

Cardinal Pole had summoned a National Synod of both Provinces for the restoration of religion. Dr Watson was present ; and it is a clear proof of the estimation in which he was held for his character, learning, and eloquence, that when the Council assembled on the 21st January 1555–56, in the Archbishop's Chapel in Lambeth, to hear the promulgation of the legatine constitutions, Dr Watson was the orator selected to deliver the sermon in Latin, in presence of the Cardinal legate, the bishops and clergy, "and a great multitude of people." *

In this synod much attention was given to the subject of preaching, and it was determined that homilies should be prepared that the less learned priests might read to their people.†
I have no doubt that it was in consequence of this synod that Dr Watson set about the preparation of his book of " Sermons on the Sacraments."

We may suppose that the greater part of the years 1555 and 1556 was spent by Watson in Durham. On December the 7th, 1556, the Queen issued a licence for filling up the see of Lincoln, and Watson was elected to that bishopric. On the 24th of the same month he had a grant of the temporalities, with all the profits accruing since the vacancy. His bull of confirmation by the Pope is dated 24th March 1557, but he was not consecrated till August.

Lincoln had formerly been one of the richest, as it was the largest, diocese in England. But during the episcopate of John Longland (1521–47) Henry VIII. had carried off all the treasures of the cathedral, 2621 ounces of gold, 4285 ounces of silver, and an immense number of pearls, diamonds, and other precious stones.‡ Longland's successor, Henry Holbeach, surrendered in one day to the Crown all the episcopal estates,§ and reduced the see to utter poverty. He also abandoned the episcopal palace in London. During his time the church was again plundered of the few ornaments that remained.

Holbeach died in 1551, and was followed by John Taylor, whose acquaintance we have already made as Master of St John's. Taylor was deprived on the accession of Mary, and John White elected on April 1, 1554. It was the translation

---

* Wilkins, Concilia, vol. iv. p. 132.
† I have treated of this subject more at length in the Preface.
‡ A complete list is given by Dugdale, vol. viii. pp. 1279–86.
§ Rymer, vol. xv. p. 66.

of White to the see of Winchester which caused the vacancy which was filled by the election of Dr Watson. Owing to the poverty of the see, Cardinal Pole (29th May 1557) empowered him to hold the deanery of Durham *pro tempore in commendam* with his bishopric. He did so till his consecration. He succeeded in recovering many rich vestments, articles of plate, and other furniture, of which his Church had been despoiled ; and on 9th November 1557 obtained, by letters-patent, a re-grant of certain of the estates which had been alienated by Holbeach, and also the patronage of certain benefices in his diocese which had belonged to the dissolved religious houses. But his Protestant successors did not much profit by his zeal, since Nicholas Bullingham, who usurped his place in January 1559, "surrendered all that his predecessor had obtained," says the historian of Lincoln ; * "and when he had stripped the see of its recent wealth, he procured himself to be translated to a richer one, Worcester, leaving to his successor the pious opportunity of conforming himself more strictly to the apostolical example of contentment with little."

I have not been able to discover any documents throwing light on Dr Watson's spiritual government of his diocese, and must be content to give, in chronological order, the few scattered notices of him which occur in the last two years of his freedom.

Shortly after his election to Lincoln he was named by Cardinal Pole as one of his delegates to visit the University of Cambridge, of which the Cardinal had been elected Chancellor after the death of Gardiner.

The incidents of this visitation have been recorded day by day, and almost hour by hour, by an eye-witness, John Mere, the Esquire Bedell, and, with more than usually blasphemous commentary, by Foxe.†

The account of the inspection of the various colleges has no general interest. The event that has made this visitation memorable was the burning of the bodies of Bucer and Fagius.

* History of County of Lincoln, by Allen, vol. i. p. 151.
Willis, in his Survey of Cathedrals, enumerates the benefices (about 150 in number), all in the diocese of Lincoln (vol. iii. p. 65).

† Mere's Diary was published in 1838 by Dr Lamb, in his Collection of Letters, &c., illustrative of the History of the University of Cambridge. A very full account, taken from Lamb and Foxe, is also given by Cooper in his Annals of Cambridge.

Martin Bucer and Paul Fagius, two foreign heretics, had been invited to Cambridge in 1549, and appointed Professors of Divinity and of Hebrew. Their stay was not very long, for Fagius had died the November after his arrival, and Bucer in February 1551. They had both had public funerals given to them by the University, and Fagius was buried in St Michael's, Bucer in St Mary's Church. Cardinal Pole considered that the university ought to make a solemn act of reparation for this apostasy from the Church, and had given instructions for the reversal of all the honours paid to the foreign reformers. They were consequently accused and tried as heretics, then exhumed, and their coffins and bones burnt in the market-place with heretical books. This act will probably seem barbarous; but at least it was more humane than the burning of living heretics; and it would seem to have been the wish of Pole, as well as of the visitors, to spare the living, while vindicating the faith. It is, however, probable that the effect was misjudged, and that the burning of these dead bodies caused greater disgust and indignation than the burning of one or two obstinate disputants would have done. The latter course would have been defended as necessary severity; the former was generally condemned as a needless outrage.

Watson, however, was not the principal visitor. He was accompanied by Scot, Bishop of Chester, and Christopherson, Bishop of Chichester, and by Nicolas Ormanet, an Italian prelate who had accompanied the Cardinal into England, and who is commonly called in the records by his title of Datary. He seems to have guided the English theologians in their proceedings.

I need merely add that Foxe gives a summary of a sermon preached on Candlemas Day 1557 during the visitation, by Dr Watson, which any one who has read his published sermons will at once see to be utterly untrustworthy. Dr Watson also preached in St Mary's Church while the bodies of the reformers were being burned in the market place, "setting forth Bucer's wickedness and heretical doctrine," says Mere. Foxe has also given an abridgment of this sermon, but as he himself was then on the Continent, and only knew what some sympathising friend of Bucer's chose to report, it would be useless to reproduce it here. The day after, the Church of St Mary's, which had been interdicted as regards the mass, was reconciled; the

Blessed Sacrament was brought to it in solemn procession and mass was celebrated, the Bishop of Chester preaching. On the 17th February the Bishop (elect) of Lincoln returned to London.

Of his stay in the capital we have the following notices in the diary of the worthy citizen Machyn :—

" The 17th March, preached afore the Queen, the new Bishop of Lincoln, Dr Watson." *

" The 3d day of April, did preach Dr Watson Bishop of Lincoln, at All Hallows the More, at afternoon, where was great audience of people." †

" The 22d of April, did preach at St Mark's, Spital, Dr Watson, new chosen Bishop of Lincoln, a godly sermon." ‡

He was consecrated on the Feast of the Assumption (August 15th, 1557), at Chiswick, by Nicolas Heath, Archbishop of York, acting under a commission from Cardinal Pole, assisted by Thomas Thirlby, Bishop of Ely, and William Glynn, Bishop of Bangor. §

His duties in Parliament and in Convocation would often require his presence in London, and it was probably on such an occasion that he preached another sermon thus noticed in Machyn's diary :— ‖

" The 20th day of February (1558), did preach at Paul's Cross, Doctor Watson, Bishop of Lincoln, and made a godly sermon, for there were present ten bishops, beside my Lord Mayor, and the aldermen and judges, and men of the law, and great audience there was."

But we have now to turn to very different scenes.

CHAPTER IV.—IN THE REIGN OF ELIZABETH.

ON the 17th November 1558, Queen Mary died, and a few days later Cardinal Pole. Though Elizabeth's plans were already formed for the establishment of Protestantism, yet she acted cautiously at first, hoping to gain over the Bishops. The Protestant exiles at Strasburg, Frankfort, and Zurich, as soon

---

* Machyn's Diary (Camden Society), p. 128.
† Ibid. p. 131. ‡ Ibid. p. 132.
§ Stubbs—Registrum Sacrum Anglicanum, p. 82.
‖ Machyn's Diary, p. 166.

as they heard of Mary's death, came back into England ; and Elizabeth, with the advice of her Council, appointed a solemn conference to be held between them and the bishops, professedly to prepare the minds of the nobility and legislators for the questions which would come before them in the approaching parliament regarding public worship. The conference having been resolved on, the disputants on the Catholic side were the Bishops of Winchester (White), Lichfield (Bayne), Chester (Scot), and Lincoln (Watson); and theologians, Drs Cole, Harpsfield, Langdale, and Chedsey. On the Protestant side were Scory, Coxe, Whitehead, Grindal, Horne, Guest, Elmer, and Jewel.

The place was Westminster Abbey, where a table was set for the Bishops and Catholics on one side of the choir, and for their opponents on the other, the Lords of the Council being seated at a cross table. The nobility and members of Parliament were to be present.

The points to be urged against the Bishops were these :—

1. That it is against the Word of God and the customs of the ancient church to use a tongue unknown to the people in common prayer, and in the administration of the sacraments.

2. That every church hath authority to appoint, take away, and change ceremonies and rites, so the same be to edification.

3. That it cannot be proved by the Word of God that there is in the mass offered up, a sacrifice propitiatory for the living and the dead. *

Of what happened in these conferences we have only a one-sided statement, all to the disadvantage of the bishops. The third article never came into discussion, and there was no orderly disputation regarding the others. It had of course been intended that the Bishops should be worsted or declared so. Hayward concludes his account by these words :—" Then the Assembly was dissolved, the expectations frustrated, the purpose defeated." The contrary would be the truth. " It is very probable," continues Hayward, " that the Bishops could either not be provided in so short a time, their minds being somewhat clogged with former pleasures and present cares ; or else, that they discovered such an inclination against them that all their

* Letter of Jewel to Peter Martyr (March 20, 1559), Zurich Letters ii. Also Hayward's Annals of Queen Elizabeth (Camden Society), p. 20.

hopes did plainly vanish. And being men no more able to endure adversity than they had been to moderate prosperity, they weakly yielded, and abandoning both their credit and their cause, gave full way to their own ruin." So far the annalist. Whether Watson's mind was clogged by pleasure the reader knows, and whether he was not able to endure adversity the rest of his life will declare. "Afterwards," says Hayward, "the Bishops of Winchester and Lincoln, who behaved themselves, especially Lincoln, more indiscreetly than others, were for this contempt committed to the Tower."

Camden has given another, and in some respects, fairer account of these proceedings.* He says the bishops complained that Bacon, the Lord Keeper, was appointed judge in such matters, of which he knew nothing, and that no good ever came of such disputations which do always bend that way that the sceptre inclines.

But Camden adds, that the Bishops of Winchester and Lincoln threatened the Queen with excommunication, and this statement has been since copied by a multitude of writers. It is intrinsically improbable, for the excommunication of the Queen would not belong to a simple bishop ; nor is it in harmony with anything we know of Watson's character, to suppose him thus hastily uttering such a threat. Besides this, Camden's statement rests on no previous and contemporary authority, nor is it borne out by other historians who lived nearer to the events. Hayward has nothing of it, nor has Holinshed,† who, however, copied his account from a statement published soon after the conference by authority of the Queen. The original memorandum, signed by Bacon, the Chancellor, the Earls of Bedford, ¦Shrewsbury, Pembroke, by Cecil and others, is still in existence,‡ and has not a word about excommunication. This paper says :—"Afterwards for the contempt so notoriously made, the Bishops of Winchester and Lincoln having most obstinately both disobeyed common authority and varied manifestly from their own order, and specially Lincoln, who showed more folly than the other, were condignly committed to the Tower of London."

If it be said that the Council would not make public so great

---

* History of Elizabeth, Book i.
† Holinshed, vol. iii. p. 1183 (ed. 1586).
‡ P. R. O., Dom. Eliz., vol. iii. n. 52.

d

an outrage on the Queen as a threat of excommunication, I reply that most certainly the eyewitnesses of the conference, who wrote an account of it in private letters at the very time, could not have passed over such a matter. Now Coxe and Jewel, two of the disputants, each wrote independent accounts of what took place within a few days of the events, and yet neither of them, while dilating on the contempt and contumacy of the Bishops of Lincoln and Winchester, mentions any threats against the Queen. Yet Jewel gloats over their punishment. " White and Watson," he writes to Peter Martyr, " were committed to the Tower. There they are now employed in castrametation." *

For some months the Bishop of Lincoln had been suffering from a severe attack of ague. The report of his death had reached Strasburg in January.† This will explain why his name does not occur in the journals of the House of Lords, in the debates in which the other bishops nobly defended the Catholic Faith. He had not yet entirely recovered, as appears by the letter of the Council to the Lieutenant of the Tower for his committal :—

" He is willed to keep in sure and several ward the two bishops, suffering them nevertheless to have each of them one of their own men to attend upon them and their own stuff for their bedding and other necessary furniture, and to appoint them to some convenient lodgings meet for persons of their sort using them also otherwise well, specially the Bishop of Lincoln, for that he is sick, for which respect also and because this is his sick night, the said lieutenant is willed to have the rather regard unto him, and to spare him some of his own lodging and stuff for this night, and also to suffer his surgeon and such other as shall be needful for his health to have access unto him from time to time.

" My Lords of the Council did this day appoint Sir Ambrose Cave and Sir Richard Sackville to repair to the houses of the said Bishops of Winchester and Lincoln here in London, and both to peruse their studies and writings, and also to take

* Letter, April 6, 1559, in Zurich Letters, i. p. 13. Coxe's letter to Weidner is dated May 20, 1559. Ib. i. p. 28.
† Letter of Jewel, written from Strasburg, January 26, 1559. Zurich Letters, i. 6.

order with their officers for the surety and stay of their goods." *

Another letter written on the 27th of April gives instruction to the lieutenant " to suffer the Bishop of Lincoln to come, at such times as he by his discretion shall think meet, to his table for the better relief of his quartan ague ; and also to have that liberty of the house, as prisoners heretofore having the liberty of the Tower hath used, the ordering whereof is referred to his discretion." †

On the 26th June the Queen deprived the two bishops of their sees. For this purpose they were brought, says Machyn, " to Master Hawse, the King's (*i.e.*, Queen's) Sheriff, in Mincing Lane, and the Bishop of Winchester to the Tower again, and the Bishop of Lincoln delivered away." ‡ If this means that he was set at liberty, whither he then repaired I can only conjecture. It was probably to his brother's house in London. This brother is mentioned in 1556 in Mere's Diary as having come to Cambridge during the visitation. § His name was John. It was probably to him that a lease was granted, when Dr Watson was master of St John's, of a tenement belonging to the college, mentioned in the college registers. || He is then called " John Watson, of London, gentleman," and he has permission to alienate the lease to William Roper, of Lincoln's Inn, probably the son-in-law of Sir Thomas More.

In the State papers of 1578 there is a list given by an informer of the names and addresses of certain Papists in London, with particulars of those who keep chaplains, attend mass, &c. Among these is mentioned Watson, of Great St Helen's, attorney of Guildhall. ¶ This is all the information I can glean about this brother, unless he is the same John Watson who is mentioned in 1579 as laying complaints before the Privy Council against the Protestant Bishop of Lincoln, and who is said to be *non compos mentis*. ** But to return to the year 1559.

---

* Council Register, vol. i., A. 1558–1559. Mary. Elizabeth, p. 263. Machyn notes in his diary that the two bishops were sent to the Tower by the guard by water, to the Old Swan, and to Billingsgate after. (Diary, p. 192.) † Ibid. p. 278.
‡ Ibid. p. 201. § Lamb's Collection, p. 207.
|| See Cooper's Notes to Baker's History of St John's, vol. i. p. 374, n. 163, 165, and p. 377, n. 182.
¶ P. R. O., Dom. Eliz., Addenda, vol. xxv. n. 118.
** Privy Council Register, 16th October 1579, p. 641.

Elizabeth was disappointed in her hopes that the bishops would accept her supremacy. The only one who yielded was Kitchin of Llandaff. Jewel writes to his friend, Peter Martyr, on August 1st :—" The bishops, rather than abandon the Pope, whom they have so often abjured before, are willing to submit to anything. Not, however, that they do so for the sake of religion, of which they have none, but for the sake of consistency, which the miserable knaves now choose to call their conscience." "Now that religion is everywhere changed," continues this amiable gentleman, " the mass priests absent themselves altogether from public worship, as if it were the greatest impiety to have anything in common with the people of God." *

Dr Lingard has summed up in a few words the history of the Catholic hierarchy :— †

" It should be observed," he says, " that deprivation was not the only punishment inflicted on the Catholic bishops for their nonconformity. They were objects of persecution, with, perhaps, one exception, as long as they lived. Those who had attended in Parliament were deprived immediately, the others were sent for from the country, and shared the fate of their brethren. All were placed under custody ; and during the winter the sentence of excommunication was published against Heath (of York), and Thirlby (of Ely), and in the summer against Bonner (of London). By that time Tunstall of Durham, Morgan of St David's, Ogilthorpe of Carlisle, White of Winchester, and Baines of Coventry, had died of the contagious malady which prevailed. Scot of Chester, Goldwell of St Asaph, and Pate of Worcester, found the means of retiring to the Continent. Of the remaining seven, Heath, after two or three months' imprisonment in the Tower, ‡ was

---

* Zurich Letters, vol. i. p. 39.—This testimony is noteworthy, since it is generally thought that most of the priests conformed. This is refuted statistically by Mr Simpson in his " Life of Campion." Jewel also writes (November 2, 1559) after visiting Reading, Abingdon, Gloucester, Bristol, Bath, Wells, Exeter, Cornwall, Dorset, and Salisbury—" If inveterate obstinacy was found anywhere it was altogether among the priests, those especially who had once been on our side. Let them make what disturbance they please, we have in the meantime disturbed them from their rank and office."—Letters, i. 45.

† History of England, vol. vi. note B, p. 668 (ed. 1849).

‡ This seems erroneous. In June 1562, Heath was still in the Tower

permitted to live on his own property at Cobham, in Surrey where the Queen, by whom he was greatly respected, occasionally honoured him with a visit. Bonner, after a confinement of ten years, died in the Marshalsea ; Watson of Lincoln remained a prisoner twenty-three years, and died in Wisbeach Castle. Thirlby of Ely lived in the custody of Archbishop Parker, and Bourne of Bath and Wells in that of Dr Carew, Dean of Exeter. Turberville of Exeter, and Pool of Peterborough, were suffered to remain at their own houses on their recognisances not to leave them without licence. Feckenham, Abbot of Westminster, passed from the Tower to the custody of the Bishop of London, then to that of the Bishop of Winchester, and was at last confined in Wisbeach Castle."

Watson survived all his brethren with the exception of Goldwell of St Asaph, who died a few months later.[*] Our attention must be limited to Bishop Watson, and even as regards him I must now omit all the events which took place around him, and merely trace him from prison to prison till his death.

If in truth he was left in liberty, after his release from the Tower on June 25th, 1559, which I do not think likely, he was once more sent to the Tower on 20th May 1560.[†] Strype tells us [‡] that he was committed thither by the Archbishop of Canterbury (Parker) and other ecclesiastical commissioners. There were at the same time five other bishops, the Abbot of Westminster, and Dr Boxall.

A letter from the Privy Council to the Archbishop allowed them to come together for their meals, if he approved of it ; the Archbishop of York (Heath), the Bishop of Worcester (Pate), the Abbot of Westminster (Feckenham), and Dr Boxall, at one table ; the Bishop of Ely (Thirlby), the Bishop of Bath (Bourne), the Bishop of Exeter (Turberville), and the Bishop of Lincoln, at another table. Strype adds, that " after a while they were all committed to easier restraints, and some restored to their perfect liberty." This is incorrect, as we have seen. As to Dr Watson, he is returned by the Lieutenant of the Tower [§] a year afterwards,

---

[*] His life has been written by the Rev. F. Knox, in the " Month."
[†] Machyn's Diary, p. 235.
[‡] Annals of the Reformation, vol. i. pt. i. p. 211.
[§] P. R. O., Domestic Eliz., vol. xvii. n. 13.

May 26, 1561, as still under his charge; and so far from the restraint becoming easier, in June 1562, the lieutenant writes to "put their lordships of the Privy Council in remembrance that the late bishops, with Mr Feckenham and Mr Boxall, being all eight in number, be close and severally kept, for the which they continually call upon him to make in their names humble suit to have more liberty," and he informs their lordships that "it is very troublesome to serve so many persons so long together." *   What result this application may have had as regards the others I cannot say. The Bishop of Lincoln was still in the Tower in September 5, 1562. †   In March 1563, an Act was passed ‡ enabling the Protestant Bishops to require the oath of the Queen's supremacy from any who had ever held office in the church during the last three reigns, or who should say or hear a private mass, &c.   The refusal to take this oath when tendered the first time subjected the refuser to perpetual imprisonment; a second refusal subjected him to death, as in cases of high treason.   The Queen, however, secretly warned the bishops not to proceed to tender the oath a second time without her leave.   Had this not been the case, Watson would be now ranked among the martyrs instead of the confessors.

When this law passed, or shortly afterwards, Watson was given into the custody of Edmund Grindal, Bishop of London, one whom he had known at Cambridge, and whom he had met more than once in disputation since. §   But if he had been ready to discuss with him when they met on equal terms, he wisely refused to renew the encounter with one who was his jailor.   This we learn from the following letter of Grindal to Cecil (October 15, 1563):—"I thank you that . . . ye remembered to ease me of one guest . . .   My Lord of Ely received him on Sunday last past, and writeth that he is welcome for their sakes that send him, otherwise not.   I signified to Dr Watson that, if he had tarried, I was willing to have conferred with him in divers points, but he answereth that he will not enter in conference with no man.   The reason is, he will not incur penalties of laws.   I said only one

---

* P. R. O., Domestic Eliz., vol. xxiii., n. 40.
† Ibid, vol. xxiv. 39 i.   ‡ See Lingard, vol. vi. p. 83.
§ *e.g.*, at Sir Richard Morison's in 1551, at the Convocation of 1553, and at the Westminster Conference in 1559.

law was penal,* that might be forborne ; but he persisted in his opinion. I here said, ' Mr Feckenham is not so precise, but could be contented to confer.' The Bishop of Winton,† when he was with me, said that if he should have any, he could best deal with Feckenham, for in King Edward's days he travailed with Feckenham in the Tower, and brought him to subscribe to all things, saving the presence, and one or two more articles. Ye might do very well (in my opinion) to ease the poor Dean of Westminster,‡ and send the other also " (*i.e.*, Feckenham), " to some other bishop, as Sarum or Chichester, &c. It is more reason that we bishops should be troubled with them than the poor dean." §

It appears from the above letter that Watson, after being some time, we do not know how long, in the custody of the Bishop of London, had been transferred in October 1563 to that of Coxe, Bishop of Ely. With him he remained rather more than a year, for by a letter from the Privy Council,‖ dated 9th January (apparently of the year 1564—5), the Bishop of Ely is ordered to send him to the Tower again, while at the same time the Lieutenant of the Tower is instructed " to keep him in safe ward, without having conference with any."

This is an indication of what we shall see explicitly stated by the Government on another occasion, that Watson both had and exerted great influence in keeping Catholics faithful to God and His Holy Church, in spite of persecution.

Five years after his recommittal, a return of the prisoners in the Tower, made April 1570, shows him to have been still confined in the state prison.¶ Baker says that, on the publication of the bull of excommunication against the Queen by St Pius V. in February 1570, Bishop Watson was interrogated together with Feckenham, Cole, and Harpsfield, concerning the bull, and that his answers (given under his hand) were

* Denying the Queen's supremacy by statute, 1 Eliz. c. 1.
† Horne.
‡ Goodman, in whose custody Feckenham then was.
§ Grindal's Remains, p. 281 (Parker Society). Feckenham was sent to Horne, who was not so successful as he had hoped. For an account of the controversy between Horne and Feckenham see Stapleton's Counterblast.
‖ Privy Council Register, Eliz., vol. i. p. 143.
¶ P. R. O., Dom. Eliz., vol. 67, n. 93.

very temperate, and with due regard to his allegiance to the Queen.*

Baker refers to Goldast, a German, who has preserved the answers of Watson, which I do not find in the State Papers. I give them as Goldast has translated them in Latin.

"Respondeo me eam rem non aliter quam ex auditu compertam habere. Neque enim Bullam præfatam aut legi unquam aut vidi. Confiteor reginam nostram Elizabetham, non obstante Pontificis Romani bullâ, aut declaratione quacunque, veram nostram esse et legitimam Angliæ et Hiberniæ Reginam, eique ut Reginæ ab omnibus suis subditis obedientiam debere præstari. Confiteor me, non obstante bulla præfata, vel quacunque alia jam facta aut deinceps facienda, Reginæ Elizabethæ, ut subditum legitimæ principi suæ, obedientiam et fidelitatem debere." †

It does not become me to discuss so delicate a matter, or to criticise either a canonised pope or a bishop who was confessor of the faith. Dr Milner has treated the question of the bull of excommunication in his Sixth Letter to a Prebendary, and defended the loyalty of Bishop Watson both to the Queen and to the Pope. He observes that "Pius V. did not require the English Catholics to receive or observe his bull;" that "he never published or signified it to them," and that "Gregory XIII., his successor, explicitly declared that the bull did not regard the consciences of English Catholics." But to return to the record of the bishop's imprisonments, I may here insert a letter written about this time by Grindal, Bishop of London, to Cecil, on February 3, 1569-70:—

"Sir,—I pray you most instantly to be a mean that I be not troubled with the Bishop of Ross.‡ He is a man of such quality as I like nothing at all. If needs I must have a guest, I had rather keep Mr Hare § still. If it please you to know mine opinion *in genere*, surely I think it were good that such as deserve to be committed should be sent *ad custodias publicas*. Experience declareth that none of those are reformed which are sent to me and others, and by securing of them the punishment lighteth upon us." ||

* History of St John's, p. 140.
† Goldast, Monarch, tom. iii. p. 66, ed. Francof, 1613.
‡ John Leslie.   § Michael Hare, Esq., a Catholic gentleman.
|| Grindal's Remains, p. 320.

Whether in consequence of this remonstrance or for other reasons, Watson, as I have said, was kept in the Tower. In July 1574, we find him in the Marshalsea. I have not been able to discover the time of his removal thither from the Tower. At that date the Privy Council * sent "a letter to the Bishop of Canterbury in the behalf of Dr Watson, prisoner in the Marshalsea, that upon sufficient sureties and bonds taken to the Queen's Majesty's use, that the said doctor shall not by speech, writing, or other means, induce or entice any person to any opinion or act to be done contrary to the laws established in the realm for causes of religion, to give order that he may be delivered to his brother John Watson, to remain with him at his house, and not to depart from thence at any time, without the licence of the lords of the Council; nor that any person shall resort to the said Doctor Watson any time, other than such as shall have occasion to resort to the said John Watson."

These various imprisonments have taken but a few pages to relate, but they had extended over fifteen years. When the bishop was sent to the Tower at the close of the Westminster Conference, he was scarcely forty-three years old; he is now fifty-eight. We know that at his first committal he was suffering from a severe attack of ague; he can scarcely have escaped relapses in such places as the Tower and the Marshalsea. In a letter of Grindal's, written 15th August 1569, he says, " The prison sickness reigns usually at this time of the year. Milerus the Irishman in my custody is very sick of an ague." Yet it is probable that the bishop's prisons were less unhealthy than the Tower. Nothing can be more piteous than the description which Richard Creagh, Catholic Archbishop of Armagh, who was confined there at the same time as the Bishop of Lincoln, gives of his various infirmities brought on by bad air, bad food, and confinement.† We have no details of the nature of Watson's imprisonment, of the books allowed him, or persons who could resort to him. In those days prisoners sometimes purchased the connivance of their jailors and managed to say or hear mass; and priests found their way to them in disguise and heard their confessions and gave them holy communion.

* Privy Council Register, Eliz., vol. ii. p. 246.
† Published by the Bishop of Ossory in his Spicilegium Ossoriense, from the State Papers.

Whether and how far the Bishop of Lincoln gained any such consolations can only be a matter of conjecture. We can, however, easily imagine the joy of the venerable confessor when, in the security of his brother's house, he might once more offer the holy sacrifice, recite his breviàry, study and converse with Catholics. He could not indeed go out, and visitors were forbidden under penalties to communicate with him. Dodd writes as if he " administered confirmation and gave advice on matters regarding government and discipline " to the afflicted Catholics now without a bishop to direct them, and with only fugitive priests to instruct or feed them with the sacraments. But perhaps Dodd is here writing from conjecture.[*] He says also in his short biographical notice : " While Bishop Watson lived, he was consulted and regarded as the chief Superior of the English Catholic clergy, and, as far as his confinement would permit, exercised the functions of his character." [†]

This, at least, is fully borne out by the documents I am about to produce. After the bishop had remained three years with his brother, viz., in July 1577, the following letter was sent by Walsingham to the Bishop of London :—

" After my very hearty commendations unto your lordship, the inconvenience and mischief being daily found to increase, not only to the danger of her Majesty's person, but to the disturbance of the common quiet of this realm ; and the lenity that hath been showed to such persons as obstinately refuse to come to the church in the time of sermons and common prayer : It is resolved, therefore, that for the redress thereof, there shall be some consultation, and thereupon some general order to be set down, which shall not be changed. And because it is intended that your lordship shall be present at the said consultation, I am for that purpose also appointed by my lords to require you to be there upon Thursday, and to. bring with you Mr Doctor Hamon, your Chancellor, and such as you shall think meet. And forasmuch as the special point of the said consultation will stand upon the order that may be taken generally with all them that refuse · to come to the church, and in particular what is meetest to be done with Watson, Feckenham, Harpsfield, and others of that kind

* Dodd's Church History, vol. iii. p. 45 (ed. Tierney).
† Ibid. Part iii., book 2, art. 3. (orig. ed.)

that are thought to be the leaders and the pillars of the consciences of great numbers of such as be carried with these
errors, whether it be not fit they be disputed with, all in some
private sort, and after disputation had with them, and they
thereby not reduced to conformity, then whether it shall be
better to banish them the realm, or to keep them here together
in some strait sort, as they may be kept from all conference to
the further maintenance of this corruption. . . . . . I have
thought meet to give you of the same these short remembrances, that by thinking thereupon, and of some such other
things as may further this good intention, your lordship may
come the better prepared to the furtherance of so good a purpose.   And so I bid your lordship most heartily farewell."*

Enclosed with this letter were the following memoranda†:—

*How such as are backward and corrupt in Religion may be
reduced to conformity, and others stayed from like corruption.*

" For the reducing to conformity of such as are corrupt in
religion, and refuse to yield obedience to the laws of the realm,
provided in that behalf, and the staying of others from falling
into like corruption, three things principally are to be put in
execution.

" 1. The first in taking order generally with such as are
recusants, as that they may be brought to obey the laws.

" 2. The second in providing, either by banishment or restraint, that Watson, Feckenham, and the rest upon whose
advice and consciences the said recusants depend, may do no
harm.

.   .   .   .

" Touching the second point for the restraining or banishing
of Watson and the rest: if banishment be not thought meet,
then it is to be considered how they may be restrained in such
sort as there may be no access had unto them, which may be
performed by putting these things following in execution :—

" First, in making choice of some apt place for the keeping
of them.

" Secondarily, in appointing some man of trust to take
charge of them.

" Lastly, in taxing upon the bishops and clergy such as are

* P. R. O., Dom. Eliz., vol. xlv. p. 21.   † Ibid. p. 10.

non-residents, and have pluralities, some yearly contribution
for the finding of them, and a convenient stipend to be given
to their keeper."

The result of all these deliberations was that the following
letter was addressed by the Council to those into whose charge
the poor Catholics were committed.*

" After our right hearty commendations unto your lordship,
whereas her Majesty heretofore, after the restraining of Feckenham, Watson, and others, very backward and obstinate in
religion, upon persuasion and some opinion conceived that by
granting them liberty they might be drawn in time to yield
themselves conformable unto her Highness' laws, she was contented to have them enlarged, and bonds taken of them for
their good behaviours, as that they should refrain all manner
of conference, secret practices or persuasions, to seduce her
said subjects by withdrawing of them from the religion presently received within this realm, and their dutiful obedience
towards her Highness and her laws : forasmuch as it is in-
formed that Feckenham, Watson, and the rest, contrary to their
bonds, promise, and hope conceived of their amendment, have
and do daily and manifestly abuse the liberty granted unto
them, whereby many of her Highness' said subjects are by
their secret persuasions lately fallen and withdrawn from their
due obedience, refusing to come unto the church, and to perform that part of their duties which heretofore they have been
dutifully contented to yield.   Upon consideration whereof her
Majesty foreseeing of what consequence the effects of these lewd
persuasions and practices may be, if in time they shall not
conveniently be met withal, hath thought it convenient again
to restrain them of their liberties, and to make choice of some
of your calling, unto whom they might be committed, and
carefully looked unto, and, namely, hath appointed the person
of A. B. unto your lordship's custody, to be straitly kept
and dealt withal, according to a form which we send your
lordship herewith in writing, requiring you in her Majesty's
name, at such time as the said A. B. shall be sent unto you to
receive him, and in all points to do your endeavour strictly to
follow the said form for the usage of him during the time he
shall remain with you, unless upon some good report made by

* P. R. O., Dom. Eliz., vol. cxiv. n. 69.

you of hope of his conformity, it shall be by her Majesty or us ordered, that he shall be more favourably dealt withal.

" Wherein not doubting but you will thoroughly perform the expectation had of your care in this behalf, we bid your lordship right heartily."

A form to be observed by my Lords the Bishops in the ordering of such as were committed to their custody for Popery.

" 1. That his lodging be in such a convenient part of your house, as he may both be there in safe custody, and also have no easy access of your household people unto him, other than such as you shall appoint, and know to be settled in religion and honesty, as that they may not be perverted in religion or any otherwise corrupted by him.

" 2. That he be not admitted unto your own table except upon some good occasion to have ministered to him there, in the presence of some that shall happen to resort unto you, such talk whereby the hearers may be confirmed in the truth ; but to have his diet by himself alone in his chamber, and that in no superfluity, but after the spare manner of scholars' commons.

" 3. That you suffer none, unless some one to attend upon him, to have access unto him ; but such as you shall know to be persons well confirmed in true religion, and are [not] likely to be weakened in the profession of the said religion by any conference they shall have with him.

" 4. That you permit him not at any time and place while he is with you to enter into any disputation of matters of religion, or to reason thereof otherwise than upon such occasion as shall be by you, or in your presence with your good liking by some other, ministered unto him.

" 5. That he have ministered unto him such books of learned men and sound writers in divinity, as you are able to lend him and none other.

" 6. That he have no liberty to walk abroad to take the air, but when yourself is at best leisure to go with him, or accompanied with such as you shall appoint.

" 7. That you do your endeavour by all good persuasions to bring him to the hearing of sermons, and other exercise of religion in your house and the chapel or church which you most commonly frequent."

I do not think that it is a rash conjecture that Watson's old antagonist Grindal was at the bottom of these severe measures. In 1570 he had been promoted from the see of London to that of York, and in the beginning of 1576 to that of Canterbury. We have seen him express his opinion that the recusants should be confined in the public prisons rather than in the bishops' houses. When he was Archbishop of York (in November 13, 1574), he did not disguise his vexation, in a letter to Lord Burghley, at the news which had reached him of the greater measure of freedom lately granted to Dr Watson. I give a long extract from this letter, because it contains some interesting details regarding one of Watson's old companions at Cambridge, Thomas Vavasor, a physician, and one who had harboured Campion in 1572 :—

" My very good lord,—We of the ecclesiastical commission have here sent a certificate to my Lords of the Council of our proceedings this term. Only five persons have been committed for their obstinacy or papistical religion. For the number of that sect (thanks be to God !) daily diminisheth in this diocese especially. None of note was committed, save only your old acquaintance, Doctor Vavasor, who hath been tolerated in his own house in York almost three-quarters of a year. In his answer, made in open judgment, he showed himself the same man which you have known him to be in his younger years : which was sophistical, disdainful, and eluding arguments with derision, when he was not able to solute the same by learning. His great anchor-hold was in urging the literal sense of *hoc est corpus meum*, thereby to prove transubstantiation, which to deny, saith he, is as great an heresy as to deny consubstantiation,* defined in the Nicene Council. The diversity was sufficiently declared unto him by testimonies of the fathers. *Sed ipse sibi plaudit.* My Lord President and I, knowing his disposition to talk, thought it not good to commit the said Dr Vavasor to the castle of York, where some other like affected remain prisoners ; but rather to a solitary prison in the Queen's Majesty's castle at Hull, where he shall only talk to walls.

" The imprisoned for religion in these parts of late made supplication to be enlarged, seeming, as it were, to require it of right, by the example of enlarging Feckenham, Watson,

---

* The consubstantiality of the Son with the Father.

and other papists above (*i.e.*, in London). We here are to think that all things done above are done upon great causes, though the same be to us unknown. But certainly my Lord President and I join in opinion, that if such a general jubilee should be put in use in these parts, a great relapse would follow soon after." [*]

It is not rash to suppose that when Grindal became Archbishop of Canterbury, he should have looked with a jealous eye on the liberty enjoyed by Dr Watson, however restricted it was, and should have used his influence to destroy it.

In July 1577 then Bishop Watson was given over to the custody of Dr Horne, Bishop of Winchester, with the instructions given above.[†] At the same time, Young was sent to the Dean of Canterbury, Harpsfield to the Protestant Bishop of Lincoln, and Feckenham to the Bishop of Ely.

Robert Horne, who was now Bishop of Winchester, has been already mentioned as one of the Fellows of St John's, contemporary with Watson. He had been one of the leaders of the Protestant movement, and had been made Dean of Durham during the reign of Edward. He had been deprived because of his marriage and heresy, and had been succeeded by Watson. He would naturally, therefore, not look very favourably on his theological opponent and ecclesiastical rival. Mr Cooper thus gives his character : "Bishop Horne was no doubt a man of considerable learning and ability, although he appears to have had an imperfect control over a somewhat unhappy temper. His memory is obnoxious for his furious zeal in defacing the monuments of the piety of a former age." [‡] Horne had also brought an action against the Bishop of Lincoln for some goods and books which he said had been unjustly taken from him when he was deprived of his deanery of Durham. This was in February 1560, after Watson himself had been deposed from his bishopric.[§] It seems then quite natural that he should not have relished the company of Watson, any more than Watson his guardianship.

In August the Council wrote to the Bishop of Winchester, " that whereas Dr Watson hath been a suitor unto their lord-

[*] Grindal's Remains, p. 350.
[†] Privy Council Register, Eliz., vol. iv. p. 1.
[‡] Cooper's Athenæ Cantabrigienses.
[§] See Letter of Horne to Cecil, P. R. O., Dom. Eliz., vol. xi. n. 16.

ships to have a man of his own to attend upon him during his being in the custody of the said bishop, whereof although their lordships made difficulty, for that his man is of his religion, they are notwithstanding upon consideration that it is less danger to let one already corrupted than a sound person to attend upon him, he is required to permit his said man to attend upon him so he shall be contented to repair unto the church ; and withal his lordship to take heed that in using the company of his men, none of them do receive infection from him." *

Bishop Watson seems to have been sent to Bishops-Waltham, Farnham, or Winchester, places where he had been familiarly known and respected in a different character. Horne was not long before he seized on a pretext to get rid of his unwelcome guest, as we find from the following letter, written to the Bishop of Winchester by the Council (16th January 1578–9) :—

"That whereas he desireth to be discharged of the custody of Dr Watson, in respect that his lordship intendeth for recovery of his health to repair to London, his lordship is required to bring the said Watson thither with him, who for like infirmity desireth to go thither ; and further orders shall be taken for his custody."†

Their lordships resolved to transfer him to the custody of the Bishop of Rochester, John Young, who had been appointed to that see in 1578. They accordingly wrote to him (on 19th February 1578–9) :—

"That whereas Dr Watson, committed to the keeping of the Bishop of Winton, is by occasion of sickness of the bishop to be removed, and is ordered to remain with the said Bishop of Rochester; his lordship is required to take him into his charge, to use all good means to bring him to conformity, and to have regard that he have no such conference nor repair as he may corrupt others.

"To Bishop of Winton to give him notice what is done, and to require him to give order that the said Watson may be safely delivered into the custody and charge of the Bishop of Rochester." ‡

* Council Register, Eliz., vol. iv. p. 10.
† Ibid. p. 376.
‡ Ibid. p. 403. Also Strype's Annals, vol. ii., part 2, app. p. 660.

The only incident on record connected with Dr Watson's imprisonment under this official is, that a certain Portuguese, named Antonio Fogaça, induced the Bishop of Lincoln and the Archbishop of Armagh, then imprisoned in the Tower, to sign two letters, one to the King of Portugal, the other to his Majesty's Confessor. These were intercepted. Antonio, on being interrogated, declared that he himself indited the two letters in Spanish, and gave money to Dr Watson's servant to obtain his master's hand to the letters.*

This was in April 1580. The Bishop's servant was also interrogated, and as his answers contain some interesting particulars I will transcribe them. I omit the questions for brevity's sake, as the answers will speak for themselves.

The answer of William Whiting, unto such interrogatories as were ministered unto him the 17th of March 1579–80.

" To the first interrogatory he saith, that he knoweth Fogaça if he see him, and hath only known him but since one month before Christmas, and never saw him before that time, nor ever since but once, meeting him by chance in the streets ; and sith that at the first time of his acquaintance with the said Fogaça he came unto him in the streets, but where about in the streets he cannot remember, at which time the said Fogaça demanded of him if he were not Dr Watson's servant, and this examinate answering ' yea,' the said Fogaça desired him to carry two letters from him to his master, and to procure him to sign them ; which at the first he refused, for that (as he saith) his master had forbidden him to bring him any letters, but afterward (at the earnest instance of the said Fogaça, declaring unto him that the contents of the letters were only to signify what good deeds he had done here to good men, and that the commendation thereof confirmed by Dr Watson would do him much good), he was contented, and did thereupon carry them unto his said master.

" To the second he saith, that he knoweth no Catholic prisoner by name, but only some few in the Marshalsea—Wood, Bilson, Pound, Bluet, Webster, with whom he came acquainted, being himself prisoner in the Marshalsea by the space of one-half year, committed upon suspicion to be a priest. And to these men he hath sundry times repaired since his en-

* P. R. O., Dom. Eliz., vol. cxxxvii. pp. 647, 649.

largement as of himself, but never carried or received anything to or fro between his master and them.

"To the third he saith, he hath had recourse unto his master since the time of his commitment unto the Bishop of Rochester, at the least every week once, but never carried any letters or writing unto his master from any man; neither ever brought any letters or writings from his master to any other person.

"To the fourth he saith, that he knoweth not any man from whom his master hath ever received any exhibition or relief, but only from John Watson, his brother; but what he hath had from him, this examinate knoweth not.

"To the fifth he saith, that he never delivered any other letters, writings, or papers unto his master than the two letters he received from Fogaça, unto whom he restored them after his master had subscribed them, within one day, at his house in Mark Lane, where (as he saith) he never was before, but had notice of the place of Fogaça's dwelling at the time when he received the letters of him; of whom he had a crown in money at the bringing of the letters unto him: and no speeches he had with Fogaça, but was asked of him how his master did, and he answered him that he was well, and no more.

"To the sixth he saith as in the first, that the letters contained only matters of Fogaça, his commendation.

"To the seventh he saith, that he knoweth not by whom the letters were penned, nor whose handwriting they were, and were received by him and delivered as is above said.

"Signed by me,

WM. WHITING."*

When the Archbishop of Armagh was interrogated why he signed these letters, he replied that "he was persuaded that thereby there should grow some relief unto such as are in prison for religion."† Hugh Kenrick, a Sheriff's Protonotary, who had helped to convey the letters, being questioned, "confessed that one William Whiting, servant to Dr Watson, did bring unto him, a little before Christmas, a letter, written in a Roman hand, directed unto the King of Portugal, . . . and touching the reading of the said letters, he saith he never read

* P. R. O., Dom. Eliz., vol. cxxxvi. n. 62.   † Ibid. n. 54.

them, for that he conceived that being subscribed by Watson, they did contain no undutiful matter."

There are other papers on this matter, which may be truly described as " much ado about nothing." The incident is interesting, as bringing together two great confessors of the faith, and in proving the truth of the long imprisonment in the Tower of the Archbishop of Armagh, which Mr Froude has recklessly denied.

There exists, among the State Papers,* a memorandum, in Lord Burghley's handwriting, apparently made in July 1580. It runs as follows :—

" Things to be considered—That all the deposed ecclesiastical Papists be collected together, and sent to divers castles, as to Wisbech [or] Banbury. That all the papistical laymen, being manifest recusants, remaining upon bonds, may be sent for by the commissioners, and be bestowed into some convenient places near London, under sure guard.

" That their armour be seized.

" That generally all such others as will not come to the church, may be fined and imprisoned by virtue of the ecclesiastical commission."

The result of the Council's deliberations was the choice of Wisbech Castle, in Cambridgeshire, as a fit receptacle for the unfortunate priests, and thither in consequence Bishop Watson was committed in August or September.

Strype says that " when certain Roman emissaries came into the realm, and began to disturb the church, Watson (being too conversant with them) was committed to Wisbech Castle a close prisoner."†

These " Roman emissaries " were the seminary priests from Douay, and the Jesuits. Into the history of this movement I must not enter. It is being illustrated by better hands than mine. I will merely say that the epoch of Catholic martyrdoms had now begun. " Cuthbert Maine had led the way in 1577, the first of the glorious holocaust of Douay priests. In 1578 one priest had been martyred, John Nelson ; and one layman, Thomas Sherwood, a Douay student. Four priests

---

* S. P., Dom. Eliz. Addenda, vol. xxvii. n. 21.
† Annals of the Reformation, vol. i. part i. p. 214.

suffered in 1581, Campion's year; and in 1582 no less than eleven." *

Baker says, " Upon the alarm given by the coming over of Parsons and Campion, Jesuits; Watson and others were committed to Wisbech, where they lived in a collegiate and friendly manner, no one assuming authority over the rest till after the Jesuits coming among them."†

He also tells us that Bishop Watson " greatly disliked the violent proceedings of the Jesuits." This is also repeated by Mr Cooper. A few words must be said in explanation of these statements, which are likely to be misunderstood. By " violent proceedings " is meant the method of acting of the Jesuit missionaries, adopted generally in England. By " assumption of superiority," reference is made to an unhappy dispute which arose among the prisoners at Wisbech. Though these two matters are perfectly distinct, yet they were confounded and worked up together in some passionate pamphlets published in the years 1601–3, and it will be necessary at least to disentangle the truth regarding Dr Watson, though I have no intention of reviving the memory of former quarrels. I begin then with some extracts from a pamphlet, printed in 1601, called " Important Considerations by the Secular Priests," which gives a review of the policy of the government, and of the treatment of Catholics, from the schism until the death of Bishop Watson.

" It cannot be denied," say these writers, " but that for the first ten years of her Majesty's reign the state of Catholics in England was tolerable, and after a sort in some good quietness. Such as for their consciences were imprisoned in the beginning of her coming to the Crown were very kindly and mercifully used, the state of things then considered. Some of them were appointed to remain with such of their friends as they themselves made choice of. Others were placed, some with bishops, some with deans, and had their diet at their tables, with such convenient lodgings and walks for their recreation as did well content them. They that were in the ordinary prisons, had such liberty and other commodities, as the places would afford, not inconvenient for men that were in their cases.

* The Troubles of our Catholic Forefathers, by Father Morris (2 series 1875), p. 13.
† History of St John's, vol. i. p. 140.

"The Catholics here continued in sort, as before you have heard, till the said Rebellion brake forth in the North, 1569, a little before Christmas; and that it was known that the Pope had excommunicated the Queen, and thereby freed her subjects (as the bull importeth) from their subjection. And then there followed a great restraint of the said prisoners.

"Their [the Jesuits] first repair hither was Anno 1580, when the realm of Ireland was in great combustion, and then they entered (viz., Mr Campion, the subject, and Mr Parsons, the provincial) like a tempest, with sundry such great brags and challenges, as divers of the gravest clergy then living in England (Dr Watson, Bishop of Lincoln, and others) did greatly dislike them, and plainly foretold that (as things then stood) their proceedings after that fashion would certainly urge the state to make some sharper laws, which should not only touch them, but likewise all others, both priests and Catholics.

"Besides, to the further honour of her Majesty, we may not omit that the states of the whole realm assembled in Parliament, Anno 1576, were pleased to pass us over, and made no laws at that time against us. The ancient prisoners that had been restrained more narrowly in the year 1570, were (notwithstanding the said enterprises in Ireland) again restored to their former liberty, to continue with their friends as they had done before.

"But when the Jesuits were come, and that the state had notice of the said excommunication, there was then within a while a great alteration, . . . thence was a greater restraint of Catholics than at any time before. Many, both priests and gentlemen, were sent into the Isle of Ely, and other places, there to be more safely kept and looked unto. . . .

"The same month [January 1581] also a Parliament ensued, wherein a law was made agreeable in effect to the said proclamation, but with a more severe punishment annexed; for it was a penalty of death for any Jesuit or seminary priest to repair into England, and for any to receive and entertain them, which fell out according to Bishop Watson's former speeches or prediction, what mischief the Jesuits would bring upon us.

"Such of us as remained in prison at Wisbech (and were committed thither 1580, and others not long after committed

also thither, to the number of about thirty-three or thirty-four),
continued still in the several times of all the said most wicked
designments, as we were before ; and were never brought into
any trouble for them, but lived there, college-like, without any
want, and in good reputation with our neighbours that were
Catholics about us."*

On these extracts I would observe that it is certainly true
that the persecution of Catholics in the latter part of Elizabeth's reign was more severe than in the first twenty years,
and that the change was produced in part by the action of the
Sovereign Pontiff, of the seminary priests, and of the Jesuits.
But this is easily explained without blaming any for "violent
proceedings." At the beginning of Elizabeth's reign, those
who remained faithful to the Church waited to see what would
happen. They had been accustomed to changes in the reigns
of Henry, Edward, and Mary. Elizabeth might die and
another change occur in favour of the Catholics. But as
years rolled on, it became clear that the whole policy of the
Government was to bring about external conformity at least
to the state religion, and that no toleration would be granted
to nonconformity. The priests, therefore, who by the efforts
of Cardinal Allen and others were educated with a view to
this new state of things, came into England with the clear
purpose of resisting this absorption of the Catholics into the
national schism and heresy with all their power. In this work
the Jesuits zealously co-operated. Their policy was exactly
the same as that of the seminary priests, of Cardinal Allen
and of the Holy See. It would perhaps be rash to assert that
Dr Watson never let fall any expression of fear as to the
results of Father Campion's public challenge, which was afterwards distorted by the enemies of the Society into a dislike
for their general policy. But to say that he really blamed the
boldness, the zeal, and self-sacrifice with which the new race
of priests sought to arouse the faith and constancy of the
Catholics, as well as to bring back heretics, would be absurd.
He had himself suffered in that cause for twenty years. He
is mentioned in state documents as one of the most active in
persuading Catholics to refuse any compromise, and in winning
back those who had yielded. In 1577 he was called by

* Important Considerations by the Secular Priests, A.D. 1601.
From a Reprint : London, 1688. Pp. 34-49.

Walsingham one of "the leaders and pillars of the consciences of great numbers;" while Strype tells us that the very reason why he was committed to Wisbech was that he was too conversant with the new "Roman emissaries."

I conclude therefore that, in the heat of subsequent disputes, the little party of schismatical priests, who resisted the archpriest, and complained of the rigour of the persecution, willing to strengthen their cause by an appeal to great names, exaggerated some casual expression of Dr Watson, or wrested it from its meaning, just as they in the same way, after Cardinal Allen's death, reported that he too had made use of some expression in conversation derogatory to the illustrious Society of which he has been always the warmest friend. These appeals to the unwritten *obiter dicta* of great and holy men *after their decease*, are very uncertain grounds on which to base historical conclusions.

As it is evident that the writers of the pamphlet highly over estimated the small amount of liberty or comfort, granted to Bishop Watson and the others in their long imprisonments, for the sake of contrasting with it the fierceness of the subsequent persecution which they laid to the charge of the Jesuits; so would they exaggerate the quiet endurance of the holy bishop into a condemnation of the aggressive activity of the younger men who came into England at his death. The truth, however, is, as we shall see directly, that in many respects the imprisonment which the bishop endured at Wisbech was far more severe than that of which these writers speak. Some time after his death a good deal of freedom was granted to the prisoners and even facilities for public worship, but I find no trace of this during his lifetime.

In 1582 Father Parsons wrote an account of the persecution, which he published. In this he describes the treatment that the Bishop of Lincoln and his companions were then enduring at Wisbech—that they were deprived of all their books, and not allowed any intercourse one with the other, except at table.[*] Whether even that degree of freedom was granted at first I should doubt from the following letter[†] written October 16th 1580 by the keepers of Wisbech to the Privy Council:—

[*] De Persecutione Anglicana Libellus, p. 60 (ed. 1582).
[†] P. R. O., Dom. Eliz., vol. 143 n. 17; given by Father Morris in his Life of Weston, p. 226.

"All duty and obedience unto your honourable Lordships—
We crave pardon in that we have not so shortly observed your
honours' direction in advertising the state of the recusants in
Wisbech Castle as was set down. The greatest reason for
our excuse is to crave more time than the allowance of one
month for certifying the state of our proceedings therein ; for
else, by not searching into the particular conditions of the
parties, we might inform more for order than for matter, and
so in vain. Let it therefore please your honours to understand
that the recusants here now imprisoned are eight in number,
namely, Watson, Feckenham, Young, Windham, Oxenbridge,
Metham, Wood, and Bluet. And we, according to your
lordships' letters and articles to the same adjoined, have (as
duty have charged) performed carefully what was enjoined, as
well to the Bishop [of Ely], Gray the keeper, as the prisoners
themselves. Advertising further that the lord bishop hath
appointed a preacher unto the recusants, a man of holy life,
learned, and able to give account of his doctrine strongly.
The men restrained before us both, and others have been
called divers times, and as often required to hear the preacher,
and abide the prayer ; but they all with one voice generally,
and after that every man particularly answering for himself,
denied to allow either, saying that they are not of our
church, or, they will neither hear, pray, nor yet confer with
us of any matters concerning religion. Yet as touching conference we must confess that Oxenbridge, Metham, and Bluet
(being privately dealt with) were contented to abide some
conference with the learned ; but when the place and time
was appointed for disputation upon their own questions, the
first of them that spoke made his protestation that, for
obedience' sake and our pleasings, they were content to
dispute before us, upon divers causes between their church
and ours now in question. Nevertheless, with such minds,
as what and whatsoever could be said against them, they
meant not to be reformed. The disputation held by the space
of two hours, the Lord be thanked ! to the great profit of us
and such as stood by, though to them a hardening.

"We have also, according to the article, with the preacher
perused their books and writings, of which we restrained all,
saving the canonical Scriptures and the allowed writers,
which to forego (together with their Romish notes upon the

same) was a great grief unto their hearts, alleging that the Book of God simply carrieth not such force and comfort to their consciences as when the same is unfolded by the Councils and Church of Rome.

"It may further please your honours that divers of the recusants have their servants to attend upon them, and yet for them to be allowed is not warranted. We have suffered them (as restrained only within the walls) to attend their masters till we know your further pleasure, and in the meantime we find that their repairing together and not so abridged as their masters, is in manner all one as if their masters might as well confer as eat together, which conferring, as it is restrained, so we wish their eating together were. For if they be such offenders as in your honours' letters appear, ordinary meeting at meals doth not only strengthen them in error, but also layeth a persuasion before them that this late earnest restraint, with such favour added, will end with restoring of their former liberty. But it were too much boldness for us to show any further our opinions before your wisdoms, what we think meet for such obstinates, without further understanding of your honourable minds herein.

"Even thus, therefore, beseeching the Lord our God to endue your honours with all knowledge, judgment, and obedience, of and to His will in this behalf, and that even upon these monsters somewhat may be wrought by your authority that may yield to His glory and the godly peace of this part of His Church, in the preservation of the life and continuance of the prosperous government of her most excellent Majesty, with increase of all grace, we most humbly take our leaves from Wisbech Castle the 16th of October 1580. — Your honours most humbly in the Lord at commandment,

"GEORGE CARLETON.
"HUMPHREY MICHELL."

The Castle of Wisbech was an old, dilapidated palace of the Bishops of Ely, surrounded by a moat, and being situated in the fens was a most unwholesome residence for an old man (Dr Watson was now sixty-four years old) subject to ague. It is no wonder that he did not survive more than four years.

But few events connected with these four years have been recorded. Not long after the arrival of the prisoners at

Wisbech, Dr William Fulke, a busy and disputatious Puritan, was sent by order of the Privy Council, for the purpose of conferring with them, and persuading them to resort
to church. They had had enough of these unprofitable discussions, and refused to gratify this man's vanity. Parsons,
in the book above referred to, charged him with thrusting
himself upon them without authority, in order to get the credit
with his party of disputing *cum magnatibus*, and of having
put out a foolish and false account of the occurrence. An
account indeed had been published, but if we may believe
Fulke, without his knowledge. The matter is of no importance.*

If we may give credit to a letter,† written in 1581, in Latin,
by a Catholic prisoner in the Tower, the venerable bishop had
to bear worse insults than the intrusion of Dr Fulke. " Not
many days since," says this letter, " an infamous woman, the
tool of some ruffians, was introduced into the chamber of the
Bishop of Lincoln (who remains still in prison at Wisbech),
and dared in the most shameless way to solicit to sin that
holy man, worn out as he is with cruel treatment. When the
old man with all his might endeavoured to drive the impure
beast from his cell, her evil instigators, who awaited the result,
even threatened him with blows." This history seems almost
incredible, but unfortunately it is not without parallel in the
records of those days.

One more paper existing in the public records‡ throws some
light on the character of the bishop's jailors. It is anonymous,
but from internal evidence seems to have been written by the
Bishop of Ely, and to be addressed to Lord Burghley.

" My right honourable Lord, I am in some conscience
moved to write, but yet this world liketh me so ill, that I have
no hope of good success therein. The recusants of Wisbech
Castle are the men of whom all the rest do depend. They
are sworn against Christ, and His Church here. I see how it
fareth amongst our grave Reformers. I like them so well that
I will not trust them in so good a service. Therefore upon
your lordship and the rest of my lords, and upon the consciences of you all, do I lay this burden. The former letters

* Fulke's version is in Strype's Annals of the Reformation, ii. 342.
† P. R. O., Dom. Eliz., vol. 149 n. 61.
‡ P. R. O., Dom. Eliz., vol. clxviii. n 1.

from the lords to me directed, was to lay upon the recusants a learned preacher, to offer them conference and disputation, and withal to bring them to the service of our church. They refuse all, they obey nothing, they regard not what ye enjoin.

"If my boldness might not be disliked, I would make my suit thus: The care shall be mine, much charge shall be mine, and the danger shall be mine. Let the lords then make Gray's number of the recusants to be twenty. They and their lodgings shall be all enclosed within a brick wall : they shall eat and speak together : they shall conspire, and do what they list. I and mine, my lands and goods, shall answer for all. For I mean if walls, locks, and doors will separate them from out practice, they shall not want a sufficient provision of such. Now let it not be thought, and as some bishops have reported, that I have, or ever mind to make, trade or gain by overruling such wretches. Only Thomas Gray is faithful in his calling ; to him, therefore, let that belong. I have obtained of him a consent, if his number might be twenty, certain and special, to give out of his commodity rising from them, unto two preachers, fourscore pounds by year. For the considerations before, and my care therein, let me then have the favour of naming the preachers, upon which point all hope of doing good and winning glory to God doth consist ; for your honour must know that formality and goodly words of consent to all traditions whatsoever screeneth not the reins [?] of an obstinate mind. But it must come from them, that by holy life and deep judgments are able to set down God's anger and wrath to come.

"May it therefore please your lords to be a mean that of these four here named two of them may be preferred to preach, confer, and dispute within—viz., Lancelot Andrewes, of Pembroke Hall; Lawrence Dewse, of St John's College; Bartholomew Dod, of Jesus' College; and William Flood. The assembly shall be in Wisbech Castle hall. The recusants shall be conveyed thither by a secret way without seeing any; they shall have a secret place for themselves to be in, to hear and not be seen.

"The lords must give me authority to see all this performed, and what else they shall think good and meet to be done. This is the holy ordinance of God. He will bless His own ways. Other courses have not prospered with them. If it please God to move your hearts to consider hereof, you shall try the success. And as I have thus boldly presumed upon your lordships, so have I done the like with Mr the right honourable Secretary. Thus most humbly I take my leave, this first of February 1583 " [*i.e.*, 1584].

Whether the suggestions contained in this letter were acted on I cannot say. To force money out of poor Catholic prisoners, in order to pay preachers to annoy them, was a device worthy of the Reformers. But to say, " This is the holy ordinance of God, He will bless His own ways," was a consummation of impudence that must have startled even the Privy Councillors of Elizabeth.

The other question touched on in the pamphlets already alluded to, is the demeanour of Bishop Watson to his fellow-prisoners. Happily I can extract what they have said of him without concerning myself with the purpose for which they brought it forward.

A book published in 1600 asserted that the fear of incurring a *premunire* " made the late reverend Bishop of Lincoln to refuse all external jurisdiction offered him over his fellow prisoners." In answer to this, another book called " A Brief Apology " accused the writer of misstatement. In 1603 a reply was published to this Apology, and the statement is reiterated on the authority (alleged) " of those who were priests and fellow-prisoners with Bishop Watson, and who were present at the offer and his refusal, and are ear-witnesses thereof."*

We are, however, left in the dark as to the nature of this jurisdiction. If it were episcopal, he still had it by right in his own diocese, but how could priests offer it to him in the diocese of Ely ? If, as it seems more likely, they merely asked him, being a bishop, to rule them as a community, it seems far-fetched to connect his refusal with fears of *premunire.*

However this may be, I am glad to extract the following account of Dr Watson from the ugly controversy in which it is related ; a controversy which began long after the bishop's death, and in which he is in no way concerned :—

" In the year 1580," says an anonymous writer, " Doctor Watson, Bishop of Lincoln, Doctor Feckenham, Abbot of Westminster, Doctor Young, Master Metham, Doctor Oxenbridge,

* A Reply to a Notorious Libel intituled, A Brief Apology, p. 127.

and Master Bluet, were sent to remain as prisoners in the Castle of Wisbech, where they lived in great unity and brotherly kindness; every man intermeddling only with his own affairs and private meditations. They were all in commons with the keeper, and for their recreation had a garden there to walk in, and to solace themselves as they thought good. Such money as was sent to any particular man he had himself the disposition of it, as he thought it convenient; that which came for the common use was by all their consents delivered still to Master Bluet, who divided the same to every man alike. There was then no affectation of superiority, but every man yielded of his own accord that duty and precedency which to every one was due, the keeper having the commandment over them all. Afterwards within about three years, eight or nine gentlemen were likewise sent to remain there as prisoners, upon certain speeches that the Duke of Guise had some intendment against England, whereby the number of the prisoners increased, without any disturbance at all to the foresaid unity. These gentlemen lived at their own charges, and as most dutiful children demeaned themselves towards their fellow-prisoners and spiritual fathers. If at any time some little indiscretion happened in any, a word (especially of his ghostly father) was more than sufficient to reform it: or if upon such like an occasion Bishop Watson were moved to reprove this or that, his answer was: 'What, are we not fellow-prisoners? Are we not at the commandment of another? Shall I add affliction to one that is afflicted? Are we men who profess ourselves to be examples to others in suffering for our consciences, and shall we not be thought then able, without controllers, to govern ourselves? Be content; I will not take upon me to reprove my fellow-prisoners.' And indeed this was the course that every man held, so as by submitting themselves one to another, every man had a commanding power one over another; such was the most Christian and brotherly affection amongst them. In this sort they lived till all were either dead or gone, but Master Metham and Master Bluet, which was for the space of about six or seven years." *

We have now exhausted our information regarding Bishop

* A True Relation of the Faction begun at Wisbech, printed in 1601, (p. 1–3).

Watson. We know nothing of the length or nature of the disease of which he died. We do not know who assisted him, though it is probable that one or other of the priests then in Wisbech was not denied access to him in his last moments. It is related of Bishop Gardiner that "when he was lying on his death-bed, he caused the Passion of Christ to be read unto him, and when he heard it read, that Peter after the denying of his Master, went out and wept bitterly, he, causing the reader to stay, wept himself full bitterly and said, *Ego exivi sed nondum flevi amare* : I have gone out, but as yet I have not wept bitterly." * Gardiner died in the possession of dignity and wealth ; his chaplain Dr Watson was more happy. The sincerity of his repentance for the schism of his early years, of his love to the Church, and fidelity to the Holy See, had been proved by twenty-five years of suffering. He died on 27th September 1584, at the age of sixty-eight. He was the last survivor of the Catholic bishops in England, and with the death of Thomas Goldwell, Bishop of St Asaph's, in the year following, the ancient hierarchy of England ceased to exist. He was buried in the parish church of Wisbech. The register, still in existence, contains simply the entry "1584, 27th September : John† Watson, Doctor, sepultus." No memorial was ever erected,‡ owing to the circumstances of the times ; but I will venture to express a hope that before many years each diocese of our restored hierarchy will commemorate by some fitting monument its confessors and martyrs ; and that Hexham in which Watson was born, and was dean, Nottingham which contains his see, and Northampton which contains his university, as well as his prison and his grave, may each inscribe on its list the name of Thomas Watson. I have sought in vain for any portrait, nor am I aware of any description of his personal appearance. His character may be gathered from his life and writings, Strype calls him "altogether a sour and morose man," § prob-

---

* Stapleton, Counterblast, p. 368.

† By mistake for Thomas. He may have died that day or the day before.

‡ Cole, the antiquarian, searched for one in vain in 1748. See Cole's MS., vol. xviii. p. 90 (British Museum).

§ Annals of the Reformation, vol. i. p. 214. He has merely copied Godwin in this, and Burnet and others repeat the same thing on the same authority. Mr Cooper says that the reflection on Watson's

ably for no other reason than his refusal to sully his priesthood by a sacrilegious marriage, like some of his fellow collegians, or to preserve the honours and revenues of his episcopate by apostasy. On the other hand, Thomas Nash bears testimony, not merely to his merit and scholarship, but to his wit and good humour. There is a calmness and absence of invective in his sermons very unusual in those days ; and in the various disputations in which he was engaged you will seek in vain for a word of bitterness against an opponent. Even Foxe, who rails incessantly at all the Catholic champions, makes no charge of unfairness or overbearing temper against Watson. The only apparent exceptions that I have met with are his treatment of Rough, which I have discussed already, and his resistance in the Westminster Conference. But even then he is not charged with pride towards the disputants, but with contumacy towards those who had power to commit him to prison, and "his folly and violence," as they are called, were merely the bold vindication of the dignity of his office and the rights of the Church. He was a man who by his learning, his talents, and his energy would in all probability, had God allowed him to govern the church of Lincoln longer, have left a name in that see as famous as that of Robert Grosteste. But in the prime of his age and beginning of his career, God permitted him to be torn from his flock ; and as men might say, to waste his mature years in inactivity. But though his pen was wrested from his hand and his tongue was silenced, he glorified God and edified the Church by patient suffering and invincible constancy as the opponent of heresy and schism, and his name will ever be in benediction in the Catholic Church in England, as the last and not degenerate successor of St Hugh.

temper is not only entirely unwarranted by facts, but the very reverse of the truth.

WHOLESOME AND CATHOLIC DOCTRINE.

---o---

THE FIRST SERMON.

OF THE NUMBER OF THE SACRAMENTS OF CHRIST'S CHURCH, AND THE EFFECT OF THE SAME.

THE Catholic Church of God (good people) doth extend her doctrine concerning the matter of our belief, not only to the Articles of our Creed, and such points as by revelation from God it teaches us to believe of God, and the works of our Saviour Christ, which He did or suffered for the redemption and salvation of man ; but also to the holy sacraments of God, by the worthy using whereof, He poureth abundantly His manifold graces into our souls, and by them maketh us people meet to receive the fruits and benefits of His passion. And as ye have been instructed partly concerning the Articles of our faith, so it is expedient ye be likewise instructed concerning the holy sacraments of His Church, to the intent ye might not only know the manner of God's working in curing of your souls, but also prepare and dispose yourselves to the fruitful receiving of His medicines which be ministered to every man by His holy sacraments. And therefore, at this time, by God's help, I intend to declare unto you the number of the sacraments of Christ's Church, and also the effect of them all in general, and at other times every one of them in special.

It is to be believed, upon pain of damnation, that there be seven sacraments of Christ's Holy Church, institute and ordained of our Saviour Christ, in His New Testament or Law, which be—Baptism, Confirmation, the sacrament of the Altar, Penance, Extreme Unction, Order, and Matrimony. The first five be ordained for the making good and the perfection of every man and woman, as by Baptism we are justified and made members of Christ's mystical body; by Confirmation, we are increased and strengthened in grace ; by the sacraments of Christ's Body and Blood we are nourished to everlasting life, and made fat with God ; by Penance, we are restored to our former righteousness* and goodness, if in case we fall after Baptism ; by Extreme Unction, we are made whole spiritually, and also corporally, if it be thought to God expedient to our souls. All these five sacraments be ordained to begin or restore our righteousness and to bring it to perfectness for our salvation. The other two last be ordained for the common state of the Holy Church, as Matrimony, to increase and multiply the Church corporally by

---

* In the original throughout the book this word is written "right-wisnesse "—*i.e.*, right-wise-ness.

generation ; and Order, to multiply the Holy Church spiritually by regeneration, and also by the ministry of God's word, sacraments and discipline, to rule and govern it after the will of Almighty God.

And whereas the Scriptures in many places compare man's life to a war (Job vii. 1, 1 Tim i. 18, 2 Cor. x. 3, 4), we may well, by that same similitude, understand the number and division of God's sacraments, and the true effect of the same. For Christ, our Lord and King, Who hath for us overcome the devil, the flesh, the world, hell, death, and all His enemies and ours, laboureth to make all us for whom He hath prepared triumph, and the inheritance in the kingdom of heaven, to be His soldiers, and by His power and help to fight against the said enemies, and to overcome them in our own persons, and so to attain the promised reward.

The first thing that a worldly prince doth, intending to make war against his enemy, is to muster and choose out his soldiers, and to take their names, and to apparel them with his livery and badge, that they may be known from the soldiers of his adversary. Even so Christ, our chief Captain, by Baptism hath called and chosen out of all the people of this world which He hath wholly redeemed, certain to be His soldiers to fight against His enemy the devil; which soldiers, thus called, have given their names to Christ their King, and have renounced the service of their old master the devil, who was a tyrant, delighting only in their death, and have promised to serve only Christ, like true soldiers, against the devil ; and by this sacrament of Baptism are par-

doned and washed from their old spots of original
sin, and have received the white livery of innocence,
and the badge of Christ by the impression of the
holy cross in divers parts of their bodies, and so
are known throughout the whole world to be the
soldiers of Christ their Lord and Captain.

The second thing that a worldly prince doth in
his war, is to provide that every soldier be able to
fight, and have harness and weapons meet for his
body, both to bear off the assaults of his enemies,
and also to invade them as cause shall require.
Even so Christ, our heavenly Prince, hath ordained
the sacrament of Confirmation, to make us strong and
able to fight with our ghostly enemies, and has armed
us with a sevenfold harness, that is to say, with the
seven gifts of the Holy Ghost, whereby we be sufficiently preserved, defended, and encouraged ourselves,
and also able to help and comfort our fellow soldiers,
which by chance shall come into any distress or
danger of their enemies.

The third thing a worldly prince doth in his war,
is to foresee and provide that his whole army be
well victualled and furnished with plenty of wholesome meat and drink, lest for hunger their strength
decay, and they in process famish and die. Even so
Christ, our spiritual Captain, hath provided victual for
us His soldiers, both good and plenty of it; not meat
that will perish and be consumed with once eating,
but meat that will remain and nourish to everlasting
life; that is to say, His own natural flesh and blood,
which He giveth to His soldiers in a sacrament
under the forms of corporal bread and wine, con-

descending therein to our infirmity, and by that spiritual and most wholesome and precious food, He repaireth all our decays in grace and spiritual strength, He openeth our eyes to see the trains of our enemies, He swayeth the rage of our inward enemy the flesh, and preserveth our bodies and souls from famine and eternal death.

The fourth thing that a worldly prince doth in his war, is to ordain over his whole army one chief lieutenant (if he be absent himself from the field), and under him officers and captains, some of more, some of fewer, such men as be expert in war, who can instruct the rest in all feats of war, how to fight and overcome their enemies, and can set the whole army in good array, and also can by the law-martial correct and punish all traitors and offenders. Even so Christ, our Lord and King, after He hath Himself overcome all His enemies in His own person, and is now triumphing with God the Father in heaven, and yet hath His Church in battle and conflict with their enemies on earth, being absent by His visible Presence, and invisibly and spiritually present among us, hath ordained the sacrament of Order, and by that sacrament hath elected and chosen out certain expert and cunning men, to whom by imposition of hands of priesthood, He hath given authority and commandment to instruct His soldiers in all feats of spiritual war against the devil, and to admit others into the rooms of them that die or depart, and to comfort and encourage them that be in conflict, and by unity of faith, charity, and obedience, to cause the whole army to keep good array, and to punish by excommunication such as by apostasy, heresy, or schism, break the peace and good order, and by the discipline of this war of the Church, to correct all other offenders, and to receive them again that will amend. And of these men there be certain degrees and orders, one chief lieutenant of the whole army which was S. Peter, and now is his lawful successor in the chair of Christ, governing the whole army of Christ's Church here in earth; and under him there be in every province one Archbishop, and in every city one Bishop, and in every parish one Priest or Curate, to feed, order, encourage, and to govern the whole army and every soldier of Christ's Church in every place.

The fifth thing that a worldly prince doth in his war, is when his army is assembled, well armed, well victualled, and well ordered and ruled by good captains, then to march forward and to join in battle with his enemies; in which conflict if any of his soldiers chance to be hurt and wounded, then to cause a surgeon to search his wounds, and to lay plasters and medicines on to them, that he, being made whole, might enter into his place again and fight afresh against his enemies. Even so doth our Saviour Christ with us, when all we be assembled into one Church and spiritual army by Baptism, and be well harnessed with God's graces and the gifts of the Holy Ghost by Confirmation, and be well victualled with the precious foods of His own body and blood in the sacrament of the Altar, and be set in good array, and well instructed and encouraged by the rulers and ministers of His Church, having authority so to do by the sacrament of

Order : then we be led by God's Spirit into the wilderness of some good purpose or work, there to be tempted and assaulted of the devil. For they that have the Spirit of God be not idle but occupied in some good work, which the devil withstandeth and fighteth against, as much as he is able to do ;—in which conflict, if any of us be overcome with evil, which cannot be, except we will be overcome, and voluntarily suffer the devil to prevail against us (for no man sinneth actually against his will), yet our merciful Lord will not see us utterly trodden underfoot and slain, but if we love to be healed and be sorry for our voluntary hurt and wound, He hath prepared a present medicine and plaster for us, which the spiritual surgeon, when he hath searched the wound by our own confession, layeth and bindeth to our sore by the sacrament of Penance, and so, restoring us to our perfect health, maketh us able to enter the field again, and to fight afresh against our enemies.

The sixth thing that a worldly prince doth in his war, is when any of his soldiers waxeth aged and feeble, and can fight no more, then specially to comfort him, and to set a watch that his enemies steal not privily upon him and kill him, when he is not able to defend himself. And if the same soldier hath lightly offended in any small matter, and hath not at all times been so vigilant as the laws of war required, yet then gently to forgive him, and to shew him that honour at his death, that he shall be of all the army accounted to have been a faithful soldier, and to have died in his prince's favour. Even so

Christ our Lord doth with us His soldiers, when any of us waxeth aged or feeble by sickness, and is in danger of bodily death, which death is the escaping of all dangers, the end of all labours, the entry to the possession of eternal inheritance in heaven which God promised to all His faithful soldiers. And knowing that our enemy, the devil, is most busy and fierce then craftily to assault His soldier in his last conflict, when he is least able to resist (because the body that corrupteth and dieth, doth make heavy the soul) : then, I say, our Saviour Christ, by the sacrament of Extreme Unction, doth inwardly anoint the sick soldier, whereby He doth replenish him with grace, comfort and strength of the Holy Ghost, against the manifold and violent temptations of the devil, and doth relieve his heart with spiritual joy against the horror of death. And if he hath lightly offended in any venial sin, He pardoneth him. And if he thinks it so expedient to his soul's health, He doth also sometimes relieve his corporal disease. And if not, yet He sheweth him that honour, that He doth and would the Holy Church should account him as a faithful soldier ; and if he hath not refused the benefit of His other sacraments, to have departed this transitory life in His most gracious favour, and to have changed the short and light afflictions of this time with the weighty and everlasting glory in the kingdom of heaven.

The seventh and last thing that a worldly prince doth, is, if the time of his war be prolonged and further continued, and many of his soldiers be slain or departed, then to provide that his army be fully

restored again with some new and fresh soldiers, and
to use them as he did the other before. Even so
doth our Saviour Christ ; because all the time of this
world is the time of our battle and conflict of our
ghostly enemies, in which time a great number of
the soldiers of Christ depart out of this transitory
life, some in the favour of their Prince, and so to be
remembered, and some in His displeasure, such as
have fled traitorously to the devil their enemy, and
have turned their face against Christ their Prince :
therefore He hath ordained the sacrament of Matrimony, specially for this cause, to restore His army
again, that new men and women may be born by
generation in lawful conjunction and chaste matrimony, of whom, by Baptism and spiritual regeneration, He might choose and appoint out new soldiers
to furnish His army again, and to fight in the place of
them that be departed, during the time of His war,
which is the time of this present world.

By this example and similitude of war, I have
declared unto you (good people) both the number of
the sacraments of Christ's Catholic Church which be
seven, and also generally the effects and virtues of
them all, and what fruit and benefit we take thereby.

Furthermore ye shall understand, that like as in a
man there be two things, a body and a soul, so in
every sacrament there be two things, one that is outwardly seen, another that is inwardly perceived and
believed. The outward visible thing is the element
or matter of the sacrament ; the inward invisible and
spiritual thing is the grace and virtue of the sacrament. The inward grace is signified, contained, and

given by the outward part of the sacrament. The graces of the sacraments be spiritual, and ordained of God to heal the sins of the soul of man ; and because man principally did sin by the consent of his reason, and yet took occasion to sin of the sensuality and desire of his flesh : therefore hath God tempered the medicine of His sacraments according to man's disease, that the chief part, which is the inward grace, being spiritual, might be ministered to man in a sensible and visible sign of a sacrament, as it were a secret medicine delivered to a sick man in a visible glass or vessel, and such a vessel as doth teach the receiver what is contained within it, and is also given by it—as for example, the spiritual grace of regeneration is given to a man by the use of Baptism, whereby he understandeth by the property of the water, which is to wash away the filth of the body, the nature of the inward grace which is the washing and purging of the soul from all spots of sin and iniquity, so that now the body by the receiving of the sensible sacrament, is made an occasion for the soul to rise from sin by receiving of the spiritual grace, as in the beginning it was an occasion for the soul to fall to sin. For which cause now the flesh is washed, that the soul might be purged, the flesh is anointed, that the soul might be consecrate and hallowed, the flesh is marked and crossed, that the soul might be armed and defended, the flesh is covered by imposition of hands, that the soul might be lighted with the Spirit of God, the flesh is fed with the body and blood of Christ, that the soul might be nourished and made fat with God ; and as these two be now joined in their works, so shall they be afterwards joined in rewards.*

And although these marvellous graces and spiritual medicines be given unto us by the sacraments, yet God is only the Author and Giver of them, Who healeth the soul of man now joined with the body, with His spiritual grace ministered in corporal signs and sacraments: and it is not the outward visible things that give that which is given by them, but God doth give grace by them, that commandeth us to seek grace in them. And this is the very difference between the sacraments of the Old Testament and of the New, that the old sacraments did signify and promise Christ the Saviour, and the new sacraments do give the salvation ; and the sacraments of the Old Testament did profit the fathers then, not by any virtue that was in the sacraments, but only by the virtue and efficacy of their faith in Christ to come, which was signified and promised by those sacraments. But the sacraments of the New Testament do profit the receivers, not by the faith and devotion either of the receivers or of the ministers— although faith and repentance and conversion to God, and the preparation of the heart, and the aptness of the person be necessarily required in the receivers (being of age and discretion)—but they profit by the virtue which they have of the merits of Christ's passion already suffered upon the cross, Who useth them as instruments of His grace and mercy, and hath decreed to work infallibly by them such effects of grace as they signify.

* Tertullian.

And it is not the goodness or naughtiness of the minister that can further or hinder the virtue of the sacraments in working of their effects, for neither he that planteth, nor he that watereth is anything, but God that giveth the increase (1 Cor. iii. 7). Even as it maketh no matter whether the physician be sick or whole, or whether the box be of silver or of wood, so the medicine be apt and good. For if the effect of the sacrament did depend upon the goodness of the minister, which to men is unknown, then could not a man be sure of whom to receive, and should always be in doubt of the virtue of that he receiveth, which no man may be. And although the true sacraments of Christ may be ministered and received out of the Catholic Church among heretics and schismatics; yet they cannot be profitable to the receivers, until they come again to the unity of Christ's Catholic Church.

Wherefore (good people) let every man and woman that desireth to be made whole from his sin, or to be preserved or sanctified by Christ, and to be partaker of His blessed passion, prepare himself with all reverence and humbleness of heart to receive these most holy sacraments in such form, and for such purpose and intent, as our Saviour Christ and His blessed spouse, the Holy Catholic Church, have appointed and ordained ; seeing that otherwise to misorder and abuse them, or wilfully to deny or refuse them, is to deny or refuse Christ that made them, out of Whose bloody side they came forth, and also to deny or refuse the benefits of His death and passion, which by them be applied and be brought into our souls. As the worthy and reverent using of them is the means to grace and salvation, so the misusing or contempt of them is heinous and detestable sacrilege, because without them no religion can be perfect, which perfectness every man is bounden to procure with all his diligence during the time of this present life, that in the end thereof he might enjoy life everlasting, to the which He bring us all, Who has so dearly bought it for us, to Whom be all honour, praise, and glory, world without end. Amen.

THE SECOND SERMON.

OF BAPTISM.

BECAUSE the holy sacrament of Baptism is the first gate or entry into the Church of Christ, and the ground of all the other sacraments, which cannot be given to any but to such as be baptized before : therefore (good people) I shall now begin with Baptism, and declare unto you what ye ought to think of it, and what fruit ye receive by it.

First, It is to be known that our Saviour Christ did institute and ordain this sacrament, when, after His resurrection, appearing to His disciples, He said to them : "All power in heaven and in earth is given unto Me : Go ye therefore and teach all nations and people, baptizing them in the name of the Father, and of the Son, and of the Holy Ghost, and teaching them to keep and observe all things which I have commanded you, and I am with you always to the world's end" (Matt. xxviii. 18–20). By which words of our Saviour Christ we learn that power is given unto Him only, to institute and ordain sacraments, which the Church receiving of Him and of His Spirit, doth faithfully deliver unto us, to be observed and used. 'And also we learn that the form and manner of baptizing, is to do as He commanded, and in so doing, to say these words "I baptize thee in the name of the Father, and of the Son, and of the Holy Ghost." And we learn also that Christ doth by His promise assist the doing of His minister, and worketh the same effects by Baptism, when it is duly ministered of a man, as if He did minister it Himself. And last of all, we learn that Baptism is not an idle ceremony, but that every person which is baptized, and being of age and discretion, ought to be taught before the faith of Christ, and to believe the same, and then after Baptism ought diligently to observe and keep all things which Christ hath commanded. And if they that be baptized be infants or otherwise cannot believe themselves, lacking the use of their reason, seeing our Saviour Christ said that children pertain to the kingdom of heaven (Matt. xix. 14), and the door into the kingdom of heaven is Baptism, at which door no person can enter in ordinarily, but such as be born again of water and the Holy Ghost : therefore such be offered to be baptized in the faith of the Church, and in receiving Baptism, they are made faithful by the sacrament of faith : but of this thing I shall, God willing, speak more another time.

Secondarily, It is to be understanded that Baptism ought to be ministered in water, as Christ hath ordained, and in no other liquor, and that is because Baptism is a sacrament of necessity, and water is a common element throughout the whole world, and therefore it is ordained to be ministered in water, that no man might excuse himself for lack of matter, and so come in danger of damnation for lack of Baptism. And also it is ordained to be in water

for signification of the effect; that men might learn
in this Sacrament, as they do in all other, by the
property of the element, what is the virtue and effect
of the same—that like as water washeth away the
spots of the body so Baptism washeth away the
sins of the soul.   And also because the general flood
in the time of Noe, and the Red Sea (1 Peter iii. 20,
21), through which Moses and all the people of Israel
went, and thereby escaped the danger of King Pharao
that persecuted them, were figures of Baptism (1
Cor. x. 1–4): therefore it is ordained to be in water,
that the truth might agree with the figure, and God's
people might be now saved from the devil and
drowning in deadly sin (Eph. v. 26), by the water
of regeneration joined with the word of life, as Noe
and his children were saved by the water of the flood
and his ship, and as Moses with God's people were
saved from the sword of Pharao by the water of
the Red Sea and the cloud.   Yet the grace that is
ministered in the water, proceedeth not from the
nature of the water, which without the word of God
is but only water still, but it proceedeth from the
presence of the Holy Ghost, that descendeth upon
the water, and doth consecrate the water, and by
it doth wash and purify the soul.

   Thirdly, It is to be known, that a man by the
virtue and efficacy of Baptism truly ministered and
received, is washed from all kind of sin, endued with
God's Holy Spirit, apparelled with Christ and His
righteousness, and is made with Christ an inheritor
of the kingdom of heaven.

   First, Baptism washes away all sins, in thoughts,

in words, and in deeds, both original sin, and actual
or personal sin, which be done either of ignorance or
knowledge; both the sin itself, and the guiltiness
thereof, and also the eternal pain in hell due for
the same; as the prophet sayeth, "In that day (of
Christ) there shall be a fountain set open to the house
of Jacob and to all the inhabitants of Jerusalem for
the washing away of sins" (Zach. xiii. 1). And S.
Paul sayeth to the Corinthians, that they were great
and heinous sinners, but now they be washed, they
be sanctified, they be justified in the name of our
Lord Jesus Christ and in the Spirit of our God
(1 Cor. vi. 2), and that there is no damnation now
remaining to them that be in Christ (Rom viii. 1),
and walk not after the flesh. And although original
sin, both in infants and all others, be taken away and
fully remitted, so that, in them that be baptized duly
as they ought to be, no sin remaineth, nor no other
thing that doth offend and displease God, but that
the infection which every person taketh by carnal
generation from the first earthly man, Adam, is now
washed and clean purged by spiritual regeneration,
in the blood of the second heavenly man, Christ our
Saviour; yet it is to be understanded that there
remaineth in every person after Baptism a certain
infirmity or inclination to sin, which is commonly
called concupiscence of the flesh, whereby a man is
made weak and less able to withstand sin, and his
appetite is much inclined to sin, which, though it be
sometimes called by the name of sin (as a man's
writing is called his hand, and his speech is called his
tongue), yet it is not sin and hateful to God, nor

B

imputed to us as sin, so long as our will doth not consent unto it, but by grace withstandeth it (Rom. viii. 17–20); and God hath suffered it to remain in our flesh, not that we should obey it and be ruled by it, but that we should resist and fight against it ; which is left in us for our exercise as an inward familiar enemy, making continual civil war against us, which if we, by the aid of God's grace and His Holy Spirit, do finally overcome and subdue, shall be a matter and occasion of our great glory and everlasting reward.[1]

And that we may so do, God, as He hath by this sacrament of Baptism forgiven us all sin, so by the same sacrament He doth give us special grace to overcome sin, and to suppress this bitter root of sin, that it spring not and bring forth in us the wicked fruit of sin, making us more able to withstand the carnal lusts and desires of our flesh than is any other man that was never baptized.

The next effect of Baptism after remission of sin is our spiritual regeneration, in that we are born again of water and the Holy Ghost, and made new men in righteousness and holiness, and by adoption are made sons and children of Almighty God ; as S. Paul sayeth, " God, according to His mercy, hath saved us by the water of regeneration (or new birth) and the renewing of the Holy Spirit, which He hath poured upon us abundantly by Jesus Christ our Saviour, that we, being justified by His grace, might be heirs of eternal life" (Titus iii. 5–7); or like as a foul vessel, if it be never so well washed and scoured, yet it will still keep some mark or taste of the evil humour which was in it before, but if the vessel be put again into the furnace, and be there with the flame renewed, it will have no scent remaining of the old corrupt liquor; even so God doth put us into the fountain of water as into a furnace, and with the grace of His Holy Spirit, as it were with flame of a fire, doth renew us and make us brighter than the sunbeams. And as we were born when we came forth of our mother's womb, even so we are born again when we come forth of the water of Baptism, whereby God hath delivered us from the power of darkness, and hath translated us into the kingdom of his well-beloved Son (Col. i. 13), and hath of His own will begotten us by the word of truth (James i. 18), and of Him we have received the spirit, not of bondage, to fear Him as a tyrant, but the spirit of adoption of the children of God, by which, as being now chosen to be His children (Rom. viii. 14), we lovingly and with humble reverence call Him Father, which spirit also beareth witness with our own spirit that we be the children of God, if we suffer with Him, that we might likewise be glorified with Him.

The third effect of Baptism after remission and regeneration is to be apparelled and clad with Christ and His righteousness. For like as when a child is first born, then hath he a coat put on him to cover his nakedness and to adorn him, so when we be born again of the water and the Holy Ghost, we have a spiritual coat put upon us, which is our Saviour Christ; as S. Paul saith, "All you that be baptized in Christ have put on Christ as a garment" (Gal. iii. 27), which garment covereth the deformity of our corrupt nature, defendeth us from the storms of all tempta-

tions, and maketh nothing appear in us but the image
of Christ in godly and virtuous conversation.   For
like as a table, being made plain and smooth, and
having the picture of the King's image printed in it,
is esteemed of all men, not according to the value of
the matter, be it gold or silver, but according to the
cunning workmanship, in that it lively representeth
the very face of the King, and therefore causeth the
lookers-on to honour it and to be in love with it ; even
so a man that hath by Baptism put off his old man
with his acts and corrupt living, and hath put on the
new (Col. iii. 9, 10) man, which is made new in the
knowledge of God, and in righteousness and holiness
of truth in that part of his soul where the image of
God is printed (Eph. i. 24), by turning his love wholly
from temporal and carnal things to eternal and
spiritual things above, is now much esteemed of
Almighty God, and accepted of Him as a loving child,
because in all his conversation he is made like to
the image of Christ and followeth Christ's footsteps,
that did no sin, nor no deceit was found in His mouth,
(1 Peter ii. 24), and so hath put on Christ, in that his
faith is imputed to him as righteousness.

The fourth effect of Baptism after remission of sin
and the making of us the children of God by our new
birth and the apparelling of us with the righteousness of Christ, is to be made heirs of God and of
His heavenly kingdom, and fellow-heirs with our
Saviour Christ ; as S. Paul saith, " We be the children of God (by Baptism), we be also the heirs of
God, and fellow-heirs with Christ" (Rom. vii. 16, 17),
which inheritance we have not yet in full possession,

but only by hope of eternal life. And as Christ God's Son by nature, came to His inheritance by suffering His passion, so our hope shall be sure, that if we suffer with Christ, and patiently bear the afflictions of this world, and forbear and contemn the vanities of the same, we shall, without fail, enjoy God's inheritance with Christ as God's children (Rom. viii. 17), for whom the same inheritance was prepared before the beginning of the world.

Many more effects of Baptism I might rehearse unto you, seeing all other graces take their beginning here, and be builded upon it; but in these four which I have rehearsed they may be considered ; as how in Baptism we are made free from sin ; we are sanctified by grace ; we are made just men by righteousness ; we are made God's children by adoption ; we are made heirs of the kingdom of heaven ; we are made fellow-heirs with Christ, God's Son ; we are made members of Christ's mystical body ; we are made the house and temple of God ; we are made the instruments of the Holy Ghost ; we are grafted in Christ to grow and bring forth the fruit of sanctification, and to receive the reward of our fruit, everlasting life. All these graces Almighty God worketh by Baptism, as by a peculiar instrument for that purpose, in the hearts of all infants that, by the Church and in the faith of the Church, be offered to God and baptized, where nothing of the infant's part doth stop the grace of the sacrament. But if he that is baptized be of age and discretion, having the use of his reason, it is required necessarily of him before Baptism to have faith and repentance of his former naughty living; as Christ saith, " He that believeth and is baptized shall be saved, but he that believeth not shall be condemned " (Mark xxi. 16); and as S. Peter saith, "Do penance, and be every one of you baptized in the name of Jesus Christ in remission of your sins, and ye shall receive the gift of the Holy Ghost " (Acts ii. 38); whereby we learn that the lack of true faith and repentance do stop the grace of the sacrament, that it can take no place in the heart of him that hath the use of his reason when he is baptized. And yet the Baptism is good, and may not be iterate and given again, although it be unfruitful to the receiver at that time, till afterward he receive by true faith and penance and imposition of hands the gift of the Holy Ghost.

Thus (good people) when we have considered what we ought to think of Baptism, and what fruit we receive by it, now our duty is to put the same in practice all our lifetime, and to live so that this good work be not in vain begun in us, and to show ourselves thankful for so great a treasure and so precious a jewel given unto us, and to labour and pray diligently that God's Spirit, given unto us in Baptism, be not driven away by our naughty living, but that His grace in our hearts be daily continued and more increased, that, by the virtue thereof, the righteousness of the law might be fulfilled in us that walk not after the flesh, but after the Spirit, till this mortal nature of ours put on immortality in the day of our Lord Jesus Christ, to Whom, with the Father and the Holy Ghost, be all honour and glory. Amen.

THE THIRD SERMON.

OF THE NECESSITY OF BAPTISM, AND THE MINISTERS OF THE SAME.

THE necessity of Baptism (good people) is known by the plain words of our Saviour Christ, Who saith to Nicodemus, that came to Him in the night, "Except a man be born again of the water and the Holy Ghost, he cannot enter into the kingdom of God " (John iii. 5), whereby we learn that no man is incorporate to Christ, and made one body with Him, but he that is baptized, if he may be baptized.   And S. Philip also, declaring that Baptism is a sacrament of necessity for salvation, when he had fully taught the Eunuch the faith of Christ, whose heart was replenished and fulfilled with the Holy Ghost, did not cease there, but, to show the necessity of Baptism, when they came to water, Philip went down from the chariot with the Eunuch, and did baptize him and let him go.   And S. Peter likewise, preaching the faith of Christ to Cornelius and his family and friends, when he perceived that the Holy Ghost did inspire their hearts with His grace before Baptism, was not content only with that, but, to declare the necessity of water, said, " Can any man forbid water that these men should not be baptized that have received the Holy Ghost as we have?" (Acts x. 47).

Therefore be a man never so well instructed in the knowledge of Christ's religion, yet he beareth the burden of his iniquity, which shall not be forgiven him, but when he shall come to Baptism if it may be had. And children which be born in original sin, and therefore be the children of God's anger and displeasure, cannot be saved and delivered from their sin but by the water of regeneration. And this is true whether they be born of faithful parents or unfaithful; for whatsoever is born of the flesh is flesh (John iii. 6), and like as by one man, Adam, sin came into the world, and by sin death, and so death came upon all men that sinned in Adam (Rom. v. 12), even so by the righteousness of one man, Jesus Christ, grace came into the world, and by grace life, in whom many be made righteous, which righteousness only they have that have put on Christ by Baptism.

And yet (good people) it is to be understanded that this general rule hath but two exceptions, which be martyrdom and conversion of the heart by faith when Baptism cannot be had. For martyrdom, which is to suffer death for Christ's cause or in the quarrel of Christ, doth supply the stead of Baptism, both in those that be children and also in those that be of age, when only necessity and not contempt excludeth the sacrament; as our Saviour Christ saith, "He that confesseth me before men, I shall also confess him before my Father which is in heaven; and he that loseth his life for me shall find it;" so that whosoever cannot receive the sacrament of regeneration, but dieth before for the confession of Christ, it is as much available to the remission of his sins as if they were washed away by the holy fountain of Baptism. For who doubteth but that the Holy Innocents, whom the wicked king Herod slew for Christ, are numbered among the martyrs of God, who made a good confession of Christ, not by their mouths, but by the shedding of their blood for Him? Likewise he that hath his heart fully converted to God by true and lively faith, and cannot be baptized in water, but is prevented by death before, is in that case excused for not having Baptism. For Christ saith, "He that believeth in me shall not see death for evermore." And where faith is, where hope is, where charity is, where the full and perfect virtue of Baptism is, there salvation cannot lack, if the sacrament be had in purpose and will, and cannot be had in deed.

So that we see that children have but one remedy to supply the lack of Baptism, which is martyrdom, and they that have the use of reason have two remedies, both martyrdom and also the full conversion of the heart by lively faith, and that only in time of need, when the sacrament, not of contempt, but of necessity, cannot be had.

And because this sacrament is of such necessity, therefore the ministration of it is not extended to such a small number as it is in other, for of the other sacraments the minister ought at least to be a priest, saving in matrimony, which the two parties may contract between themselves; but in Baptism the ministration is not only reserved to priests and to deacons in the absence of the priests, but is also permitted to lay men and lay women, that be faithful themselves, if extreme necessity so require. And if there be no necessity nor danger of the death of the child, and yet lay persons do take upon them to minister this sacrament (which pertaineth not to them to do but in time of need), although they themselves do sin in that doing, for their presumption, where need compelled not, yet the child is truly baptized, and may not in any wise be baptized again.

And because it often chanceth that children newborn be in danger of death, and so be baptized of the midwives or of other women at home ; therefore I will show unto you how they must do when they will minister the said sacrament of Baptism.

First, when the child is born (for the child that is not born, but yet in his mother's womb, cannot be born again by baptism till he be once born *), if there come a chance of danger, that verily they think it will not live till it be brought to the solemnisation of Baptism, then a lay man or lay woman in that need going about to baptize the child, must unfeignedly intend to do therein that which the Catholic Church doth, and taking some honest name, as John or Thomas, or some other, if it be a man-child, and if it be a woman-child then taking Joan or Catharine or such like, let the person that shall christen the child, take water, as well-water, sea-water, or rain-water, or other common water (for no other liquor, as oil, blood,

---

* On this point see Benedict xiv. *De Synodo*, lib. vii. cap. 5, and S. Alphonsus in *Theol. Mor.*, lib. v. n. 107.—ED.

wine, rose-water, or other artificial water, can be the matter of this sacrament *), and then let the christener begin to cast or pour the water upon the child's head, calling it by the name they give it, saying thus, " John, I baptize thee in the name of the Father, and of the Son, and of the Holy Ghost. Amen." † And if it be a woman-child, then let the christener say thus, calling it by the woman's name: "Joan, I baptize thee in the name of the Father, and of the Son, and of the Holy Ghost. Amen."

Now that man or woman that thus doth say, and cast or pour water upon the child's naked head in the time that he is saying the foresaid prescript words, doth minister well this sacrament of Baptism in the time of need. And let the christener take heed that he leave out none of these prescript words, nor change none of them, nor add no more to them, and also let him remember to cast or to pour water upon the child's naked head in the time before he make an end of those foresaid words, " John, I baptize," &c., for if the water be cast upon the child's head before the christener beginneth to say those words, or else after that he hath said the words, then the child is not christened.‡ For the words without the water is no

---

* Theologians distinguish between such liquors as oil, blood, wine, which are certainly invalid matter of the sacrament of Baptism ; and others, such as rose-water, which are only doubtfully invalid. In case of extreme necessity, the latter should be used conditionally, but not the former. See S. Alphonsus, *Theol. Mor.*, lib. v. n. 103, 104.—ED.

† " The word Amen is not given in any correct edition of the Ritual," says Kane ; " it is not permitted, therefore, to add it to the form." Notes on the Roman Ritual, n. 168.—ED.

‡ This was the opinion of Cajetan, but it is rejected by Suarez as

sacrament, nor can do no good, nor yet the water without the words, and therefore they must be joined and go together after the manner beforesaid.

Moreover, ye must note that there may not two persons do these two foresaid things ; that is to say, one may not speak these words, "John, I baptize thee," &c., and another pour the water upon the child in the meantime, and whilst the words be in saying ; for if they do, then is the child not christened, and therefore it must be but one person that must both say the words, without any long interruption or pause, and pour on the water.

And whereas the water of Baptism hath been used, ever since the time of the apostles, in Christ's Church to be hallowed and sanctified by the priest's prayer and invocation of God's Holy Spirit by the sign and mystery of Christ's cross, and in the name of the Holy Trinity, and by the infusion of the holy oil into it, that by the use of it the sins of him that is baptized might be washed away and be made clean ; yet in the time of need and of sudden danger, where such hallowed water cannot be had, other clean and common water will suffice.

Furthermore, like as the Holy Ghost came down from heaven in the Baptism of Christ, when He was baptized by John, and visibly rested upon Christ (Mark. i. 10), declaring all grace to be in Him, and

---

unfounded, too severe, and giving rise to unnecessary scruples, *De Bapt.* disp. ii. sect. 2, n. 6 ; as also by S. Alphonsus, *Theol. Mor.*, lib. v. n.' 9. A moral union of matter and form is sufficient. A layman, however, baptizing in case of necessity, should be careful to pronounce the words while pouring the water.—ED.

all grace to proceed from Him; even so we be taught, that always when this sacrament is duly received and ministered in the name of the Holy Trinity, the Holy Ghost descendeth from above, and doth invisibly rest upon him that is baptized, and worketh special grace in his heart to obey God and His commandments. And as the Father of heaven by His voice which He sent from heaven testified that Christ was His well-beloved Son, in whom He was well pleased, so our heavenly Father in this sacrament testifieth to his conscience that is baptized that he is His loving child, and that nothing is in him that is displeasing to God.

Therefore (good people) considering that this sacrament of Baptism is of such necessity that no child (except the case of martyrdom) can be saved and enter into the kingdom of God but by it, because every one, being born in original sin, and so the child of God's anger by his nativity, cannot be partaker of the promise of salvation, and have the merits of Christ's passion applied to him, but either by his proper faith, or else by the sacrament of faith ; and seeing that young infants have not the use of their reason and will, whereby they may understand the doctrine of our faith, and so believe themselves in their own persons ; and therefore, if ye will have your children come to Christ, as He commandeth they should be brought to Him (Mark x. 14), and rebuked them that forbade them to be brought, and promised the kingdom of God to the only followers of the innocence of children, whom He embraced and laid His hands upon them ; ye must procure with all your diligence to have your children brought to Baptism, and to receive the sacrament of faith, whereby they be set in the state of salvation, and be made partakers of Christ's merits. Let not your children for your negligence accuse you in the last day for the loss of their salvation, which they might have had by Baptism, if ye had showed your full endeavour.

And lest any man should excuse himself for lack of matter, or of a minister, or of doctrine, God and His Holy Church hath ordained Baptism to be ministered in water, which is an element not far to seek anywhere, and hath permitted that, in time of need, any man may be minister of it, and for lack of them any woman, yea, the very mother of the child if the case so required ; and for doctrine, a little sufficeth, for the form of the sacrament consisteth. but in three or four words which be soon learned. And like as children were made guilty of original sin and damnation for another man's fault, so they may be reconciled again to God and have remission of sin in Baptism by other men's faith. For which cause every child that is baptized professeth Christ's faith by the mouth of the Church, which is represented by the godfathers and godmothers, and likewise maketh his covenant with God to renounce the devil and all his works and vain pomps. And therefore all you that have been or shall be godfathers and godmothers by offering of children to Christ by Baptism in the name and faith of the Church, which you represent, and, by answering for the children, have made yourselves surety for the same, take heed to your charge, that when the said children shall be able to take knowledge, ye teach, or procure them be taught, that faith and profession which they have made by you, and to be exhorted diligently to live a godly and virtuous life according to that profession which they have made in their Baptism by you, and to observe the commandments of God and all things which they have promised and vowed by you, so that both you and they might pass over the time of this present life in the well-using of God's graces given in Baptism, labouring daily to continue and to increase the same in the fear and love of God and good works, that at the end and term thereof ye may attain the crown of righteousness, which God will give, as He hath promised, to all them that love Him ; to whom be all praise, honour, and glory for evermore. Amen.

THE FOURTH SERMON.

*OF THE ANCIENT AND GODLY CEREMONIES PER-
TAINING TO BAPTISM, AND WHAT IS MEANT AND
TAUGHT BY THEM.*

IN Baptism (good people), beside the very ministration of it, which consisteth in speaking of a
few formal words over the child baptized by the
minister of God, and in dipping the same child the
same time in the element of water, or, in time of
need, by pouring water upon him, which two things
be required of necessity to the true ministration of
this sacrament, there be also other ceremonies used
which be called sacramentals, and have been used
universally throughout the Holy Church of Christ from
the Apostles' time till this day, and were ordained to
be used, partly against the power of the devil, partly
for the devotion and instruction of us and them
that be baptized. For that cause I think it good to
declare unto you at this time which be those godly
and ancient ceremonies of Baptism, and what is meant
and taught by them.

The first ceremony, which is called exorcism, is
done without the church-door, because the child that
is brought to be baptized is as yet no part of Christ's
Catholic Church, but the child of God's wrath, by his

nativity conceived in sin, and is under the power of
the devil till he be admitted into the Church of Christ
by Baptism, and be made a member of the same
Church by regeneration and the renewing of the Holy
Spirit. For which cause the Holy Church universally
and after one manner useth first of all exorcism, which
is adjuration of the devil in the name and power of
the Holy Trinity to depart from that creature of God
which he possessed before ; whereby the child is delivered from the power of the devil (that stoppeth him
all that he can from the sacrament and the grace of
the same), and is prepared to be translated and brought
into the kingdom of Christ. Here plainly appeareth
how the prince of this world is cast forth (John xii. 31,
Luke xi. 14), and how the strong prince is bound,
and his vessels be reft from him, and brought into the
possession of the stronger conqueror that hath taken
captive the captivity itself, and hath given gifts to men
(Eph. iv. 8). Like as King Pharao in Egypt, oppres-
sing the people with importable works and keeping
them in thraldom and slavery, and not suffering them
to depart from Egypt at the message of God by
Moses and Aaron, was sundry and divers ways
plagued by Almighty God, and yet still did obstinately
withstand God, till he and all his army was drowned
in the Red Sea : even so the devil, keeping in bondage
and thraldom the reasonable creatures of God, is continually plagued and scourged by these exorcisms
and adjurations, in the power and name of God, and
yet he, being obstinate in his malicious tyranny, doth
not wholly dismiss and suffer the said creatures of
God to depart out of his dominion, till they come

C

to the water of Baptism (whereof the Red Sea was a figure, 1 Cor. x. 2–11), and then is he overthrown, and the child baptized set at liberty by the mighty hand of God, to serve Him all the days of his life.

In this exorcism there be used divers things. First, the party that is baptized giveth his name to Christ, either by himself, if he be of age, or by his godfathers and godmothers, as representing the Church; whereby we be taught, that he renounceth utterly the devil his former possessor, and now giveth his name to be taken as a soldier of Christ, and to be from henceforth under His dominion and obedience. So long as he remained in the possession of the devil, he bare no name, but as soon as the name of God is called upon over him, then he taketh a name, and beginneth to be written in the book of life. Next the giving of the name, the child baptized is marked with the sign of the cross in divers parts of his body ; whereby we understand that now he is received into the army of Christ, and taketh his soldier's coat and his badge upon him, which is the cross of Christ, under which he professeth to make war against the devil during his life. Which cross the devil feareth marvellously, because he was once beaten and overcome with that rod. And as God when He plagued the Egyptians, would not suffer the Angel to kill any person, nor yet to enter the house, but to pass by the house, where the blood of the Paschal lamb was sprinkled upon both the posts of the door (Exod. xii. 7–13), even so the devil, that is, the destroying Angel, dare not come near to kill, but flieth from him that professeth to fight under the cross, and so in very deed taketh his cross upon him and followeth Christ.

The like is shewed in the prophet Ezekiel, how that all they in the city of Jerusalem that were marked with the letter thau—T—in their forehead (Ezech. ix. 4) (which is the very sign and print of the cross), were saved and delivered from the plague and sword of God's Angel. And this sign of the cross is marked upon the child's forehead as in the place and seat of shamefastness, to the intent he should never be ashamed to be a Christian, and to follow the doctrine and word of the cross, which was an offence to the Jews and thought foolishness to the Gentiles, but to us and all them that be saved it is the virtue, the power and the wisdom of God (1 Cor. i. 18.) The same sign also is marked upon the child's eyes, whereby we be taught that he is elected and prepared to see God in this world by true faith, and in the next world to see Him face to face in the fruition of His glory. His ears be also signed with the cross, declaring that he is now dedicate to God, to hear His word and to learn the truth of His Catholic doctrine, and to obey the same in his living, and to stop his ears from the hearing and believing of error and the false doctrine of heresy. Likewise his nose is signed with the cross, to the intent he should always remember to live so, that his doings and works be a sweet savour to Almighty God (2 Cor. ii. 14–16). Moreover, his breast and mouth be signed with the cross, that by the virtue thereof he should conceive and believe in his heart the true faith of Christ to

his righteousness, and should with his mouth speak
and confess the same faith to his salvation (Rom.
x. 8–10), without fear of any danger or trouble that
might worldly come to him thereby.   And last of
all, his shoulders be signed with the cross, to the
intent he should take upon him to bear the sweet
yoke and light burden of God's service, according
to the commandment of our Saviour Christ, saying,
"Take my yoke upon you, and learn to be meek
and humble in heart, and ye shall find quietness
and rest in your souls" (Matt. xi. 29).

After the sign of the cross followeth the ceremony
of putting salt in the child's mouth ; whereby is
signified that the child is prepared and made the
salt of our Lord, and a sweet vessel to receive into it
the salt of God's heavenly wisdom, of His spiritual
grace, by the presence of God's Holy Spirit, and that
all his words and deeds ought to be savoury and
well-seasoned with the said heavenly wisdom and
grace, not putrefied by the worms of sin, nor yet
smelling evil by the corruption and poison of
abominable iniquity.

After this, like as our Saviour Christ when He
healed the deaf and dumb man, He put His fingers
into his ears, and with His spittle touched his mouth
and said, "Be thou opened" (Mark vii. 34), even so
after that manner, the priest in the person of Christ
doth open the ears and touch the nose of the child
that is born spiritually deaf and dumb, that he should
now begin to hear the voice and word of God, and
to obey His most holy commandments, having the
ears of his heart opened to understand and approve

that which is the good, well-pleasing, and perfect will of God (Rom. xii. 2) ; and also that he should have discretion by the opening of his inward smelling, to discern the good smell of life from the evil smell of death, and to receive the sweet savour of God's knowledge by the virtue of the incarnation of God's Son (2 Cor. ii. 14–16), (which is signified by His spittle), and to think continually upon such things as be true, chaste, just, holy, and of good name and fame (Phil. iv. 8), and that the power and illusions of the wicked spirit, the devil, might be restrained, and that the grace of God might be given to the child, whereby the spiritual effects and all that is taught by these godly ceremonies might be wrought in the child's soul.

The priest, with them that represent the whole Church, say the " Pater Noster " and make their most humble prayer to Almighty God, and in spirit and truth do call upon His name; and after all these things done without the door of the "visible " church, whereby is signified the true Church and mystical body of Christ, out of which the child remaineth till he be baptized, at last they enter the church, and bring the child to the fountain of Baptism, and there is made the solemn league and covenant between God and man. First the league and vow of the man's part with God, when he voluntarily by three solemn professions, renounceth the devil and all his works, and all his pomp and pride. The pomps of the devil be the unlawful desires that defile the soul, as the desires of the flesh, the desires of the eyes, and the ambition of the world. He that will over-

come the world, must overcome these three things
which be in the world, and thereby shall he overcome
the devil, that by persuasion of these three deceived
the world. On the other side, the league of God's
part with man, is to remit his sins, to receive him as
His son, to endue him with His Holy Spirit, and to
bring him to eternal salvation. This league and
covenant is never broken of God's part, but whosoever believeth and is baptized shall be saved (Mark
xvi. 15); which promise of our Saviour Christ is ever
fulfilled, except the man break his vow and promise
before by serving the devil and doing his works, and
so finally lose by sin the grace which is given unto
him in Baptism.

After this league made, the child is anointed with
oil upon the breast, to the intent he should understand when he cometh of age, that the Holy Ghost
(which is signified by the oil) should always possess
his heart by faith, and always dwell in that heart by
charity as in a holy temple, ever, in all adversities,
comforting it with the oil of spiritual joy and gladness. And he is also anointed in the back, that he
should understand that the same faith which he hath
received into his heart, ought to be exercised with
good works to the glory of God and the edifying of
his neighbour. And so is he anointed as a champion
of Christ, as one that even then entereth into the
battle of this world, to fight with the devil and all his
wicked angels. And because Christ saith " He that
believeth and is baptized shall be saved," therefore
the party that is brought to be baptized, is inquired
and asked what he believeth concerning the Holy

Trinity and all other articles of our common creed. And if he be of age and discretion, he professeth his own faith in his own person, without the which profession he may not be admitted to the holy sacrament of Baptism. And this form was always observed in the beginning of the Church, when men of perfect age were baptized. But after that the multitude of the Gentiles were converted to the faith of Christ, the holy Church providing for the salvation of their children, which cannot be saved but by regeneration of the water and the Holy Ghost, hath ever used to baptize them in the sacrament of faith, that like as they were alienated from God by another man's sin, so they might be reconciled again to God by other men's faith. So that the holy Church, our mother, answereth and professeth the true faith for the children, and maketh the promise for them, till they may understand that faith and keep that vow which is made in their names by the Church their mother. Then after the profession of this faith, the party is asked whether he will be baptized or no, because no man having the use of his will is saved without the consent of his will, and when he answereth, or it is answered for him, that he will, then is he put into the water thrice, and baptized in the name of the Father, and of the Son, and of the Holy Ghost, in which thing consisteth the great mystery or sacrament of Baptism, where the flesh is washed and the soul made clean, where the inward man is made new, and Christ is formed in the mind of man, where the devil, the old tyrant and usurper, is driven away, and God, the right owner

and possessor, is brought in.   Then are we (as S.
Paul saith) buried with Christ by Baptism into death,
that as He rose from death by the glory of the Father,
so we should likewise walk in a new life.   Whereby
we understand that like as Christ died, and rose
again the third day, and liveth evermore, so every
man, when he renounceth the devil, he dieth to sin,
and killeth the works of the flesh in himself, and
when he is dipped and put under the water, then is
he buried to sin as Christ was put within the earth in
the Sepulchre, and when he is thrice put under the
water, he representeth the three days of Christ's
burial, and when he is taken forth of the water again,
then doth he rise a new man, as Christ rose out of
the Sepulchre, and ought to die no more by serving
of sin, but to live continually in righteousness and
holiness all the days of his life.

And although the old and ancient tradition of the
Church hath been from the beginning to dip the
child three times in the water, as Christ lay three
days in the grave, yet that is not of such necessity,
but that if he be but once dipped in the water, it is
sufficient, yea, and in time of great peril and necessity, if the water be but poured upon his head, it will
suffice.*   Now when the Baptism is done, the child

---

* It would seem from this passage, that Baptism by immersion was
the usual practice in England in the sixteenth century ; though Baptism
by effusion, *i.e.*, by pouring water on the head, had already become the
more common mode throughout the Latin Church, at least since the
thirteenth century.   The mode indicated in the Roman Ritual is that
of effusion, although instructions are given for immersion, "where such
is the custom."   See Kane,   Notes on the Roman Ritual, 175–178,
and 346.—Ed.

is anointed on the crown of the head with the holy chrism; whereby we be taught that he is, by the unction of the Holy Spirit, incorporated and grafted into Christ who is the Head of His mystical body the Church, and there is he anointed and made a spiritual king to rule and overcome his own carnal affections, and also is anointed and made a spiritual priest to offer up spiritual sacrifices to God in a pure heart; and so he taketh of this holy chrism and of Christ, the name of a Christian man, being anointed into everlasting life, which he is bounden to seek and procure all the means he can, although it were with the loss and spending of this temporal life here.

And by and by after he be anointed with the holy chrism, he hath a white vesture or chrisom put upon him, which declareth that the child hath now put off the foul and filthy clouts of sin, and hath put on the chaste garment of innocence and cleanness of a new life, which he ought with all diligence to keep undefiled and to present it before the judgment-seat of Christ, for the attaining of eternal life. And also a wax candle burning is put in his hand, whereby is signified the light and truth of Christ's doctrine, and that his duty is to fulfil that in his life, which Christ taught in His gospel, saying " Let your light shine so before men, that they may see your good works and glorify your Father which is in heaven" (Matt. v. 16), and he that preserveth and keepeth this candle unquenched till the day of our Lord, shall amongst the five wise virgins enter in with the Spouse to the heavenly marriage.

Thus I have declared unto you (good people) all

the ceremonies used from the beginning of Christ's Church universally in the ministration of Baptism, and also the duty of him that is baptized, which I pray you and exhort you in God's name both to remember yourselves, and also to teach your children them as soon as they can understand, and amongst all other, specially that solemn covenant, promise, and vow, which they have made for the renouncing of the devil, his works, and all his pomps and pride. Teach them that this promise is made, not to an earthly man but to God Almighty and all His holy angels, Who hath power to destroy and cast into hell both body and soul of him that keepeth not his promise, And teach them to renounce and forsake the devil, not in words only, but in their deeds, not in the sound of their tongue, but in all their conversation, And teach them that they have to do in their conflict with an old crafty and mighty enemy, against whom if they prevail, as they cannot without their own great diligence, and the special aid of God's Holy Spirit (whereof they be always sure), then will God keep His part of the league and promise, that is to say, He will save them by grace in this world, and by the fruition of His glory in the next world, through the merits of Christ His Son, to whom with the Holy Ghost be all glory and praise.   Amen.

THE FIFTH SERMON.

OF THE SACRAMENT OF CONFIRMATION.

AFTER that a man by receiving the sacrament of Baptism is born again, and made a member of Christ's mystical body, it is ordained by our Saviour Christ and His Holy Spirit, that he should also receive the sacrament of Confirmation, and thereby be confirmed and made strong in that grace which he received before. For which cause I think it good at this time (good people) to declare unto you what ye ought to think of that sacrament of Confirmation, and what spiritual grace and effect it worketh in his soul that is confirmed, and what is every man's duty to do that hath received it.

We ought to think that our Saviour Christ did institute this sacrament, concerning the grace and effect of it, first when He did promise to send His disciples the Holy Ghost, and also when He did perform the same promise by giving to them the Holy Ghost (John xv. 26, Acts ii. 4). Many times did He promise to send them the Holy Ghost, but specially before His ascension, when He said " I shall send unto you My Father's promise, but remain you in the city till ye be indued with strength and power from above " (Luke xxiv. 49). And again He said

" Ye shall receive the virtue of the Holy Ghost coming upon you, and ye shall be witnesses of Me in Jerusalem, and in all Jewry and Samaria, even to the world's end " (Acts i. 8).

This promise he performed upon Whitsunday, when the Holy Ghost came down and rested upon the Apostles in a visible sign as in fiery tongues ; whereby we may understand, that as the Apostles were confirmed immediately by the Holy Ghost Himself without the ministration of any minister, even so the same grace and strength is given by the sacrament of Confirmation to us all that be baptized before, according to the measure of God's gift. Which thing is proved manifestly by the doings of the Apostles, for when they heard tell that the Samaritans had received the word of God, and were baptized by S. Philip, they sent thither S. Peter and S. John, who when they came they prayed for them, and laid their hands upon them, and they received the Holy Ghost in a visible sign (Acts viii. 17). And another time S. Paul baptized certain men at Ephesus (Acts viii. 6), and when he had laid his hands upon them they received the Holy Ghost, and they spake with tongues and did prophesy. By this imposition or laying of the Apostle's hands upon them, is meant this sacrament of Confirmation, by which the Holy Ghost is given, of whom they receive increase of their former grace given in Baptism, and spiritual strength against all temptations. And this grace in the 'aning was given in visible signs of fiery tongues, 'y spake also miraculously in divers tongues, y prophesied. But when this visible sign did cease and appeared no more, and yet the same grace was given that was given before : then the fathers of the primitive Church and successors of the Apostles, by the inspiration of the Holy Ghost, and by the tradition of the very Apostles, did minister this sacrament with the holy chrism ; so that the imposition of the bishop's hands, outwardly anointing the party baptized with the holy chrism upon his forehead, with the words thereunto belonging, is the sacrament of Confirmation signifying and working in the soul of man the inward unction of the Holy Ghost, with the greater and further gifts of His manifold grace.

The necessity of this sacrament of Confirmation is not of such importance as it is of Baptism. For without Baptism (if it may be had by any means) it is impossible to be saved. But if a man or child after Baptism chance to die in his innocency without deadly sin, his Baptism and regeneration only is sufficient to his salvation, and his death is to him a Confirmation, because after death a man can sin no more. But if the child or man do live after Baptism, because he is then led into the wilderness of the world, and there is tempted of the devil his ghostly enemy (Matt. iv. 2–8), who goeth about like a ramping lion seeking whom he might devour (1 Peter v. 8), and also tempted by the wicked world—sometimes by the terror of adversity, other times by the flattering and deceitful face of prosperity—and hath also within himself lurking a secret and busy enemy of his flesh always rebelling against his spirit (Gal. v. 17), therefore hath he need of further aid of grace to be more able to withstand his enemies, which aid of grace God giveth him by this sacrament of Confirmation, where he receiveth the same Holy Spirit that he received before in Baptism, but to a diverse end and in diverse gifts. For in Baptism he was born again spiritually to live ; in Confirmation he is made bold to fight. There he received remission of sin, here he receiveth increase of grace ; there the Spirit of God did make him a new man, here the same Spirit doth defend him in his dangerous conflict ; there was he washed and made clean, here is he comforted and made strong. In Baptism he was chosen to be God's son, and to be an inheritor of His heavenly kingdom ; in Confirmation God hath given His Holy Spirit to be his tutor, to instruct him and preserve him, that he lose not by his folly that inheritance which he is called unto. In Baptism he was called and chosen to be one of God's soldiers, and had his white coat of innocency delivered unto him, and also his badge, which was the red cross, the instrument of Christ's passion, set upon his forehead, and other parts of his body ; in Confirmation he is encouraged to fight, and hath the armour of God put upon him which be able to beat off the fiery darts of the devil, and to defend him from all harm, if he will use them in his battle and not put himself in danger of his enemies by entering the field without them.

By this we may understand the goodness and effects of this sacrament, and how necessary and expedient it is for a man that would live well in this world, and to be able to avoid sin. For what doth it profit a man to arise when he is fallen, except

he be stayed from falling again? As in Baptism a
man lying in sin was set up upon his feet, and made
able to walk in the ways of God which be mercy and
truth, so in Confirmation he is stayed from falling
and made able to endure the pains of the journey,
and to pass through the straits and dangers that
may chance.

And also there is given in this sacrament by the
Holy Ghost great consolation in all troubles and
adversities, both to take comfort himself, and with
gladness to bear his cross with Christ, and also to
give comfort to all others that by any occasion shall
come in distress. Experience of this we may see in
the very Apostles themselves, and specially in S.
Peter that was the first and chief of all the others.
For when our Saviour Christ had declared that he
was clean (John xiii. 7), and had showed unto him so
much of His glory in the mountain as he could bear,
when he heard the voice of the Father testifying
Christ to be His Son (Matt. xvii. 5), and saw with his
eyes His marvellous works, and did miracles in the
name of Christ (Luke ix. 6) himself, and walked upon
the sea at Christ's commandment (Matt. xiv. 29), and was
so familiarly used of Christ, that he said he was ready
to go to prison with him (Luke xxii. 33), and though
he should suffer death with him he would never deny
him (Matt. xxvi. 35), yet for all this, lacking as yet
the strength of God's Spirit, he was afraid of one little
maid, and by-and-by denied Christ, and sware twice
that he knew Him not. And besides this, after
Christ's resurrection, when he had received a message
from Christ, and had seen Himself, and was much

comforted by Him, yet he kept himself privily in a house with the rest of the Apostles for fear of the Jews. But after that he had received the Holy Ghost, which Christ promised to send, and was confirmed and indued with spiritual strength from above, then began he with the other Apostles to speak boldly the word of God, and to bear witness of Christ's resurrection, and was nothing afraid of the mighty princes of the world, but contemned all their threatenings, and gloried in their tribulations, and rejoiced that they were thought worthy to suffer either shame or death for the name of Jesus, taking this for a rule of their living, rather to obey God than man.

For this same intent and spiritual effect (good people) receive we the Holy Ghost in our Confirmation, that we should be established in the gifts and graces before received in Baptism, that we lightly fall not from them again, that we should be made hardier and more bold to confess our faith, not regarding any danger or peril that might come to us thereby ; and that we should constantly withstand all the assaults and temptations of the devil, the world, and the flesh, and neither shrink for fear, or give over for pain, nor cease for shame, but with patience and continuance keeping our promise, bearing our cross, and not yielding to our enemy, should with sure hope look for the crown of righteousness which God will give to all them that love His coming (2 Tim. iv. 1).

These godly effects be taught and signified unto us by the matter of this sacrament, and by the other ceremonies which be used in the ministration of it. The matter of it is the holy chrism which is mingled and made of two things—olive oil and balm. By the olive oil is signified the infusion of grace, and the fervent zeal and charity towards the maintenance of Christ's faith, wherewith he is indued that is confirmed. By the balm is signified the sweetness of God's Holy Spirit, wherewith Christ doth allure us, and draweth us to His service, and also whereby we are made a good and sweet savour to God, replenished with the fruit of righteousness to the glory and praise of God (Phil. i. 11), and to the good example and edification of our neighbour. With this holy chrism the man or child is anointed in his forehead, by the imposition of the bishop's hands, with the sign of the cross. By the imposition of hands, is signified the strength of the Holy Ghost, wherewith we be indued in our Confirmation, to the intent we might be able to stand in our faith, to abound in hope, and to grow in charity in good works. And the cross is signed in our forehead that we should never be ashamed of our Lord Jesus Christ, nor of our religion, but should steadfastly resist the temptations of the devil, and overcome with patience the troubles of this world, always glorying in the cross of Christ, and labouring to come to the fellowship of His passion, that so we might be partakers of His glorious resurrection.

After Confirmation the party confirmed hath a blow of the cheek given him by the bishop, to the intent he should know and remember, that his religion and confession is meekly and gladly to suffer the shame, rebuke, and tribulation of the world for the name of Christ, and for righteousness' sake, without grudging against God (Acts v. 41), or revenging of his own

D

quarrel, and so in peace and patience to possess his soul.

Therefore I beseech you, brethren, do not neglect this wholesome and profitable sacrament, but diligently consider what aid and what grace is given unto you in it, and if by your negligence and fall ye have lost that grace for a great part, yet it may be recovered again, not by a new Confirmation, which may not be iterate, but by your inward conversion and faithful penance, and after ye be risen and have recovered your strength again, then take better heed, and do not make heavy nor drive not away the Holy Ghost from you, who flieth always from feigned hypocrisy, and will not dwell in that body that is subject and servant to sin. And likewise be you careful and diligent to have your children confirmed in this grace, and to be indued with these excellent gifts of the Holy Ghost, by receiving this holy sacrament in the Catholic Church, and specially those whose children were baptized of heretics in the time of any schism and out of the Catholic Church. For although they did then receive the sacrament of baptism which may not be ministered to them again, lest we should shew ourselves to crucify Christ again ; yet they did not then and there receive the grace of baptism being out of the Church,* but may now receive the grace which

---

* It is of faith that baptism may be validly administered by heretics. The Council of Trent has decreed :—" If any one saith that the baptism, which is even given by heretics in the name of the Father, and of the Son, and of the Holy Ghost, with the intention of doing what the Church doth, is not true baptism ; let him be anathema."—Sess. vii., can. 4. But there can be true baptism without the grace of baptism,

they lacked before, and be reconciled to God, and be made members of His Holy Catholic Church, and so in time be admitted to receive the blessed Body and Blood of our Lord Jesus Christ—which things if you procure for them, and both they and you stand steadfastly in that same grace to your lives' end, ye may perfectly trust to attain that glory which shall be revealed and given to all God's elect people in the last day by the merits of our Saviour Christ, to whom with the Father and the Holy Ghost be all honour and praise, for evermore. Amen.

---

as in the case of adults baptized in heresy, or even in the Catholic Church without the necessary dispositions. To assert, however, as Watson seems to do, that the infant *children* of heretics and schismatics receive in baptism no sanctifying grace, is very singular, and quite contrary to the common teaching of theologians. The matter will be treated in an appendix.—ED.

THE SIXTH SERMON.

OF THE SEVEN GIFTS OF THE HOLY GHOST GIVEN IN THE SACRAMENT OF CONFIRMATION.

WHEREAS it is declared unto you (good people) that in the sacrament of Confirmation, the Holy Ghost is given to him that is confirmed, not for the making of him a new man or the child of God, and the inheritor of the kingdom of heaven, for which purpose He was given before in baptism, but to confirm him in that grace he hath received, and to aid him in his spiritual battle with his ghostly enemies, and to defend him in his conflicts, and to comfort him in his travail, and to be his tutor in keeping him from falling, and to make him strong and able to resist and overcome his enemies, all which things the Holy Ghost worketh in the heart of the party confirmed by induing him with His seven principal gifts : therefore I intend, God willing, at this time to declare unto you, which be those seven gifts, and how they be used to avoid the suggestions and assaults of the devil.

The seven gifts be set forth by the prophet Isaias (chap. xi. 1, 2), where he saith of our Saviour Christ, "that there shall a rod or branch spring forth of the oot of Jesse, and a flower shall ascend from that

root, and the Spirit of God shall rest upon him, the
spirit of wisdom and understanding, the spirit of
counsel and strength, the spirit of knowledge and
piety, and the spirit of the fear of God shall replenish
him."

Which seven gifts do not only rest upon Christ as
man, being the head of His mystical body the
Church, but also upon every one of us that be made
members of the same body, and the Holy Ghost
dwelleth in his soul that hath these gifts, and always
defendeth him from his enemies, and when he
loseth or quencheth them by yielding to his enemy,
then the Holy Ghost withdraweth His gracious presence from him, till he by penance and prayer recover them again. And these gifts (after the manner
of Holy Scripture) be termed and called by the
name of spirits, not that they be the substance of
the Holy Spirit of God, but that they be wrought
in our souls by His motion, inspiration, and spiritual
unction, and do make that man a spiritual and
godly man that hath them and useth them.

Now, for what intent the Holy Ghost doth give
them to a man that is confirmed, you shall plainly perceive if ye will consider the manner and order of the
devil's temptation in us. There be seven capital vices
called deadly sins, from which, as from seven wells or
fountains, all other vices and corruptions of the soul
do spring and proceed. These be the net and snares
that the devil layeth to entrap and catch a man in.
And considering that he is so mighty, being the
prince of darkness, and so malicious, never ceasing
to devour us, and so crafty, knowing in what point

we are most weak to withstand, and being practised
from the beginning of the world in such feats, he
will not fail to entangle us with these vices his snares,
except we have the assistance and aid of God's Holy
Spirit to help us, and be vigilant ourselves to take
heed to our feet, and with faith and prayer put away
his darts. And because we be weak of ourselves,
and not able to match and overcome this our mighty
and crafty enemy, therefore the Holy Spirit of God,
our tutor and defender, being of more strength than
the devil is, hath armed us with seven other gifts
contrary to the devil's seven snares or darts, and
hath also bound him that he shall not tempt us
further, than we being thus armed and aided be able
to withstand (1 Cor. x. 13). And because these His
seven gifts be as it were the seeds of godly living
sown in the ground of our hearts, He causeth
out of them other seven virtues to grow, whereby
a man is made able not only to avoid the seven
snares of the devil, but also is inwardly beautified,
and enriched, and made a happy man : for which
cause these virtues be called beatitudes. And in
case a man lose these gifts and virtues, our Saviour
Christ hath taught us a mean to recover them again,
which is prayer, and for that every man is not of
that wisdom and learning, as he can particularly and
in proper terms ask that which he needeth, therefore hath He taught us one form of prayer containing
seven petitions, whereof every one of them is directed
in order to the asking and attaining of one of the
foresaid seven gifts and virtues. Thus are we every
way on God's part provided for sufficiently, and may

easily overcome the devil our enemy, if we list to take pains and fight, as our duty to Almighty God and regard to our soul's health do require.

And that ye may the better understand this that I have spoken in general, I shall by God's help for your edifying, declare shortly and particularly how every vice is overcome with the contrary gift of the Holy Ghost.

And first, to begin at pride, which is the root and beginning of all sin (Eccles. x. 15), the mother of death and misery (Isa. xiii. 8), and the very cause why the devil was expelled out of heaven and man out of Paradise, ye may consider that the devil by pride laboureth to take God from us, whom we are most bound to love and serve, and daily tempteth us, either to think and esteem that good quality, which we have, to come of ourself and not of God, or else that it is not freely given but fully deserved of our part, or else to boast ourselves to have that we have not, or else to despise others and to labour to appear singular, or else by one means or other he provoketh us to contemn God, and not to regard our state and condition. By this dart he laboureth to wound our souls : against the which the Holy Ghost hath armed us with His gift of the fear of God, not only with the servile fear of the pains of hell, which is the beginning of wisdom (Prov. ix. 10), and goeth away at His coming by charity (1 John iv. 18), but also with the reverent and chaste fear of God's majesty and goodness that remaineth for ever, whereby a man forbeareth to offend God, and is careful to please and serve God, as the wise man counselleth, saying, "Son, when thou comest to God's service stand in fear, and prepare thy soul to temptation" (Eccles. ii. 1). This fear of God is the root and keeper of all religion, in which except a man keep himself steadfast, the house of virtues builded in his soul will soon decay and come to ruin (Eccles. xxvii. 4). And it is given us by the Holy Ghost as a present remedy against pride, as S. Paul saith, *Noli altum sapere, sed time*—be not proud and high-minded, but fear (Rom. xi. 20). For by fear a man is awaked out of the sleep of negligence, his conscience is examined if any fault be done, and he is made careful for this life present, and desirous of the life to come.

Out of this root of fear springeth the goodly flower of humility, which is called poverty in spirit (Matt. v. 3), whereby a man giveth God the glory of that virtue he is endued withal, and is content with the fruit of the same, and is esteemed but little in his own sight, be he never so high in knowledge and dignity, and putteth his trust and glory neither in himself, his strength, his virtues, his works, or his riches, nor yet in no other creature, but in his Lord God alone, and is therefore made most happy, and put in fair hope to attain Christ's promise of the kingdom of heaven. And if he shall perceive by his negligence these two gifts of fear and humility to be diminished or decayed in him, then let him straight run to prayer, and ask them of God in the first petition of his "Pater Noster," which is "Hallowed be Thy name;" wherein he asketh that he may, in all things, glorify God's name in humility, and not

his own name by pride, acknowledging all goodness
to proceed from God, and labouring to honour Him by
his good life.

The second dart of the devil is envy, for of pride
groweth envy, and as he by pride robbed man of the
love of God, so by envy he robbeth man of the love
of his neighbour, and always tempteth man to bear
gall in his heart and poison on his tongue, to rejoice
in the adversity of his neighbour and to be sorry at
his prosperity, to wish his neighbour evil and to speak
evil of him behind his back. Against this dart of the
devil the Holy Ghost hath armed us with the gift of
pity [or piety], whereby we be armed and instructed
to have compassion of our neighbour's adversity, to
bear the infirmities of others, to wish well to all men
for God's cause, to procure as much as we can their
commodity and preferment, and with devout affection
to honour and to do our duties, next God, to our
parents, to our country, to our princes, to our masters,
to our children and family, to our neighbours all, be
they friends or enemies ; that is to say, to shew reverence to our superiors, to shew conformity to our
equals, and to shew relief in word and deed to our
inferiors.

But of this root of pity springeth the godly virtue
of meekness ; for he that is well affected towards the
service and honour of God, and studious to do his duty
towards all degrees of men, shall shew himself to be
not heady, stiff-necked and envious, but meek, gentle
and tractable, not resisting evil, but with good overcoming evil, and therefore this meek man may well
be called happy, which by God's promise shall inherit

and possess the land of the living. And if this gift of pity, or the virtue of meekness, chance to decay or be lost by the envy of the devil, then let him pray the effect of the second petition, which is " O Father, let Thy kingdom come," either to us that we may be as Thou art, and teacheth us to be humble and meek in our own hearts, and so have Thee (Who art eternal rest) dwelling in our souls, or else let Thy kingdom come from heaven to earth in the clearness of the glorious coming of our Lord Jesus Christ, when the meek men shall hear Him call the blessed people of His Father to His kingdom (Matt. xxv. 34), and therefore shall rejoice and be glad for evermore (Ps. xxxiii. 3).

The third bolt that the devil shooteth against a man is ire, for of envy groweth ire ; when he envieth his equal or superior upon a small occasion either given or taken, he is stirred to indignation, malice, swelling of mind and evil looks, or else to chiding and brawling, and so in process to injury, vengeance, or murder ; wherein appeareth his great folly, for naughty anger resteth nowhere but in the bosom of a fool (Eccles. vii. 10), because it is great folly to thrust a sword through his own heart, to the intent he might hurt the coat of his enemy, which thing every angry man doth that, usurping the office of God, seeketh to revenge his own quarrel. And thus the devil, as he by pride robbed him of his love to God, and by envy of his love to his neighbour, so now by ire he robbeth him of the love of himself.

Against this fiery dart of the devil, the Holy Ghost hath armed us with the gift of knowledge, whereby we know how to walk uprightly and without offence in the midst of this wicked generation, and also that we should behave ourselves to them that have by wrong done us injury, as we would to sick folks, children or madmen, of whom their parents and other friends and physicians often times will suffer diverse injuries, till their youth or infirmity be gone away.

Out of this gift of knowledge springeth the virtue of mourning ; for when we know in what miseries we be wrapped, what a great heap of evils be round about us, which we of ignorance desired as good things and profitable for us, then we fall to mourning, and lament the lack or prolonging [*i.e.*, postponing] of the very true and eternal goods and riches that be stored up for us in heaven, and begin to set little by those vain and transitory things which we esteemed as food in earth : for which cause our Saviour Christ esteemeth us happy that so do mourn, and hath promised us the comfort of the Holy Ghost, that for contemning these temporal things here we should enjoy eternal gladness in heaven.

And for restitution of this gift and virtue when it decayeth or is lost by us, we may pray the third petition, "that God's will might be done in earth as it is in heaven," that when our flesh as earth and the desires of it, do in all things without rebellion obey our spirit—the lack of which obedience is the cause of our mourning, as the having of it is the performance of God's will on earth—then we might have this promised comfort presently in our hearts as a pledge of that gladness which is to come.

The fourth dart of the devil is idleness and slothfulness, when he tempteth a man to esteem the fulfilling of God's commandments either impossible or very hard and painful, and so to forbear the doing of his duty, or to be weary in the beginning, and sad ever after. Against this dart the Holy Ghost hath armed us with the gift of fortitude and strength, and thereby persuadeth us to think God's commandments not to be heavy or grievous, but to be a light burden and sweet yoke, and encourageth us to set upon that work which is excellent and worthy praise. And for avoiding of faintness or weariness, He kindleth our hearts with His love to continue steadfast and immovable from the hope of the gospel, increasing in good works and knowing that our labour is not in vain in Christ (Col. i. 23, 1 Cor. xv. 58). Out of this gift cometh the virtue which is called the hunger and thirst of righteousness, which consisteth in true faith and perfect obedience to God's law, the earnest and vehement desire whereof causeth a man to be moved neither with the flattery nor adversity of this world, nor to be sad when he doeth well, but to hope as a lion (Prov. xxviii. 1), and not to give place to his adversary. Therefore, seeing that fortitude is the gift of the Holy Ghost, whereby they be happy that be hungry and thirsty, that is to say, greedy and desirous of righteousness, because they shall be made full with the meat of Christ, which is to do the will of His Father, and also with that drink which causeth a fountain of water to be in them, springing up to everlasting life, if at any time we lack these virtues, or be slack in using of them, then let us pray that our daily bread may be given unto us this day, by virtue whereof we being sustained and made strong, might come to that perfect fulness and satiety which shall admit no hunger or thirst any more ever after.

The fifth dart of the devil is covetousness; for when he perceiveth a man encouraged to do good and serve God, by the gift of fortitude and strength, he laboureth all he can to turn that his constancy and strength to a wrong end, that is to say, from the fulfilling of God's law and maintaining of His truth, to the greedy and insatiable appetite of fulfilling the desires of the world, and to the maintenance of vice and error, and tempteth him further to be obdurate and stony-hearted in unmercifulness, and so in process, for hope of gain not to regard craft, deceit, violence, or treason.

Against this dart of covetousness the Holy Ghost armeth us with the gift of counsel, that our courage and strength may be stayed and directed to the right end, that is to say, to the contempt and despising of the vanity of this world, and not to trust in the uncertainty of riches, but to trust in the living God (1 Tim. vi. 17), and to do good to all we can, and to be rich in good works, being ready to give part of that God hath sent, and to store up a good treasure in the next world, to the attaining of everlasting life. And by this gift of counsel we be armed not to lean to our own strength, nor to the power of any multi-tude, nor to the obstinacy of mind, but to the help of God and for the glory of His name. So that this gift of fortitude worketh the virtue of mercifulness, whereby a man useth the world, not as the devil

tempteth him, to fulfil his greedy appetite, which like
dropsy will never satiate, but to the relief of the
poor, the defence of the innocent, the forgiving of
the offender, and the maintenance of the truth ; for
such a man is happy, and shall receive greater mercy
at God's hand.

And therefore when we lack this gift, or do not use
it, let us first forgive them that have offended us,
and then pray that our debts may likewise be forgiven unto us, and that is the very practice of this
gift of counsel and the direction of our spiritual
strength and fortitude.

The sixth dart of the devil is gluttony ; for when he
hath moved a man to take pleasure and joy in these
outward and worldly things, he tempteth him specially
to follow that pleasure that is most natural to his
flesh, and not to be content with that the necessity
of nature requireth, but to let pleasure have its will,
either in exceeding measure, or in too much delicate-
ness and preparation for the same, whereupon followeth the decay of health and subversion of reason,
for commonly where there is a full belly there is
also a dull wit. For that cause the Holy Ghost
hath armed us with the gift of understanding, out
of which proceedeth the virtue of cleanness of heart,
that our spiritual eyes may be simple, and refuse to
be made dull with the stuffing of our bellies, and our
hearts may be clean and pure from the corruption of
the flesh, not loaden with surfeiting and drunkenness,
to the intent we might escape the said vice of
gluttony, and be promoted to so great happiness as
to see God, which no man can do except the mist of

ignorance, error and unclean living, be taken from his eyes by faith and the gift of understanding.

And therefore, lest these temptations of the flesh specially concerning the nourishing and pampering of the same, do hinder us from true understanding, and the sight of God which He hath promised to all that be simple and clean of heart, let us diligently pray that He suffer us not to be led into temptation.

Finally, the last of the devil's darts is lechery, which is the vilest kind of sin of all other, and the soonest is a man tempted unto it, if the devil have any entrance before, either by idleness, covetousness, or drunkenness. For (as the prophet saith) the cause of the iniquity of Sodom was pride, too much eating, wealth, and idleness (Ezek. xvi. 49). And his voice blindeth a man's soul, taketh away his reason for a time and the consideration he should have of death, and bringeth him into hatred of God, and in mistrust or desperation of the life to come.

And for remedy against this most beastly vice, the Holy Ghost hath armed us with His greatest gift, which is wisdom ; whereby a man pulleth away his mind and pleasure from the corruption of his flesh, and refuseth to be subject to his unnatural sensuality, and to defile his body, the temple of God, and setteth his whole joy, felicity, and rest in his Lord God, having his mind occupied in heavenly thoughts, where nothing is that can displease. And this is the wisdom of God that cometh from above, which is chaste, peaceable, gentle, easy to be entreated, agreeable to goodness, full of mercy and good fruit (James iii. 17). Happy are they that have this wisdom, out of which springeth the virtue of making peace, because the fruit of righteousness is sown in peace to them that be peacemakers, to whom God hath promised that they shall be called His sons and children; for which cause when we lack this gift of wisdom, or wax slack to use it, let us pray to Almighty God to deliver us from all evil, which deliverance setteth us at liberty, and maketh us freemen, that is to say, the children of God, indued with the spirit of adoption, whereby we may boldly call God our Father.

And thus I have declared unto you the seven gifts of the Holy Ghost, given unto us in our Confirmation, which for lack of our good and virtuous bringing up when we were children, do not so much appear and shew themselves in our deeds, as it were expedient they should, but if we raise them up again by our prayer and diligent exercise, as I have partly told you, we shall be sure to overcome our spiritual enemy, and in the day of our Lord receive the crown of glory, through the merits of our Saviour Christ, to Whom with the Father and the Holy Ghost be all honour and praise. Amen.

THE SEVENTH SERMON.

*OF THE REAL PRESENCE OF CHRIST'S BODY IN
THE SACRAMENT OF THE ALTAR.*

AS a man by his carnal generation is not only
born to temporal life, but also in process of
time waxeth strong, which life and strength cannot
be preserved without nourishment and wholesome
meat ; even so a man by his spiritual regeneration
is not only born again to a spiritual life in Christ by
Baptism, but also waxeth strong in Christ by receiving the gifts of the Holy Ghost in Confirmation,
which spiritual life and strength cannot be preserved
and continued without spiritual nourishment and
wholesome meat. For which purpose our Saviour
Christ, who loved us so vehemently, that, to bring us
to life, was content to die, and for the price and
ransom of the same life vouchsafed to give His own
Body to death, doth still vouchsafe to nourish us, so
redeemed and brought to life, with the sweet and
wholesome milk of His own Blood, and giveth us His
Flesh to eat and His Blood to drink, that we might
be fed and nourished, for the continuance of our
spiritual life, with the same precious things that we
were redeemed withal before.

And because our souls be as yet joined with our

E

bodies, therefore for the time of this life our Saviour Christ giveth unto us His invisible graces in sensible sacraments. And as in Baptism by water (which is a sensible thing), is given to us the invisible grace of regeneration ; even so in the sacrament of the Altar, under the visible forms of bread and wine, is given to us the substance of all grace, which is Christ Himself, that is to say, His Body and His Blood ; which, though they be corporal things in their own nature, yet now being glorified, they be spiritual, and therefore not sensible, but where it pleaseth our Saviour by miracle to have them appear.

This is then most certainly and constantly to be believed of us all, upon pain of damnation, that in this blessed sacrament of the Altar (whereof I entreat at this time) is verily and really present the true Body and Blood of our Saviour Christ, which suffered upon the cross for us, and is received there corporally by the services of our mouths, not in the same form of His Body as it was upon the cross, but in the forms of our daily and special nutriments of bread and wine, the substance of which bread and wine, is converted and changed into the substance of Christ's Body and Blood, by the omnipotent and secret power of His word, assisting the due admini- stration of His minister.

This marvellous and heavenly doctrine is not invented by man's wit, but revealed by God's Spirit in His Holy Scripture, and taught us by the mouth of our Saviour Christ, who instituted this Holy Sacra- ment in His Last Supper, saying to His disciples, " Take, eat ; this is my Body, which is given for you ;

this is my Blood of the new testament, which is shed for many, and for you, in remission of sins" (Matt. xxvi. 26–28). Of these words, and the like which be written in the Gospels of S. Mark (xxii. 22–24) and S. Luke (xx. 19, 20), and in the Epistle of S. Paul to the Corinthians (1 Cor. xxiv. 24, 25), the Holy Catholic Church hath ever from the beginning understanded and believed that, after the speaking of those words by Christ, or by His minister in His person, sufficiently authorised so to do by His commandment, is made present the natural Body and Blood of our Saviour Christ, there to be received of His faithful people, to the increase of all grace, and immortality both of body and soul. For the Church esteemeth these to be the working words of God, making the thing to be as it was not before, and not as the words of only man, which can only declare the thing to be as it is before. For if Christ's word be of such strength that it can make things to be that were nothing before, how much more hath it strength to make a thing that was before to be changed into another thing that it was not? Like as the heaven was not, the earth was not, and yet He said the word, and they were made; even so the sacrament before the consecration was not the Body of Christ, but after the consecration it is now the Body of Christ, for He hath said the word and the thing is made. And He that is the Author of the gift is also the Witness of the truth of the same gift, so that our faith in this thing is grounded not in man's reason or sense, but in the almighty power of God's word. For if Christ, the speaker of this word, were not God's Son, and the Word of God, by Whom all trees and herbs do bring forth fruit, it could not be certain to us that this blessed and sanctified bread of the sacrament were Christ's Body and the cup of His Blood. Therefore, seeing that He hath said, "This is my Body, this is my Blood," who can neither deceive nor be deceived, let us without all doubt steadfastly believe it to be so, and look upon it with the eyes of our understanding. For our faith in this matter is induced by His only authority, and not by our wit, whose words require necessarily our faith, and in no wise do admit our reason : they require a simple believer, and reprove a wicked reasoner; so that we must believe simply that which we cannot search profitably. Wherefore, like as we may not curiously search how it is done, so we may not Jewishly doubt whether it be done, but reverently prepare us to receive that by faith which we are sure is done.

And furthermore, the Holy Church esteemeth those words of Christ, " This is my Body, this is my Blood," to be the formal words of a sacrament of the New Testament, working inwardly the same grace that is signified outwardly, which is the property of every sacrament of the New Testament, whereby they differ from the other shadows of the Old Testament. And because the grace that is signified by these formal words is the very Body and Blood of Christ Himself, the Author and fountain of all grace, therefore we must certainly know by faith that God, assisting the true ministration of this sacrament, according to His promise, doth inwardly work in the holy sacrament the real presence of His said Body and Blood. It is not the power of the priest, being a man, that, in the creatures which be set upon the altar to be consecrate, causeth the Body and Blood of our Lord to be made present, but it is Christ Himself that was crucified for us. The words be⁻ pronounced by the mouth of the priest as His minister, but the oblations be consecrate by God's power and grace, who is now there present, and sanctifieth the creatures, and changeth them, by the invisible working of the Holy Ghost; which miraculous change must be imputed to Christ, who by His word worketh this His presence above the reach of man's carnal understanding.

And we ought to think of this consecration far above the consecration of other things. For other things in the Church used about the holy sacraments be by prayer sanctified and called holy, for that they be dedicated to some holy use, and the soul of man is by grace consecrate and sanctified, because it is a substance wherein holiness and virtue remaineth; and a good man's body is also sanctified, being made a member of Christ and the temple of the Holy Ghost; and the other sacraments be sanctified and holy, for that they be the instruments whereby God worketh holiness in the soul of man; but above all other things, this blessed sacrament of the Altar is most holy, being (as S. Chrysostom saith) not only a thing sanctified, but also very sanctification and holiness itself. For in that it is the Body of Christ by sanctification, whereunto is annexed the Godhead by unity of person, it musts needs be holiness itself, not in quality, but in substance, out of which proceedeth all holiness, virtue, and goodness. And the Holy Church also esteemeth those formal words of our Saviour Christ to be the performance of His promise which He made at Capernaum to His disciples, when He said : " The Bread that I shall give unto you is my Flesh, which I shall give for the life of the world " (John vi. 52); which promise He that is the very truth, and cannot lie, did never at any time before perform but in His Last Supper, when He gave His Body and His Blood to His disciples to eat, and said that which He gave them was His Body and His Blood.

And as He promised to give unto them His Flesh, that should be given for the life of the world, and not a figure of that Flesh, or a sign; so He gave in very deed the same Flesh, and not a figure or sign of it, and said precisely that it was the same Body that should be given to death for their redemption; to which word every true Christian man giveth credit, and he that believeth not that it is His very true Body, as He said it was, he is fallen from all grace and salvation. And no man ought to be in doubt of the truth of this real presence of Christ's Body in the sacrament, because he hath either read himself in certain holy writers' books, or hath heard say of other, that they say how in this sacrament is a sign or a figure, or a similitude of Christ's Body. For those same authors, either in the places where they use those words, or else in some other places, declare most manifestly their faith concerning the real presence to be all one, agreeable with the common faith of the universal Church of Christ. And for your better in-

struction in this matter, ye shall understand that
there be two things which be parts of this sacrament—
the visible forms of bread and wine and the invisible
Body and Blood of our Lord Jesus Christ.

The outward form of that which is seen is a figure
and sign of that hidden truth which is there contained, believed, and not seen. Ye shall also understand that in the sacrament there be two graces to be
considered : the one is the substantial grace of Christ's
Body there present and contained, the other is the
accidental grace only, signified and not contained,
which is wrought in the soul of the worthy receiver,
whereby he is more inwardly joined to Christ's
mystical body, not only spiritually by faith and
charity, but also by natural and corporal participation with Christ and His Church. This unity of
Christ's mystical body, the Church, is as well signified
by Christ's natural Body there present, as it is by
the visible element of bread, which, as it is made one
loaf of many grains, so the Church is made but one
body of Christ, consisting of many men and women.
And thus is Christ's natural Body in the sacrament
a figure of His mystical body in the Church and of
the unity of the same.

And further, whereas our Lord commanded His
disciples and all us to do the same that He did
(1 Cor. xi. 25, 26), that is to say, to consecrate and
to receive His Body and Blood in the remembrance
of His death and passion till His last coming, ye
may therefore understand that the invisible, spiritual,
and intelligible Flesh and Blood of Christ in the
sacrament signifieth and representeth the same

visible, mortal, and palpable Body of Christ upon the cross; for which respect the sacrament of divers doctors is called a figure or sign. Finally, because all things that be in this present world, be they never so true, yet they be called figures and images in respect of the same things in heaven, which be seen as they be, without all shadows or coverings; therefore, like as the very oblation of Christ upon the cross, which is a thing of most truth, is called an image in respect of that oblation which He the same time, and at all times, maketh in heaven before His Father, where He appeareth as an Advocate for us, even so the natural Body of Christ in the sacrament, which cannot here be seen but by faith, may well be called a figure or image of the same Body in heaven, which is there seen without cover, and received by perfect fruition of all the blessed angels and saints that be there in the kingdom of God. For here the Church hath Christ her Spouse in a sacrament, and there she shall have Him without all sacrament. Both here and there, is the truth, but here it is covered, and there manifest without cover: in earth we eat the bread of angels in a sacrament; in heaven we shall eat the same bread evidently without a sacrament, where the presence of the Most High Priest shall show itself openly to all men as it is. For these respects which I have rehearsed, no man ought to be in doubt of the truth of Christ's real presence in the sacrament, because of these words (*figure* or *sign*) found in certain authors, which words (as I have declared) do in no wise deny the truth of the presence, but either they declare the secret and covered manner of it in the sacrament, or they signify the unity of Christ's mystical Body, or else they bring into our remembrance the passion of Christ's Body which is past, or the clear fruition of the same in heaven, which to us is yet to come. And here ye ought to mark diligently that which I have said concerning the two manners of being of Christ's Body— the one in heaven at the right hand of His Father manifestly without all cover or sacrament, the other the same moment of time here in earth amongst us in a sacrament, to be received of us for our spiritual sustenance ; in which thing we may not consider the nature of a man's body, but the infinite power of God, that can do with His Body what He will, and doth with it what He saith. And because He saith evidently that He giveth to us His Body that suffered and His Blood that was shed, therefore we ought to believe His word, which cannot deceive us, seeing that all things be possible to God, which be impossible to man (Luke xviii. 27 and Mark x. 27).

Christ's Body is but one, and although it be consecrate and offered in many places, yet there is but one Christ in every place, being both full Christ here and full Christ there, one body. And whereas Christ, God's only-begotten Son, goeth into every man divisibly that receiveth Him, and by His Flesh sanctifieth their souls and bodies, yet He in His Flesh remaineth whole without division in every one, being but one wheresoever He be, by no means divided. And in this miracle our Saviour Christ excelled Elias and all the prophets, for Elias left his mantle unto his disciple, but the Son of God ascending left to us His Flesh. Elias ascended without his mantle himself, but Christ hath left His Flesh unto us, and ascended having it also with Him. And this is not of our deserts, but of His exceeding mercy and goodwill, that, being whole in His majesty and glory at the right hand of God His Father, yet doth vouchsafe the same time to be with us on earth invisibly, being but one in divers places, not only comforting us that be here travailing with the presence of His divinity and Holy Spirit, but also feeding and nourishing us with the heavenly food of His Body and Blood to everlasting life. This feeding of us with Christ's Body and Blood we must understand that it is not only spiritually by faith, when we remember and think upon His passion and death, but also corporally with the service of our bodies and senses, when we receive it in the sacrament. For as in the old law the blood of the paschal lamb was commanded to be sprinkled upon both the posts of the door; even so the Blood of Christ, our Paschal Lamb, is sprinkled upon both the posts of our door, when it is received not only with the mouth of the body for redemption, but also with the mouth of the heart for imitation. Which Blood is not now shed upon the hands and coats of the soldiers that crucified Him, but is poured into the mouths of the faithful that receive Him. And this new doctrine was not known to the world till our Saviour Christ taught it Himself in His gospel. For the old law did forbid the eating and drinking of blood with their mouths, and the new law doth command it so to be drunken, for which cause we that pertain to the new law do use often times to drink of this Blood, knowing that except we eat His Flesh and drink His Blood we shall not have life in us (John vi. 54). Wherein we are called to more dignity than any of the prophets of the Old Testament was. For David did never eat of this Body, nor never drank of this Blood, although he believed in Christ as well as we, or rather better ; and so was only partaker of them spiritually by faith, and not corporally by the sacrament as we be. See with what great dignity Almighty God doth honour our mouths, by which, as by certain gates and doors, Christ entereth into us when we communicate and receive His Body, and so having Christ within us by His Flesh, and in Him corporally united by the sacrament of perfect and natural unity, we shall likewise be partakers of His property, which is life everlasting.

I will no more at this time (good people) occupy you with any longer process concerning this most true and evident matter, but shall speak of it at other times, beseeching you, in our Lord's name, not to waver in your faith like reeds blown aside with every wind, but to stand steadfast in the certain belief of this most Holy Sacrament, which is set forth to us by the mouth of our Saviour Christ Himself and the sacred books of all His holy Evangelists, and is confirmed with the blood of His martyrs, with the miracles of God and His saints showed for that purpose, with the testimony of all Catholic writers in every age, and with the authority and consent of the whole Church of Christ throughout the world, as well in General Councils assembled in the name of our Lord Jesus Christ, as in every particular province and realm ; which is the pillar of truth, and the surest staff to lean unto for a Christian man to hold himself steadfast in truth, so that the most manifest word which was spoken by Christ our Lord upon this Holy Sacrament, and the true meaning of the same word, declared from time to time by His Holy Catholic Church, delivereth us from all ignorance as to what it is, and assureth us that in His most holy sacrament is present, by the omnipotent power of God, the real and true Body and Blood of our Saviour Christ, God and man, under the sensible forms of bread and wine, and is there received of the faithful people not only spiritually by faith, but also corporally with their mouths, for the attaining of immortality and everlasting life both of body and soul ; the which God of His infinite goodness grant us through the merits of His Son Jesus Christ, and the sanctification of His Holy Spirit, to whom be all praise, honour, and glory, world without end.   Amen.

THE EIGHTH SERMON.

OF THE CHANGE OF THE BREAD AND WINE, THAT IS TO SAY, OF TRANSUBSTANTIATION.

WHAT is the substance of this blessed sacrament, we have learned (good people) of our Saviour Christ's own words, who the night before He suffered, at His Last Supper with His disciples took bread, and brake it, and gave it to His disciples, and said, "Take and eat; this is my Body;" and taking the chalice, He gave thanks, and gave it to them, saying, "Drink all of you of this; for this is my Blood of the new testament, which shall be shed for many, for remission of sins" (Matt. xxvi. 26–28). Upon these words of Christ all true Christian men ground their faith concerning this blessed sacrament, and believe verily that the inward substance of this sacrament is the Flesh of our Saviour Jesus Christ which suffered for our sins, and that in the chalice consecrate is the same Blood that did run forth of Christ's side when it was opened with the spear.

And furthermore, upon the same words of Christ, the Holy Church, and all true Christian men her members, do ground their faith concerning the change

which the Holy Ghost by His unspeakable power
worketh in this sacrament, where the inward sem-
blance of bread and wine is changed into the substance of the Body and Blood of Christ, the outward
forms of the said bread and wine, with the quantity
and qualities of the same, still remaining unchanged.
Which manner of change, because it is singular, and
hath none like it, either in nature or otherwise, therefore the Holy Church doth call it by the name of
Transubstantiation, the which word was invented by
the Holy Church in the greatest General Council that
ever was; which was called the Council of Lateran,
where there were present seventy Archbishops and
four hundred Bishops, and they spake of this change
by that name, to the intent that like as the Holy
Church of Christ in every age did agree and was of
one mind concerning this change of the bread and
wine, even so they should agree and be of one
tongue in the uttering and speaking of that change,
that the diversity of many words uttered diversely in
the books of learned men should not impair and
bring in doubt the old known truth revealed to the
Church by the Holy Ghost.

This old truth the Church learneth of Christ's own
words.   For whereas it was but one thing of substance
which our Saviour Christ gave out of His hand to
His disciples to eat, which one thing He said plainly
Body which should be given for them, and
so made it so to be by His almighty word;
cause the Holy Church believeth that it is
ad, but His very Body indeed.   And also,
as it appeareth to all a man's senses to be

very bread (which senses be not deceived so far as they can skill of and reach unto, which is only to the outward appearance and qualities or quality, and not to the inward substance), therefore the Holy Church believeth that the change which is in the sacrament is made in the inward substance of the bread, and not in the outward form of the bread, which remaineth as it was ; for which cause the Church calleth that change Transubstantiation. For that bread which our Lord reached to His disciples, being changed in nature and not in form, by the omnipotency of His word, was made flesh. And as in the person of Christ, His humanity was seen and His divinity was secret, unseen, even so in this sacrament the outward form of bread appeareth to man's sight, and the inward substance of Christ, God and man, appeareth not to a man's corporal eye, but to the eye of his soul, which is faith, which faith is stayed upon the omnipotent power of God. For He that can create all things of nought with His word, can also change things that be created with His word : and if the benediction of man can change the nature of things, as appeared when Moses changed his rod into a serpent (Exod. vii. 10), what shall we say of the consecration of God, that worketh marvellously in His holy sacrament ? If the word of Elias was able to bring fire from heaven, shall not the word of Christ be able to change the substance of bread ? Therefore, upon this ground of God's almighty power, we submit our reason to our faith, and above the reach of reason we believe Christ's word, and that there is not the substance of bread which nature formed, but the substance of Christ which benediction hath consecrate. And so we esteem this sacrament otherwise than an infidel doth. Like as an unlearned man when he looketh upon a book, he understandeth not the meaning of the writing, but a learned man will find much matter hid there, as the lives and stories of men ; the unlearned man will think there is nothing else but paper and ink, the learned man will understand another's speaking, and speak to one being absent, and ask by his letters whatsoever he would have ; even so it is in these mysteries. The infidels, although they hear what it is, yet they seem not to hear. But the faithful man, who hath experience of the Holy Ghost, can behold the virtue and power of God in the secret mysteries, where the substance of bread is consumed by the substance of Christ's Body and ceaseth to be there any more, even as wax when it is put in the fire, it melteth away, and the substance of it remaineth no more. These similitudes (whereof the books of the old writers be full) be not to satisfy the subtle wits and curious questions of men that lack faith, whose reasons brought out of natural experiments, may in no wise be admitted of a Christian man to disprove any part of our faith received, but they be brought in to declare what is our faith in this point, to which faith God's pleasure is, that every man's reason should be taken captive (1 Cor. x. 5), and serve to the belief of His wonderful works and sacraments, even as the natural inclination of our will should serve to execute the commandment of godly charity. For whatsoever flesh and blood doth bring forth, or the subtleness of man's wit, not indued with the Spirit of God, can invent, is to be rejected from the judgment and discussion of this holy mystery, and only that is to be admitted which the Father of heaven by the mouth of His Son, and the inspiration of His Holy Spirit, hath revealed to His Church. And therewith is every good Christian man contented and satisfied, not like the unfaithful Jews asking how it can be so, seeing nothing is impossible to God, but giving full credit to the Church of God in the presence of Christ in this sacrament, as the blessed Virgin Mary did to the angel of God in the Incarnation of Christ in her womb. And as she gave full consent to the angel's word when he told her that the Holy Ghost should come into her, and the power of the Most High God should overshadow her: even so ought every faithful soul to give full credit to God's Church, when it teacheth by the Word of God that the Holy Ghost overshadoweth this mystery, and maketh present the Body of Christ above the speech and reason of man, and changeth the bread and wine into Christ's Body and Blood, the outward forms remaining still, so that now there be not two substances remaining, but one and the selfsame that was given for our redemption, otherwise the manner of it is not searchable. And it ought to believe also, that like as the Church of God in the first General Council at Nice did very well when it did invent the word of Consubstantiality, to express the old truth that Christ was no creature, but equal God and of one and the same substance with the Father, to the confusion of the heretic Arius and all his adherents:

F

even so that the same Church of God did very well
in the General Council at Lateran, when it invented
the word of Transubstantiation, to express the old
truth, that there is but one substance of Christ in the
sacrament, and that the former substances of bread
and wine be converted and changed into the Body
and Blood of Christ, the qualities and figure of the
same remaining still unchanged, to the confusion of
the heretics Luther and Zwinglius, and all their
adherents.

Furthermore, it is to be considered, that in this
change of the bread, God did show His great merciful goodness towards us, that for our relief, bearing
with our infirmity, He hath suffered the outward
forms of bread and wine to remain unchanged. For
as our nature abhorreth the killing of a man's
flesh, and the shedding of a man's blood, so
much more it abhorreth the eating of man's raw
flesh and the drinking of man's lively blood ; and
whereas our Saviour Christ declaring the necessity of
this sacrament to the attaining of everlasting life,
said : That except we did eat His Flesh and drink His
Blood we should not have life in us (John vi. 54),
therefore hath He by His godly wisdom invented
this way to give us His Flesh to eat and His Blood to
drink, and yet our nature should not abhor the eating
and drinking of it, but comfortably and obediently
receive it. For He giveth it in such instruments of
bread and wine as we be daily accustomed to be fed
withal ; and so condescending to our infirmity lest we
should abhor the sight of His Flesh and Blood in their
own likeness, He reserveth the outward forms of the

bread and wine, but their substances He changeth into His Flesh and Blood. Beside divers other commodities that come to us thereby, as that our faith is more exercised in believing that to be there present, which we see not with our corporal eyes, and the property of the sacrament is retained, which is to teach by the composition and nature of the outward element, what the Holy Ghost worketh inwardly in the soul of him that worthily receiveth it, which is the unity and perfect conjunction of Christ's mystical Body. And also the holy sacrament itself is kept and conserved in His due honour, which otherwise should be contemned and despised of the pagans and infidels, if they perceived how we Christian men did eat the Flesh and drink the Blood of Christ our Lord God. For these causes He hath ordained it to be ministered in the forms of bread and wine.

And although our Saviour Christ when He did first institute this sacrament in His Supper, did minister it to His Apostles whom He then made priests, under both the kinds of bread and wine, to the intent His death and passion might be declared and remembered thereby, where His Blood was separate from His Body, as the bread was separately consecrate from the chalice, which manner is yet continually observed in the sacrifice of the Church which is the mass : yet for divers weighty considerations, as well concerning the honour of the sacrament and the avoiding the effusion of Christ's Blood which might chance, as for the more commodious administration of the sacrament to the people, the Holy Church hath used, even from the time of Christ Himself and His Apostles, to minister this sacrament under the form of bread only, both to laymen and women and also to priests, saving when they do consecrate and minister to themselves with their own hands, in which doing it hath the example of Christ, Who, the day of His resurrection, ministered this sacrament to two of His disciples in the castle of Emmaus (Luke xxiv. 30), under one kind alone, and also the people be defrauded of no part of Christ's Body and Blood, nor of no effect or grace that cometh by the worthy receiving thereof; for it is most certain that the whole Body and Blood of Christ is as truly contained under the one kind of bread, as under both the kinds of bread and wine, seeing that Christ's living Body cannot be without His Blood, nor His lively Blood without His Body.

And it is also most certainly true that if the outward element of bread be divided into small parts, there is the whole Body of Christ contained in every part, as it was in the whole element before it was divided, even as the soul of man is but one and whole in the whole body, and is likewise one and whole in every part of the body ; and also as a glass when it is broken into pieces, the whole image of a man's face appeareth in every part severally, which before in the whole glass appeared but one, even so the whole Body and whole Blood of Christ is given under every part of the outward forms ; equal portion is given to every one ; it is whole delivered ; it is distributed to many, and not dismembered ; it is incorporate to the receivers, and suffereth no injury; it is received and not included ; it dwelleth with weak persons, and is not made weak ; and is much de-

lighted with the pure faith and clean mind of him
that receiveth.

For these most weighty and godly considerations,
when the sacrament is ministered to other than
to himself that consecrateth it, it is delivered under
the form of bread only ; and the chalice is not
consecrated,* nor yet delivered as any part of the
sacrament, but for the more commodious receiving
of the other part wherein was contained the Body
and Blood of our Saviour Christ. Therefore seeing that the doctrine of Transubstantiation is (as I
have shewed) a truth necessarily deduced of Christ's
manifest words, saying, " This is My Body," declaring
the singular and only substance of that (which) He gave
to them to eat, to be His Body, and so not bread ;
seeing the universal Church of Christ hath determined
this to be-God's truth, and for final ending of all
controversies, that all men might speak one thing, and
be of one tongue, hath ordered it to be spoken of and
uttered in this term of Transubstantiation ; and seeing
the testimonies of ancient doctors to be all agreeable
in this point, that the bread is changed into the Body
of Christ, whereby appeareth the consent of the
universal Church, which is the pillar and upholder of
all truth : for that cause let every man that loveth the
truth, and the salvation of his soul, steadfastly keep
himself in the belief of this truth, and so to be a member
of Christ's Catholic Church, without the which there is
no salvation ; and let him not join himself to any

---

* The Bishop here speaks of the cup of wine which was then distributed to all communicants, not of the chalice reserved to the consecrating priest.—ED.

faction of men out of the Catholic Church of Christ, that for singularity or gain of the world trouble the peace of the Church, and stir up the ashes of old heresies, which by the greatest authority that ever Christ left in His Church, that is to say, by the judgment of the successors of S. Peter in the chair of Christ, and of Bishops and pastors of Christ's flock, called from all the parts of the world in a General Council, have been discussed before this time and fully determined. Let us not shew so much dishonour to our most certain and heavenly religion, as to think that it may be variable after the wilful and furious appetite of a few men, which is one and uniform, and so hath been from Christ's time till this day, being, by God's Holy Spirit, the schoolmaster of His Holy Church, inspired, revealed, multiplied, ordered, continued, and so stablished that hell gates, that is to say, tyranny, schisms, and heresy, shall never prevail against it. He that by unity of faith in doctrine, and by the peace of charity in good living, keepeth himself within the fold of God's Catholic Church, as a lively member of the same, may be sure of the protection of God's Holy Spirit, in grace, and be in good hope to attain the glory of God in the kingdom of heaven by the merits of Christ, to Whom, with the Father and the Holy Ghost, be honour and praise, world without end. Amen.

THE NINTH SERMON.

OF THE EFFECTS OF CHRIST'S BODY AND BLOOD IN THE WORTHY RECEIVER.

HOW much (good people) are we bound to love our Lord Jesus Christ, that like a good shepherd hath given His Soul for His sheep, and His Flesh to be our meat, and His Blood to be our drink, and so is He both our redeemer, and redemption, our feeder, and our daily food. Greater love can no man shew (John v. 13) than this which Christ our Lord hath shewed to us. But if we would consider for what cause and purpose He feedeth us with His Flesh and Blood, and what wonderful graces and effects He worketh in us both in body and soul by those heavenly meats, our love towards Him should be a great deal more increased, and our desire should be more inflamed to fill our hungry souls with so profitable and precious meats. In which matter I intend, God willing, to labour at this time, and to make but a short recital of certain benefits which the worthy receiving of this most blessed sacrament worketh, first in our souls, and then in our bodies. For to speak perfectly at length of it, and as the worthiness and dignity of the matter requireth, would ask a great process 'and a long time, which I verily hope your good affection in perceiving the truth and in following the same in your lives will supply.

First of all this holy sacrament is ordained and given to man to nourish him to eternal life. For when our Saviour Christ was dead upon the cross, and His side was pierced with a spear, there came forth of it water and blood, whereupon He founded and built His spouse the Church : for by the water He giveth to us our being, because by it we are brought to be Christian men, and by the blood He giveth to us our life, because by it we are nourished and fed and preserved to continue Christian men. For by eating of Him, which is eternal life, we are sure that He giveth to us the same thing that He is Himself, which is life, which of ourselves we had not before. It is not given to repair the ruin and decay of this temporal life, which like a vapour continueth but a while, but to repair the decay of our spiritual life in Christ, and to give unto our souls eternal life, and to bring us thither again from whence we take our beginning. This decay of our spiritual life is sustained by consenting to sin, and like as he that hath a wound will seek for a medicine, even so when we are in sin, we may have this heavenly and honourable sacrament for a medicine. I mean not of him that lieth dead in his soul by deadly sin, for as no man giveth corporal meats to him that is dead in body : so this spiritual meat of Christ's body and blood may not be given to him that is spiritually dead in his soul by deadly sin, for then he receiveth it unworthily to his further judgment and condemnation, being guilty as Judas was of the Body and Blood of Christ (1 Cor. xi. 27).

Therefore, if the wound of sin be so great that this sacrament cannot then be worthily received, let him then go to penance, and by that medicine procure himself to be restored to life again. For no doubt of it he receiveth this blessed sacrament unworthily, that receiveth it at that time when he should do penance. But if his sins be but venial, and such as this mortal and frail life cannot be passed over without them, then let him not forbear the wholesome medicine of this sacrament, which is profitable to the life and health of the whole man, being both a medicine to heal infirmities, and a sacrifice to purge iniquities. And because a man doth daily offend, and so decayeth in his spiritual life : therefore ought he often to receive this spiritual medicine, which is called our daily bread, and thereby to recover that health and strength he had lost before. For as Adam and Eve, contrary to God's commandment, by eating of the fruit of the tree which was forbidden them, were made mortal and subject to death, both of body and soul : even so every Christian man and woman, according to Christ's commandment, by the worthy eating of the Body and Blood of Christ, Who is the true vine of the tree of life, is made immortal, and hath a pledge of eternal life, both of body and soul. And if God preserved the temporal life of the people of Israel forty years in the wilderness without any bread of sown corn, but with manna that came from above : how much more will God preserve our spiritual life in this world with the heavenly bread of His own Flesh which was made of the blessed Virgin's pure substance. For this meat is the strength of our soul, the sinews of our mind, the knot of our trust, the foundation of our hope, our health, our light, our life. If we depart out of this life armed with the strength of this meat, we shall ascend to the heavenly palace of God with great trust and boldness, and as it were apparelled with a coat of gold.

The figure of this meat which was the blood of the paschal lamb, by the virtue of this blood which it figured, did purge the sin of the people and saved them from the sword of the angel ; and if the figure had such strength, and was so sovereign a remedy against death, what shall we think of the truth, which is the health of our souls, whereby our souls be washed, they be adorned, they be kindled, they are made clearer than the fire and brighter than gold.

For as a man buyeth his servant with gold and also *anourneth* * him with gold likewise : so Christ hath bought us with His precious Blood, and doth *anourn* us and apparelleth us with the same Blood, which is not now sprinkled upon us outwardly, and washed away again as the blood of the sacrifices of the Old Testament was, but it entereth into our souls, and maketh them spiritually clean and strong, and worketh in them an unspeakable beauty. So that this heavenly food is a protection and safeguard for us in all the pilgrimage of this life, and a safe

---

* *I.e.,* adorns.

conduct for our free passage out of this wicked world, and a strong vital, making us able to endure the painful journey to the kingdom of heaven.

And moreover, the worthy receiver is inwardly lightened and sanctified, for as they that did crucify Him, and put Him to death, were darkened and blinded by Him, we that worthily receive Him be lightened and our eyes be open to know Him. For the Flesh of Christ to that effect hath marvellous and unspeakable virtue, as appeareth in His two disciples that knew Him in the breaking of the heavenly bread, and this virtue hath Christ's Body, not in that it is a creature of God, and the body of man, but in that it is the Body of God united in the Godhead of Christ in unity of Person, and being sanctified itself by the virtue of Christ's divinity joined to it, it is able thereby to work sanctification in them that worthily receive it, being made by the mystical prayer a body, not only holy and sanctified in itself, but also sanctifying them that receive it with a pure mind.

And as by drinking of common wine a man's mind is refreshed, and his weariness driven away: so by the eating and drinking of Christ's Body and Blood in the sacrament, the remembrance of the old man, and the heaviness that for his worldly conversation and sinful life grieved a man's heart, is put away, and his godly affection is made drunken with spiritual wisdom and the knowledge of God, and is endued with gladness for the remission of his sins, and is no more cumbered with the cares of the world, nor the fear of death.

Thus have I declared unto you certain godly effects, which this heavenly meat of Christ's Body and Blood worketh inwardly in the soul of the worthy receiver, which effects and a great many more be set forth at large in the books of the holy fathers of the Catholic Church, and as I have shortly touched those that pertain to the soul, so shall I, God willing, with like shortness, touch those that God worketh by the worthy receiving of this sacrament in the body of man. For as the spiritual disease and death of a man is in the soul, the occasion whereof cometh by the corrupt affection of the flesh : so this spiritual medicine of Christ's Body and Blood in the sacrament worketh his effects, not only in the soul of man, but also in the body of man, by healing it, by defending, sanctifying, strengthening, and reducing it to immortality.

First, seeing that we mortal and sinful men be flesh and blood, we cannot be reformed in the corrupt and weak nature of our bodies and souls, nor come again to the likeness and similitude of God in purity and life, except a convenient plaister be laid to our old disease, and, in the healing of our desperate infirmity, one contrary be removed by another, and like things be applied and made agree unto like, as Christ's lively and sanctified Body to our mortal and sinful flesh. Which thing is done in the receiving of this most blessed sacrament, when the virtue of so great and wholesome a medicine doth pierce all parts of body and soul, and doth renew and make whole whatsoever sickness the corruption of old naughty living had before caused and engendered in the flesh or in the spirit. For the Body of Christ our Lord received into us by the mystical benediction (which is the sacrament) and remaining in us, driveth away not only death, but also all sickness, and the poison that was brought in by original sin, and it pacifieth and keepeth under the raging law of our members, it strengtheneth devotion, it quencheth the froward and sinful affections of the mind, and those small sins we be in, it regardeth not, but healeth the sick, restoreth the bruised, and from falling it lifteth us up.

In Baptism we were washed from all sin, and the writing of our damnation was cancelled, and grace was given unto us, that the concupiscence and carnal desire of our flesh should not hurt us, if we abstain from consenting to it, and so the corrupt and putrified matter of our old sore was removed and taken away. But who is able to overcome the violent motions of his flesh, and to quench the heat and itch of such a sore? Surely no man of his own strength. But we may be bold, for grace helpeth us, wherewith we be endued by receiving Christ's blessed Body and Blood in this sacrament, which hath in us two effects, the one to take away our small sins that we feel them not, the other to take away or refrain our consent from great and mortal sins that we do them not. So that if any of you all do feel and perceive in himself, not so great motions, or so violent provocations to anger, to envy, to lechery, or to other vices, or not so often times as he did before : let him give most humble and high thanks to the Body and Blood of our Lord, for the virtue of the sacrament doth work in him, and he may be glad that the rotten sore and old disease of his sensual concupiscence, is better amended and well-nigh brought to health, and that the commotion and rebellion of his sudden passions and carnal affections be so well ceased and pacified.

Furthermore beside the healing of our sinful flesh, it sanctifieth and strengtheneth it in virtue and godly living, for like as material bread doth comfort and make strong a man's body : even so the bread of life that came from heaven, which is Christ's Body one Person with the Godhead, doth likewise make strong our bodies in grace, and more than that, it sanctifieth both body and soul. And like as wine maketh glad a man's heart, even so the Blood of Christ doth fulfil a man's heart with spiritual gladness, and beside that, is made a great stay and a sure defence for it ; which to a godly man, is as it were a shield against his enemy. And therefore in all dangerous and perilous times, in remembrance of Christ's passion, by which all grace and strength was purchased for us, we receive Christ's Body and Blood for the defence and preparation of our bodies and souls, whereby the power of the devil is resisted and his fiery darts of temptations be driven away. So the Church of Christ useth to do with her faithful soldiers, in all persecutions either of furious tyrants, or deceitful heretics, for when it provoketh and exhorteth them to fight against their enemies, it doth not leave them naked and unarmed, but doth harness and defend them with the protection of Christ's Body and Blood. For seeing this sacrament is ordained for this purpose to be a defence to the receivers, therefore it armeth all them with the harness and shield of our Lord's meat, whom it would have to be safe from the hurt of their enemies. For after a man hath worthily received the heavenly meat of our Lord's Body and Blood, the devil forsaketh him and flieth away quicker than the wind, and dare not approach near. When the angel that destroyed the first-begotten in Egypt, saw the door-posts sprinkled with the blood of the paschal lamb, he passed by and durst not enter in to kill (Exod. xii. 13). How much more will the wicked angel, the devil, run away when he shall see, not the blood of the figurative lamb sprinkled upon the posts, but the Body and Blood of the true Lamb of God in the mouth of a Christian man? If the angel gave place to the shadow or figure, how much more will the enemy be afraid when he seeth the truth? when he shall see the house of the soul occupied with the brightness of Christ's heavenly presence, and all entrances for his temptations shut away?

Thus are we made strong against our enemies, by the virtue of this heavenly food, whereby also our bodies, being purified and refreshed, be set at liberty, and doth freely follow the soul and the motions of our spirit, being delivered from the heavy burden and weakness which our carnal nativity did cause, and finally, they be made no more corruptible, having this heavenly meat for their hope and pledge of their resurrection to life everlasting, whereby they be preserved and prepared to the attaining of the same life. For how can our flesh come to corruption and perish for evermore, and not receive eternal life, which is fed with the Body and Blood of our Lord, as our Saviour

Himself taught us, saying: "He that eateth My Flesh, and drinketh My Blood, hath life everlasting, and I shall raise him up at the last day," that is to say, My Body which is eaten, being the Body of life, shall raise up his body to eternal life in the last day. For the very cause of our life is, that we have Christ by His Flesh remaining and abiding in our flesh. And it were not possible for this corruptible nature of our flesh, being subject to corruption and death, to be brought to incorruption and immortality in the kingdom of heaven, except an immortal nature, such as is the Body of Christ, being God and eternal life itself, were joined to it after the way of meat, by participation whereof it might be delivered from the possession of death and corruption, and be endued with the property of Christ's Body, which is eternal life. For as Christ reduceth our souls to life eternal, by giving to them His Holy Spirit in the sacrament of Baptism, even so He reduceth our bodies to life eternal, by giving to them His living and immortal Body to eat in the sacrament of the Altar. And this is the ordinary way of God's working in us, although He be not always bounden to His sacraments, but that He saveth men sometimes of His absolute power before Baptism, and raiseth some to life eternal without this sacrament, such as for lack of age cannot prove themselves, or depart in the faith of Christ without contempt or refusal of the said sacrament, when by some violence or other impediment they were letted to receive it in deed.

These be (good people) some of the effects Christ worketh by this sacrament in man's body, which in

very deed be marvellous, but above all other this is
the greatest that He maketh us all that worthily
receive Him to be one body with Him, endued with
His Holy Spirit, whereby the perfect influence of
His grace, being our Head, is derived and deduced
unto us that be members of His Body, flesh of His
Flesh, and bones of His bones. For, as S. Paul saith,
we that be many, are made one bread, one body,
because all we do receive and eat of one bread (1 Cor. x.
17), which is the natural Body of Christ, the Bread of
Life that came from heaven, which He promised to give
to us all, as He gave it to death for us all (John vi. 52).
In nature we be all divers persons, and have sundry
and divers substances, but because we be all fed
with one singular substance of Christ's Flesh which
cannot be divided into parts, and also are sealed with
one Holy Spirit that likewise cannot be divided,
therefore these singular things indivisibly received
into our bodies and souls, draw us to their unity, and
make all us one body mystical with Christ—which
unity is to be called true and natural unity, and not
only in will and affection by faith and charity—where
(according to Christ's prayer immediately after His
last supper) He is in the Father by the nature of His
divinity and we in Him by His corporal nativity,
and He in us by the sacrament of His Flesh and
Blood, and so by Christ is made a perfect unity (John
xvii.) Like as when two waxes are melted at the
fire, one whole thing is made of them both ; even so
by the communion and receiving of Christ's Body
and Blood into ours, He is in us and we in Him, and
so by receiving the virtue of this heavenly meat, we

G

are incorporate into His Flesh, that for our salvation was made our flesh. Therefore (good people) considering these glorious and wonderful graces and effects which by this holy sacrament He worketh both in our souls and bodies, let us not defraud ourselves of them, neither by too long abstaining from it, nor yet by the unworthy receiving of it, but as His exceeding love towards us moved Him to give it to us, so let it and the benefits we receive by it increase our love towards Him. And as He that giveth His life for us, and His Flesh to us, will deny us nothing that may do us good, so let us serve Him with heart and will, and omit nothing that may please Him; so shall we finally enjoy the special fruit of this most blessed sacrament in the kingdom of God, which is incorruption and immortality of body and soul by His grace and free gift, to Whom, with the Father and the Holy Ghost, be all honour, glory, and praise for evermore. Amen.

THE TENTH SERMON.

AN EXHORTATION FOR THE WORTHY RECEIVING OF THE HOLY SACRAMENT.

BEING sufficiently and most manifestly taught (good people) by the mouth of our Saviour Christ, that in His most holy sacrament He giveth His Body and His Blood, that was slain and shed upon the cross for the life of the world, let us faithfully believe God by His word, and not repugn against Him, although it seem not so to our senses and our carnal thoughts. For His mysteries exceed our reason, wherein we ought to consider not what our eyes sheweth us, but what His word teacheth us. For our eyes may easily deceive us, but His word cannot deceive us, who in sensible things giveth us heavenly and intelligible things, which our senses cannot judge and discern, but giveth place to our faith directed by God's word to the knowledging of this infallible truth.

Therefore it is now our parts to prepare and make clean our bodies and souls from all filth of the flesh or spirit, that we may receive His heavenly meat worthily, considering the manifold graces that come by it, and the eternal damnation that hangeth over their heads, that unworthily presume to re-

ceive it. Remember how every man is displeased
and angry with the traitor Judas and them that
crucified our Saviour Christ, and so beware that
you be not likewise guilty of the Body and Blood
of Christ. They most cruelly shed His Blood, but
he that unworthily receiveth Him with a foul and
sinful conscience, spitefully treadeth His precious
Blood under his feet. No filth or mire is so unworthy His pure and heavenly body, as is the
body or soul of man defiled with mortal sin. And
as the thing we come unto is most honourable, so
the worthy receiving of it is most profitable. But if
a man come unto it with a guilty and naughty conscience, it increaseth his fault and damnation, for he
that eateth and drinketh the Body and Blood of our
Lord unworthily, eateth and drinketh judgment and
damnation to himself (1 Cor. xi. 29) ; for as they
that do defile the King's purple robe, are worthy
to be punished as well as they that cut or rend
it, even so it is no marvel if they that receive
Christ's Body with an unclean conscience, do suffer
the same punishment that they do which did nail
Him to the cross. See how terrible a pain S.
Paul threateneth to the unworthy receiver, saying,
" A man that transgresseth the law of Moses, being
convict by two or three witnesses suffereth death "
(Heb. x. 28), how much more and greater punishment deserveth he to suffer, that treadeth under
foot God's Son, and with no reverence regardeth
the Blood of His testament, by which he was
sanctified, but taketh it as common meat, and doth
injury to the spirit of grace, and in that he be-

trayeth and delivereth Christ as Judas did, not now to the sinful Jews, but to his own sinful members, wherewith he presumeth to dishonour so inestimable a sacrament. S. Peter and Judas at one table, in one supper, did both eat of one consecrate bread which was Christ's Body; but Peter received by it life, Judas death: to Peter it was an increase of goodness, to Judas it was a testimony of his naughtiness: Peter being good and clean, took it for his salvation, Judas being a traitor and unclean, took it to his damnation. The thing that was given was not evil, but a good thing was naughtily received of an evil man to his damnation. For after the receipt of our Lord's Body, the devil entered into Judas. Not that the devil did despise or contemn our Lord's Body, but the impudent wickedness of Judas made entry for the devil to dwell there. Whereby we be taught that the devil lieth in wait and prevaileth over them that use these secret mysteries with a corrupt mind. So that Judas, as soon as he with his traitorous mind touched the heavenly food, and the sanctified bread entered into his cursed mouth, his mischievous mind, not able to bear the strength of so great a sacrament, was blown forth like chaff out of a barn, and so headlings * he ran to his treason and money, and so to desperation and hanging. Mark the great mercy of our Saviour Christ, and the madness of Judas; for Judas bargained for thirty pence to sell his Master, and Christ did minister to him the same blood which he sold, to the intent he should have had remission of

---

* *I.e.*, headlong.

sins, if he would have forsaken his wickedness. O
cruel heart of this traitor ; with what eyes could he
look upon Him Whom he had in his mouth to eat,
being both at once to Christ a murderer and a guest,
selling his Master for a little money, and losing God
and himself for evermore. Even so, at this day,
there be in the Church of God good men as S. Peter
was, and naughty men as Judas was. The good
receive the blessed sacrament to their salvation, the
evil men, being like dogs and swine, to their damnation. They be dogs that unreverently come unto it,
and therefore they depart in God's high displeasure.
For they that live after the flesh, and be fettered in
the chains of sin and vice, they receive with Judas,
the traitor, poison, and run to the halter of spiritual
hanging in hell, being condemned both for their other
manifold sins, and also for the contempt of Christ's
most precious Body, which in very deed they receive,
but in substance only, and not in any profitable or
wholesome effect.

Osee, the priest, in the Old Testament put to his
hand to the Ark of God to stay it when it was like
to fall off the cart, and God, being displeased for his
rash enterprise, did smite him by and by with sudden
death. Where we may evidently see and understand
how much he offendeth, that rashly with a guilty
conscience cometh to the body of our Lord, when the
devout priest was punished by death, that with less
reverence than he ought to have done did touch the
Ark, which was but the figure of our Lord's Body.
In the old law it is said, that if a man do eat of the
sanctified meat of the sacrifice by ignorance, his sin

and iniquity shall be imputed unto him, for which cause S. Paul doth warn us to come unto this most holy sacrifice of the New Testament, with much caution and wariness, lest we take it to our damnation. For if ignorance in the old law be condemned, how much is a guilty conscience in the gospel condemned? Look how much Christ Himself passeth and excelleth the material temple of God which Solomon builded: even so much more grievous and terrible is it to receive Christ's Body in deadly sin, than to eat rashly of the sacrifices of the old law. Therefore, let no false and covetous man, as Judas, let no man that useth simony or usury, as Simon Magus, let no man bearing a malicious heart to his neighbour, as King Herod, come to this board of our Saviour Christ. This sacrifice is spiritual meat. For like as common meat when it findeth a man's stomach full of evil humours, it doth him no good, but great hurt, even so this heavenly and spiritual meat, if it find a man's heart full of iniquity, it maketh him worse not for any fault of the meat, but by the fault of the receiver. If he be worthy punishment that kisseth the king's hand with a foul mouth, what pain is he worthy that kisseth the mouth of the King of Heaven with a stinking soul? And lest men should think that these were but vain threatenings of S. Paul and other holy men, and that God would not enter into judgment with them that so villanously and contemptuously abuse Christ's Body, S. Paul doth further shew, as it were, an image of God's judgment to come against such unworthy receivers, declaring how that for that same heinous fault, many now in this world are punished with sickness, with infirmities, with mischances, with great adversity, and also with sudden death of the body, to the intent that the multitude should be afraid and learn by the example of a few, knowing that God will not leave the contempt of His Body unpunished. And although many escape free here, yet they may be sure to be more extremely handled there, both for abusing Christ's Body, and also for contemning the example of others. And these plagues of sickness and death chance to many, because they will not judge themselves, nor will not understand what it is to communicate with the Church, and to come to so high and so heavenly sacraments, and so they suffer that which men that be in a fever be wont to suffer, when they kill themselves by presuming to eat of whole men's meat. And also these plagues chance because they will not judge Christ's Body, that is to say, they will not discern and consider the greatness and majesty of this present mystery, but negligently and contemptuously take Christ's Body as other common meat. For if they did but consider and esteem of what excellency and majesty He were that is perfect there before them, and given them to eat, they should need no other persuasion to make clean their hearts, and to receive Him with His most honour and reverence, but He alone would cause them to take heed and to purge themselves. For they would consider that they receive and taste upon His Body and Blood, that sitteth in heaven, that is honoured of angels, that is of infinite power, that made both heaven and earth, that redeemed and governeth the whole world, that shall judge both quick and dead. And on the other side, they would consider that if God did give unto us the heaven, the sea, the earth, and all the riches and treasures that be in these, and if He did send unto us His patriarchs, His prophets, His angels, He should neither give nor send to us anything equal with this, which is the head of all goodness, Who spared not His only begotten Son to save us that were His fugitive slaves. And Christ our Lord was not only content to be made man and to be whipped and slain for us, but also hath brought us (as it were) into one heap of leaven with Himself, and not only by faith, but also in very deed, hath made us His body : what thing then ought to be so clean as he that should receive that sacrifice ? Yea, the very beams of the sun be not so pure as his mouth ought to be, that should receive this marvellous Body and Blood of our Saviour Christ. Remember, man, how God honoureth thee, of what meat art thou partaker? Thou art fed with the same thing that the holy angels tremble at, and be not able to behold it, for the brightness that cometh from it. What shepherd ever fed his sheep with his own body ? Many mothers do commit their infants to be nursed of other women, but Christ doth not so, Who feedeth and nourisheth us His sheep, or rather children, with His own Body, and so doth join us to Him in one body. And as young infants with great gladness do suck the breasts of their mothers or nurses, even so with greater gladness ought we to come to the breast of our Saviour, there to suck the grace of the Holy Ghost, and to take it most heavily and with most sorrow, if we be for our deserts excommunicate and deprived of that spiritual food.

Therefore let us pull down the wall that maketh division between God and us, let us by penance remove our sins, and wash our consciences, let us amend that kind of beastly living which we be ashamed should be laid to our charge, and let us withdraw our minds from the unsatiable greediness of this world. For what shall it profit a man to gain the whole world and lose his soul? The three wise men came out of the east country of Persis to seek Jesus the King of the Jews, but let us go forth from our worldly cares and carnal desires to see Jesus. It is no great journey. We need not to pass over the sea, nor to climb over the mountains, but sitting at home, if we be compunct in heart, and bent towards godly devotion, we may pull down the wall of our sins, and make short the long way of our journey and see Christ. For God is a God nigh at hand, and not afar off (Jer. xxiii. 24), and nigh unto all them that call upon Him in truth. Yet now-a-days there be many Christian men that be so full of sin, and do so contemn godly religion, that they take no care for their soul's health, not considering that the time to receive this most holy sacrament is not this day or that day, but when their consciences be pure and purged from sin. For as he that is clean may come every day, so he that is unclean, and is not penitent for his sin, he may not come at those days which by the Church be appointed. For to come once a year doth not deliver us from our sins, if we come then

unworthily, but rather it increaseth our damnation.
For which cause I shall exhort you all in our Lord's
name that ye come not to these fearful and terrible
mysteries for a custom, as compelled by the appointment of the Church, without diligent preparing of
yourselves; but that ye purge and wash your souls
divers days before by penance, by prayer, by alms,
by spiritual exercise, and that ye do not turn afterward to your old sins, as a dog turneth back to
eat again his casting. Is it not against all reason
to have so much care of worldly things, as when the
feast draweth near to prepare new and costly apparel,
to prepare great and sumptuous fare, and by all
means to trim up the body, and to have no respect
of the soul, but to suffer it to be ragged and torn and
to die for hunger? And the body is decked for the
sight of the world, but the soul is always in the sight
of God, that most grievously punisheth the neglecting
of it. If any man have an enemy by whom he is hurt
or offended, let him dissolve his enmity, and refrain
his hot affection and swelling of mind, that his soul
be quiet without trouble or tumult. For by this
blessed communion thou shalt receive the King into
thy soul, and when the King entereth, there ought to
be great quietness, silence, and peace. And although
thine hurt or injury shewed by thy enemy be very
great, yet thou must remit it. Because thine enemy
hath hurt thee, wilt thou therefore hurt thyself
more? Whatsoever he hath done, it cannot be so
great harm to thee, as thou doest to thyself, if thou
be not reconciled to him. Wilt thou shew spite and
villany to God because thy neighbour hath shewed

the like to thee before? For to retain displeasure
against him that offended thee, is not so much to
avenge thy quarrel against him, as it is a spiteful
contempt of God, the author of this law and commandment, that we should be reconciled to our
enemies before we come to His altar. Therefore
have no respect to thine enemy, nor to the greatness
of thine injuries sustained by him, but to God
Almighty, and printing His fear deeply in thy heart,
consider this, that the greater violence thou dost use
to thine own heart in compelling it to forgive thine
enemy and to be in friendship with him, the greater
reward thou shalt receive of God that commandeth
thee so to do, and as thou dost after that sort receive
God with much honour, so shall He make the reward
of thine obedience a thousandfold.

This is the duty of a Christian man, when he
cometh to God's board to procure himself to be
purged from all corruption of the flesh or spirit, and
to have perfect holiness in the fear of God and the
charity of Christ, and to have no spot or wrinkle or
any such thing, and to have a perpetual memory of
Him that was dead and rose again for us, and to
make clean his soul with faith, baptism, virtue, and
the doctrine of the gospel, that the corrupt manners
of such as be strangers and not God's people, and the
manner of living which was used in Egypt, in the
time of King Pharao, that is to say, the whole heap
of vice, be not now used, but banished away. And
so let him come to this heavenly bread, which was not
brought forth of the ground by tilling and sowing,
and labour of man, but which came from heaven, and

is the true bread of life, and causeth the worthy
receiver never to be hungry again but to live always
in immortality. If no man dare lay his bread on a
foul cloth or put it into a foul vessel, how much
more may it not be received in a foul heart, which
filthiness above all things He most abhorreth, as
the greatest injury that can be done to His Body.
For as Joseph, the just man, wrapped Christ's body
in a clean cloth, and buried it in a new sepulchre, so
ought we to lay it in a clean heart and a chaste
body. Which thing if we diligently procure, as it
may be done in little time, and make ourselves not
unworthy receivers of so great a treasure, then shall
Christ, our Lord, with the Father and the Holy Ghost
come unto us, and dwell with us, and work in us all
the godly and wonderful effects of this blessed
sacrament both in our souls and bodies, and nourish
us into Christ's mystical body with His own natural
flesh, which as a pledge maketh us to be in sure hope
of life everlasting, to the which He brings us that
made us, to Whom be all honour and glory for
evermore. Amen.

THE ELEVENTH SERMON.

HOW A MAN MAY COME WORTHILY TO RECEIVE THE BLESSED SACRAMENT.

I PURPOSE, by the grace of God, in this sermon to instruct you (good people) how to prepare yourselves to come worthily to receive this holy sacrament. Ye know the great and marvellous benefits, which Christ our Lord worketh in their souls and bodies that worthily come unto it, and also ye know the dangerous and damnable state of them that come to it unworthily; and that ye may the better avoid the one and be partakers of the other:—First, ye ought certainly to know that it is required that ye do come to it and receive it. For as the unworthy coming is perilous, so not to be partakers of this mystical supper at all is a great offence, and a very destruction of a man's soul, as our Saviour Christ taught us, saying, "Except ye eat the Flesh of the Son of man, and drink His Blood, ye shall not have life in you, and he that eateth My Flesh and drinketh My Blood hath life everlasting" (John vi. 54, 55), which is to be understanded of him that eateth Christ's Flesh as it ought to be eaten. For many eat it that do not dwell in God nor God in them, because they eat it not with a clean heart, and after that manner which Christ saw when He said so. Many forbear to come to it, because they perceive their conscience grieved with deadly sin, and in that they do well, if they can forbear justly, without offence of other persons. But if they forbear because they have a wrong and false opinion of this holy sacrament, or because they will not be reconciled to their neighbours, or intend not to amend and forsake their naughty living, then besides their heresy and other damnable living, they offend deadly divers ways, both in contemning Christ and His sacraments, which He hath ordained to be instruments wherewith He might give unto us grace and salvation; and also in contemning the Church of Christ, which hath ordained that every man and woman being of years of discretion, should faithfully confess alone to his own curate, or by his permisson * to some other meet and learned priest, all his sins, once in a year at least, and should to his power fulfil that penance and satisfaction which is enjoined him, receiving reverently, at least at Easter, the blessed sacrament of the Altar, expect perchance by the counsel of his own curate, † for some reasonable cause, he think meet for a time to forbear the receiving of it. And that he which contemneth this ordinance, should be accursed and kept from the entering into the Church amongst Christian men, and when he is dead should be kept from Christian men's burial. This is the discipline

---

* At the present day no explicit permission is required.—ED.

† The confessor can give this counsel or permission at the present day.—ED.

and ordinance of the Church at this day, which is not a restraining of a man to come but once a year, but correcting of him that cometh not once a year. The oftener he cometh the better it is, and the more is he nourished to everlasting life. And the better a man is, the more desirous is he to be joined to God corporally by this sacrament. For as Christ, by giving to us His Flesh and His Blood, declared most of all His exceeding love towards us, even so declareth he his love most of all towards God, that the oftenest and with most reverence cometh to receive this precious food of His Flesh and Blood. So did the holy man, Job, say of his servants that loved him most, repeating their words which were these— " Who shall give us of his flesh to eat, that we may be full withal " (Job xxxi. 31), which no man ever did but Christ our Lord, to the intent He might bind us to Him with more charity.

Such was the fervent charity of the people in the beginning of the Church, that came every day, or in a manner every day, to this holy sacrament, and afterwards when devotion decreased, they came every Sunday, and further, as the charity of the people waxed cold, the fewer times they prepared themselves to receive this sacrament, insomuch that it was decreed by certain Provincial Councils, that he that came not thrice a year, that is to say, at Easter, at Pentecost, and at Christmas, should not be taken as a Catholic man. But after that, when devotion decayed and charity was cold, and iniquity did abound, so that men giving the bridle to the flesh, were careless of their salvation, then the Church our mother being careful for her children, and compelled by love, partly to condescend to the infirmity of the people, and partly by discipline to reduce the people again to their duties, did in a General Council decree that every person of discretion should fulfil God's commandment in receiving this sacrament once a year at least, as I have said before, under the pain of excommunication, which is the spiritual sword of Christ to compel men to do their duties, which need not to be drawn but for the hardness of our hearts, that love the world more than God, and to serve the devil rather than Christ, the author of all grace, which is given to us in this blessed sacrament.

Whereunto I shall most earnestly exhort every man and woman as they love their own souls, and to be preserved in grace and the favour of God, to dispose themselves oftentimes effectually to receive the Body of our Saviour Christ, which is every day both offered to God the Father for the sins and infirmities of the people, and also is prepared and offered to all them that will with a pure heart receive it. For they that wilfully abstain from it, they deprive themselves of all the graces and godly effects which be given by it, they lose their spiritual strength to fight against the devil, and they waxe rotten and dead members of Christ's Body, lacking their food and spiritual nourishment, and so are meet for nothing else but to be cast into the fire.

And they that be in conscience of deadly sin, let them by penance make clean their conscience, for otherwise we that be ministers may not minister but to the worthy receivers, so far as we know, for if we

H

know any man to come to it unworthily, we ought rather to shed our blood, than to give Christ's Body and Blood to dogs and beastly livers. And that every man, when he is disposed to receive this most holy sacrament, may do it worthily to his salvation, he must observe three things before he come to it ; he must prove and judge himself when he cometh to it, he must judge and discern the Body of our Lord after he hath received it, he must imitate Christ and communicate with Him in His passions.

First, he that intendeth to eat the Lamb of God, he must have the innocency of a lamb, and may not be a wolf having wolfish manners, because this is the bread of the children of God, and not of filthy dogs or ravenous wolves. And no person may be partaker of it, but he that believeth all things to be true that be taught of the Catholic Church, and is baptized in the water of regeneration, and frameth his life after that manner which our Saviour Christ did set forth in His life and gospel. For as in the Old Testament three sorts of people were not admitted to eat of the Paschal Lamb, as strangers born, such as were not of the stock of Israel, and they that were not circumcised, and such as by touching any dead or unclean thing were made themselves unclean (Exod. xii. 43, &c.) : even so there be three sorts of men in the New Testament that may not be admitted to eat of Christ's Body in the sacrament, which was figured by the Paschal Lamb, first, all infidels such as be not true Israelites and of the house of Christ's Church by receiving His law and faith ; secondly, they that be not baptized and so circumcised in heart, not having the vain thoughts and works of the flesh cut away by the Holy Ghost; and thirdly, they that be not clean and pure in conscience but privy to their own guiltiness, or in will to remain in sin still.

These three sorts of persons be not worthy to receive the Lamb of God, our Saviour Christ, in the blessed sacrament, but if they presume so to do, they do it to their own damnation.

Therefore whosoever will come worthily to so great a mystery, he must be a Christian man, and stedfastly believe whatsoever truth God hath revealed to His Holy Church, and specially concerning the truth of this sacrament, neither oppugning it by malicious heresy, nor being ignorant of it by lack of knowledge, but acknowledging that it is the Body and Blood of Christ, God's Son, verily and in truth as Christ's word spoken of it doth plainly testify. Moreover he must prove himself as S. Paul teacheth us, that is to say, he must search if he be guilty of any deadly sin (1 Cor. xi. 28), and if he find his conscience to reprove him, then he must refrain from the holy sacrament, till he have by true contrition and the sacrament of Penance made clean his conscience, receiving remission of all his sins, and then being clean, let him eat of this most holy sacrifice of Christ's Body and Blood. And if he find that his conscience is privy to any venial sin, and yet not having a will to sin after any more, then before he receive let him satisfy for that sin with weeping and prayer, and putting his whole confidence in the mercy of God that useth to forgive sins to all that devoutly confess them, he may boldly and fruitfully come to the blessed sacrament. The more diligence he taketh in examining, searching, and purging his conscience after that sort as is declared in the sacrament of Penance, the more boldly and worthily shall he receive. Not that any man should think himself worthy to receive the most precious Body of Christ, God and man, in respect whereof the highest angels be unclean, but that if a man do that which lieth in him to wash away the filthiness and spots of his soul and body by contrition and the sacrament of Penance, and prepareth his heart with humility and reverence to receive the Body of his Lord God, then doth God esteem and accept him as worthy, that is to say, further from unworthiness than he is that taketh no penance for his sin at all. This worthiness may be considered and known by such observations as were commanded to be used about the eating of the Paschal Lamb (Exod. xii.) For as the lamb was the figure of Christ in this sacrament, so the manner of eating that is an instruction how we should worthily eat this. They that should eat one Paschal Lamb were commanded to eat it in one house, and to carry no part of the flesh out of the doors. So we be commanded to eat the Flesh of Christ our Lamb nowhere else but in the house of God the Catholic Church, and thereby all heretics and schismatics which be out of the Church are forbidden to presume to eat of Christ's Flesh, which cannot be eaten but of them that be members of the Church. They were commanded to have their reins girded : so are we commanded to have our bodies and souls girded, that is to say, restrained and kept from the works and lusts of the flesh by abstinency and chastity, and not only from the unlawful vices of fornication, adultery, and such like : but also a man should abstain from the act of Matrimony with his lawful wife for a certain space before: howbeit he that useth his wife not for the intent to fulfil his carnal pleasure, but only for desire of an increase of children, he ought to be left to his own judgment concerning the receiving of this mystery, with this exhortation, that he presume not to come, but with a pure conscience, a chaste body, and a clean heart. Also they were commanded to have their shoes upon their feet, so we be commanded to have the feet of our souls, which be our affections, mortified by the fear of God, and preserved from the corruption of worldly things, by the love of heavenly things, to be in love and perfect charity with all men, without malice, envy or double heart towards any man. For when the King of Heaven entereth into us, there must be great peace, silence, and quietness, without trouble of worldly affection, all injuries, displeasures, enmities, and trespasses must be freely and clearly forgiven, as we would Christ should forgive us, for this is the mystery of peace and the unity of Christ's mystical Body, and he that receiveth the mystery of unity, and keepeth not the bond of peace and unity, he receiveth not the mystery for himself, but a testi-mony against himself. Therefore of all things let us be sure of this, that we be in charity, and that no anger fret us, no pride inflame us, no lechery defile us, nor no envy torment our hearts, when we come to our Lord's Table.

They also did eat the lamb with wild and sour
lettuce, even so must we take the Flesh of our Lamb
with sour contrition, we must afflict and punish
our hearts with sorrow and bitter tears for our sins,
that the bitterness of our penance might wipe away
the filthy humour of our corrupt life from our
souls.

The Jews did eat their lamb standing, having their
staffs in their hands, and in great haste ready to fly
out of Egypt : even so ought we to stand in true faith
and good life, and not to sit or lie in corrupt doctrine
or living, but to have the staff of true hope of eternal
joys to come in our hands to stay us in the dangerous
journey of this world, that we neither faint for weariness, nor give over for cowardness, to our ghostly
enemies, knowing that their journey was from Egypt
to Jewry, and our journey is from the earth to heaven,
the strong and wholesome victual of which journey is
this heavenly food of Christ's Body and Blood. And
as they were in readiness to depart out of Egypt by
and by after the eating of the lamb, so ought we
coming to this blessed sacrament to have our lives
so upright and pure from all sin, as though we should
even then depart out of this transitory world.   For
look in what state of clean life a man would adventure
his soul when he dieth, let him with all diligence provide and procure that his soul be in the same state
when he cometh to communicate.   By this comparison
ye may learn (good people) how to prove and judge
yourselves, and so to come worthily to this heavenly
food.

The next thing is to learn how to judge and discern the Body of our Lord when we come unto it, that is to say, we may not undiscreetly and negligently take it, but we ought to discern Christ's Body from other common meats, and considering the great dignity and worthiness of it, we ought to give honour and reverence due to so great a thing as is the Flesh and Blood of Christ, God and man, not the flesh of man only, for then it could not give life, but the proper Flesh of God's Son united to His Person in Divinity, and is therefore able to give eternal life to our mortal bodies. For which cause we ought with fear, reverence, and a devout mind to come unto it, which being the same in substance that suffered, is also the best witness of Christ's painful Passion. Wherefore when thou doest go up to the altar to be fed with this spiritual and heavenly meat, behold with faith the most holy Body and Blood of thy God, honour it, marvel at it, touch it with thy mind, take it with the hand of thy heart, and specially drink of it with the draught of the inward man. No man eateth worthily this Flesh, but he that first honoureth it with godly honour in the holy sacrament, considering that it is great sin not to honour it, seeing it is the Body of Him that made thee, and with it redeemed thee, and shall by it raise thee out of dust and ashes, for the which thou hopest to receive heaven and the joys that be therein, and to be associate to His holy angels.

But whereas in this sacrament there be two things contained, the outward form of bread which is seen with the eyes of the body, and the Body and Blood of Christ which is seen only with the eyes of the soul, which is faith : Therefore let every man or woman when he seeth this sacrament in the priest's hands, direct the eye of his faith and his intent, to honour only that substance of Christ, God and man, which he seeth not with his bodily eyes, but believeth it most certainly to be there present, and let him not fix his thought upon the visible whiteness or roundness of the bread, which be sensible creatures reserved there for the use of this mystery, and may in no wise be adored and worshipped with godly honour, but let him intend to honour the Body and Blood of Christ, and yet not those as only creatures, but as they be united to the Godhead and made one Person in Divinity, for only God is to be honoured with godly honour, which we do when we honour Christ, God and man present in the blessed sacrament. This honour specially consisteth in our true and lively faith which we have of Christ there present, which honour we declare outwardly by kneeling and other reverent behaviour of our bodies, protesting thereby what is our faith and judgment concerning the substance of this most blessed sacrament, and so we truly judge and discern our Lord's Body. And for further honour to be given to it, whensoever we receive it, we take it fasting before all other meats, except extreme sickness, or the instant danger of death do require otherwise to take it when and as we may. For ever since the Apostles' time, it pleased the Holy Ghost, that for the honour of so great a sacrament the Body of our Lord should first enter into the mouth of a Christian man, before all other external meats. For this manner and custom is observed universally throughout the whole world. And for that cause it is decreed by the universal Church of Christ, that this most honourable sacrament should be reserved for the necessity of them that be sick or absent, lest (where it cannot be duly consecrate at all times and places, of a priest not fasting) the sick folks should die without this heavenly food which is their strength, and the stay of their passage to the next world.

Furthermore, at the time of the receiving of this sacrament we ought to have our minds occupied in remembering the Passion of Christ. For by this sacrifice which Christ giveth to us, we know assuredly that He bought us with no worldly treasure of gold and silver, but with this same His most precious Body and Blood, and by it we are provoked to remember always His most high benefit, and therewithal to render most humble thanks to Him in devout affection and obedient service, accord to His good will and pleasure. Thus receiving the Body and Blood of our Lord, we ought thankfully to remember and confess that our Saviour Christ hath given His Body to death, and shed His Blood for us, knowing that we ought again rather to suffer our bodies to be slain, and our blood to be shed for Him, and in defence of His truth, and edifying of His people (if the case so required) than to forsake or deny Him or the truth of His gospel revealed by the Holy Ghost to the Catholic Church.*

By this (good people) ye know how to judge and discern the Body of our Lord, and how to behave yourselves when ye come to receive it. Now likewise

---

* Let it not be forgotten that Bishop Watson suffered twenty-five years' imprisonment in defence of his faith.

know what is your duty to do after ye have received
it : ye ought to keep and preserve yourselves clean
from sin, rather after than before, lest you commit anything that might displease the Presence of His majesty,
Whom ye have received, and thereby be an occasion of
His departing from you, and of withdrawing His grace
from your hearts, that have desire to have sin, which
is the mother of death, rather to reign in your mortal
bodies, than to have Christ, and His Heavenly Father
with the Holy Ghost to make Their habitation there.
As it is more shame for a man to dislodge his honest
guest, and thrust him out of doors after he hath
received him into his house, than at the first time to
have said him nay, and to have denied him lodging :
even so it is greater damnation to defile this our flesh
with the filthiness of sin, when it hath received Christ's
Flesh and Blood, and so to tread under foot God's Son :
than to have abstained and not to have received Him
before, making the last end worse than the first.
Wherein we be like cursed Absolon that called his
brother Amnon to a feast, and caused his servants to
kill him there (II. Kings xiii. 28, 29).   And also we be
like to the traitor Judas, that after with Christ in His
Supper he received Christ's Body at Christ's hand, gave
place to the devil's suggestion, and betrayed Christ
his Master to the wicked Jews.   And we be also like
to the Jews that met Christ coming to the city with
boughs of palms and olive trees, and within five days
after cried, *Crucifige* upon Him, and pursued Him even
to the death.

But our duty is to give as much reverence to Christ
being present and dwelling with us, as we did when

He was coming to us, and not to take His precious Body and Blood in vain, and without cause, but to express in our lives that we imitate and follow His footsteps, and so keep a perpetual commemoration of Him That died for us, and rose again, in that we be now mortified to sin and the world, and living to God in Christ our Lord. For this sacrament of the Altar, wherein we receive Christ's Body and Blood, doth signify and teach us that we should communicate with Christ in His passions, and follow that conversation in our manners, which He showed in His Flesh, and as His Body in form of bread is seen to enter into our mouths: so we know that He also entereth into us by that conversation which He used on earth, to dwell in our hearts by faith.

Therefore he that so remembereth Christ's death, that he according to Christ's example, doth mortify his members which be upon earth, that is to say, fornication, uncleanness, naughty· desires, covetousness, and such like, he eateth worthily Christ's Body and Blood, and hath everlasting life remaining in him, and suffering with Christ, shall reign with Christ in the glory of His Father, with the Holy Ghost, world without end. Amen.

THE TWELFTH SERMON.

OF THE SACRIFICE OF THE NEW TESTAMENT WHICH IS CALLED THE MASS.

AS Christ our Saviour hath given unto us His most precious Body and Blood in the sacrament, to be our meat to feed and nourish us to everlasting life : so hath He given (good people) unto us the same His Body and Blood to be our daily sacrifice for the attaining of remission of sins and eternal salvation, and as He commanded us to take and eat that His Body which He gave us, so hath He commanded us to offer it to God the Father in remembrance of His Passion. So that the sacrifice of the Mass, which is the proper sacrifice of the New Testament (whereupon by God's help I intreat at this time), is the execution of Christ's commandment in His last Supper, when He said to His disciples :— "Do this in My remembrance ; " wherein the bread and wine be consecrate and changed, and the Body and Blood of Christ being made present there by the almighty power of the Holy Ghost, be offered to God the Father by the Church, for the Church, and received of the faithful people. Christ our Lord God Who loved us sinners so exceedingly, that for our

redemption and salvation abased Himself to be made
man (Phil. ii. 7), and was made obedient in humbling
Himself to the most painful and vile death of the
cross, and for our justification rose again the third
day, and ascended to heaven, to the glory of His
Father, which be the wonderful works of God and
therefore marvellous in our sight: hath also instituted
and ordained a memory of these marvels, saying "So
often as ye shall do these things, ye shall do them in
My remembrance." And when said our merciful
Lord that word? verily even then when He gave
the meat of His Body to them that feared Him (Ps.
cx. 4). And then in His last Supper did He, being
our most High Priest, first of all offer a sacrifice to
God the Father and commanded the same to be
done of the priests of His Church that occupy His
office, in memory of Him, and so taught the new
oblation of the New Testament, which oblation the
Church receiving of the Apostles, doth offer to God
throughout the whole world.

And for plainer understanding of this matter (good
people) I pray you call to your remembrance, the
sum and ground of all our faith, which is, that we
believe to be saved only by the merits of our Saviour
Christ, and that He bearing our sins in His Body on
the cross, and being the innocent Lamb of God
(John i. 15, 29, 36) without all sin Himself, shed His
most innocent Blood for our sins, and by the voluntary
sacrifice of His own Body and Blood, made satisfaction for all the sins of the whole world, and reconciled the wicked world to the favour of God again.

This bloody sacrifice made Christ our Saviour

upon the Altar of His cross but once (Heb. ix. x.), and it is the propitiatory Sacrifice and a sufficient price and ransom for the sins of all people, from the beginning of the world to the last end.   All our comfort and joy is and ought to be in this sacrament and Passion of our Saviour Christ, by which only we have and may have sure hope of salvation.   All that were saved from the creation of the world and the fall of Adam, were saved by the virtue of this Sacrifice, and by lively faith in Christ that was promised to Adam, and Noah and Abraham, and the other patriarchs and fathers of the Old Testament, and all the sacrifices which they offered then, were but figures of this Sacrifice of Christ, whereby they did protest their faith in Christ to come.   And likewise all we that have been justified and saved since Christ's time, and shall be to the world's end, obtain and receive that redemption, remission of sin, and salvation by the only virtue of the same bloody Sacrifice of Christ upon the cross.   Whensoever we be in sin, we resort to that Passion to have remission ; whensoever our works be unsufficient and unperfect, we run to that Passion to have that supplied that lacketh in us ; whensoever we go about to render thanks to God for all His benefits, we cannot do it worthily and sufficiently, till we join ourselves to that Passion, that maketh our thanksgiving acceptable in the sight of God.   No tongue can particularly express the worthiness and commodities of this Sacrifice of Christ's Passion, which hath purchased for us all pardon, all grace, all righteousness, all holiness, every good gift, and eternal salvation.   The action and doing of this

Sacrifice was not long, but accomplished and ended upon Good Friday, which was the day when Christ died, and He dieth no more but liveth ever : but the operation and virtue of this Passion is a long thing, extended to the salvation of man from the beginning of the world to the last end, from the time when Christ was first promised to be the Saviour of all men, till the time when He shall come again in His Majesty to be the Judge of all men. And although the suffering of His Passion was but short, and is already ceased ; yet the effect of it which is man's redemption and satisfaction ceaseth not ; and because it is applied to every man that is partaker of it by lively faith in continual succession during all the time of the whole world, therefore Christ our Saviour willeth that the Sacrifice of this redemption should never cease, but be always to all men present in grace, and always be kept in perpetual memory.

For which cause He hath given and committed unto His Church, the most clean and pure sacrifice of His Body and Blood under the forms of bread and wine, and hath commanded it to be offered to God, and received of us in the remembrance of His Passion, till His last coming. Which thing the Church most faithfully and obediently observeth and useth, not by presumption, taking upon itself to offer that sacrifice of our Saviour which is far above the dignity of man, but by commission and warrant of His most holy Word authorised to offer Christ, God's Son, to God the Father, that is to say, to represent to the Father, the Body and Blood of Christ, which, by His omnipotent Word, hath there made present, and thereby to renew His Passion, not by suffering of death again, but after an unbloody manner, not for this end that we should thereby deserve remission of sins, and deliverance from the power of the devil, which is the proper effect of Christ's Passion, but that we should, by our faith, devotion, and this representation of His Passion, obtain the remission and grace already deserved by His passion, to be now applied unto our profit and salvation. Not that the Passion of Christ is imperfect, or needeth any work of ours to be added to supply the imperfection of it, but to comfort and relieve our imperfection, that some drop of grace may be drawn and brought unto us out of the fountain of all grace, and wellspring of His Passion. Not that we can apply the merits of Christ's death as we list, and to whom we list, but that we, by this representing of His Passion, most humbly make petition and prayer to Almighty God to apply unto us that remission and grace which was purchased and deserved by Christ's Passion before, after the measure of His goodness, to all those whose faith and devotion be known unto Him. So that the Host, or the thing that is offered, both in the Sacrifice of Christ upon the cross, and in the sacrifice of the Church upon the Altar, is all one in substance, being the natural Body of Christ our High Priest, and the price or ransom of our redemption, but the manner and the effects of these two offerings be divers, the one is the shedding of Christ's Blood, extending to the death of Christ the Offerer, for the redemption of all mankind : the other is without shedding His Blood, only representing His death, whereby the faithful and devout people are made partakers of the merits of Christ's Passion and Divinity.

Thus is Christ a Priest for evermore after the order of Melchisedech (Ps. cix. 4), Who, in His last Supper, offered His Body and Blood without shedding of His blood, and so taught and delivered to His Apostles and their successors, bishops and priests, the manner how they should offer Him, being the Lamb of God, in sacrifice for evermore to the world's end, after the order, that is to say, after the rite and manner of Melchisedech, under the form of bread and wine, Who in old time, in figure of Christ, offered bread and wine, and did dedicate and prophesy before the mystery or sacrament of us Christian men in the Body and Blood of our Saviour. Whereof also spake Malachi, the prophet, saying (chap. i. 11), that in this our time of the New Testament God would reject and detest the Jews, and all their sacrifices of brute and unreasonable beasts, and that His Name should be magnified among the Gentiles, from the rising of the sun to the setting, and that one singular and pure sacrifice, without spot or imperfection, should be of them offered to Him, not only in one place among the Jews, but in every place among the Gentiles, which sacrifice should succeed all the other sacrifices of the Old Testament, which were offered in the shadow of this to come. For the Jews, in their sacrifices of beasts, did, as it were by prophecy, declare and signify before that saving sacrifice which Christ offered upon the cross; and the Christian men now do celebrate the memory of the same sacrifice of Christ that is past, even by the offering and receiving

I

of the same Body and Blood that suffered passion.
For as Christ upon the cross, being the head of all us
His mystical body the Church, offering there Himself, did also offer all us that be of the Church to
God the Father, for the pacifying of His wrath and
indignation against our sin, so we, being His mystical body, do use to offer to God, the Father, Christ
our Head, and by His merits do beg pardon for our
offences, knowing that God, Who spared not His
only-begotten Son, but gave Him to us for our redemption (Rom. viii. 32), will now deny us nothing
for His sake that we have need upon, Who is now
also at the right hand of God, and maketh intercession for us. So that Christ in heaven, and all we
His mystical body in earth, do both but one thing.
For Christ being a Priest for evermore (Heb. ix. 11),
after His Passion and Resurrection, entered into
heaven, and there appeareth now to the countenance
of God for us, offering Himself for us, to pacify the
anger of God with us, and representing His Passion,
and all that He suffered for us, that we might be
reconciled to God by Him. Even so the Church,
our mother, being careful for all us, her children, that
have offended our Father in heaven, useth continually
by her public minister to pray and to offer unto God
the Body and Blood of her husband Christ, representing and renewing His Passion and death before God,
that we thereby might be renewed in grace, and
receive life, perfection, and salvation. And after the
same sort the holy angels of God, in the time of this
our sacrifice, do assist the priest, and stand about
the Host, thinking then the meetest time to show

their charity towards us, and, therefore, holding forth the Body of Christ, pray for mankind, as saying thus:—Lord, we pray for them whom Thou hast so loved, that for their salvation Thou hast suffered death, and spent Thy life upon the cross; we make supplication for them, for whom Thou hast shed this Thy Blood; we pray for them, for whom Thou hast offered this same Thy very Body.

O Lord, what earnest desire should we have to be present, and to associate ourselves in the oblation of this our sacrifice, which we know Christ Himself always to do, and also His holy angels and archangels, and is so acceptable a thing to God the Father, for all our sins and ignorances. For in that hour, when Christ's death is renewed in mystery, and His most fearful and acceptable sacrifice is represented to the sight of God, then sitteth the King upon His mercy-seat, inclined to give and forgive whatsoever is demanded and asked of Him in humble manner. In the presence of this Body and Blood of our Saviour Christ, the tears of a meek and humble man never beg pardon in vain, nor the sacrifice of a contrite heart is never put back, but hath his lawful petition granted and given.

By resorting to this sacrifice of the Mass we evidently declare and protest before God and the whole world, that we put our singular and only trust of grace and salvation in Christ our Lord, for the merits of His death and Passion, and not for the worthiness of any good work that we have done or can do, and that we make His Passion our only refuge. For when wisdom faileth, which only cometh by the

doctrine of Christ, when righteousness lacketh, which
only is gotten by the mercy of Christ, when virtue
ceaseth, which only is received of Him that is the
Lord of all virtue, then for supplying of these our
lacks and needs, our refuge is to Christ's Passion ;
then we run (as the prophet saith, Ps. cxv. 13) to the
cup of our Saviour, and call upon the name of our
Lord, that is to say, we take His Passion, and offer to
God the Father in mystery the work of our redemption, that by this memory and commemoration of it,
it would please His merciful goodness to innovate
His grace in us, and to replenish us with the fruit of
His Son's Passion and death.   For that commemoration of which our Lord said, " Do this in remembrance
of Me," is the only commemoration that maketh God
merciful unto us.   We are become debtors to Almighty God two ways, for our manifold sins and
iniquities done against Him, and for His manifold
benefits and graces given unto us.   As for the debts
of our sins, many pay very evil that drive off their
penance to their last age, and many pay nothing at
all that die without penance and charity, and they
that labour to pay all they can all their life, can never
fully pay their whole debt, no, scant one farthing of
a thousand pound.   What remedy, then, have we,
but to run to the rich man our neighbour that hath
enough to pay for us all ? I mean Christ our Lord
that hath paid His heart-blood, for no debt of His
own, but for our debt ; and there whilst we celebrate
the memory of His Passion, we acknowledge and confess our sins, which be without number, and grant
that we be not able fully to satisfy for the least of

them, and therefore beseech our merciful Father to
accept in full payment and satisfaction of our debts,
His Passion which (after this sort as He hath ordained
to be done in the sacrifice of the Mass) we renew and
represent before Him ; and where our sinful life hath
altogether displeased Him, we offer unto Him His
well-beloved Son Jesus in sacrifice, with Whom we
are sure He is well-pleased, most humbly making
supplication to accept Him for us, in Whom only we
put our trust, accounting Him all our righteousness,
and the author of our salvation. And as for His
manifold benefits and gifts of nature, of grace, and of
fortune, what have we to render to God again ?
Sinners that have taken their soul in vain, and give
both their souls and bodies to serve the world and the
flesh, and abuse the goods of the world, as sticks and
matter to kindle the fire of their vain and carnal lusts,
they be most unthankful, and deserve most punishment. But other men that consider all they have to
be God's gifts, and given to them, not to do their
wills withal, but to give an account again of the well-
using of them, and therefore bestow their external
goods in the works of mercy and piety, and bring
their bodies in bondage to their spirit, and their
souls to be ruled by the Spirit of God, and so dedicate themselves wholly to God's service, these men
be good, and make of their goods, their wills, their
bodies and souls sweet sacrifices of praise and thanksgiving to Almighty God. But yet all these sacrifices,
in comparison of the great heap of benefits which
God hath given, doth give and shall give unto us,
be but as it were one drop in the whole sea, a little

wart to a great mountain, and because they be imperfect and in many things spotted with sin and
unclean, therefore they be not worthy to be represented before God as thanks, seeing all we have done
is but our duty and scarce that.   For which cause
we resort to the Body of Christ, Whom God hath
given to us, and Him as being ours we offer to God
again, and so in Him we supply that we lack in ourselves.   For it is He that by His propitiatory sacrifice (which we celebrate in the Holy Mass) doth
reconcile us to God, and with the plenty of His gifts
maketh us thanksgivers, and in all things taketh upon
Him our person, and supplieth that which we ought
to do, and by the very nature of His sacrifice, which
is His Body, stirreth us to the continual giving of
thanks.   So that our sacrifice being Christ's Body,
as it is the greatest gift that God gave man, so it is
worthy and a real giving of thanks for all His other
gifts.   And therefore it is also called "Sacrificium
Eucharisticum," a sacrifice of thanksgiving, not only
for that we by it give thanks to God in words and
prayers, but also for that it is itself a sacrifice of
thanks for our redemption, for the hope of our health
and salvation.   And whereas sacrifice is the greatest
and chiefest kind of adoration that can be, pertaining
to godly honour called "Latria," therefore we do
make sacrifice to no creature, neither to saint nor
angel, but only to the Holy Trinity, which is the
only and true God, and all our temples and altars be
builded, erected, and dedicated only to God, there to
do sacrifice to God, and to no saint, although in our
sacrifice we name and have remembrance of the holy

martyrs and saints, both to thank God for their victories, and also to provoke ourselves to imitate them in the overcoming of our ghostly enemies.

By this (good people) that I have declared unto you, ye ought truly to understand and believe that Christ's natural Body in the blessed sacrament, is the proper sacrifice of Christ's Church, and that Christ Himself, both by His own deed, and also by His express word and commandment, did institute and ordain that the Church, His spouse, should by her public ministers being priests, offer to Almighty God the Father, with the Son and the Holy Ghost, in sacrifice the same His natural Body in remembrance of His Passion. Which Passion the Church now daily to the world's end doth renew in mystery, and doth represent before God in the Holy Mass, for the attaining of all the graces and benefits purchased by the same Passion before, after the measure of His goodness, and as our faith and devotion is known unto Him. And in all her needs and troubles it resorteth to God, trusting to have relief and mercy, only for the merits of that Passion which it representeth to God as a full satisfaction for all her offences, and as a full perfection of thanks for all His former benefits and gifts. And finally by this sacrifice of Christ's Body and Blood in the Mass, we certainly declare that nothing doth exercise our faith in the knowledge of God and of ourselves, more than this sacrifice of the Mass doth and that nothing doth more increase our charity and hope in the mercy of God ; and it declareth that we believe that there is no Saviour but only Christ our Lord, and that we have no refuge but to Him, ascribing altogether to the merits of His Passion, and so by it we most of all set forth our humility and the glory of Christ and His true honour.

Which sacrifice if we daily and devoutly exercise and come unto, and behave ourselves as becometh Christian men, and in such affection and intent as I have declared now how the Church doth, no doubt of it but we shall perceive great comfort in our hearts, great amendment in our lives, and great furtherance to the attaining of everlasting life; to the which He bring us, that by His Passion redeemed us, to Whom with the Father and the Holy Ghost be all honour, glory, and praise for evermore.—Amen.

THE THIRTEENTH SERMON.

OF THE GODLY PRAYERS AND CEREMONIES USED IN THE SACRIFICE OF THE MASS.

IF in that sacrifice which is Christ, no man is to be followed but Christ, it is meet for us to be obedient, and to do that thing which Christ did and commanded to be done. And therefore (good people) considering that this our sacrifice of the Mass is (according to Christ's commandment) the commemoration of Christ's Passion, the Holy Church of Christ, ever since the time of His Passion hath obediently used to do as He did. He did consecrate the bread and wine with His omnipotent blessing, and made there present His very Body and Blood, and also He offered that His Body and Blood after the order and manner of Melchisedech to His Father, and thirdly received it Himself, and gave it to His disciples. Even so the Holy Church in Christ, and Christ by the Holy Church, doth the same in all points at this day ; for the special and substantial part of the Mass consisteth in these three points, in consecrating the bread and wine into the Body and Blood of Christ, in offering of the same Body and Blood of Christ to God the Father,

and in receiving of the same by the devout and faithful people.

Christ also, after His Supper and before His Passion,
did say a hymn before He went forth to the Mount
Olivet (Matt. xxvi. 30), and He taught His disciples
many necessary things, and promised to send unto
them His Holy Spirit (John xv. 26), Which should
teach them all truth Which they could not bear (John
xvi. 12), and afterwards prayed long and fervently for
His faithful disciples, and for the whole Church that
should by their word believe in Him, and specially for
their peace and unity in God and among themselves
(John xvii.)

In these things also the Holy Church doth follow
the example of Christ her Head, which in the
ministration of this sacrifice useth to join almost all
the other inward sacrifices of a Christian man—as
confession of sins, invocation of God's mercy, the
praise of God, petitions for things needful, the doctrine of the people, the profession of our common
faith, the giving of thanks to God, prayers for all
states of God's Church, the honouring of Christ, the
asking of God's peace, the exhorting to the same,
with divers other godly exercises, which I shall
(God willing) at this time shortly and particularly
shew unto you, to the intent you may know how
there is nothing contained in the Mass, but a heap
of all godliness and spiritual sacrifices, and thereby
to be the more provoked and disposed to the often
using and frequenting of the said Mass.

First of all, the holy vestments wherewith the
priest goeth to the altar, beside other mysteries which

they teach and signify, they renew the memory of Christ's Passion in our hearts. For as the Jews did first cover Christ's face, and did mock Him and buffet Him (Luke xxii. 63, 64), so hath the priest in memory of that an amice put upon his head, and also the white alb put over all his body, doth bring us in remembrance how Christ was condemned of King Herod, who, in mocking Him, put upon Him a white apparel, and sent Him back again to Pilate (Luke xxiii. 11). And the maniple upon the priest's arm, and his girdle about his white alb, and the stole about his neck, do shew a man how Christ was bounden fast to a pillar when He was whipped and scourged (John xix. 1). And as Christ was crowned with thorns, and had His hands and feet nailed to the cross, so in the amice and alb of the priest there be tokens of these five wounds. And the upper vestment of the priest putteth us in memory of the purple robe that Pilate's soldiers put upon Christ after they had scourged Him. And upon the back of this vestment commonly there is made the sign of the cross, teaching us how Christ was compelled to bear His cross upon His back through the city; so that, whensoever we see the priest thus apparelled, go up to the altar to celebrate the commemoration of Christ's Passion, we may remember how cruelly Christ was handled of the Jews, and after what sort He went up to the Mount of Calvary to suffer His Passion for the redemption of man.

The priest, coming to the altar, beginneth first of all with the sacrifice of a contrite heart, without the which no man can do the work of God worthily, and The Con-fession.

there, beside the sacramental confession, which he hath made before (if his conscience did reprove him of any deadly sin), he maketh also a general confession of all his sins, not excusing his fault or laying the blame upon God or any other thing, but, knocking upon his breast, accuseth and judgeth himself. And, because our deadly offences be done against God and His whole Church, therefore he maketh his confession to God and to the whole Church, both triumphant in Heaven, and militant here in earth, requiring of God pardon and remission, and requiring of the Church aid to join with him in prayer. And as they that do there assist him, do pray for him in his hearing, so is he sure that the blessed angels and saints in heaven are, of their abundant charity, glad of his penance, and pray for his pardon and amendment.

The Office. In the meantime, the choir and the priest also at the altar, do begin the office of this ministration with a hymn or psalm, or some part of a psalm, as the Church doth in all other service. And with it he **Kyrie Eleison.** useth another inward sacrifice, which is the invocation of God's help and mercy, which, for fervent desire to have his petition granted of Almighty God by the merits of Christ, he repeateth it divers times.

Gloria in Excelsis. And for such certain and sure confidence, which he hath of God's mercy for Christ's sake, he beginneth by-and-by after that the sacrifice of praise, and useth the same words that the angels praised God withal, when they brought the glad tidings of Christ's nativity to the world, which the priest and the choir do prosecute and continue for joy that God hath wrought mercifully among men.

And then the priest, saluting and wishing well to the people, to stir their hearts to devotion, and to join with him in the common prayer, saith the Collect, which is a sacrifice of prayer for all such things as the people hath need upon, and is called a Collect, for that the common petitions of the people be collected and gathered together in one prayer, and uttered only by the mouth of the priest in all their names, whereunto the people answering "Amen," giveth their consent, praying God to grant that for all their salvation, which is required in all their names. *Dominus Vobiscum. The Collect.*

After these sacrifices of confession, invocation, praise, and petitions, the priest converteth his words to the doctrine of the people, and first beginneth with some part of the Law and Prophets, or of S. Paul's Epistles, wherein is shewed the true meaning of the Law and Prophets, preparing their hearts to the most perfect and most wholesome doctrine of the Gospel of Christ, the spiritual food of men's souls, to the intent that such as be not partakers of Christ's Body and Blood corporally in the Sacrament, may yet, by the instruction of the Holy Word of God, be fed spiritually in their souls by faith, that like as the Holy Mass is the exercise and practice of good living, so it might also be the teacher and school of true faith. And between these two doctrines of the Law and the Gospel, are said or sung certain Canticles, or songs of God's praise, according to the condition and nature of the time—as the Gradual and Tract for *Epistle. Gospel. Gradual Tract.*

the time of penance, when men lament their sins and
misery of this life, and the prolonging of the life to

come ; or else the Alleluia, which is a song of God's
praise for the time of joy and gladness, when men
rejoice, considering the state of their eternal felicity
to come, using still the old strange word without
interpretation, declaring thereby that as yet they be
ignorant of such joys as God hath prepared for them
that love Him.

At the rehearsing of the Gospel the priest saluteth
the people, preparing their hearts to the hearing of
God's Word, wishing grace to be given to them of
God, to receive His Word with humility and meekness, which is able to save their souls. And the
people rising up, and standing reverently bareheaded,
declare themselves to be attent and ready to hear the
Gospel of Christ, and do glorify God that hath
vouchsafed to make them partakers of His Gospel,
which is the virtue of God for the salvation of all
them that believe (Rom. i. 16). And the priest,
making a cross upon the book and his forehead,
declareth that this doctrine is not invented by man,
but revealed by God, and pertaineth to the mystery
of Christ's cross and our redemption, and also pro-
testeth with the people, that their duty is not to be
ashamed of the Gospel of Christ's Cross, but to
believe in their heart and to confess it with their
mouth. And for proof of the same, that faith cometh
by hearing of the Word of God (Rom. x. 17); by-
and-by, after the reading and preaching of the
Gospel, the priest beginneth to profess and offer the

sacrifice of faith, which the choir or people also profess with great gladness, in such form of words as the ancient and holy fathers assembled in the First General Council at Nice did utter their faith, to the confusion of all heretics that were before them, declaring that they have the foundation of their faith nowhere else, but of Christ's mouth, and the preaching of His Holy Word.

Here endeth the Mass of them that be but only learners of our faith, and be not yet christened, which in old time were not admit to be present among Christian men, in the time of the sacrifice of Christ's Body and Blood, but after the prayers and doctrine ended, were secluded from the Church. But this manner is not used now in the Church, because every one is christened being a child, and learneth our faith afterward. *Missa Catechumenorum.*

And the priest proceeding forward, exhorting all the people to pray, doth offer to God the matter of the consecration, which is bread of wheat, and wine mixed with water, which be not yet consecrate, but prepared to be consecrate, and directing his eye and intention to the Body and Blood of Christ, that afterward be made present by the consecration, as Christ prayed before His Passion for all them for whom He suffered, so the priest before the mystical oblation saith that he offereth it to God, in the honour of God and all His saints, for his sins and offences, for the salvation of all that be living, and for the rest of all them that be departed, and prayeth that God would so accept it. For to this end every sacrifice that we make, and every good deed that we do, is intended and directed, which they be not able to bring to pass *Offertory or Oblation.*

but by the merits of Christ's bloody sacrifice upon the cross.

And here, beginning this most holy and Sacred mystery, for reverence to the holy sacrament, the **Washing of hands.** priest washeth his hands, that no outward filthiness should seclude him from the communion, and therewithal prayeth to be made clean from all uncleanness of body and soul, that in clean life he might perform the holy work of God, which is also a lesson to the people, and to put away naughty thoughts out of their hearts, lest God, offended with their sinful thoughts, do turn His face away from their oblations and prayers.

And as the priest before exhorted the people **Secret Collect.** secretly to prayer, so doth he pray secretly himself, with much devotion, that their common sacrifices may be acceptable to God for them, and that it would please Almighty God to grant that the influence of His grace might descend and sanctify the oblations, that when they be sanctified and received, the heavenly virtue and effects of the blessed sacrifices may take place in the hearts of them for whom they be offered. To which prayer, when the people hath consented, saying "Amen," the priest saluteth the people, and wisheth well to them, and they to him again; and he exhorteth them to lift up their hearts to God, and so to prepare their hearts to the sacrifice of thanks, which they by their whole consent promise to do.

Therefore, I beseech all you (good people) to take heed to your promise, and be ashamed to be found liars in the presence of God, specially in the time of the terrible sacrifices. Put away all carnal and worldly thoughts, and think upon nothing but upon that ye pray. For the priest in this preface Preface. of the Mass before the canonical prayer, doth exhort the people to lift up their hearts to God (which they answer they do), to admonish them that they ought to think upon nothing but upon God. Shut the door of your hearts against the devil, and let it be open only to God, and let not God's enemy enter in the time of prayer. For this is the subtle craft of the devil to call our minds from God, and so to make void our prayers, that we should have one thing in our mouth and another thing in our heart; whereas God ought to be prayed unto, not with the only sound of the voice, but with a pure intent and a vigilant mind, earnestly thinking upon that he prayeth. For no man can worthily give thanks to God that hath not his heart lifted up to God. And because the true honour and worshipping of God standeth in this most of all, that our soul be not unthankful to Him, therefore, in the most true and singular sacrifice, we are admonished to give thanks to our Lord God, which is most seeming and right we should do, seeing he cannot be called thankful that ascribeth to himself that which is given to him of God. And then the priest beginneth the Eucharistical sacrifice of general thanks, as a public person in Eucharistic the name of all the Church before the consecration, tic thanksgiving. following the example of Christ, Who in His last Supper gave thanks to God the Father, and then blessed and distributed His Body and Blood to His disciples.

In this giving of thanks by Christ our Lord, for whose merits they be only acceptable, he prayeth to

K

be joined and associated with the angels and arch-angels, and all the whole army of the blessed spirits in heaven, who then do assist the priest, and be present there in the honour of Him that is offered, praying, honouring, and adoring the Majesty of Almighty God, and with them singeth the hymn of the angels and evangelists, giving honour, glory, and benediction to the Lord God of Hosts (Apoc. iv. 11), using also the same words of praise that the children and the people of the Jews used in praising Christ when He came riding to Jerusalem as a King, and yet humbly upon an ass (Matt. xxi. 9), not to take upon Him the kingdom and pomp of the world, but with His Passion and death to redeem the world.

Canon.   The rest of the Mass that followeth is that part which is called the Canon, which is spoken in silence, to declare unto us the heaviness of Christ's Passion, and that the priest may the better convert and set his whole mind and attention upon the work of God, and the words of his prayer and consecration. And he useth very few ceremonies, saving only certain crosses upon the Host, partly to move the people that stand by to consider the Passion, and partly to declare that our redemption was wrought by the voluntary will of God the Father, that gave His Son for us, and also by the will of the Son, that having such power of His own soul that no man could take it from Him, yet offered Himself by the Holy Ghost a clean sacrifice to God, to purify our hearts from sin.

In this Canon all invocations, all prayers and

petitions, be made and directed to God the Father, for His Son Jesus Christ's sake our Lord, and be made to no creature, neither in heaven nor earth, but to Him ; and in it be expressly declared what we offer to Him, for whom we offer, with whom we offer, and to what end we offer.

The thing that we offer to God is Christ Himself. Nothing have we that is perfect and pure to offer to God, but Christ that is given unto us for that purpose. Whom we do not now offer in figure as the Jews did in the old law, but in very truth, and yet in a sacrament. For what is more meet to be offered for man than the flesh of man ? And what flesh is so acceptable as the flesh of our sacrifice, being the body of our Priest ? For Christ remaineth one God with Him to Whom we offer, and hath made Himself one with them for whom we offer, and He is one with us that do offer, and He is the one and the self-same thing that is offered ; so that our external sacrifice that pertains now to the New Testament, is the innocent Lamb of God that taketh away the sins of the world, which sacrifice lieth upon the altar, and is offered now of the priests without shedding of His Blood, and is the holy bread of eternal life, and the cup of everlasting salvation.

Secondly, because Christ suffering His Passion, offered His Body and Blood for the whole Church, both those that were alive and those that were dead, therefore the Church, renewing in mystery Christ's Passion, offereth likewise the same Body and Blood for the whole Church, both for the quick and the dead, and that in special words. First, generally for the whole Catholic Church of Christ, secluding all those that be out of the Church (for no man offereth the Body of Christ but for them which be the members of Christ), and then particularly for the governors of the Church and of commonwealths, as for the Pope's Holiness, the successor of S. Peter, to whom Christ did commit the cure and charge of His universal Church throughout the world—for bishops, for kings and princes, and in especial for such as the minister any way is bound to pray, and for them that be present and communicate with the priest in true faith and devout affection. And also the Church offereth Christ for the souls of them that be departed, "having at their departing the signs of faith," which be the Holy Sacraments and good works, "and sleeping in the sleep of peace," which is the peace of conscience towards God, with sure hope and trust of remission by Christ; that is to say, for such as in their lives obtained so much grace of God, that our charity and sacrifices might help and relieve them after their death. For seeing the souls of such be not separate from the Church, which is the kingdom of Christ, among the members of which kingdom there is a mutual communion of all good deeds and godly works or sacrifices, therefore the Church commendeth them to the mercy of God, and the intercession of Christ's oblation, verily believing that the precious Blood of Christ, as it is profitable for the salvation of the living, so it is also available for the absolution and perfection of them that be dead, that they being for a time detained in the temporal afflictions and purgations, might the sooner, by the virtue of this blessed sacrifice, be delivered and brought to the place of light and eternal peace, where nothing entereth that is spotted and imperfect.

Thirdly, because the blessed Virgin Mary, the Mother of God, and the holy martyrs and saints in heaven, be also our brethren and members of Christ's Church, for the which Christ suffered His Passion, and being knit to us in one communion by the band of perfect charity, and being careful for us, and they be sure for themselves, cease not to communicate with us in prayer, and to require of Christ the perfection of His Body, which is the Church ; therefore in our oblation of Christ's Body and Blood, we join with them, and with honour and reverence we remember them at our Lord's Table, not to pray for them, as we do for others, that rest in peace, but rather that they should pray for us, that we may follow their footsteps, and in all our affairs be defended by God's protection, and that by the merits of Christ, Whom we pray not to weigh our merits but to pardon our offences.

And last of all, in the Canon is expressed for what end we offer Christ, that is to say, in remembrance of His Passion, His Resurrection and glorious Ascension, most humbly beseeching that God of His mercy would accept Him for us and our salvation, and whereas He is for Himself most acceptable in His sight, that likewise He would accept us, that be His Body in earth, for Him, that by participation of His most precious Body and Blood, we might be fulfilled with all grace and heavenly benediction.

Thus doth the Church offer Christ, her Head, to God the Father, as a worthy sacrifice of praise and thanks for her redemption, for the hope of health and salvation, and for all His other benefits; and also it offereth Him as a sacrifice propitiatory, by the virtue of His Passion, for all her sins and offences, that we in this world might live in peace with God, and afterward be delivered from eternal damnation, and with His elects be rewarded in the kingdom of heaven.

And to conclude this canonical prayer, the priest having Christ, God's Son, in his hands before him, Who is the only Mediator between God and man, trusting to obtain whatsoever he asketh in His name, and being instructed by Him ever to pray to the Father, saith boldly the "Pater Noster," in which prayer is contained all that is good and needful for the life of man, both temporal and eternal, and so maketh an end of the Canon.

And because this is the mystery of unity and peace, which cannot be had but by the mercy of Christ, therefore the priest turning him to the Lamb of God, Who only taketh away the sins of the world, prayeth devoutly for the peace of conscience which cometh by remission of sin, and for the peace of his affections which cometh by the mortification of the flesh, and also for the peace of brotherly charity, which is poured into our hearts by the Holy Ghost, and so taketh and giveth to the people the kiss of peace, the token and testimony of unity and Christian charity.

The other prayers that follow in the Mass pertain to the devotion of him or them that receive the blessed sacrament, that they may receive it worthily to the profit and salvation both of body and soul, and that it might be acceptable to God for all them for whom it is offered.

Therefore (good people), seeing that I have now by God's help declared unto you, as shortly as I could, the whole sum of all that is said and done in the Mass, which is all most godly and most comfortable, pertaining all to this end, to set forth the benefit of Christ and the virtue of His Passion, and containing in it almost all the spiritual sacrifices of the new law, and the exercises of true faith, as confession of sin, invocation of God, prayer, doctrine, giving of thanks, and such other as I have rehearsed, I shall most heartily require you (as you are most bounden) to have this work of God in such estimation as becometh Christian men that be members of Christ's Church, redeemed with His precious Blood, and that by using of this sacrifice of the Church, which is a commemoration of Christ's Passion most acceptable in the sight of God, and commanded by Christ to be done of us, ye might thereby receive plenteous and abundant grace and mercy, both for you that be alive, and also for them that be departed in the faith of Christ, and in all your necessities and distresses, relief and succour. And when the consecration of the very Body and Blood of our Saviour is made by the power of His omnipotent Word, and the price of our redemption is lifted up for you to see by faith, under the several forms of bread and wine, to be adored and worshipped with godly honour, then call to your remembrance how that Christ for your salvation was lifted up in the air upon the cross to be seen of all the world, and how His precious Blood ran forth abundantly out of all the wounds of His Body, and then pray that God the Father would look upon Him for us, and accept Him for a full satisfaction of all our sins, over and beside all that we can do and suffer, and for a perfect supplying of all our negligences and imperfectness, and for a worthy sacrifice of thanks for all His benefits given unto us.

And to the intent ye might be more entirely joined to Christ, and be more replenished with His gifts and graces, I would wish and exhort you the oftener to prepare yourselves to receive corporally the blessed sacrament, which is ever ready prepared for you to receive, and when as of reverence you forbear to receive Him, as the Centurion said that he was not worthy that Christ should enter into his house (Matt. viii. 8), yet at least resort to this sacrifice, and with faith and devotion receive Christ spiritually, and giving thanks for all His gifts, commit yourselves wholly to the custody and tuition of Almighty God, Who is always ready to shew us mercy for Christ's sake, to Whom with the Father and the Holy Ghost be all honour, praise, and glory, world without end. Amen.

THE FOURTEENTH SERMON.

OF THE NECESSITY AND COMMODITY OF PENANCE IN GENERAL.

OUR Lord and Saviour Jesus Christ Which came into this world to call and save sinners (Luke v. 32, and 1 Tim. i. 15), dealing patiently with them (2 Peter iii. 9), not willing any man to perish, but all men to be converted and turned to Him by penance, after that John Baptist, whom God sent before His face to prepare His way by preaching penance, was apprehended and cast into prison, then (I say) our Saviour Christ began to preach the Gospel of His grace and glory, after this form, saying, " Do penance, for the kingdom of God draweth near " (Matt. iv. 17), teaching us both by His Word and deed. And like as John Baptist goeth before, whose ministry was to preach penance, and Jesus cometh after, by Whose death we have redemption and remission of sin, even so in the heart of every sinner, the effect of John's preaching, which is true and unfeigned penance, must go before, that the effect of Christ's Passion, which is grace, mercy, and remission of sins, may come after.

And as this doctrine of penance was first of all other

taught by our Saviour Himself, and by John His most holy Prophet, as a thing most necessary for the instruction and salvation of all men, even so His holy Apostles in the beginning of their preaching, observed the same matter and form of doctrine, as S. Peter in his first sermon made at Jerusalem in the day of Pentecost, when he had opened the work of the Holy Ghost in the gift of tongues, and thereby took occasion to set forth the mystery of Jesus Christ ; at the last end his doctrine to the people which were smitten by compunction of heart by his words, was this : " Do penance, and be every one of you baptized in the name of Jesus Christ, for the remission of your sins, and ye shall receive the gift of the Holy Ghost " (Acts ii. 38).　And in his next sermon, written in the third chapter of the Acts (verse 19), he taught the same doctrine in these words : " Do you therefore penance, and be converted, that your sins may be taken away."　S. Paul also calleth the doctrine of penance the foundation of all other doctrines in the heart of a godly man (Heb. vi. 1), out of which do spring such other virtues as bring a man to the perfection of a Christian life.　Likewise S. John Evangelist began with the same doctrine of penance, writing in his revelation to the seven churches that were in Asia, saying thus to the Church of Ephesus in the person of Christ :　" Remember from whence thou hast fallen, and do penance, and do the first works, or else I shall come to thee soon, and shall remove thy candlestick from its place, except thou do penance " (Apoc. ii. 5).　And this doctrine also did all the Apostles first and principally set forth to

all them that received the faith of Christ as most
necessary for their salvation, being taught and commanded so to do by our Saviour Christ Himself, when
before His Ascension He opened to them their wits
and understandings ·to understand the Scriptures,
saying to them, that it was so written that Christ
so should suffer and rise from death the third day
(Luke xxiv. 46), and that penance should be preached
in His name and remission of sin, throughout all
people, beginning at Jerusalem. For which cause and
consideration I, as a minister of our Saviour Christ, to
whom He hath committed the word and ministry of
reconciliation (2 Cor. v. 18), using as it were His
embassage to exhort you to be reconciled to Him,
intending to teach you at this time what things to do
for the saving of your souls and the attaining of
everlasting life, have thought it most expedient for
satisfying of my duty in following the example and
commandment of our Master Christ and His Apostles,
and for your erudition to be taught the straight path
and high beaten way for our Christian religion, to
speak of penance, and first to declare the necessity
and commodity of the same, and then in order the
parts of it, and how to do it in such manner as it
may be acceptable to Almighty God, and a mean to
attain His mercy and remission of sin.

First of all consider you (good people) that penance
is a gift of God, as the Scripture saith, God hath
given and granted penance to the Gentiles for life
and salvation (Acts xi. 18), and it is God that standeth
at the door of our heart and knocketh (Apoc. iii. 20),
by Whose inspiration we have the beginning of our

conversion, without Whom we be not able and sufficient of ourselves as of ourselves to think any good
thought (2 Cor. iii. 5). This gift of penance is a
perfect and marvellous great gift, being (as S.
Chrysostom saith) the mother of mercy, whereby
(as the wise man saith) God doth dissimulate the sins
of men for penance ; that is to say, God of His mere
mercy and fatherly affection, doth bear with the sins
of men, and deferreth to avenge and punish them
justly according to their defects, patiently looking for
their conversion and penance, by means whereof He
might remit their offences, deliver them from many
dangers, give unto them plenty of grace, and conduct
them to the fruition of His glory. For if God should
by-and-by punish all offenders, neither Zaccheus
should have had space to have done penance, nor yet
S. Matthew nor many others ; being taken away to
eternal death before the time of their penance. But
our most meek Father, calling every one to penance,
doth abide and tarry for us, which patience whosoever
abuseth and contemneth by remaining still in his
former sins, according to the hardness and obstinacy
of his own heart, doth store up to himself God's indignation in the day of God's anger and just judgment
(Rom. ii. 5), when He shall render to every one according to his works. And as He saith Himself, except
in very deed we do penance we shall all perish and
be condemned (Luke xiii. 5), whereby we understand
how profitable and necessary a medicine penance is,
without the which sins be not remitted to them that
have the use of their understanding and reason. The
serpent in Paradise moved Eve to sin, penance loosed

her again, and from thence came good and evil to man. Our father Adam was expulsed out of Paradise for sin, and we and all others that be his children be called thither again by penance. For penance openeth that which sin hath shut, and the merciful goodness of God doth call us thither again, from whence His anger hath cast us out. What a great power and virtue hath this virtue of penance, which by the mercy of God remitteth sin, openeth Paradise, healeth the contrite man, maketh glad the heavy, revoketh a man from destruction, restoreth him to his former good state, reneweth his old honour, repaireth all the decays of virtue, maketh him acceptable and bold with God, and doth purchase of God more plenty of grace than he had before.

This virtue is like a fruitful field, the fruit whereof when an hungry sinner doth eat, he is well refreshed in his soul, groweth in credit and trust with God, and after remission of his sins, waxeth fat in good life, and speaketh to God after this manner:—Lord, before Thee is all my desire, and the mourning of my heart is not hid from Thee; the fear of sin vexeth me, the weight of my conscience oppresseth me, in myself I have no hope to live, nor boldness to die, at Thy judgments I tremble, and fear the pains prepared for the wicked spirits. Hear me, I beseech Thee, whilst time is, and pardon that I fear before I go, and shall be no more (Ps. xxxvii.) To such a penitent heart is remission given and life granted.

And for better knowledge of penance, it is to be considered that the doing of penance is three ways spoken of in Holy Scripture: one is for all kind of sin before baptism. For he that is judge and ruler of his own will, when he cometh to baptism, he cannot begin a new life, except he take repentance for his old, and he must have hope and love to be made that he was not, and hate that he was. From this kind of penance before baptism only young children be free, which as yet cannot use their free will, and for their consecration and remission of original sin, the faith of the Church, which is professed by the godfathers and mothers as representing the Church, doth profit and suffice, and so by the sacrament of faith which is baptism, they are made faithful and members of Christ's mystical Body. Of this penance speaketh S. Peter, saying thus, "Do you penance, and let every one of you be baptized in the name of our Lord Jesus Christ, for the remission of your sins" (Acts ii. 38).

The second way of doing penance is, for venial sin after baptism, and is daily done, or ought to be done, throughout a man's whole life, so long as we be in this weak, frail, mortal, and sinful flesh. For which cause we knock upon our breasts, saying, "Forgive us our trespasses, as we forgive them that trespass against us." For we require not to have those sins forgiven us, which we be sure were forgiven in baptism before, but those which, through our frailty and sensuality, by little and little, continually creep upon us, which being many, if they were all gathered together against us, and we contemned to avoid * them, in time they would so grieve and oppress us as one mortal sin. For what difference is it to have a man's

* *i.e.* To cast them out.

ship drowned at once with one great surge and wave of the sea, or to suffer the water to enter into small holes by little and little till the ship, by contemning to draw the pump, be full, and so sink, and be drowned ? For the which cause we fast, do alms, and pray, wherein when we say, " Forgive us as we forgive " (Matt. vi. 12), we declare that we have something to be forgiven ; by which words we humble our souls, and cease not after a certain manner to do daily penance.

The third way of doing penance is, for such deadly sins after baptism as be prohibited by God's ten commandments, of which the Apostle saith, " All they that do such shall not possess the kingdom of heaven " (Gal. v. 21). And this penance ought to be more grievous and painful, because the fault is great, causing a deadly wound in our souls, as adultery, murder, or sacrilege. But although the wound be great, grievous, and deadly, yet Almighty God, as a good Physician, after the suggestion of sin by the devil, the delectation of the flesh, the consent of our mind and freewill, and also the doing of the sin in deed, as though we had lain in grave stinking four days, as Lazarus did, doth not so leave us, but crieth " Lazari veni foras," Come forth, O Lazarus (John xi. 43), and by-and-by misery gave place to mercy, death to life : Lazarus cometh forth, and is bounden as men be in confession of their sins, doing penance. Of this speaketh S. Paul to the Corinthians (2 Cor. xii. 21), saying, I am afraid lest, when I shall come again, God do humble and afflict me among you, and lest I lament and mourn for many of them that have sinned before, and have not done penance for their fornication and unclean life they have used.

This last kind of penance is that whereof we specially treat upon at this time, and is called by the holy father the second table or board after baptism; for all sinners being, as it were, drowned in the flood of sin by reason of original sin, that from Adam overfloweth all the world, or else by their own actual sin, which they have done in their own persons beside, may be saved and escaped out of this flood if they will take hold of the first board which is baptism. But after the sacrament of baptism, if they fall into the waters again by deadly sin, there is no remedy to be saved from drowning and damnation; but only penance, which is the second board that God hath ordained to save us by; so that whosoever taketh hold of it unfeignedly during the time of this natural life, no doubt of it, it will, by God's merciful grace, bring him to the haven of salvation, were his sins never so great and heinous, whereby we may understand how necessary this is, as being the only remedy now left us to restore us to the favour of God, which by sin we had lost before.

Wherefore I do exhort every man and woman in the name of our Lord Jesus Christ, as they tender the health and salvation of their souls, to be diligent and careful to use this special remedy ordained of God for remission of sin, neither contemning His justice, nor despairing of His mercy, which two be the lets * of true penance, and enemies to the grace of God in remission of sin (Ps. vii). For God is a just, mighty,

i.e., Hindrances.

and patient Judge, for hearing and forgiving the penitent sinner, judging and condemning the obstinate sinner. As the consideration of His mercy should speedily provoke us to amendment, so the fear of His just judgment should utterly take away all delays. We be in danger on both sides, both by too much hoping and by despairing. He is deceived by hoping that saith, God is good and merciful, promising pardon whensoever we convert, therefore I will do that which pleaseth me, I will give the bridle to my lusts, and satisfy the desires of my mind. On the contrary side, he is deceived by desperation, that falleth into grievous sins, and, thinking them not able or worthy to be forgiven, saith to himself, I shall be damned, therefore I will do that which pleaseth me. The one is in danger by presuming of God's mercy, promising to himself long life ; the other is in danger by indiscreet fear of God's justice, and horror of his great and manifold sins. But every Christian man and woman ought to go circumspectly in the midst, and beware for falling on either side, remembering that the Scripture saith to him that is in danger by too much hope, " Be not slack to turn and convert to God, nor do not defer from day to day, for God's anger will come suddenly, and in the day of vengeance He will destroy thee " (Ecclus. v. 8, 9). And to him that is in danger by despair, God saith, " In whatsoever day a sinner shall be converted, I shall forget all his iniquities " (Ezek. xviii. 21, 22). For him that despaireth God hath set open the haven of forgiveness, to him that

L

vainly hopeth and delayeth his conversion, He hath made the day of death uncertain.

Thus taking heed to ourselves, not abusing God's mercy by delaying our amendment, nor mistrusting His goodness, for fear of His judgment, but speedily, while time is now offered unto us, embracing this necessary and present remedy of fruitful and true penance, we shall be reconciled to Almighty God, and be partakers of His heavenly kingdom, through Jesus Christ our Lord, to Whom with the Father and the Holy Ghost be all glory for evermore. Amen.

THE FIFTEENTH SERMON.

AGAINST DESPERATION.

EVERY sinner (good people) that intendeth to obtain of God by the merits of Christ's Passion remission of his sins, must expel and put out of his mind all manner of despair, and all fear and doubt that should or might move him to think that he shall have no mercy and forgiveness at God's hand, what sins soever he hath done, be they never so many.

Two things there be that bring a sinner in despair. One is, if he think that his sins be so great that God cannot forgive him ; and this is very false and against God's omnipotence, Who hath power and is able to do what He will. Another is, if he think that Almighty God will not forgive his sins; and this is also false, and against the righteousness and goodness of Almighty God, Who hath promised to forgive the penitent sinner always his offences (Ezek. xviii. 21), and if we confess our sins (Ezek. xxxiii. 14, 15), God is faithful and just to remit unto us our sins, and to make us clean from all kind of iniquity (1 John i. 9). And in witness of this our Saviour Christ hath ordained the Holy Sacrament of Penance, that is to say, the sacramental absolution (John xx. 23), which the priest giveth unto the penitent person truly con-

fessing his sins, which absolution is allowed and confirmed in heaven, and the penitent restored to the
state of salvation ; so that to mistrust or fear that
God cannot or will not forgive the penitent sinner his
sins, is deadly sin in itself, blasphemy to Almighty
God, and damnation to the party with Cain and others
that did despair (Gen. iv. 13, &c.)

There is another kind of despair of mercy and
salvation, which they have that intend or do kill
themselves, which they take, not in remembrance of
the multitude or greatness of their sins, but for the
heaviness and thought of the world, as the wise man :
—" Multos occidit tristicia, et non est utilitas in ea."
Sadness and thought hath killed many, and there
is no profit in it (Ecclus. xxx. 25), and S. Paul
saith, " The sorrow of the world worketh death "
(2 Cor. vii. 10). These men come to this despair
thus :—

First, they take sorrow and thought for such things
as have chanced against their minds, and then they
do not put that thought away, but rather set it
wondrous deep and fast in their hearts, and let it
continue there still, and so it groweth, till it be so
great and so painful unto them, that they be weary
of their lives and would fain be dead. And because
they cannot die by sickness so shortly as they would,
nor by course of nature, therefore they determine
to kill themselves, and so they despair to have
everlasting life in heaven, or else think not of it, and
also do not believe that they shall have damnation in
hell, but think that if they were once dead, that then
they should have no more sorrow nor pain in their

mind. And so upon that ungracious and false belief, they kill themselves one way or other, and then be their souls damned in hell, there with Achitophel (2 Kings xvii. 23), and Judas (Matt. xxvii. 5), and other of that sort, in more vexation and pain in their minds than all the wits in the world can devise.

The remedy against both these kinds of despair, is to be well and thoroughly persuaded of hell, and the infinite greatness of the pains that be there, and how they never have end, but endure for evermore; and in the beginning to avoid and put out of mind all thought and heaviness for loss of worldly goods, or for any mischance, or for any rebuke or shame deserved by them, or otherwise, which they may do by opening the cause of their sorrow to some one discreet person or more. For the longer the cause is kept secret, the more grief and pain it worketh, and shall be the harder to put away.

Therefore let every man and woman understand this, that the devil doth move a man to despair of obtaining, for this end, that he might cut off all hope of goodness, which is the anchor of our health, the foundation of our life, the guide of our journey, whereby we return again to Almighty God. For the Apostle saith, "By hope we are made safe, and that hope which is seen, is no hope" (Rom. viii. 24). It is hope, therefore, wherein our salvation consisteth, which hope as a chain cast down from heaven, draweth our souls that hold fast by it up to heaven, and delivering them from earthly griefs, maketh them to forget and contemn this present life. But if a man, having his mind wholly set and fixed upon sin and worldly cares, let slip out of his hand the anchor of hope, he must needs fall into the pit, and in the bottom of all evils be drowned and slain, which, when our enemy perceiveth, and seeth us abhor the multitude of our sins, and to be afraid with the biting of our guilty conscience, straightway he cometh near, and doth suggest the thoughts of despair, making us heavier than any sand or lead, which thoughts, if we receive and agree upon, by-and-by letting go the hold of our salvation, we must needs by the very weight of them be drowned in the bottom of all mischief, contemning the commandments of a meek and good Lord, obeying the will of a cruel and fierce tyrant and enemy to our salvation.

For to conversion and penance desperation is utter enemy; which if it once rest and dwell in a man's mind, have he never so earnest an intent and fervent desire to be saved, yet the same desperation shall let his purpose and stop the ways and passages to the salvation of his soul. If the way penance be once stopped, then is the door that leadeth to salvation shut also. And how can he that is out of the way, and to whom the door is shut, do any good work, when as he can find no entry, entry to goodness being let by desperation ? For this cause the devil, by all means he can, goeth about to plant such thoughts in our hearts. For when desperation has carried us far from the way of truth, then hath the devil no more contention against us. Against whom should he fight when no man withstandeth? But if the man can loose this band, by-and-by his strength cometh again, and taketh delight to renew his battle afresh. For he shall perceive how he chaseth away the devil, whom he fled before, and shall have a pleasure to pursue his old persecutor. And if perchance his foot slip and he fall (as oftentimes the condition of war is), he may not by-and-by despair for shame of a fall, but he must remember that this is the law of fighting, not never to fall, but never to yield, for men do not call him overcome that oft falleth, but him that at last yieldeth. Likewise he that is overcome by the thoughts of desperation, how can he recover his strength, or withstand his enemy, seeing he runneth away and will not turn back to fight again? I would not that ye should think that I speak only of those that were a little blotted with a few small spots of sin ; but I speak of him that hath given place to all kind of sin, that for the outrageousness of his wicked living hath excluded himself from the kingdom of heaven, and not of infidels, but of Christian men, and such as have before times pleased God highly, but afterwards have fallen to adultery and other filthy living, such (as the Apostle saith), is shame to speak of. These men, I say, ought not to despair of salvation, although they had lain wallowing in such like filthiness even to their extreme age. What the reason of this saying is, ye shall hear.

If God's anger were a passible affection,* we might well say that the flame of it could not be quenched, which was kindled with so many and great offences. But when the truth of God's Word doth define the nature of God to be impassible, we must

* *i.e.,* Were of the nature of a human passion.—ED.

understand that now, although God doth punish and afflict us, yet He doth it not with passible anger, but with most unspeakable clemency, with the affection of him that healeth, and not of him that punisheth, and for that cause He very gladly receiveth the penitent, seeing that God doth not punish for Himself's sake (as I said before), as it were avenging His own quarrel and injury against the sinner (for God's nature receiveth no such passion into itself), but He doth all for our profit. For our profit and correction He doth punish, not to revenge Himself, but to amend us. He that abideth still in the hardness of his heart, is like to a man that turneth his eyes from the light, which doth no harm to the light, but bringeth himself into darkness. Even so he that through an impatient heart thinketh to contemn the power of God, trusteth in God nothing, but secludeth himself from all health and salvation.

If a physician suffer a little injury of his patient vexed with a frenzy, or distempered in his brain, yet is he not grieved with the same, nor yet angry, but doth all things that his art of physic requireth, although his patient seemeth to be grieved with his medicines, which grief is not avenging of the physician's injury, but a curing of the patient's malady. And if the sick man begin a little to amend in his health, ye shall see by-and-by the physician rejoice, and with more gladness do the rest of his cure, not remembering the injury he suffered before, but procuring the patient's health more and more. How much more Almighty God, when we fall into extreme madness of the soul, is not moved with the affection

of vengeance for the offences we have done against
Him, but is desirous to heal the old rotten sores of sin
that are corrupted within us, for the which He saith
and doth all things, as only tendering our health, not
delighted with our pain. Such is the goodness of God
towards man, He never refuseth penance if it be
simply and purely offered unto Him. Although a
man were come to the height of sin, and yet from
thence would return again to the way of virtue, He
receiveth him, He most fatherly embraceth him to his
first state again, and also (which is greater and more
excellent than all this) although a man could not
fulfil all the order of satisfaction, yet He refuseth not
his penance how small, how short, soever it be done,
but accepteth the same, and suffereth him not to lose
the reward of his conversion, be it never so little.

This seemeth Isaias to shew where he speaketh
such like of the people of the Jews: "For his sin I
have a little made him sad, and have smitten him,
and have turned my face from him, and he is sad and
walketh an heavy man, and I have healed him, and
have comforted him" (Isa. lvii. 17, 18). But the
wicked King Achab giveth us a more evident testimony, which through his wife's wickedness obtained
the prey of his own covetousness, but afterward, being
troubled with the great enormity of his own sin, did
repent, and putting on hair and sackcloth wept for his
offence, and provoked so the mercy of God towards
him that He pardoned him of all his sins. For thus
said God: And God said to Elias, "Hast thou not
seen the contrition of Achab before me? and because
he hath wept in my sight, I will not bring in these

plagues in his days" (3 Kings xxi. 29). Manasses also that passed all other tyrants in cruelty of wickedness, that filled God's temples with idols, that overthrew the service of God in true religion and the observation of the law, this man, I say, exceeding all men in abomination of sin, yet, because he repented he was afterward numbered among the friends of God (2 Parali. xxxiii. 13 and *ante*). And therefore, if either this man, or the other we spake of before, considering the greatness of their sins, had despaired to come to God's favour again by conversion and penance, they had lost all these benefits that chanced to them by their amendment. But they, casting their eyes upon God's unspeakable mercy, and the deepness of His infinite goodness, loosed the devilish chains of desperation from their necks, and lifting up themselves, were converted to the way of virtue.

Thus much have we spoken of the examples of holy men. Hear now how we are provoked of God to conversion by the words of the prophets. Even this day (saith David) if ye hear His voice, do not harden your hearts as in the day of provocation in the wilderness (Ps. xciii. 8, 9). In that he saith this day, he meaneth all the time of our life till we come (if it so chance) even to the extreme age; for penance is not weighed by length of time, but by pureness of·affection. Have we not read how the Levites washed away their most grievous sin in the wilderness, not in a great long continuance of time, but in a little short hour of one day? The thief also that hung upon the cross, needed no long space to enter into Paradise (Luke xxiii. 43), but so much

space sufficed as would serve for the speaking of a
few words; so that in a little moment of time, obtaining remission of the sins of his whole life, he did enter
into Paradise before any of Christ's Holy Apostles.
What shall we say of martyrs? Have we not seen
them oftentimes in one day, yea, sometimes within
the space of an hour receive the crowns of eternal
reward? We must therefore begin only, and set
upon it with a manly courage. And first, let us be
moved and angry with that harlot, our own lust, that
deceived us, and then let us turn our whole affection
and love to the exercise of virtue. For that is it that
God willeth and requireth of us. He seeketh not
that length of time, but specially looketh to this if
our conversion be true and pure. For which cause we
often see that many which began last, are by their
faithful endeavours made foremost. It is not so evil
to take a fall, as it is to lie still after the fall and not
to rise again, and with a certain pleasure and
determination of mind to *wallow* * still in sin, and at
last to cloak and cover his naughty purpose of sinning still under the words of desperation. Against
whom the prophet crieth out with a certain indignation, saying, Doth not he that falleth rise again? or,
Is not he that turneth backwards converted again?
(Jer. viii. 4). If thou say, the state of our question
is, whether any faithful and Christian man, if he fall,
may be restored again? to this question I answer,
In this same that we say he fell, we grant that once
he stood before he fell. No man saith that he is
fallen, that ever did lie and never stood. Yet let us

---

* Walter, in original.—ED.

bring forth Holy Scripture concerning this matter, if any thing be spoken either in parables or in plain sentences. What other thing, think you, is meant by the sheep which, going astray from the other ninety and nine, was afterwards sought and brought home upon the shoulders of the shepherd ? (Luke xv. 4–6). Doth it not plainly declare both the fall and the restitution of a Christian man, for that sheep ´ and the other ninety and nine were all of one flock and under one pastor ?

It fed upon the same pasture, drank the same water, and was lodged within the same fold that the other were, but it wandered a great way, it strayed far through the hills and hard rocks and many crooked ways of error, yet the Good Shepherd did not leave it nor suffered it to perish, but seeketh it, and bringeth it home again, not compelling it by pricks and beating, but bearing it upon His own shoulders.

And not only this parable doth shew unto us the commodity of returning, but also that other of the prodigal and riotous son. And that was a son, and not a stranger, and brother-german to him that never went from his father. He was a son which is reported to have gone to the furthest borders of all sin, for he went into a far country, far from God, that was the rich man, and being a nobleman born was made worse than a bondman or slave ; but yet returning home and repenting him, was received into his former state, and restored to his former glory (Luke xv.) But if he had despaired, and considering those miseries that chanced unto him, had been ashamed

to return to his father, and had bidden still in the
far strange country, he should never have attained
these things that he hath, but by penury and famine
should have suffered most miserable and unhappy
death. You see now how great hope there is of conversion by penance. The prodigal son received his
former state of glory by penance, which his elder
brother kept still by perseverance.

Therefore, dearly beloved, having these examples
of penance, let us not continue in evil nor despair to
be reconciled, but let us come again to our Father,
and draw near to Almighty God. Believe me, He
will never turn His face from him that turneth to
Him, if we do not make ourselves strangers to God.
For God Himself saith, "I am God that is near
hand, and not God afar off" (Jer. xxiii. 23). And
again, by another prophet, "Your sins," saith he,
"make distance between you and me" (Isa. lix. 2).
If we, therefore, take away this wall, that is to say,
our sins that separate us from God, there is nothing
that can let* us to be joined to God. Will you that
I show you these things not only spoken in parables
but fulfilled in deeds? There was a certain man
among the Corinthians, as it seemed of no small consideration. This man had committed such a sin, as
is not wont to be done among the heathen, and he
was one of the number of the faithful and familiars
with Christ. What then? Did S. Paul cut him
from the number of them that be in hope of salvation? Nay, rather when he had sufficiently rebuked
the Corinthians for him, willing again to declare that

* *i.e.*, Hinder.

there is no wound, no disease, which giveth not place and is not healed by the plaster of penance, he commandeth him to be delivered to Satan to the destruction of the flesh, that his spirit may be saved in the day of our Lord Jesus Christ (2 Cor. v. 5). Yet he commanded this before he knew anything of his penance. But when he had done penance, he saith, let this correction and rebuke suffice, which was given to him of many. And he added more, I beseech you conform your charity towards him, lest Satan have him in full possession, for we be not ignorant of his crafty subtleness (2 Cor. ii. 7-11).

Also the whole Church of the Galatians, after that it believed in Christ, and had received the Holy Ghost, so that in spirit it did many virtues and miracles, and had suffered much persecution for the faith of Christ, after all this (I say) it fell from the faith, and was restored again by the good exhortations of the Apostle. And that thou mayest know that by the Holy Ghost they did miracles, hear how the Apostle saith : Who then gave you the Spirit, and wrought these miracles among you ? was it of the works of the law, or of the hearing of faith ? (Gal. iii. 2) ; and again, that they did suffer much after that they had received the faith he declareth in this, where he saith, " Have ye suffered so great affliction in vain, if it be in vain ? " After they had walked and profited thus much in the faith, they did commit such a sin that was able to alienate them clean from Christ, whereof the Apostle spake, " Behold I, Paul, say unto you, if you use circumcision, Christ will profit you nothing " (Gal. v. 2), and again,

"You that be justified by the law be fallen from grace" (Gal. v. 4). Yet after these decays of faith, after so great falls, he calleth them back again, and with motherly affection doth cherish them, saying, "My dear little children whom I labour to bring forth again as a mother doth of her child unborn, whilst that Christ be formed in you" (Gal. iv. 19).

What other thing is taught by these, but that it is possible that Christ may be formed and dwell in him again by penance, that hath fallen from Christ by extremity of sin before. Almighty God willeth not the death of a sinner, but that he convert and live (Ezek. xviii. 32). Let us therefore be converted, and let us yield ourselves to the accomplishing of God's will. For so long as we be in this life, how great sins soever we commit, it is possible to wash them all away by penance, but when we shall be taken out of this world, there although we repent us, for we shall repent very much, yet we shall have no profit of our repentance. And although there be gnashing of teeth, howling and weeping, although we pray and cry out with innumerable obsecrations, no man will hear us, no man will succour us, no, not so much as with his finger's end pour a little water upon our tongue that burneth in the flame, but we shall hear that which the rich man heard of Abraham, that a great vast distance is put between us and you, so that none from thence may come hither, nor from us to you (Luke xvi. 26). Let us, therefore, good brethren, cast up our eyes to our Lord Jesu Christ, and let us like good and profitable servants seek Him, and not despair so long as we enjoy this life, by penance to obtain pardon for our sins; only in hell, as I said, the medicines of penance will profit nothing; but in this life, although it be in the last crooked age and in the extremity of sin, yet, believe me, it will cure us and bring us to perfect health. For this cause the devil moveth and doth all that he can to bring desperation into our minds. He knoweth full well that if a man do penance but a little space, be it never so short, yet his conversion shall not be unfruitful. Only let us now begin to do better. Ever the beginning seemeth hardest. At the first step the way of virtue seemeth to be hard, and not able to be come unto. For so is the nature of all things; all labour seemeth painful so long as it is weighed only in the consideration of a man's mind. But when we come to the experience of the thing, and begin to go through a little of the labour, there is all the fear of the grief driven clean away. The success of the work bringeth sweetness, and the increase of virtue new repaired bringeth gladness to our minds, and by-and-by maketh us stronger, when the hope of salvation beginneth to seem nigh at hand. For that cause the devil took Judas out of this life, lest knowing there was a way to turn to salvation, he might by penance reform his fall. Therefore let us now enter the journey of life, let us return to the heavenly city, wherein we be elected and appointed as free citizens. The gates of this city desperation doth shut, but hope shall open them, and sure confidence shall make the entry large and broad. When the soul beginneth to despair of salvation, it regardeth not thereafter what

sort, or into what vice it cast itself, it feareth to do or
to speak nothing that may be contrary to her salvation. And as we see often in them that be mad,
when they have once lost the stay of their right mind,
then they fear nothing, but are bold to speak and do
whatsoever they list; though they should fall into the
fire, or into a deep pit, they stick not nor pull not
back their foot; even so they that be taken with desperation, are made intolerable, and run through the
ways of iniquity, neither shame nor fear letting them,
neither present misery doth stop them, nor pain to
come doth affray them, only death, which they cannot avoid, endeth the execution of their malice.
Wherefore I most entirely beseech you (if there be
any here that despair or be in doubt to attain mercy
and forgiveness) to take again the sweet yoke of our
Saviour Jesus Christ and His light burden, and not
to suffer so great a treasure of God's former gifts and
graces utterly to perish. It will perish if we continue in sin, provoking God more and more with our
naughty deeds. Let us arise, therefore, now without
delay, and believe me, our adversary will fly away;
our boldness shall make him afraid; the more fierce
we be, the more fearful * will he be; and God will be
present, and both diminish the conscience of our sins
and undermine his might and strength. So shall we
faithfully serve Him here, and reign with Him eternally in the next world through Christ our Lord, to
Whom be all glory for ever. Amen.

* *i.e.,* Timid.

M

THE SIXTEENTH SERMON.

AGAINST PRESUMPTION OF MERCY.

LIKE as penance is the mother of mercy, and a virtue most agreeable to the will of God, even so (good people) an impenitent heart is an enemy of mercy, and most repugnant to the fountain of all goodness, and such a vice as only can never attain forgiveness at God's hand, Who daily through His unspeakable mercy provoketh sinners to penance, Whom obstinate sinners, delaying their conversion, do provoke to anger. Many there be that purpose to continue still in their sins, upon hope of remission and forgiveness at the last end, or in their old age, abusing God's goodness, and contemning His justice. These men go from evil to worse, and abuse the precious treasure of time, by their continuance in sin, which God granteth to man as a special remedy against sin.

From this most detestable vice, the consideration of God's inestimable and infinite benefits should withdraw us, lest our unkindness do appear, which stoppeth the ways of grace, and suffereth remission to have no entry into our souls.

God the Father hath so loved us, that to redeem

us, His servants, He hath not spared His only-begotten Son (John iii. 16). God the Son hath so loved us, that to make us His servants, He hath redeemed us not with corruptible gold or silver, but with His own precious blood, which He hath shed forth abundantly (1 Peter i. 18, 19). They both have sent and given unto us their Holy Spirit, God the Holy Ghost, Who hath endued us with heavenly and marvellous gifts, by Whom we have strength of good life, light of true knowledge, and assurance that we shall inherit the kingdom of heaven if we convert from sin and continue in grace, which conversion God most patiently abideth, and most fatherly provoketh by many and sundry ways, Whose conception maketh clean ours, Whose life instructeth ours, Whose death destroyeth ours, Whose resurrection is cause and example of ours, Whose ascension prepareth ours, Whose Spirit helpeth our infirmity. What obdurate unkindness is this, not to recognise these so great benefits, but the more He heapeth precious gifts upon us, the more to displease Him, to disobey Him, and to increase our own damnation? The better He is to us, the worse to be to ourselves, and so spitefully to abuse His mercy, by making it (which of itself is the cause of all our wealth and salvation) to be, by our prolonging, the cause of our sin and the continuance of the same?

Knowing that the time of this frail and mortal life is but short (Job xiv. 5), and as it were a vapour or smoke appearing for a time (James iv. 15), and shortly vanishing away, and that death tarrieth not (Ecclus. xvi. 12), nor man knoweth not his end; but as fishes be taken with the hook, and as birds be taken with the net, even so men be taken in the evil time when it cometh upon them (Ecclus. ix. 12); so that the considering of the certainty of death which no man can escape, and the uncertainty of the time of death, which God hath made uncertain to man, lest he should live worse under hope of forgiveness, should be a great cause to move every man to make haste to amend his sinful life. For like as in the firmament a star doth soon rise and suddenly setteth again, and as a sparkle of fire is soon quenched and put out, even so endeth a man's life when he liveth in this world most pleasantly, and thinketh he shall live many years, and disposeth things to be done by long times, and suddenly is he caught by death, and at unawares the soul taken from the body.

Therefore, I pray you consider every man with himself, where those men be now that not long ago were so wholly set upon the world, and given to satisfy the pleasures of their flesh and private wills. Nothing remaineth of them here but ashes and worms. Mark diligently what they be, and what they have been. They were men as thou art, they did eat, drink, laugh, and led their lives in pleasures, and went to hell in a moment of time (Job xxi. 13); here their flesh is committed to the worms, and their souls to the fire, until they both be knit together again, so to be joined in eternal pain. What profited them their vainglory, their short mirth, their authority of the world, their pleasure of the flesh, their false riches, their great family, and their naughty desires? Of so great gladness what heaviness doth ensue; out of that great wealth and pleasures they fell into great misery and torments. Whatsoever happened to them, the same may happen to thee, being a man as they were. For thou art made of earth, and dost issue of earth, and shall return into earth when thy last day shall come, which cometh suddenly, and perchance shall be to-morrow. It is certain that thou shalt die, but uncertain when, how, or where. Wherefore, seeing death doth always look for thee, if thou be a wise man, see that thou look always for it. The justice of God cannot judge otherwise but as our works deserve. For he that loveth the world more than God, gluttony more than abstinence, lechery more than chastity, shall follow the devil, and go with him into eternal fire and pain. Which pains every wise man will fear and so avoid them, lest by contemning of them he fall suddenly into them.

Therefore, remember the horrible throne of God's judgment, which is compassed about with a burning flood of fiery flame, where is weeping and gnashing of teeth, where is outward darkness and the worm of conscience that never dieth, and the fire that never is quenched. For the fire here consumeth and wasteth all things it receiveth; the fire there, whatsoever it receiveth once, it always tormenteth and reserveth it in continual pain, and is therefore called a fire unquenchable, not only for that it is never quenched itself, but also that it never destroyeth and bringeth to nought those it once receiveth. The Scripture saith, that sinners put on and are clad with incorruption (1 Cor. xv. 53), that is to say, not to the honour of life, but to the eternity of pain. The

violence of this pain and the power of this fire no
tongue can express ; for in corruptible things there
is nothing like that can be compared to things incorruptible, whether it be good or evil. Yet let us
imagine at least some image of that fire and pain.
Remember, when a man is inflamed with the vehement
heat of a burning ague, what anguish, what torment
is both in the body and soul.* Now of this temporal
pain, measure how great the pains be which that
eternal fire doth cause, which the fiery flood that
runneth before the horrible judgment-seat of Christ
doth overflow with flaming waves. What shall we
do there ? What may we answer ? There - shall
nothing be there but gnashing of teeth, but howling
and weeping and late repentance, where help shall
cease, and pains increase on every side, nor there is
no comfort anywhere, no man [shall come to our
sight, but only the ministers of pains, and the ugly
faces of the tormentors. And that which is most
grievous of all, there shall be no comfort of the
air and light ; for round about the places of pains
shall be outward darkness, and that the flaming fire,
which as it hath the nature not to consume and
destroy, so it hath not to give light, but it is a dark
fire and a black flame to them that remain therein.
What horrible trembling, what resolution,† and as it
were a melting of his body and bowels, what rending

---

* Dr Watson had a severe attack of ague in the beginning of
1559. Jewel wrote to Peter Martyr on January 26 :—" It is reported
of Watson, Bishop of Lincoln, that he is dead " (Zurich Letters, 1.
7).—ED.

† *i.e.,* Breaking up.—ED.

of his flesh and members, what and how great affliction is in all senses, no speech can express. There be divers and sundry fashions of pains, and in every man and woman, according to the number and greatness of sins, are multiplied the pains.

And if thou would say, how can a body suffice to endure so great pains which knoweth no end of time, consider what chanceth sometimes in this life, and of a little, conjecture the great. How sometimes we see some wasted with a long disease, and yet can find no end of their wretched and hateful life. But although the body is sometime dissolved by death, yet the soul is not consumed. Whereupon it followeth, that when the body likewise shall receive immortality, neither then the soul nor the body can with any pain be utterly destroyed. For in this present life it cannot chance that the pain of the body should be both vehement and perpetual, but the one giveth place to the other, because the frailty of the body cannot sustain both. But when both are made incorruptible, then may the pain rage at will and find no end. Let us not think that the extremity of our torment shall make an end of our sorrow, but as we said, our sins shall kindle our pain, and incorruption of body and soul shall without end continue the same.

And if it were so, that equal time and all one space were appointed for the pleasure here and for the pain there, should there be any man so foolish and so mad that would choose for one day of pleasure to suffer one day of pain, when as the sorrow of one hour and every torment of the body is wont to make us forget all time passed in pleasure before?

But now, whereas it is possible in a short time, if we convert to God, to escape all these torments of pains, and to attain eternal joy, why do we linger? Why do we tarry, and do not use the largeness and free gift of God? The unspeakable and infinite goodness of God hath already provided, not to extend the time of our labours and conflicts, nor to make it long or eternal, but short, and, as I might say, a moment of an hour.

This is even the life present, if it be compared to the life eternal. The goodness of God hath therefore provided that in this little short life should be our conflicts and labours, and in that which is eternal should be the crown and reward of our merits, that our labour should soon be ended, and the reward of our merits should endure for ever. But this, like as it rejoiceth them that, through patience of labour, receive the crown, so it tormenteth and afflicteth them in time to come that see themselves for a short time of pleasure to have lost eternal glory, and to have gotten perpetual misery. And lest we come into this vexation of mind, let us now awake while we have time. Lo! now is the time acceptable, now is the day of repentance (2 Cor. vi. 2). But if we neglect our life, there remaineth for us not only those evils which we shall suffer in hell, but an evil more grievous than all that. To be excluded from all goodness, and to be deprived of such joys as be ordained for saints, doth engender such a grief, such a sorrow, that if no other did otherwise vex us, that alone might suffice. The lack of the glory we had in our power to enjoy passeth all the torments that be in hell. For when the whole universal world shall come to judgment to be judged of that Judge that needeth no witness, that seeketh no proofs, that admitteth no orators, but, all these set apart, He Himself discovereth and sheweth abroad both deeds, words, and thoughts, and everything, as it were painted in certain tables, He layeth open before the eyes of them that did them and of them that stand by, how shall not every creature then shake and stand in great fear? And if then the flood of fire did not overflow the world, nor the terrible angels assist God, and if there were no face and horrible sight of torments, but only this, that if men were called forth before the King, and some should be accounted worthy praise and honour, and others with shame, rebuke, and confusion abjected out of sight; if men should only suffer this kind of punishment, would not it in a manner exceed all the pains of hell, that other men receiving rewards of the King, they had deserved shameful repulse with confusion? How great pain this is, although my words cannot fully teach it now, yet when it shall come to experience of the matter in deed, then we shall plainly know it, because we shall painfully feel it.

Add also to all these, the sorrows of the torments, and not only the confusion and shameful reproach, but also put before thine eyes the way that men be drawn to the fire and pains; think upon the cruel and horrible ministers of the pains that throw down headlong sinners into all kinds of torments, and that (too) the same time that other (which lived well) are borne up by the most clear and pleasant angels, before the high seat of the eternal King, and are rewarded with crowns of glory and immortal reward. It is no marvel if the infidels, and they that believe not the general judgment and the resurrection to come, care not how they live, and have no compunction of heart nor remorse of their sins; but for us that see things to come surer than things present, to live so wretchedly and to take no remembrance of the judgment to come, but to fall into utter contempt of it, it is extreme madness, and one of the greatest sins of all, when we that believe, frame our lives like unto them that believe not.

To fall into sin is a point of man's infirmity, but to remain in sin still is a point of the devil's obstinacy. Thus let us put before our eyes the last day, and make haste to amend our lives till* we have time. For He that hath promised pardon unto us whensoever we convert, doth not promise unto us long life and to live while† to-morrow. Watch therefore (saith our Saviour Christ) because ye know not the day nor the hour (Matt. xxv. 13). Ever ought we to be afraid of the last day which we cannot foresee. We ought therefore to seek our Lord God whilst He may be found, and not to lie sleeping in sin as the five foolish virgins did, till the Spouse come and the door be shut. For then shall the door be shut to them that too late and unfruitfully shall lament, which now standeth open to all that truly and betimes will be penitent. There shall be repentance then, but not fruitful; for then shall he find no pardon that now wilfully loseth the time of pardon. If we then pray

---

* *i.e.,* While.   † *i.e.,* Until.

with the foolish virgins, Lord, Lord, open the door to us, we shall hear Him say again, I know you not. For there is no man can obtain that which he asketh which here would not fulfil that which God commanded. He that will be out of all doubt, and avoid the danger of eternal death, let him do true penance whilst he is in health, and hath space and occasion of God offered to do it, and then may he be sure, because he hath done penance in that time when he might have sinned more. But if he will then take repentance when he can sin no more, then sin doth forsake him, and he not it, and then it is no marvel though God condemn him in his death, that ever before condemned God in his life.

It is easy for a sinner at the beginning to arise, but if he delay his conversion, the longer he remaineth in sin, the harder it will be for him to arise. The longer the devil possesseth a man, with the more difficulty will he let him go. David smote Goliath in the forehead, and so killed him (1 Kings xvii. 49). Whereby we be taught that the devil is soon killed if we smite him in the forehead, that is to say, at his first entry into us by sin and in the beginning of our life. If by heaping one sin upon another we accustom ourselves to the same naughty living, in process of time sin will wax strong in us and prevail over us, and make us as bondsmen and slaves unto it, and to follow that way whithersoever the devil shall lead or move us. Then shall God's special grace go from us, God's Spirit forsake us, and we be left to ourselves, when one sin shall be a punishment for another. A custom in everything is marvellous violent, specially when it hath bodily pleasure joined with it, first to entice, and then to enforce the soul to sin.

First, a man that is not careful how to live and please God, by negligence and not regarding his deeds, suffereth the fear of God to go away, and then beginneth he curiously to search and love things without himself, as worldly vanities and estimation, whereby inward devotion in the heart decayeth. After that curiosity, he findeth soon that pleaseth his will, and doth practise that is evil and hurtful to his soul. Thus proceeding from vice to vice, he is led by his own lust, not stopped by any shame, leaving that which is lawful and following that which liketh him. In this damnable lust is he bounden by custom, which maketh those vices that he practiseth to be as it were natural to him, and so from custom falleth into contempt of sin, giving lust the bridle, and running headlong whithersoever it carrieth him. This contempt bringeth in extreme malice, and causeth him to be glad when he hath done evil, and to rejoice in all iniquity. This is the pernicious and deadly chain of sin that draweth a man even down to the pit of hell, which cannot be broken when it is once surely linked, except he stop at the beginning and loose the links before they be knit one by one. This chain made Lucifer, an angel of light, to be a devil in hell, which falling from God by presumption, increaseth in malice by obstinacy. This way go all they that be children of the devil, first by presumption, not caring to sin, and then by obstinacy, refusing to rise. But let us consider with ourselves the danger which we be in that have sinned and not done penance.

Now is the axe put to the tree-foot ; if we fall by death, having evil fruit and not good, we shall perish for evermore (Matt. iii. 10). Let us consider the casualty of our frail life, the malice of the devil our ghostly enemy, the nature of sin, wherein the longer we tarry the harder it is to come out, the goodness of God, that so patiently provoketh us to return, the unspeakable joy that by God's grace lieth in our power to attain, the horrible pains of hell, which by our . sin we justly deserve, and let us without any deliberation or counsel, but in all haste, fly out of Egypt, and run out of Sodom, that is to say, out of the kingdom of darkness and sin, by the way of penance, using God's patience to our amendment, not abusing it to His anger and our confusion. For if we say with the wicked servant, My Lord prolongeth His coming, and begin (as he did) to beat the servants and maids, our fellows, by any oppression or injury, and also begin to eat, drink, and be drunken (Luke xii. 45), the Lord of us and of that servant shall come in the day when we look not for Him, and in the hour when we know not, and shall give us our reward amongst infidels and unbelievers. But if we by-and-by, at the hearing of God's Word (as the Ninivites did at the preaching of Jonas), do not harden our hearts, but convert to Him unfeignedly by penance, as they did (Jonas iii.), then may we be sure of His mercy and remission, then shall be great gladness in heaven among the blessed angels of God for our conversion, and we, for well using of His grace, be brought to the fruition of His glory, the which God give us through Christ our Lord, to Whom with the Father and the Holy Ghost be all honour. Amen.

THE SEVENTEENTH SERMON.

OF CONTRITION.

YE have learned (good people) by the words of Holy Scripture, and by the public and uniform preaching of Christ's universal Church, that penance is the only medicine to heal the diseases of our sinful souls, and the only means ordained of Christ to reconcile us again to the favour of Almighty God, Whom by our sin and the transgression of His law we had grievously offended. And to the intent that every man might use this wholesome medicine after the true sort, and in such wise as it may be acceptable to God and profitable to his health and salvation, I shall (by God's grace) declare unto you at this time which be the parts of penance, and principally rest in the declaring of the first part.

Penance which is perfect and fruitful hath three parts, Contrition in heart, Confession in mouth, Humility or satisfaction in work. For seeing this sacrament of Penance is like a judgment, where there is both accusation, witness, and sentence, we may understand that God is the Judge in this court of our conscience, where our thought is our accuser, our conscience witness against us, confirmed with the confession of our own guiltiness, which presupposeth the sorrow we take for our offences, and contrary to the manner of all worldly courts, because we do not stand in defence of our own deeds, but plead guilty before God, Who hath promised to pardon all them that convert and humble themselves before Him, therefore sentence of absolution and free pardon is granted to us by Him that willeth not the death of a sinner, but rather his conversion and life. Which sentence is put in execution when the party guilty submitteth himself voluntarily to the correction and discipline of His merciful judge or of His minister in His name. And by this we may perceive that of this sacrament there be the three parts we spake of before.

Now concerning the first part, it is to be known that contrition is an inward sorrow and repentance which a sinner willingly taketh for his sins for the love of God, Whom he hath so unkindly offended, for the which he fully purposeth to sin no more, but to keep Christ's commandments truly, and to make restitution, and to confess his offences, and to do satisfaction for them, as he shall be enjoined. This is the contrition and repentance that every sinner must take for his sins, and (for better knowledge of the same) let every man mark well every point and part of it.

First, that is an inward sorrow which is taken, not for any natural inclination, as for that sin of itself is dishonest, or bringeth infamy and slander to the doer ; for such sorrow is not true contrition, because it proceedeth not from faith, which is the foundation of penance, which no man can do except God with His grace prevent him, and freely by His mercy convert him ; nor yet only proceedeth from fear of punishment either temporal or eternal ; for that declareth that the sinner doth not nor would not forsake his sin, if he knew that he might continue in the same still without any pain or punishment ; but it proceedeth from the love of God, Whose majesty we have offended,* and therefore are angry with ourselves, and hate that our naughty sin wherewith we did offend, and had rather suffer any pain, be it never so great, than to offend Him again. This is the true sorrow of contrition which is taken for our sins, principally for this respect, that we have offended our most merciful Father, which contrition He will never despise, but receive to mercy all those that with so pure an heart do turn to Him.

Blessed S. Peter, in the repentance that he took for his sin, left an example how we might have true contrition, which is to do as he did ; for he was very sorry, and wept bitterly for his offence alone by himself (Matt. xxvi. 75). And yet he did not so for any bodily hurt that he had for denying of his Master, our Saviour Christ, nor for any loss that he had of worldly goods, nor for any rebuke that was given him for his denial, nor yet for any fear that the Jews would have put him to shame because he had denied his Master, for he knew they would neither hurt him nor blame him, but rather favour him for it. But these

---

* The Bishop does not reject the imperfect contrition which is aroused by the fear of God's justice (though he rightly rejects the mere dread of eternal pain). He alludes with approval to the motive of fear in several places. There will be found nothing in these sermons on penance, when they are read candidly, and one place weighed with another, that is not in harmony with the teaching of the Council of Trent.—ED.

N

things caused him to be sorry and to weep for his sin. First, he did remember and consider the great perfection, holiness, and goodness of his Master, and how He was the very Son of Almighty God, and also he remembered how He had taken him and made him His disciple, and how great favour and singular kindness He had shewed him, for the which he considered how fervently he loved Christ, and how greatly he was bounden so to do. And then he remembered the promise he had made unto Him, and how unfaithful he was in breaking that promise, and unkind in denying and forsaking His Master. And thus the remembering and considering of these things caused S. Peter to be contrite and to weep for his sins, and to wish that he had not denied Christ, and further to will that he would never offend again nor break his promise any more, but ever keep and fulfil justly all that ever his Master, our Saviour Christ, did command him to do. And so S. Peter did. After this manner should we consider our sins, and be sorry and contrite for them.

Surely, if we sinners did call diligently to our remembrances the great goodness of our Saviour Christ ever shewed unto us, as how He redeemed us with His most precious blood and painful death, and hath chosen us to His disciples, and made us inheritors unto heaven, and how merciful and gracious He is always to us, and how holy, just, reasonable, laudable, and how easy a law He hath given us, and then consider further, particularly, and more in special, His goodness, and that He hath done and doth daily for us, we should then see that we ought to love, laud, and honour Him above all creatures, and fulfil His commandments, which we have vowed and promised to do. And then, if we did consider the vileness and naughtiness of our sins, and how much we did against natural reason and honesty in doing of them, and how greatly we did offend God in presuming to do so evil in His presence and sight against His law, and in breaking our solemn promise of keeping His commandments ; and then, if we did consider that in doing of our sins we did not regard His gracious goodness and favour, nor fear His power and most dreadful punishment,—if we did well consider these things, and were fully persuaded of God's mercy, which He is ready to shew to all that unfeignedly will forsake their former naughty ways and turn to Him, we should then take this contrition, and see that we ought to be more sorry for our sins than S. Peter ought to have been for his. For our Saviour Christ had shewed us more kindness, and had done more for us, than He had done for S. Peter at that time. For He died afterward for our sakes, and redeemed us, and delivered us out of the hands of the devil. And again, our sins be more, and we have oftener broken our promise than S. Peter did, for he brake it but once, and that was for fear, and we have sinned oftentimes without any fear or compunction, but rather willingly, yea, and divers times we have desired to sin, and studied how and where we might fulfil our ungracious lusts and desires. And thus ye may see that we ought to be more contrite and sorry for our offences than S. Peter ought to have been for his. By this example ye may know for what cause and by what mean ye may have contrition. And surely the sinner that doth well weigh and consider this that I have spoken, shall be sorry that ever he sinned, and did against the will and commandment of our Saviour Christ, Which is so good and gracious, and he shall will that he had never offended, and he shall hate sin, and purpose and attend to live well, and to make amends and restitution of that he hath wrongfully taken or done, and shall humble himself by acknowledging and confessing his faults, and submit himself wholly to the correction and discipline of God and His holy Church, not doubting but that he shall be received to grace and mercy and remission of all his sins.

Furthermore, it is to be noted that the sorrow and repentance which a thief taketh for his theft when he shall suffer death for it, and the repentance that misliving man or woman taketh for their misliving when they shall be brought to any open shame, or shall get any painful disease thereby, is not that true contrition that we speak of, nor yet any other like sorrow that men may have and take for their offences in other like cases; because such like sinners and offenders be not sorry, for that they did against God's law and offend Him, but they be sorry for the death, or shame, or other pain, which they shall suffer for their naughty living.

Yet, notwithstanding these other pains whereunto they come by order of law, they may also be sorry for their sins, specially and most principally because they did offend God in despising Him in doing their sins, more than for any shame or pain they shall suffer here for them, and if they so do, having the mind and will to sin no more, but to make restitution, and to confess and make satisfaction for the same, then they have true contrition, and may be sure of mercy and be saved if they die in that mind.

And although a man is not truly contrite when he is sorry only for the fear of pain, be it corporal pain or everlasting pain, yet the fear of pain is an introduction preparing the way for true contrition. For charity, without the which no man liveth in soul by grace, is builded upon fear of God's judgment, when a man is glad to be loved of God Whom He feareth, and dare be bold to love Him again, and is afraid to displease Him Whom he loveth, although he might do it without punishment. For no man cometh to God that is not smitten with some fear. For which cause S. John Baptist, preparing the way for Christ and remission of sin (Matt. iii.), beat into the people's heads the horror of their sins and the fear of God's judgment. And S. Peter in his first sermon, after that he had brought the Jews in fear of God's anger, by declaring unto them how they had crucified and killed Jesus Whom God had made Christ their Lord, and so had smitten their hearts with fear (Acts ii. 22–27), then he taught them to do penance, and to take true contrition for their sins. Thus, when a sinner looking upon God's law, either written in the book, or written in his own heart, whereby he seeth, as in a glass, what pleaseth or displeaseth Almighty God, and seeth also by faith that God threateneth damnation and everlasting death to all sinners, and then is accused secretly by his own

conscience, that he hath broken that eternal law of
God, not only in thought but also in deed, and perceiveth the vileness and greatness of his own sin, how
often he hath offended, and into what misery he hath
brought himself, and of what great graces and joys
he hath deprived himself thereby, being then separate
from the spiritual communion of Christ's Church, and
guilty of eternal damnation, then, if there be any
sparkle of grace left in that man, if he be not obdurate
and clean forsaken of God, he will begin to fear and
tremble, which fear will break the hardness of his
heart, and prepare the way for wisdom and grace to
enter it. Without the which fear no man can receive
remission of sins and be made righteous (Ecclus. i.
27, 28). Which fear of hell is not in charity, but prepareth a place for charity, and as charity increaseth
in a man's heart, so it decreaseth till perfect charity
possess the whole. (1 John iv. 18). After this fear a
sinner beginneth to hate and abhor his sin, whereby
he was brought into so great danger and misery, and
so proceedeth to lament and be sorry for his offences.
And as in the doing of his sins there were two
things, the naughty deed and the carnal pleasure
that was joined with the same, so in the forsaking of
his sins there must be two things, ceasing from the
deed, and sorrow for the sin past. For so the prophet crieth, " Quiescite perverse agere " (" Cease to
do evil," Isa. i. 16). He that continueth still in his
naughty doing is far from all kind of true penance.
For how can he turn to God that is not turned from
his sin, nor he cannot be sorry that still is doing
the thing for the which he is sorry. And it is to be

understood that this sorrow of contrition is inward in the heart, and not feigned, only pretended in the outward behaviour. Which the very word contrition doth signify; for that is called contrite that is bruised and beaten into small pieces or powder. Even so when the hardness of a man's heart is mollified with sorrow and tears for that he hath by sin displeased God, then is his heart contrite. A hard heart is that which is not cut with compunction, nor made soft with pity, nor moved with prayers, nor yieldeth to threatenings, but is unkind after benefits, without shame of dishonesty, without fear of peril, giving no place to any good motion, but withstanding by continuance in will to sin. Even so on the other side a man's heart is contrite, when he is cut with compunction, mollified with pity and devotion, moved with prayers and exhortation, is afraid by threatenings, allured by kindness, ashamed of dishonesty, giving place to God's inspiration, putting away the will and love to sin, abhorring his former filthy living, displeasing himself and lamenting for the same, and with sure trust of God's mercy submitting himself wholly in all points to obey His will and commandment.

An heart after this sort contrite and humbled, God will never despise nor reject (Ps. l. 19), but accept it as a sweet sacrifice ; of the which the prophet saith, " Be ye turned unto me in all your heart in fasting, in weeping, and lamenting; cut your hearts and not your garments " (Joel ii. 12, 13); and our Saviour saith, " Blessed be they that mourn, for they shall receive comfort " (Matt. v. 5) ; which mourning is not from

the lips outward, to say or pretend themselves to be
sorry, but to declare it outwardly in deed as much
as they can by weeping and lamenting.

And this contrition is the cross of Christ, which
every Christian man and woman that followeth Christ
in this world beareth voluntarily upon his own back,
and so sheweth the virtue of Christ's cross in his
own flesh, ever carrying about the mortification of
Jesus Christ in his body (2 Cor. iv. 10), that the life
of Jesus may be shewed in his body.   And because
we must turn to God with our whole heart, and the
quantity and greatness of this sorrow is to be measured
by the quantity of our crimes, so that he which
hath sinned much do lament much, that his penance
be found no less than his crime, and the more that
he doth humble himself by sorrow, the more shall
he be exalted to grace ; the more abject he is in his
own sight, the more accept in the sight of God.
Therefore our Saviour Christ forgave S. Peter his sin
by-and-by, because he wept bitterly and did not
increase his fault by driving off his amendment.   For
a true penitent loseth not time.   For the time past
he redeemeth again, whilst that he calls to remembrance all his years past in the bitterness of his soul.
The present time he doth fully possess by sorrow
and exercise of that virtue which is contrary to that
he offended in.   The time to come he loseth not, by
constantly endeavouring himself to perform that good
purpose of sinning no more which he hath godly
begun, remembering the sayings of the Apostle,
While we have time let us do good (Gal. vi. 10), and
he that continueth to the last end shall be saved

(Matt. x. 22). For except a sinner determine surely with himself in his mind to leave and forsake all sin, and intend never to do any again, but to keep God's commandments justly from that time forward, he shall not obtain forgiveness of his sins at God's hand, nor his contrition is not perfect and profitable unto him. Wherefore it is to be feared that many, yea, and all those which shortly after confession turn to their sins again, did not will and intend to forsake all sin before they were confessed ; for if they had so intended, either they would have so continued, or if it had chanced them sometime to have fallen, they would have risen again by-and-by and forsaken their vice.

And this contrition, although it seem to a carnal man a painful thing, yet to him that is truly penitent it is very sweet and pleasant, and is the very joy of the Holy Ghost in his heart. For, as the prophet saith, "According to the multitude of sorrows in my heart, Thy comfort hath made glad my soul" (Ps. xciii. 19).

The more the sorrows be in a contrite heart for the love of God, the more doth comfort abound, when he knoweth and seeth that he shall have mercy and for-giveness for all his offences, according to God's most loving and merciful promise. And also he that hath this contrition, his good deeds which he shall do afterward be acceptable to God, and profitable for his salvation, so long as he hath it and is in that mind. And if it should chance him to die before he can be shriven and make satisfaction, yet then shall he have mercy and for-giveness and be saved, what sins soever he hath done, for the contrition which he had, and for the good mind and purpose that he died in, and as the prophet saith, "The iniquity of the wicked man shall not hurt him, in what day soever he shall be turned from his iniquity" (Ezek. xxxiii. 14, 15). For in this case God accepteth a man's good mind instead of that he should have done; which our Saviour Christ shewed in pardoning and saving the contrite and penitent thief that suffered with Him (Luke xxiii. 43).

Therefore (good people) let us not neglect our souls, which is that precious treasure God hath committed to our care, seeing we may return easily and repay it with small labour. Howsoever we esteem this affliction of penance, yet in very deed it is but light and short; as S. Paul saith, "The light shortness of our affliction in this present life worketh the eternal weight of glory in time to come, in us that look not to things which we see, but to things we see not; for things that we see be temporal, things that be not seen be eternal" (2 Cor. iv. 17, 18). It is now only required of us to leave that most shameful bondage of sin we were in, and to return to our former virtue, considering the pain that followeth riot and the glory that is reserved for virtue; and as we have been rash in falling to sin, so let us be circumspect in the remedy, being well ware of our doings hereafter by reason of our fall before. Thus shall we mitigate the displeasure of Almighty God, Whom we have offended, and after reconciliation shall proceed further from grace to grace, till we come to the greatest grace of all, which is the glory of God, to the which He bring us that made us, to Whom be all glory and honour. Amen.

THE EIGHTEENTH SERMON.

OF INWARD CONFESSION TO ALMIGHTY GOD.

IT is to be known (good people) that true contrition, whereof ye have been something instructed, is never without humble and meek confession of a man's sins to Almighty God, which confession is truly done when we open our sins to Almighty God secretly in our own hearts, condemning ourselves and our deeds before God with much sorrow and compunction taken for them, always looking at God's mercy and free pardon for the merits of His Son Jesus Christ. And as prayer is always to be used, as S. Paul commandeth (1 Thess. v. 17), so this confession is at all times to be used, which ought to be the chief part of our continual prayer; whereby we humble ourselves before God, confessing our iniquity, blaming ourselves, and praising Him, being severe judges over ourselves, to the intent He might be our merciful Saviour.

This confession is a part of true contrition, and a distinct thing from the sacramental confession, which is made to a priest for the attaining of absolution, wherein consisteth the sacrament of Penance, which hereafter in another sermon shall be by God's grace

declared unto you.   For every man that seeth and
perceiveth his own shameful and beastly living, is
both by the law of nature written in his heart, and
otherwise by the law of God and inspiration of His
Holy Spirit, moved and provoked to be ashamed of
himself, and to accuse himself, his own thoughts accusing or defending his deeds (Rom. ii. 15); which to
a man endued with a knowledge of the true living
God, and delivered from the superstitious darkness of
the unbelieving Gentiles, is a great furtherance to cease
from his sin and to amend his life.   Seeing that the
confession of a fault is a profession to leave the same,
therefore we ought first to forsake our sin whereof we
have begun to make confession, and then to have good
hope of forgiveness.   For it is not only sufficient * to
accuse ourselves, and to be seen to declare our sins,
but to do it with this affection, that we may have
hope thereby to have some justification given unto
us through our penance.   For so we may let in shame
into our soul, confessing itself, that it fall no more
into the same crimes it confessed before.   For to
condemn and call himself a sinner is a common
thing to all, Christian men and infidels.

Many of these beastly men, and specially unchaste
women call themselves sinners and mischievous persons, but they do it not for this intent that they desire to be amended ; and therefore this is not to be
called a confession, for it cometh not forth of a contrite heart and in the bitterness of tears, nor yet with
that affection, as men that hate that which they blame,
and have a will never to do it any more, nor yet to

* The meaning is, it is not sufficient merely to accuse ourselves, &c.—ED.

hear of it ; but the thing is only in words, and in words from the lips outward, not proceeding from the inward sorrow of the heart ; so that sometimes they require to be praised for that, as they were men that would not lie, but although it were against themselves, yet would they say truth. As who say, the crime seemed not to men so grievous, when that is spoken of him that did it, as when it is reproved of another. But this do they that for much desperation lack also the feeling of sorrow, and then fear not the reproach of men, but with impudent boldness blaze abroad their own faults, as they were other men's.

But I would have us do none of all these ; neither with desperation to confess our sinful life, but with good hope of pardon, the root of desperation being clean grubbed out. And like as a man, vexed with a grievous sickness, hath need of many medicines, and hath little to buy them withal, if a physician come unto him that is sick and say, Thou hast need of divers kinds of medicines, and knowing that thou art not able to buy them all, yet buy me one or two of the best of them and least worth,* and the rest I shall find at my own cost freely ; even so Almighty God saith to us, Give me thy confession and the tears of penance, and the rest shall I find of my gentleness and free gift.

God giveth mercy and health, and the sinner giveth the confession of his sins, which was given him before to give. A small thing, yet that he is able to give, as David said, " I knowledge and confess mine iniquity " (Ps. l. 5).

* *i.e.,* Least costly.

But on the other side, how many sinners be
there that live careless, that rob and steal, and will
not understand, that oppress the widows and father-
less, that circumvent the simple, and live other ways
wretchedly, and yet will not recognise and see the
destruction and mischief that hangeth over their
heads, and in the meantime do that evil they like
with boldness, neither mourning nor weeping, nor
confessing their faults.   How can these men be saved,
not acknowledging their sins, nor having the judgment
of God before their eyes?   Yet blessed David made
plain confession, saying, "For I know my sin, and
it is always in my sight."   He forgot it not although
it was forgiven, but had the adultery and murder
which he committed painted in his conscience as in
an image, and every day he saw the corruption of it,
and therefore said, "My sin is always in my sight."
Lord, I see it, do not Thou consider it ; I write it
in my conscience, Lord, put Thou it out.   This is it
that Elias said, If thou remember it, God will forget
it ; if thou forget it, God will remember it ; for God
saith of Himself, I am He that blotteth out thine
iniquity (Isa. xliii. 25), but be thou always mindful
of it.   Why would God have a man always to remember his sin ?   That His mercy should be to the
sinner more thankful, and that he should perceive the
better what God hath forgiven him.   He that always
remembereth the heap of his sins, shall also remember
the greatness of God's merciful benefits.

Such were the holy men in old time ; they did not
call to their remembrance their virtues but their sins,
and did not as men do now, forget their sins, being

desirous to hide them and keep them close, and shew forth to all men their good deeds if they have done any, and boast themselves of them. But if thou hast done any good, keep it secret that thy Lord may see it and praise thee for it. For if thou boast thyself of any good deed, thou hast received glory of men. If thou hast done evil, remember it, that God might forget it; if thou shalt tell thy faults, thou hast made them less; but if God shall tell them and lay them to thy charge, He shall increase them. If thou be ashamed to tell thy sins to thy neighbour, then tell them daily inwardly in thine heart. I do not bid thee tell them to thy neighbour and fellow-servant, to the intent he should upbraid thee with them, and utter them again to thy confusion, but tell them to thy Lord God, that shall not upbraid thee with them, but heal them and take them clean away. Not for that God doth not know them, seeing He knoweth all things, and was present when thou didst them, and knew them before they were done, but for that He would have thee to know them, and by confessing of them, to recognise the greatness of God's mercy in pardoning of them, and so afterward warily to avoid them and humbly to thank Him. This medicine is neither costly nor grievous, and yet restoreth a man perfectly to his former health; for he that would have his disease healed and be brought into health, let him put out of mind all worldly cares, and with repentance go to God the Physician, and before Him pour forth his warm tears, and with much diligence confess his sins against himself, and bringing steadfast faith with him, let him trust and put his confidence in the art and cunning of the Physician. What cost or grief doth this merciful Physician require of us? He requireth contrition of heart, compunction of mind, confession of our fall, careful and humble continuance, and He doth not only heal our diseases, but maketh us righteous men which were laden with sin before. What great mercy and excellent goodness is this, when he that offended confesseth his fault and asketh forgiveness, is by-and-by pardoned and made righteous! And for plain declaration hereof, hear the prophet's words, " Tell thou thine iniquity first, that thou mayest be justified " (Isa. xliii. 26). He saith not only, Tell thine iniquities, but tell them first ; that is to say, tarry not till they be laid to thy charge and thou reproved for them, but prevent thou thine accuser and have the first word, and so thine accuser shall be dumb.

See the excellent mercy of this Judge. If a man should do so in worldly judgments, and should confess before he were accused, were the judge never so merciful, yet he should have sentence of death ; but such is the clemency of our merciful Judge and the Physician of our souls, that if we prevent our adversary the devil, which at the last day shall stand before our face, and in this present life before judgment fall to confession, and preventing all other, be our own accusers, we shall provoke our Judge to so great mercy that He will grant us not only to be delivered from our sins, but also to be accounted in the number of just men.

For if Lamech, which had no law whereupon he might learn, nor heard no prophet, nor had no other admonition, but even by the judgment which was given to him in nature, being privy to his naughty murder, confessed openly against himself that he had done, and condemned himself (Gen. iv. 23), what excuse can we have, that with all diligence will not shew our sores to the intent we might have them perfectly cured? For there is no greater enemy to a man's sin than a man's own proper condemnation and confession of his sin joined with repentance and tears. Whereof we may take an example of a thief that was crucified with our Saviour Christ, which when he was suffering for his own crimes, took no care of himself, but opened his sins to Christ. For as his sins did make him foul and vile, so the confession of them opened Paradise to him. For no doubt of it, if he had not confessed his sins here, he should have been compelled to have confessed them there where more pain and more shame should have followed. And yet the shame (if it be well and truly considered) ought rather to be in the doing than in the confession of our sins, for it is no shame to confess to God, but rather virtue and righteousness, for if it were not virtue God would never have promised a reward for it, saying (as I said before), "Tell thou thy sins first that thou may be justified." And who shall be ashamed to do that deed whereby he is made righteous, seeing God commandeth us to confess our sins, not to punish us but to pardon us? For which cause, lest a man should fear to be punished after confessing of his fault, David saith, "Make confession to God because He is good, and His mercy is for evermore" (Ps. cxvii.)

What profit should a man have if he should not

o

confess his sin ?   Can he keep it from the knowledge
of God, Who knoweth the secrets of man's heart
and all things before they be done ?   No, no ; it is
worse not to confess the sin than to transgress the
law ; it is worse to refuse our conversion than to contemn God's admonition.   It is worse not to mitigate
God's displeasure by our satisfaction than to deserve
His displeasure by our transgression.   The Ninivites
confessed their sins and lived, the Sodomites neglected
confession and perished (Gen. xix.)   The Israelites
when they sinned, they were delivered to their
enemies ; when they confessed their sins, they were
delivered from their enemies ;   for like as no man
escaped God's plague when he sinned, so every man
had God's pardon when he confessed his sin.   Through
hope of this holy David prayed to God that he might
be washed more and more, because he knew his
iniquity, and his sin was always in his sight (Ps.
l. 4, 5), not by delectation to frequent and continue it,
but by hatred to avoid and abhor it.   The publican
in the Gospel confessed his sin and went home justified, the proud Pharisee boasting his good deeds, went
home in worse case (Luke xviii. 11–14).   Confession
is the fruit of humility, which is also the mother of
grace, for the attaining whereof the Holy Ghost
teacheth us always to be occupied in this kind of
confession, saying by the prophet, " That the righteous
man is ever first of all the accuser of himself in the
beginning of his words " (Prov. xviii. 17).

Wherefore (good people) let us be as diligent in
preserving and increasing our treasure in heaven,
as these worldly merchants be in preserving their

treasure in earth. For it is a common trade of these rich men, lest the charges of household do exceed their gains, early in the morning as soon as they rise, before they go about their business, to call their servant, and to ask an account of their expenses, that they might know what is evil spent, what well, and if they see their stock decay, then to seek an occasion how to restore it again. Even so let us do in our business, let us call our servant, which is our conscience, to an account for our thoughts, words, and deeds, and search what is spent for our profit, what for our destruction. What word is evil spent in brawling, replying, jesting, and slander ; what thoughts have provoked the eye to fornication, the heart to malice, the hand to injury and mischief of our neighbour. And when our servant hath told us everything, then let us cease from wasting any more of our heavenly treasure, and seek by gain to restore that which by negligence was lost. For idle and naughty words let us bring home and store up holy prayers ; for injury done to our neighbour, mercy and alms ; for intemperate living, fasting and abstinence. For if we spend our good treasure still in waste, and restore nothing that is good again, when we shall be brought to extreme misery, and the time of our merchandise is past and gone, then shall we seek and find no help, no, not so much as one drop of water to quench the heat of our tongue's end. The merchants use to call their servants to account early in the morning, but our best time is to call our conscience to account in the evening. When thou goest to bed and hast nobody to trouble thee, then bring forth thy account book, and search diligently, if anything all the day before be done amiss, either in word, thought, or deed; for so the prophet giveth counsel, saying, "Be angry, and sin no more; those things ye speak in your hearts, be sorry and contrite for them in your beds" (Ps. iv. 5). In the day-time a man hath many lets, his labours, his offices, the care of his household, children and family, and other affairs, both private and public, which diversely do grieve or occupy a man on the day-time. But when he goeth to bed, and no man calleth upon him nor troubleth him, then let him commune with his own soul, and sit as it were upon judgment upon himself, examining what good he hath done all the day before or what evil, and if he find that he hath done good, let him humbly give God thanks, Whose grace did move him to it, assist him, and brought it to that good end.

But if he find that he hath done evil, let him cease from the evil deed, blame and accuse himself, with sorrow and compunction beat his own heart, wash his bed with tears as David did, confess his sin to Almighty God against himself, and humbly pray Him of pardon and remission, and then, using this nightly, let him pierce and smite through his soul with the fear of God, and be ashamed to come with one fault twice before Him, Who by an impenitent heart is provoked to vengeance, as by a contrite heart He is bowed to mercy, and seeketh occasion by all means to shew mercy to all men. This manner of daily confession, watered with tears of a man's own eyes, is through the merits of our Saviour Christ, a sponge to wipe away the filthiness of our sins, and a medicine preserving us from falling to sin again. Thus preventing His face in confession we may be sure of forgiveness (Ps. xciv.) For as Solomon saith, "He that hideth his sins shall not prosper, but he that confesseth and forsaketh them shall obtain mercy" (Prov. xxviii. 13). Fear of hell with hope of mercy worketh the sorrow of penance, out of which cometh forth unfeigned confession, which is a vehement voice in the ears of God, and persuadeth much to mercy and remission of sin, to increase in grace, and by continuance in the same to eternal glory, whereof God make us all partakers through the merits of our Lord Jesus Christ, to Whom with the Father and the Holy Ghost be glory and honour now and evermore. Amen.

THE NINETEENTH SERMON.

OF CONFESSION TO A PRIEST.

IN this sermon (good people) I intend by God's grace to declare unto you, wherein the sacrament of Penance consisteth and what is the matter of it. It consisteth in the absolution which by a Catholic priest is given to a penitent sinner in the name of God, Who is the principal judge and remitter of all sin, and the matter of it is that humble and true confession which a penitent sinner maketh to God before a priest, God's minister institute for that purpose to remit or retain sin. This sacrament of Penance for sins committed after baptism is necessary to salvation, which is full remission of the same sins, and it is institute and ordained by our Saviour Christ, when after His glorious resurrection, and before He ascended He gave to His Apostles priests, and so to others, power to absolve and forgive sinners their sins, saying to His Apostles thus : " Receive the Holy Ghost " (John xx. 22), the sins of those that you forgive, be forgiven, and the sins of those that you retain, be retained (verse 23) ; that is to say, are not forgiven. In which words our Saviour Christ gave

power and authority to all priests both to remit sin,
and also to retain sin, and ordained them to be judges
in His kingdom, the Church, to hear and determine all
crimes and offences which shall be committed against
Him and His laws. This power our Saviour never
gave to angels, nor archangels, nor to no worldly prince,
but only to His Apostles and those that have in His
Church the order of priesthood, which power is very
great and excellent, as pertaining to the soul of man,
and reaching to heaven, where Almighty God rati-
fieth above whatsoever sentence priests shall give in
earth.

This power no priest can exercise worthily, without the confession of the sinner himself, which is the
only way for the priest to know and understand what
he ought to forgive, and what to retain and not forgive, except he should blindly and rashly behave
himself in so great an office, forgiving that he knoweth
not what. For neither ought he to bind those that
be innocent, nor to loose those that be obstinate, but,
according to his office and commission, to exercise
the same in binding and loosing after that he hath
heard the variety of the sins confessed. For God
doth pardon them only that be truly penitent for
their offences, and begin and further purpose to
amend their living. And because the power of the
priests is two ways, to forgive the sins of some, and
to retain the sins of others, therefore our Saviour
Christ gave to them the Holy Ghost, that they might
effectually execute both the functions, and also the
better discern the one from the other. And also
considering that Christ in plain words affirmeth, that

no sin is remitted before God in heaven, which is retained and not remitted by His ministers, the priests, in earth; therefore the Holy Catholic Church of Christ, even from the beginning thereof, understandeth by the said words of Christ, that it is necessary, by God's law, that every man and woman, when they have sinned deadly, should confess their sins to a priest, if they may have one, because they cannot otherwise obtain pardon of their sins, but by a priest's absolution sacramental, except it be impossible for them to have the same, as when the sinner would confess and cannot speak, or cannot get a ghostly father; for in such cases God accepteth a man's goodwill and unfeigned contrition instead of the sacramental confession, where the sacrament is excluded by urgent necessity and not by contempt of religion.

So that the execution of this heavenly authority requireth judgment and discretion in the priest to discern what is to be remitted, what not, seeing every sin in every man is not to be remitted; whereunto is necessary the knowledge of the fault, which cannot be had of a man that seeth not the secrets of another's heart, except the party being guilty declare his own conscience, and reveal plainly his secret offences. For which cause the Holy Church teacheth that the same words that give authority to priests to forgive or retain sin, the same also do enjoin and bind all sinners to confess their sins to priests for the attaining of the said remission. Therefore it is to be believed of all men and women, that confession of deadly sins is to be made to a priest by God's law, as necessary to salvation, without the which the necessary sacrament of Penance cannot be ministered, seeing that it is the matter of the same sacrament, whereby the offender is both accuser of himself and also witness against himself, and yet may not be his own judge, pardoning himself, but ought to confess his fault not only privily to God, to Whom nothing is secret, but also, without shame or disdain, to him whom for that purpose God hath vouchsafed to make His vicar and delegate judge, and to undergo his judgment and sentence, to the intent his conscience may be quieted and he fully reconciled to Almighty God.

For men are bounden necessarily to open their sins to them, to whom the dispensation of God's mysteries is committed, for so we see that our fathers did in their penance, seeing it is also written in the Gospel that the Jews confessed their sins to S. John Baptist (Matt. iii. 6), and the people of Ephesus to the Apostles, of whom they were baptized (Acts xix. 5).

Wherefore (good people) I exhort you, in the name of our Lord Jesus Christ, that this necessary and wholesome medicine of your souls be not lightly regarded of you ; but whosoever hath his conscience loaden with the heavy burden of sin, or wounded with the dart of the devil's temptation, or infected with the poisoned contagion of deadly sin, let him run without delay to this present remedy which our Saviour Christ hath ordained and offered to all men. Let him go to the physician whom God hath appointed for his soul, and hath fully authorised and instructed what to do to the healing of the same, and let him humble and submit himself not only under the mighty hand of God, but also to a mortal man, being God's vicar and steward of His mysteries, not regarding the man for the worthiness of himself, but for the dignity of his place and administration, never accounting him to be vile whom God hath vouchsafed to make His vicar. And to him, or rather to God before him, let him open his wound, show his leper,* and humbly confess his sin, wherewith he hath offended Almighty God, and with an humble and contrite heart require remission of his sin, giving full confidence to the words of Christ, and believing that to be remitted with God in heaven, whatsoever the priest (of what state soever he be) by exercising of God's commission remitteth to him in earth, knowing that God is faithful, and neither can deceive, nor be deceived, but always assisteth the due ministration of His sacrament, working the same effect inwardly in the soul of the true penitent that the words of the priest do outwardly to his ear signify, which is remission of all his sins.

Let not shame stop this humble confession, but let every man rather be ashamed to sin than to confess his sin. For, as the wise man saith, " There be two manner of shames, one that bringeth to sin, another that bringeth to grace and glory " (Ecclus. iv. 25). The good shame is when a man is ashamed that he doth or hath sinned, and although no other creature were privy to it, yet he with reverence feareth the sight of God that always seeth him. This kind of shame driveth away confusion and reproach and worketh grace and glory, in that either he doth for-

* *i.e.,* Leprosy.

bear to sin, or else by penance punisheth, and by confession banisheth his sin committed, whereas his glory is the witness of his own conscience.

The naughty shame is when a man is ashamed to confess his sins. This kind of shame driveth away grace and glory, and worketh eternal confusion, which, like a lock or bar, stoppeth the door of his mouth, and will not let the poison of the heart to be cast out, till the soul be dead and drowned in the bottom of sin.

Wherefore this is certain and sure, he that for shame contemneth and refuseth to confess his sins here, when remedy may easily and presently be had, he shall be compelled to confess them there when greatest shame shall be in the presence of Christ, His angels, and the whole world, and endless pain shall ensue.

This is the subtle craft of our ghostly enemy the devil, who useth this naughty shame as an instrument of all mischief, in that he persuadeth a man to cast away shame, and to be impudent and careless of his living, and so to fear neither God nor man, but boldly to sin, and impudently to boast and defend the same. And on the other side, when the same sinner is smitten with the fear of hell, and is compunct in heart, and by God's grace moved to wholesome penance and confession, then the devil useth the same instrument again, restoring that he took away before, that is to say, shame, not to sin, but to confess his sin, and so keepeth him still fast bounden and locked in the chains of mortal sin, that the keys of heaven, committed by Christ in S. Peter to the

Church of God, cannot open that lock and loose the prisoner, because shame keepeth him from confession, without the which the keys cannot be used to the delivery of the prisoner.

By this we may understand that the confession of sins is the witness of a conscience that feareth God ; for he that feareth the judgment of God is not ashamed to confess his sin, and he that is ashamed feareth not. For perfect fear looseth all; shame : the suffering and avoiding whereof is a certain pain and punishment for the sin, because by this means the pride of a sinner's heart which God resisteth is broken and pulled down, and by humility is made meet to receive the grace of God. And also that pernicious security which a sinner regardeth not so long as he hath glory in himself and pleasure in his carnal living, is by kneeling down and submitting himself to God's minister taken away, whilst that he, laying his own life with all the abominations thereof before his own eyes, learneth to know himself, and how vile he hath made himself in the sight of God, and is so affected as he would wish to be if he were even then at point to depart out of this world, which is a bridle and a great stay for him to refrain from sin, and to avoid the same in time to come.

For which cause let every man confess his own sin, whilst he is yet living and remaining in this world, whilst his confession may be admitted, and satisfaction and remission which is given here by the priest, is accepted before God. If any infection of deadly sin or infidelity hath entered into his heart, let him not be ashamed to confess it to him that hath cure and charge of his soul, to the intent it might be cured by the Word of God and wholesome counsel, so that by perfect faith and good works, he might escape the pains of eternal fire, and come to the reward of eternal life. But if he that is stinged with the serpent, the devil, hold his peace, and will not do penance, and confess his wound to his brother and master that hath cure upon him, then can his master that hath a tongue to heal him profit him nothing; for how can the surgeon minister an apt and wholesome medicine, if the sick man will not open and shew his wound unto him?

For the same way is observed in the confession of sins, which is used in the wounds of a man's body. Like as the sores of a man's body be not opened to every one, but to such as can skill to heal them, even so ought the confession of sins to be made to them that can heal them, which after what sort it is done ye have heard it declared from the mouth of our Saviour Christ, Who promised to allow and accept as forgiven whatsoever His minister in His name shall forgive, and also denieth it to be remitted, which by His minister is retained and not remitted. Do what a man can, and search as much as he will, and he shall find after baptism no other table or board to save himself from the shipwreck of sin, and drowning in damnation, and to be brought unto the sure ground of grace and the state of salvation, but only by this sacrament of Penance which is ministered by a priest to him that is truly penitent, and faithfully confesseth his sin, and humbly requireth absolution for the same. And, although the contri-

tion of an humble heart may be so great that the
sentence of God in heaven may go before the
sentence of God's minister in earth, yet that true
contrition always includeth a full purpose and
determination to obtain remission at the priest's
hand by confessing his sins as soon as he may
have opportunity. For else he cannot have true
contrition before God, that proudly contemneth God's
ordinance, and never intended to require the same
of God's minister.

Thus, when a sinner forsaketh his sin, and cometh
to confession unfeignedly as he ought to do, then
doth Almighty God mercifully blot out his sin, and
forgiveth all the punishment which he deserved to
suffer in hell for breaking of God's eternal law, and
setteth him again in the state of salvation, and then
the sinner feeleth his conscience discharged of the
heavy burden of sin, and may be glad and quiet in
his conscience, knowing surely by the most sure and
merciful promise of Almighty God, that He hath of
His goodness pardoned and forgiven him all his sins,
and doth bear him again His gracious favour, and
loveth him as much as He did before, and that He
hath given him also new grace and spiritual strength,
and made him able to receive His own Son our
Saviour, God and man in the blessed Sacrament of
the Altar, and helpeth him continually in this life to
pass through the dangers of the same toward the
kingdom of heaven, to the which God bring us that
made us, to Whom be all glory. Amen.

THE TWENTIETH SERMON.

WHAT A SINNER OUGHT TO DO IN MAKING HIS
CONFESSION.

AFTER that ye have learned (good people) the necessity of confession, how every sinner is bounden to confess his sins to a priest by God's law for the attaining of absolution and remission of sin, now followeth to be declared what a sinner ought to do in making his confession. First a sinner ought, before he come to confession, to make an account with himself of his life, and to call to his remembrance how many deadly sins he hath committed since the time of his last confession, wherein such diligence must be used, as the necessity and dignity of the work of God which is absolution doth require, being willing and ready to do all things that be necessary for the recovery of grace and health of his soul, which a sick man would do for avoiding the death of his body. And this the sinner ought to do for two causes, the one that he might thereby take special repentance for every offence that he did, forasmuch as he did disobey and offend Almighty God, and had some special pleasure in every one, and therefore he ought to call his sins to his mind, and for remedy of the same to take some displeasure and repentance for every one of them. The other cause is, that he might have his sins ready and the better in his mind for to show them unto his ghostly father when he cometh to confession. The which King David did well perceive that sinners be bounden to do, and therefore when he had sinned he said thus, " I will study to remember my sin, because I will confess it " (Ps. xxxvii. 19). And the example of the prodigal son in the Gospel teacheth us also so to do, who returning to his father considered how evil he had lived, and he called then to his mind what he would confess and say to his father when he should come to him (Luke xv. 18). Thus when a sinner hath diligently examined his own conscience, and called to his remembrance how often and wherein he hath offended his Lord God, taking special repentance and contrition for every offence, then he ought to come to his ghostly father with great desire and humility, not as to a man to hear some worldly and profitable counsel, but as to the messenger or vicar of our Saviour Christ representing His person, Whose embassage he useth for making peace and reconciliation between the sinner and God (2 Cor. v. 20), to the intent he might hear of him the word of God, which is the word of absolution for his sins by past, and also be instructed by the word of God how to live well hereafter and avoid sin. And whereas the effect of God's sacraments do not depend upon the virtue or worthiness of the priest the minister, but upon the commandment and ordinance of God, who by His Spirit doth assist the due administration of the same; therefore a penitent sinner ought rather to regard the virtue and power of God that worketh by His minister, than the state of the person, be he high or low, a just or an unjust man, so long as he is a member of God's universal Church, and by toleration suffered to minister in the same; and he ought to give full credit to the words of absolution, that then his sins be clearly remitted, if his heart be then disposed and meet to receive the same remission, and if he put no stop to God's grace as they do that lack faith and true contrition.

And so the penitent sinner, coming to a priest and humbly submitting himself to him as representing the person of Christ, ought to rehearse wholly, simply, and faithfully all the deadly sins which then, after diligent searching of his life, do burden and vex his conscience. For although the Holy Church doth not burden a sinner to confess every venial sin, which is impossible or very hard to do, for who doth know all his faults? (Ps. xviii. 13); and also seeing that venial sins do not take away charity, nor do not exclude a man from the kingdom of heaven, without the which this frail and mortal life cannot be passed over, yet if a man fall oftentimes into such small sins, they ought not to be neglected but avoided * betimes, because contempt in all things aggravateth the crime, and specially in procuring the remedy, and also a man shall give an account in the day of judgment for every idle word that he shall speak (Matt. xii. 36). But all mortal sins, such as be transgressions of God's commandments, and bring a man in state of dam-

* *i.e.,* Got rid of.

P

nation, so many as come to his remembrance after diligent search and inquisition, the sinner ought to confess ; and not only such as he knoweth certainly to be mortal sins, but also such as he doubteth of, and knoweth not certainly whether they be mortal sins or no, because whatsoever thing is not of faith, is sin (Rom. xiv. 23). And he that doth or alloweth to be done anything whereof his conscience reprehendeth or condemneth him, doth therein against his conscience and sinneth deadly, and ought to confess it, and learn of his ghostly father (to whom judgment is given to discern between leper and not leper, sin and not sin) how to know and avoid the same afterwards.

Furthermore, it is to be considered that God doth not forgive one mortal sin and retaineth another unforgiven, but always when He forgiveth, He forgiveth altogether, the which He shewed in expelling all the whole legion of devils out of the man of Gerasen (Luke viii. 33), and He shewed the same again when He pardoned Mary Magdalene (Luke vii. 48). And the Scripture calleth that man happy whose sin God hath not imputed but covered (Ps. xxxi. 1, 2), and if there were any sin remaining imputed unto him and not forgiven, he should not be counted as happy, but as an enemy to God. Now, seeing the Father hath given all power to the Son, and the Son hath given the same power to the priests of His Church, whose judgment, both in binding and loosing in earth, is confirmed and ratified by God in heaven, therefore the remission which the priests give to penitent sinners, ought to be like and agreeable to the remission which is given by God (John xx. 23) that is to say, a full remission, not forgiving one mortal sin without another, but either forgiving all at once, or none at all. And because (as ye were taught before) the priest cannot worthily exercise this authority of forgiving or retaining sin, except the sinner open his conscience, and confess his sins himself, both because he cannot otherwise know what is to be remitted, what is not, and also because he may not rashly remit that he knoweth not and is not confessed unto him, therefore the sinner is bounden fully and plainly to confess all his sins, and every particular sin which, by diligent searching of his conscience, cometh then to his remembrance. For the concealing or hiding of any one mortal sin which he remembereth, is the cause why all the other which he confesseth be not forgiven. For he, then, in hiding of that mortal sin in confession, did sin deadly, and there dissemble with Almighty God, to Whose eyes all things be naked and open. A general confession, whereby a man calleth himself a sinner, is not sufficient, but a special confession and rehearsal of every mortal sin that we remember is required, that by knowing the number and quantity of our offences, we may likewise know the greatness of God's merciful goodness in remitting of them. He that is not penitent will call himself a sinner, and every just man will confess himself to be a sinner; for he that saith he hath no sin is a liar, deceiving himself, and also maketh God a liar, and hath no truth in him (1 John i. 8). But his general calling and confessing himself a sinner is not the matter of this sacrament of Penance, because it is not a faithful declaration of all

the crimes which he remembereth, but a certain crafty
colouring and cloaking of his crimes, which by a con-
fuse and general confession he dissembleth both before
God and man, as though he were but as all other
men be.   Which general confession, if it lack contrition, is a proud presumption and a glorying that he
hath done evil ; if it be joined with contrition, then,
although it be not sacramental, forgiving deadly sins
by virtue of the keys committed by Christ to His
Church, yet by virtue of the contrition, humility, and
prayer joined with it, it profiteth to the remission of
venial and daily sins, and prepareth the sinner's heart
to the attaining of further grace.   Therefore, like as
contrition ought to be without hypocrisy before God,
not of one or two sins but of all, even so confession
sacramental before God's minister ought to be whole
and perfect, seeing the death of the soul by sin cannot be taken away by parts, but wholly altogether,
when grace and life is by absolution restored and
given.   And after perfect knowledge of the whole
state and life of the sinner, the priest who hath cure
and charge of his soul, may the better in counselling,
comforting, and absolving, discharge his duty towards
Almighty God again.

And furthermore, that which I have said concerning the confession of all a man's sins, is also to be
understood of the circumstances of the same sins,
such as do aggravate the crime and make it more
heinous, and increase the contempt of God in committing them.   As a sin oftentimes used and done is
more grievous than that is but once done, and the
sin of a prince or priest is more than the same kind

of sin in a subject or layman, and sacrilege, which is robbing of churches or unlawfully taking away of that belonging to the Church, is greater crime than other robbery or theft, and he that by a malicious and naughty mind and with long study, tempteth and provoketh himself or any other to adultery or like sin against his neighbour, sinneth more than he which doth the same crime by frailty, suggestion or occasion of other: these and such other circumstances ought a sinner to express in his confession,* that his humility and shamefacedness in confessing his fault, may agree and be like to his pride and impudency in committing the same fault, always taking heed that he confess but his own faults, and do not therewith bewray the faults or persons of other, and that also without too much curiosity and scruple of conscience, and only for this intent that his sin and the greatness thereof might appear and the doubts of his conscience be taken away.

For to extenuate and make little in words that crime which is very great in deed, is likewise to diminish the glory of God that should pardon it, which is the way not to get pardon at God's hand, but to lose it ; Who doth not gladly give a benefit, which is not thankfully accepted and esteemed accordingly as it is. This is the most common and subtle craft that the devil useth with all sinners. At

---

* It is safe in practice to follow the opinion that there is no strict obligation to confess any circumstances but such as either change the species, or increase the number, or involve a censure or a reservation, or which the confessor requires to know in order to prescribe a remedy or to impose restitution.—See S. Alph., *Theol. Mor.*, lib. vi. 468. ED.

the beginning he doth cover and hide the sin he moveth them unto, and maketh it seem nothing or very little, to the intent the sinner may take boldness to do it. This boldness bringeth in use and custom to sin, which by continuance is turned into nature, so that then any exhortation or admonition can little prevail, but whithersoever the flesh and the devil leadeth him, thither he runneth headlong, only looking at the pleasure present, nothing regarding the pain to come. But at the last end when the fearful hour of death draweth near, then the devil doth not extenuate but amplify the sin, then doth he beat into the sinner's head, and lay before his eyes, the greatness of his sin and the long time he used it, and the contempt of God in doing it, and all the other circumstances that do aggravate and make it horrible, only to lead him further into desperation. From the which earthquake of desperation, the bottomless pit of all evils, I beseech God save us all.

And as we fear and abhor the end, so I pray you let us avoid and cut off the cause, which was when we did diminish our sin and esteem it but little, whereby we grew in boldness to do it, and fell into further extremity. If we stop at the beginning and know our sin, and confess it simply as it is, without any cloaking or diminishing of it of our part, we shall provoke God to cover it, to turn His face from it, and to wash it clean away.

There be many men that do not in words diminish their sin, but plainly excuse it, which doth not mitigate God's anger, but provoke it further, because they do not therein confess their faults, but defend them,

rather excusing than accusing themselves; whereby
their sins be not taken away, but more increased. A
proud heart that pleaseth itself, would not appear
guilty, and disdaineth to be corrected and convinced
when it offendeth, not abiding to accuse itself by devout humility, but seeking to excuse itself by intolerable pride, which must needs fall and come to ruin.
To restrain this pride, holy David humbly required
of Almighty God that it would please Him to put a
watch and a door before his mouth, that he do not
decline his heart to words of malice (Ps. cxl. 3); that
is to say, to excuse his sins. For what is more malicious and wicked than those words be, whereby a
naughty man denieth himself to be evil, although his
own conscience doth convict him of the same evil,
which he is not able but by malice to gainsay, and so
doth arm his tongue to kill and destroy his own soul?
Such an one was the proud Pharisee in the Gospel,
who displeased God not so much for boasting himself of his good deeds, as for excusing his naughty
deed, saying that he was not like other men (Luke
xviii. 11). And cursed Cain also, after that he had
killed his brother Abel, being asked of God where
his brother was (Who asked him that question not
for ignorance, but mercifully to give him occasion to
confess his sin and obtain mercy), answered again
that he could not tell, and further cloaking and excusing his sin, said, "Am I the keeper of my
brother?" For the which excusing, which was another sin besides his murder, he was pronounced that
he should be accursed upon earth; and from that sin
he fell further into desperation, saying that his sin was

greater than he might deserve and obtain forgiveness (Gen. iv. 9–13). Wherefore I pray you, for God's love, to lay away all manner of excuses, when ye come to confession, knowing that ye speak to God Who seeth the secrets of every man's heart, to Whose eyes all things be open and naked. If a man were the judge who might be deceived, to purge the fault with some craft, and to excuse it, might seem to be profitable for a time ; but where God is the Judge that cannot be deceived, a man may not falsely excuse or defend his sin, but truly and plainly confess his sin.

There be some men, also, that where they cannot nor do not deny the fact, yet they will lay the fault and blame upon some other thing or person from themselves, as upon youth, ignorance, sorrow, or evil counsel, or the temptation of the devil, or the inordinate desire of their bodies, or upon destiny, as though by the moving and powers of the stars and heavens above, they were compelled and forced to do evil. And some pestilent and abominable heretics there be that for excusing of themselves, do accuse Almighty God, and impute their mischievous deeds to God's predestination, and would persuade that God, Who is the fountain of all goodness, were the author of all mischief, not only suffering men to do evil by their own wills, but also enforcing their wills to the same evil, and working the same evil in them. Which words (good people) be not the words of malice only, whereof I spake before, but rather the words of blasphemy ; and therefore I will not now spend this little time in confuting their pestilent and devilish sayings. For it is better to abhor them than to confute them. Only at this time know you (good people) that these and all other such-like excuses and sayings be false. For every Christian man and woman hath so great strength in his soul, and hath his will so in his own power, that neither the devil, nor the flesh, nor evil counsel, nor any other thing can cause a man to do any sin, except he will himself grant or consent unto it. And it is always in the person's free choice that is tempted by the devil, or by the flesh, or by evil counsel, or any other thing, to consent unto the evil, or to refuse it and not to consent unto it. For if a man will not consent to do sin, there can no creature cause him or compel him to do any; and therefore when a man hath done any sin, he cannot in any wise justly excuse himself for the doing of it, for he himself was the very causer and doer, and might have left it undone if he had list. And so you may see (good people) that he which layeth any excuse for his sin in confession, doth wrongfully excuse himself, and accuseth other falsely in saying that they were the causes why he sinned, and in so doing, besides his former offences, he committeth a new sin, and thereby stoppeth the influence of God's grace, and is void of all remission.

Furthermore ye shall understand, that there be some persons that although they plainly and truly confess their faults, yet they will otherwise excuse the same, by justifying their naughty doings in comparison of other that did worse, as he that oppresseth his subjects or tenants, or will take more than his duty is for his labours or pains, and then in excusing of himself, saith that other that were before him in like authority or office were more extreme men, or took more for their labours than he. And also sellers of wares that deceived the simple buyers, will say that they were deceived themselves, and must needs utter the same again for as much as they can. Therefore let every man take good heed that he do not excuse his own fault, because he can tell of other that have done worse, but rather let him accuse himself that he hath not done so well as other that have done better, setting the virtue of good men as an example before his eyes to follow, and not the vice of evil men.

Last of all, a sinner ought to put away all indiscreet and false accusing of himself, that is to say, he may not accuse himself of more sins than he hath done, neither in special nor in general. In special, as when a man hath read in books the division of sin, how many parts and branches it hath, and then according to such books will confess himself to be an offender in the same, rehearsing every branch particularly, in so doing he lieth upon himself by confessing more sins than ever he did, and in that sinneth against God, and therefore this manner of confession is nought, and ought of every man to be refused. Likewise a sinner ought not to accuse himself wrongfully in general, as saying that he hath been the most shamefullest liver and the greatest sinner that ever was, or that can be, or any other like sayings, for they be nought and false. What knoweth he how great sinners hath been or may be ? And therefore men must put away such indiscreet sayings, and

speak soberly, truly and faithfully to Almighty God
in their confessions, and then let them not doubt but
steadfastly trust of absolution and pardon for all
their sins. Judas that betrayed our Saviour Christ,
and Cain that killed his brother Abel, confessed their
sin openly, but did not trust surely of mercy, and
therefore their unfaithful confession did nothing profit
them ; but he that avoideth and observeth all these
things which, as I have now declared unto you, ought
to be avoided and observed in their sacramental confession, no doubt of it he shall be joyful and glad in
his heart, and perceive himself eased of a great heavy
burden. And the more he remembereth the merciful
goodness of Almighty God in pardoning him his
manifold offences, the more thanks he will give Him,
and the more will he study and labour to honour
Him, and to live justly from that time forward, still
increasing in grace and righteousness by the aid and
help of our Saviour Christ, to Whom with the Father
and the Holy Ghost be all honour and glory.
Amen.

THE TWENTY-FIRST SERMON.

CERTAIN INSTRUCTIONS WHEREBY A MAN MAY CONSIDER HIS LIFE AND MAKE HIS CONFESSION THE BETTER.

AS I would wish that every person which cometh to confession, should diligently search his whole life, and examine his acts and deeds before he come, that his confession might be made in order ; whereby the minister should not be compelled to appose and examine the penitent, which in some cases may chance to do more harm than good, by putting that in the penitent's head by his questions, which he never thought of nor had experience of before, even so (good people) I think it expedient at this time, not to set forth a general form of confession how every man should confess himself, which (standing the variety of men's lives and offices) cannot agree to every person, but I think it profitable to rehearse unto you certain things wherein our Saviour Christ hath and doth shew unto us His merciful goodness and kindness, for the which we are always bounden to thank Him, and also wherein we sinners have shewed again to Him our great unkindness, for the which we are bounden to do penance and to make amends; the often and diligent remembering whereof will be a great help for every man to know the state of his life and to make his confession the better.

First, I would exhort every man and woman to thank God highly for His merciful kindness shewed unto him in his creation, in his redemption, and in his regeneration. In his creation appeareth God's kindness, in that He might have made him a mean creature sensible or insensible, which He did not, but rather of His goodness made him one of the most excellent creatures of all other under heaven, to His own image and similitude, and to be inheritor of the kingdom of heaven, and also made all other creatures to help him and to serve him here in this present life, to the intent he might the better serve God. Also a man is bounden to thank God for the benefits of his redemption, in that Christ by His painful Passion redeemed him from the possession of the devil, and made him meet by the merits of the same Passion to be brought to the state of salvation and the fruition of eternal life. And also for the benefit of regeneration, that is to say, when he was christened and received the holy sacrament of Baptism. For although Christ had redeemed him with His most precious blood, yet might he have remained still an infidel, as many do, and so should have been damned, if Christ had not called him and caused him to be christened, by which baptism He made him actually an inheritor unto everlasting life. And here also a man is bounden to thank God for that He hath not only set him in the highway to heaven, but also hath sent one of His blessed angels to be with him here, and to keep him, to help him, to admonish him, and to defend him against his mighty and most vigilant enemy. On the other side, a man ought to consider and confess his great unkindness, how that afterwards, when he came to the years of discretion, he did not obey God, nor love, laud, nor honour Him according to his most bounden duty and promise made at his baptism, but brake His most holy commandments, and so despised and dishonoured God, for the which he ought to require His most merciful forgiveness. And this a man may do particularly, perusing all the ten commandments, considering in every one and in every branch where and how he hath offended.

Secondly, a man ought to thank God highly for His great kindness, in giving unto him the special gifts of his soul, of his body, and of his worldly goods. The gifts of his soul be free will, remembrance, and reason lightened with faith, by which he may clearly perceive that God's commandments be very just and good, and very easy to fulfil and keep, and that he shall have God's gracious favour and be saved by keeping of them. And also he may see, that to live according to God's law is the most laudable, joyful, and most pleasant life that any man can have in this world, because God hath commanded nothing but that is very laudable and good, and again He hath forbidden nothing but that is evil and greatly against reason, and yet to the intent a man should avoid and forsake any such evil, God hath forbidden it under pain of damnation. Likewise a man may consider the special gifts of his body, as right shape, beauty, good proportion, strength, and such other, and also the external gifts of this world, as riches, lands or patrimony, estimation, authority, and such other, and yet over and besides all these it hath pleased Almighty God to promise him a reward in heaven for occupying and bestowing these gifts well. And here on the other side, a man ought to acknowledge and confess his great unkindness unto Almighty God, for that he hath bestowed the rehearsed gifts naughtily unto God's dishonour. Because he hath oftentimes with his reason understanded, and with his memory remembered, what God hath commanded and the goodness of it, and yet he hath refused and would not do His commandments when he ought and might have done them. Likewise he hath understanded and remembered what God hath forbidden, and the evil and naughtiness of it, and that he should lose God's gracious favour, and come in danger of damnation if he did it, and yet hath done that evil deed willingly. Also let him consider how he hath occupied his remembrance and wit in study and casting where and how he might do evil, and how he hath misspent divers times and ways the gifts of his body and also the gifts of the world, by greedy and unsatiable desires in procuring and getting them by wrong, injury, oppression, usury, ambition, and other unlawful means, and in unmerciful keeping of them by mistrust of God's goodness, and not helping his needy neighbours, and also in riotous and unthrifty spending of them for maintaining of his fleshly lust, worldly vanity and pride of life; wherein he hath shewed great unkindness, and ought to be inwardly sorry and to beseech God of His merciful pardon and forgiveness.

Thirdly, a man ought to thank God highly for His merciful kindness shewed unto him in his reconciliation, that is to say, always when he came to shrift and confessed his sins. For although it be so that a man hath broken his promise made to Almighty God at the font-stone, and hath misused and misspent God's foresaid gifts, and so greatly offended Him that he hath deserved justly to have been cast into the pit of hell, yet Almighty God, as a good Lord, of His abundant mercy is evermore content to pardon and forgive him, when he confesseth with a contrite and humble heart his offences unto his ghostly father, God's delegate judge and commissioner. For then is he there mercifully absolved and all his trespasses be clearly forgiven. And this merciful kindness is God content to shew, not once or twice, but at all times, and as often as he cometh to confession, and doth also bear him again His gracious favour, and giveth him grace to live well, and to do good works and meritorious deeds for his salvation. In this appeareth the exceeding goodness of Almighty God in ordaining this most wholesome and present remedy of penance, whereby every sinner may be delivered always from the pains of hell, and be set again in God's favour and state of salvation, for the which every man is most bounden to render thanks to the uttermost of his power. And on the other side he is likewise bounden to acknowledge, and with sorrow to confess, his manifold unkindness in that behalf, forasmuch as he hath divers times after his shrift and reconciliation turned from God, and grievously sinned again, and so hath greatly offended by breaking his promise which he made when he was shriven, for the which he ought to be sorry, and to beseech Almighty God of His merciful pardon and forgiveness.

Fourthly, a man ought to thank God for His great kindness shewed unto him, in preserving him from many sins which he might have done, and also in letting him from doing of divers which he was in mind to have done, and would have done them. For every man may consider and remember with himself that he might oftentimes have sinned when he did not, which I think he should have done, if he had not been preserved and kept from doing of them by God's special goodness. Also seldom it chanceth but that a man may understand how he hath been in mind and will to have sinned divers times, and yet he hath been let * and could not fulfil his evil purpose and desire; as sometime he hath been let by shame, sometime by fear, and sometime otherwise, which lets † (no doubt of it) God did cause him to have; for He is so merciful that He will not suffer sinners always to sin so greatly, nor to run so deeply into the hands of the devil and damnation, as they should do, if they might evermore without stop or let do so much evil and sin in deed, as they be willing to do in their hearts. And here a sinner may grant and confess, that he hath not considered this great kindness of God shewed unto him in these two rehearsed points, but hath shewed great unkindness again,

* *i.e.*, Restrained.   † *i.e.*, Hindrances.

Q

because that when he hath remembered the opportunity and the meet time and occasion that he had
to sin in time past, and might have done divers sins
without let or stop, yet he hath not given to God due
praise and thanks for his preservation from sin, but
rather he hath repented him and been sorry that he
hath not done such evil deeds as he might have done.
Likewise when he hath remembered how he hath
been let, and could not do such evil as he was in
mind and willing to do, he hath not given God thanks
because he was let, but rather he hath been discontent
and sorry that he was let ; for the which things he
ought now to be sorry and humbly beseech God of His
forgiveness.

Fifthly, a sinner ought to give God most high
thanks for His singular kindness, shewed unto him
many times when he hath been and lain in deadly
sin, for that Almighty God (notwithstanding this
manner of rebellion and obstinacy of the sinner in
remaining in sin, and not repenting him) yet did of
His great goodness and mercy come unto the sinner's
soul, and there did stand and knock, that the sinner
should have let Him in ; that is to say, God gave
him remorse of conscience, the which did grudge
against the sin that he hath done and was in, and by
that grudge of conscience he perceived, or might have
perceived, that if he would not leave and forsake his
sin he should be damned. And if he did forsake
and turn to God, and intend to live well and justly,
and to keep His commandments, that then God
would pardon him, and enter into his soul, and there
continue, and take it at his departure hence into a

better life in heaven. This merciful offer God did
always make to the sinner, upon the foresaid condition, if he would forsake his sins and keep His law.
And to the intent he should so do, God gave him
grudge in his conscience against his sin, that he
should leave it, and hate it, and take His most merciful offer. And if he did not or would not hear God
in His knocking, that is to say, if he did not forsake
his sin by the remorse of his conscience, yet God
would not actually depart and go His way, but stand
still and knock again ; that is to wit, God caused him
to have good counsel, sometime of learned men, and
sometime of his other neighbours and familiar friends,
and sometime in hearing of godly sermons, by the
which he was exhorted to forsake vice and sin, and
so to let God come into his soul. And if he did not
or would not hear Him at this second knocking, that
is, if he would not do after and follow such good
counsel as God caused him to have, yet He would
not leave him so, but did knock yet once again ; that
is to say, God did suffer him to fall in some worldly
trouble or adversity, or into some bodily disease, that
he should then remember Him and his offences, and
forsake them, and to call to God for mercy, and so to
open the door of his soul and let Him in. Thus God
in His coming and knocking hath shewed to man
great and merciful kindness, and yet man hath been
very unkind and greatly offended again. For oftentimes he would not hear God, nor let Him come in,
but rather with pleasure and desire which he had in
sin, he stopped his ears, and would not suffer his
conscience to grudge nor shew him his offences, nor

he would not do after good counsel and exhortations, nor would not esteem the adversity that came unto him as a messenger, and the knocking of God's hand; but rather fast barred the door of his soul with froward and obstinate purpose to continue and tarry still in sin, and so did keep God out. But when the devil came and knocked, and did move him but outwardly to let in pride, envy, and malice, he was then contented to open the door of his soul, and to let them and many more other vices come in. And when the world came and knocked, and moved him to· get and gather goods, not regarding how, and to keep them covetously, then he opened the door, which is the consent of his free will, and consented to let covetousness come in. Also when the sensual appetite and inordinate desire of his body came and moved him to fulfil his pleasure, as to refuse labour, and to give him ease and rest, and to nourish him in sloth and idleness, and to feed him delicately, and to put away chastity, and to follow lechery and all uncleanness, to these he set the door wide open, and at the first motion consented to fulfil their desires. And finally a sinner hath done all this in God's sight and presence, without regard of His goodness, without reverence of His majesty, without fear of His justice, and hath refused His merciful offers, and would not suffer Him to come in, but kept Him out of his soul, for the which he ought now to be sorry and to beseech God, being a most merciful Lord, of pardon and forgiveness, and not only that, but also to renounce and forsake in his heart, all manner of vice and sin, and to be in will and mind to confess

these and all other his offences, and to serve God
faithfully from henceforward in keeping His commandments, and to beseech Him to give him grace
that he never forsake nor fall from this good purpose
that he is now in, but evermore during his life to
love, laud, and honour God, according to his profession, promise, and ability.

Here (good people) I might have spoken more
largely in the rehearsing of God's merciful kindness
to us, and of our naughty unkindness again to Him,
but for this short time I judged this to be meetest
for the most part of men, seeing that after this sort
we have commonly all offended, some more, some
less, and that every man here remembering these
points that I have declared now unto you, as by the
examination of his conscience he shall find himself
culpable, so he may frame his confession, adding or
diminishing as he seeth cause. Not that I intend
hereby to prescribe a form of confession, but only to
give certain admonitions how a man might the better
make his confession, exhorting every man, beside
these admonitions, diligently to learn the commandments of God, and to search to know everything that
is there commanded or forbidden, and that by comparing his acts and deeds with God's law, which is
the rule of his life, as his conscience well examined
will bring his doings and sayings to his remembrance,
and so coming in knowledge of his offences, he may
make his confession perfectly, first inwardly to
Almighty God, and then sacramentally to God's
minister, and thereby receive pardon and absolution

of all his sins, and grace to abstain from the same
afterward, and that all we may do so, let us pray
diligently to Almighty God the Father, to Whom
with the Son and the Holy Ghost be all glory and
praise.   Amen.

THE TWENTY-SECOND SERMON.

OF CONFESSION TO A MAN'S NEIGHBOUR WHOM HE HATH OFFENDED.

WE have learned (good people) what remedy our Saviour Christ hath ordained and left in His Holy Church against the poison and infection of sin, and how that the sacrament of Penance is that only remedy whereby remission is gotten ordinarily for every deadly sin that is done of a Christian man after baptism, which sacrament of Penance consisteth in the absolution that is given by a Catholic priest to a sinner, being truly and unfeignedly contrite in his heart, and plainly and wholly confessing his sins with his mouth, submitting himself to the judgment and discipline of the Church by wholesome satisfaction, which in another sermon shall be declared unto you by God's help.

He that is thus affected, and useth this sacrament after this manner, like as he ought—steadfastly without any doubting to believe the effect of every sacrament (which by the virtue of Christ's Passion, and the operation of the Holy Ghost, doth evermore work in the worthy receiver that grace it signifieth), so he may be assured that he hath received remission of all his sins (even as the words of absolution do purport), and that he is reconciled and restored again to the favour of Almighty God, if there be no impediment and stop remaining in his heart, whereby the grace of God can take no place there, so long as that stop is not removed.

And whereas the lack of true contrition, and the hiding or excusing of a man's sins, be the special stops of this grace of remission, yet there be other stops, which, although they be generally contained within these, yet it shall be very profitable for your edifying, that they be particularly opened and declared, to the intent you may the better know them, and the sooner avoid them.

And principally because God is charity (1 John iv. 8), and the God of peace (2 Cor. xiii. 11), and not of dissension, and doth not vouchsafe to pour His grace into that heart where hatred, enmity, and breach of peace remaineth, therefore no man can be reconciled to God, Whom he hath by his sin offended, that is not reconciled to his brother or neighbour, whom by some injury, either in word or deed, he hath likewise offended. And as a sinner is bounden to confess his sin to God for absolution, so a sinner, if he have offended his neighbour, is likewise bounden to confess his fault to his neighbour, to the intent all displeasure and variance might be taken away between them, and they by brotherly love made apt vessels to receive the grace of God and remission of sin.

And although this brotherly confession be not sacramental, that is to say, the proper matter of this sacrament of Penance, as the other confession which is made to a priest is, yet it is expedient and very necessary to the attaining of the effect of the other confession, which is remission of sin, and doth prepare a man's heart and maketh it the more meet to receive the same.

So long as we live in this frail body as in earthen vessels, we cannot always be free, but sometime we shall offend and be offended, and as the offender ought humbly to ask forgiveness, so the other party that is offended ought easily and gently to remit and forgive the wrongs or injuries that be done unto him, that the members of Christ be always in peace, and most ready to keep humility and charity, the one in asking forgiveness, the other in freely forgiving. Of the first speaketh our Saviour Christ in the Gospel, saying :— " If thou offer thy offering before the Altar, and there shalt remember that thy brother hath something against thee, leave thine offering there before the Altar, and first go and be reconciled to thy brother, and then come and offer thine offering " (Matt. v. 23, 24).

In these words we may perceive the great mercy and unspeakable love of Almighty God towards men, Who letteth go His own honour, for the zeal He hath to nourish charity between neighbour and neighbour. What can be more lovingly spoken than to say, Let My service be left undone, that thy charity be kept and fulfilled ; the reconciliation of one brother to another is a sweet sacrifice to Me? And therefore, He said not, After thou hast offered, but before thou dost offer, not commanding him altogether to make no sacrifice or offering, but to prefer the reconciling of his brother before his offering, declaring by this that

He honoureth charity above all things, and accounteth it to be the most acceptable sacrifice of all other inward sacrifices, without the which He accepteth no other sacrifice, and also declaring the necessity of this reconciliation, which in no wise may be omitted and left undone, seeing no other sacrifice, neither outward nor inward in the heart of man, can be perfect so long as the enmity and displeasure between him and his neighbour is not ended and dissolved.

And therefore our Saviour Christ in these words speaketh marvellous precisely, both to affray a man and also to comfort him again. For when He had said " Leave thine offering," He rested not there, but added "before the Altar," and to fear him more He said " Go," and more than that, He said "Go first," and then (to comfort him again) " Come and offer thine offering ; " signifying by all these words, that the Altar of God doth not receive them that be at discord and variance with their neighbour. This ought to be a necessary lesson to all priests, to take heed they come not to God's Altar, and there to offer for the ignorances and sins of the people, the price of our redemption, the sacrifice of the New Testament, which is the very Body and Blood of our Saviour Christ, in the remembrance of His Passion, being at debate and in variance with their neighbours.

It ought to be a lesson also in laymen which be no priests, that they study to be reconciled to them whom they have offended, when they intend to offer to God their offerings, which be the sacrifice of a contrite heart, the sacrifices of prayer, of alms, and of thanksgiving (Ps. l. 19, cxl. 2, xlix. 14). For the

Scripture of God calleth these kind of works sacrifices made to Almighty God (Heb. xiii. 15). For which cause when a man is about to offer his prayer to God, and shall remember the offence he hath done to his brother, it were better to defer his prayer, and first to go and reconcile his brother, and then, consequently, to offer his prayer in peace and brotherly love. For the which peace and love Christ did all things that He did here in earth, to knit us all together in unity, that before were divided by enmity.

And whereas our Saviour saith not, Reconcile thy brother to thee, but be thou reconciled to thy brother, He might seem rather to speak of him that is offended and suffereth wrong, than of him that doeth the wrong. And though it be sufficient for him that suffered wrong to forgive him freely in his heart, even as he would have God to forgive him, yet it should declare the perfection of his charity, if he did go to his adversary, and not only did forgive him that wrong which he had done, but also with gentle speech did mitigate his anger, and persuaded him ever after to bear towards him a good affection. Now, if the perfection of charity doth require that the sufferer should go and reconcile him that did him the wrong, how much more is it necessary for him that of a malicious stomach doth the wrong, to go and humble himself to his neighbour, whom he hath hurt in word or deed, and to confess his fault unto him, submitting himself to make what amends shall be thought reasonable, and so to be fully reconciled and made friends again? For which cause S. James exhorteth all Christian men and women, one to confess their

sins to another, and to pray each for other, that so
they might be saved (James v. 16).

How great a fault it is to do injury to his neighbour, every man may well perceive that understandeth
the law of God, which commandeth a man, upon pain
of damnation, to love his neighbour as himself, yea,
and to love his enemy also, if any such be, and to
overcome evil with goodness, setting us the doing
of our Saviour Christ for an example for us to follow
(Rom. v. 6), Who, by His death, reconciled us to God
the Father, when we were His enemies. Hereby a
man may perceive the greatness of his fault, when
he doth injury, because then he hurteth him whom
he should love, he breaketh God's law, he contemneth the example of our Saviour Christ, he sheweth
himself the follower of wicked Cain, Saul, and the
devil, he stoppeth the influence of God's grace into
his soul, he mortifieth and marreth all his other good
deeds, if he have done any, and, finally, killeth his
own soul, and setteth it in the dreadful state of eternal damnation.

The remedy to avoid all this heap of evils is humbly, without malice or excuse, to confess his fault to
his neighbour offended, and to pacify him to whom
he gave great cause to be angry, and to make recompence so far as he may. If he have offended him in
thought, let him reconcile him in thought, if he hath
offended him in words, let him make him amends
in words, if he hath done wrong in deeds, let him
make a recompence in deeds. Look as he hath committed the fault, the same may let him make the
amends, without which reconciliation, neither his

prayer, nor his alms, nor his fasting, nor any other good work or sacrifice, is meritorious or acceptable in the sight of God, as lacking the root of charity, which in Christ giveth life to all other good works, as branches proceeding out of it. If he whom thou hast offended be far away absent, and thou canst not then go to him with the feet of thy body, then go to him with the feet of thy soul, with thine humble and loving affection, and in the sight of God, to Whom thou art about to make thine offering, require forgiveness, and then revoke thine intention to thine offering again.

No worldly thoughts ought to let this brotherly confession, as to think that thou shalt thus be despised of other worldly men, or that it is against thine honour or worship to submit thyself to thine inferior, or that it should be shame for thee so to do. These corrupt affections of the world and the flesh be the chains of the devil, to keep a man's soul still in bondage of sin, and the lets of God's grace, which should set him at liberty. We that in our baptism have promised and vowed to renounce the devil and his works, and all his pomps and pride, why should we be moved anything therewith against God's commandment, and our own soul's health, seeing we know that God despiseth a proud heart, and doth not despise an humble heart. Let us therefore regard the just judgment of God, and despise the corrupt judgment of the world.

It is not against a man's honour or worship to be the servant of God, but all dishonour and shame is it to be the servant and vile slave of sin. If God commanding us to prefer the reconciling of our brother before His oblation, did neglect His own true honour, for the commodity of man, why should not we in doing of God's commandment neglect the false and transitory honour of the world, for the service of God and the salvation of our own souls? Look what God doth more love, let us prefer that in our doings. He loveth better the concord and agreement of His people than their offerings, because their offerings cannot increase His riches, yet their charity can increase His glory. For which cause we ought most of all to regard that which God most loveth, and not to be ashamed to do well to our brother, lest God's Son be ashamed of us before His Father.

And this ought we to do without delay, as S. Paul teacheth, saying, Let not the sun set upon your anger, nor give not place to the devil (Eph. iv. 26, 27), who is most busy in the night time, taking occasion when a man is alone to kindle his anger more, and to move the man to abuse that heady affection which is void of all counsel, to further mischief, as to false accusations, murder, and such other enormities as proceed from anger.

Thus briefly ye see what he that any way hath offended his neighbour is bounden to do, which is to go to him, and to confess his fault, and to do that lieth in him to reconcile his neighbour. No heart is so hard and stiff but with humble submission it will be mollified and made soft, as the wise man saith " A soft speech breaketh bones, and an humble answer dissolveth anger " (Prov. xv. 1 ; xxv. 15), so that it lieth in our power to quench or to kindle the anger of him that is offended. On the other side, he that is offended and hath taken and suffered injury at his neighbour's hand, ought not only to forgive him heartily and freely that did the wrong, but also to pray for him, as S. James saith, "Confess yourselves one to another, and pray each for other, that ye may be saved" (James v. 16). And this is also another let and stop, that the grace which is ordinarily given by the sacrament of Penance, can take no place in the heart of him that will not be reconciled and forgive his neighbour, as he would God should forgive him.

Therefore (good people) if any of you have suffered wrong at your neighbour's hand, think and consider with himself how often he hath offended other men, and God also the Lord of all men, and so shall he be more ready and disposed to forgive again. Let him labour to imitate our Saviour Christ, Whose servant he professeth to be, Who taught all His disciples in their prayers to forgive such as were debtors and offenders unto them, if they would have God to forgive unto them their offences likewise (Matt. vi. 12). For the man of whom our Saviour speaketh in the parable that would not forgive his fellow-servant his small debt of one hundred pence (Matt. xviii. 28), did in that unmerciful behaviour much hurt himself, and brought himself in debt and danger of ten thousand talents, which his lord had forgiven him before. Whereby we be taught that when we do not forgive others, then we stand in our own light, and procure that God shall not forgive us. It lieth in our power to prescribe as it were a law to God of forgiving or not forgiving sin. If we revenge or forgive the wrongs that be done against us, even so will

God revenge or forgive that we have done against Him. For as the wise man saith, "He that will revenge himself, shall find vengeance at God's hand again, and shall retain his own sins" (Ecclus. xxviii. 1). Forgive thy neighbour that hurteth thee, and then thy sins at thy prayer shall be loosed. The man that keepeth his anger against his neighbour, can he ask a medicine of God? Therefore let every man forgive one another, if he hath any quarrel against him (Col. iii. 13), like as our Lord hath forgiven us, and let no rancour, or malice, nor no footstep of hatred remain. The greater injury that is done, the greater merit and the more praise is to contemn it. It is more glorious for a Christian man to overcome himself and his furious passion of anger, than to overcome his enemy, and so to do himself more harm than his enemy.

Against this wild beast of ire, we ought to use as a sharp bridle the fear of God's judgment to come, and when we be provoked thereto, to ask of ourselves, whether it were better to be overcome of anger than to overcome it, and to consider that when we be overcome of it, we blame ourselves, and be ashamed, although no man accuse us, and be greatly sorry for it. But when we have overcome it like a conqueror, we are glad and much rejoice. For the greatest victory against anger, is when we patiently bear our injuries, and do not cruelly revenge them. If they be worthy much blame that do injury to us, why do we make ourselves as evil as they be in doing the like to them again? Rather let us study to be like God, Who commandeth us to love our enemies, and to do good to them that hate us, and to pray for them that slander and persecute us, that we might be the children of our Father that is in heaven, that causeth the sun, His creature, to shine over good and evil, and raineth both over the just men and unjust (Matt. v. 44, 45).

God our most merciful Father hath so wholly pardoned us, and so liberally forgiven us all injuries done against Him, that He neither condemneth us nor putteth us to shame, nor imputeth them to us, whom He hath once received to mercy. But contrary, some men there be that forgive their injuries, that although they will not revenge them, yet they will upbraid them withal, and cast them in their teeth. Other some there be, that although they speak nothing of them, yet they keep rancour in their mind, ready to break out when occasion shall be given again. These men have not fully forgiven their neighbour's offences, and in so doing, be not the children of God like to their Father in heaven, Who fully and freely forgiveth all injuries, and neither upbraideth nor remembereth them any more again, so that where sin in sinners did abound, there grace in penitents doth more abound.

Therefore when we forgive, let us do it freely and wholly and from the heart, without pretended simulation, which we may know whether we have done so or not, when we perceive ourselves to be verily and heartily sorry, when our neighbour whom we have forgiven falleth into any misfortune, or is hurt or harmed by any occasion, and also when we perceive ourselves to be heartily glad for his com-

R

modity and preferment, and to labour and procure
the same as much as lieth in us.   This is that
mutual compassion that all Christian men, being
members of one body, ought to have one to the other,
in such things as be godly and proceed from charity,
always following peace and holiness of life, without
the which no man shall see God (Heb. xii. 14).   For
they shall be called the sons of God that be makers
of peace (Matt. v. 9).

Some men be peaceable that give and render good
for good, and study to hurt nobody, so much as
lieth in them.   Other some be patient that do not
render evil for evil, and yet be able to bear with them
that do them wrong.   Other some be peace-makers
that give and render good for evil, and be always
ready to profit such as hurt them.

The first kind of men keep peace, the second
maintain peace, and the third make peace and win
the souls of other, and therefore are counted happy
and worthy to be called the children of God, that do
the work of God's Son, that after they be reconciled
themselves, labour with all their power to reconcile
other to their heavenly Father.   Many kinds of alms
there be and works of mercy, both corporal and also
spiritual.   But among them all there is never one
greater, than freely, even from the heart, to remit that
another man hath offended against us.

It is nothing in a manner to love him that loveth
us and doth us no harm, for infidels and all other
men of nature will so do, but to love our enemies, and
to will to do good to them that wish and do evil
to us as much as they can, is the greatest perfection

of a Christian man. And although the number of men for the most part doth not come to that degree of perfection to love and do good to their enemies, whereunto every Christian man ought with prayer and diligence to labour and wrestle with himself to come, yet he cannot be a good man that will not freely and heartily forgive his enemy, that ceaseth to be his enemy and is sorry for that he hath done, and humbly asketh him forgiveness. For his sins be holden still and not remitted of God, that will not forgive his penitent neighbour that he hath done against him. Therefore, seeing in many things we offend all, and the angels of God be not yet come that shall take away all offences out of the world, it is not possible for peace to be kept everywhere in this world and God to be pleased, except he that in anything doth offend his neighbour lay away his pride and submit himself, and he that is offended lay away his obstinacy and be content to be entreated. For by these two means, God's peace shall be kept, without the which God's mercy cannot be gotten, and our offerings cannot be accepted. But having and using them, righteousness, peace, and joy in the Holy Ghost shall remain with us, and the kingdom of God shall be within us, and we daily in grace and fear shall work our own salvation through Christ our Lord, to Whom with the Father and the Holy Ghost be all glory for evermore. Amen.

THE TWENTY-THIRD SERMON.

OF SATISFACTION.

HAVING declared unto you (good people) the first two parts of penance, which be contrition and confession, now order requireth that I should declare at this time the third part, which is satisfaction.

And first of all, it is to be known that when a Christian man or woman hath by consent of mind, or by word or deed, done anything that is deadly sin, then hath he set himself in the state of damnation, and is bounden to suffer everlasting pain in hell, because the reward or hire of sin is eternal death (Rom. vi. 23), under which pain God in the beginning and always did forbid sin. Likewise when a sinner changeth his mind, forsaking his sin, and taketh true repentance for the same, and cometh to confession to a priest (if he may confess and have a priest), after that sort and intent as is declared before, then Almighty God doth mercifully forgive him all the pains and punishment that he had deserved, and should have had in hell, for his offences, and setteth the sinner again in the state of salvation. And this doth Almighty God evermore, after the penitent's confession ordinarily, although he take not so much and so great repentance for his sin, as he had pleasure in it, nor although he be not so long sorry, as he lay and continued in sin before. For God hath not commanded that sinners shall take as much repentance, and be as long sorry for their sins, as they took pleasure and continued in their sin. For if He had done so, the penitent sinner could not have been sure that he had mercy and forgiveness after his confession, but should rather have been always in doubt and fear of forgiveness, because he could not always certainly know that he had taken so much and so long repentance, as he had pleasure and tarried in his sin ; which fear and doubt of forgiveness, no sinner coming unfeignedly to this sacrament may have at any time, but whensoever a sinner doth forsake his sins and taketh repentance for it, be it little or much, and so cometh to confession, then he knoweth and is in surety that he hath forgiveness, and is set again in the state of salvation. And though it be true that any quantity of contrition is sufficient to have forgiveness of the pains of hell due for sin, yet the more he taketh the better he doth. And this forgiveness of sin, and eternal pain due for sin, cometh by the virtue of Christ's Passion, Who hath made satisfaction upon the cross, and rid us from all iniquity (Titus ii. 14) by His death, and is the sacrifice propitiatory for the sins of the whole world (1 John ii. 2), and hath borne our sins in His body upon the tree, by Whose wounds we are made safe (1 Peter ii. 24).

Therefore, this is to be surely believed, that only our Saviour Christ by His painful Passion on the cross is that satisfaction which deserveth remission of our sins, and the abolishing of eternal death and damnation, which remission and delivery no man is able to deserve by anything that he can do, but only the goodness and humanity of God our Saviour in Christ, not by the works of righteousness which we have done, but by His own mercy hath wrought and brought to pass (Titus ii. 14 ; iii. 5).

God of His great mercy to all true penitents, forgiveth sin, and yet of His justice and truth, He leaveth not the sins of them whom He forgiveth unpunished.   But all sins of all men and women be punished either eternally in hell, or temporally for a time (Job xxiv.), that as in forgiving appeareth His mercy, so in correcting or avenging might appear His justice.   For which cause, considering that God by the merits of Christ, forgiveth, to all that be truly penitent and confessed, all their sins, and also the pains of hell due for the same, and yet leaveth no sin unpunished although it be remitted, we may therefore certainly know that every sinner, although he hath received absolution and remission, either hath suffered, or remaineth yet still bounden to suffer, certain temporal pain according to the nature and quantity of his former fault, for that he presumed to do against God's law, and brake his promise and profession in baptism.   And this temporal pain is our debt which we are bounden to pay to God.   For as we are debtors to Almighty God for His manifold benefits bestowed upon us, and so are bounden always to thank Him, to honour Him, and to offer to Him the sacrifice of praise, so are we debtors to Him also for our

manifold sins done against Him, and so are we bounden
to satisfy the justice of God by suffering pain for the
same. Both which debts when we could not and were
not able to pay ourselves, Christ our Lord, being the
Mediator between God and man, by His painful
death hath paid it for us, and hath cancelled the
obligation of our debt, and fully satisfied God for the
sin of the world, and hath taken away eternal death
due for the same, and so hath made us now able by
Him, and in Him, both to offer that sacrifice of
praise, which for all His benefits we were bounden to
make, and also to satisfy the justice of God for that
temporal pain which remaineth for us to suffer, after
that the guiltiness of our sins and the pains of hell
be remitted through the satisfaction made upon the
cross, the benefit whereof is applied to us by true
faith and contrition. Not that we be able of ourselves
by our works or suffering to make worthy satisfaction
for the same, as Christ hath done, but that we are
made able by Christ, and in Him to do or suffer
that wherewith God is contented and satisfied and
accepteth as a satisfaction.

By this ye shall understand (good people) that the
satisfaction of penance which I have to declare unto
you at this time, is a punishment or affliction which a
sinner taketh upon him to suffer, by the assignment
of his ghostly father, after the remission of his sins,
to the intent he might thereby cut away the cause and
sequel of his sins which remain, and also either clearly
redeem, or at least mitigate the temporal pains due
for the same sins, by doing of such penal works as be
contrary to the sins committed.

This doctrine of satisfaction standeth upon these two grounds. First, that when the sin is remitted, and the sinner received into grace and favour with God again, yet oftentimes there remaineth temporal pain to be suffered for the same sin, either in this world or in the next. And secondly, that this temporal pain may be mitigated, or redeemed and taken away, by penitential satisfaction and the worthy fruits of penance. To this doctrine beareth witness the trade and process of the whole Scriptures. When the people of Israel in the wilderness grudged against Moses and Aaron, and would have gone back into Egypt again (Num. xiv. 2–4), and so provoked God to vengeance, Moses prayed for the people very fervently, at whose prayer God did forgive the people their sin, and yet notwithstanding that forgiveness, He said that He would punish them after this sort, that never one of them that came out of Egypt and had not obeyed Him in the wilderness, should see or enter into the land which He promised them. Whereby we learn that after the sin remitted, many times there remaineth a punishment temporal to be suffered for the same. Also King David when he had taken contrition, and confessed the sin which he did with Barsabee, and for the killing of her husband Urias, the prophet Nathan shewed him that God had forgiven him his sin, and that he should not die and be damned for it, but yet he should have great and long temporal punishment for those offences. And so he had, both in the death of his children, and also in the persecution of his son Absalom, and in divers other things which the prophet told him. And yet when the prophet had said that his young son begotten by Barsabee should die, trusting that his humble penance should change God's sentence in punishing of him by the death of his son, he fell to fasting, weeping, praying, watching, and lying upon the ground, by the space of seven days, and although he did not then obtain the release of that punishment which was appointed by God's immutable decree (2 Kings xii. 23), yet in another like offence he obtained the mitigation of his temporal pain. For when David for the sin of numbering the people, had taken contrition, and humbled himself before God, confessing his fault, the prophet by the message of God, for punishment of his sin after remission, gave him choice whether he would have seven years' hunger, or three months' war without victory, or three days' pestilence, and when he did choose pestilence, which might as soon fall upon him, the offender, as upon the people, he did so punish and afflict himself, that God, in respect of his penance, was satisfied and content with the plague of one day, and did remit the rest (2 Kings xxiv. 16): Even so David in his Psalms (xcviii. 8), speaking of Moses and Aaron, saith that God did hear them, and was merciful unto them, and yet punished and revenged all their inventions and sin. And the Apostle S. Paul teacheth us (1 Cor. xi. 27), that for the sin of abusing the Blessed Body and Blood of our Lord in the Sacrament of the Altar, many were punished with weakness, sickness, and corporal death, and telleth us also there the remedy how to avoid these pains, which is, if we would judge, condemn and punish ourselves, we should escape the punishment of God ; for when we be judged and punished of God, we be but corrected, Whose chastisement is rather to be called an admonition than a condemnation, rather a fatherly medicine than a final punishment and destruction. And, therefore, every sinner ought to exercise more severity against himself, that judging himself, he be not judged of God, the contemning whereof is a means to be eternally condemned with the wicked world.

It sufficeth not for a man to change his manners to the better, and to begin a new life and forsake the old, except also he make satisfaction to God for those sins he hath done by the sorrow of penance, by the mourning of an humble and contrite heart, and by alms. Whereby appeareth that the penance of a Christian man sinning deadly after baptism, containeth satisfaction by fasting, alms, prayer, and other godly exercises of spiritual life, not for the eternal pain of hell, which with the sin is remitted in the using of the Sacrament of Penance, or else (if the sacrament cannot be had) in the desire of full purpose to use it when it may be had, but for temporal pain, which (as the Scriptures teach) is not wholly always remitted to them that take the grace of God in vain.

True contrition and sorrow for sin taken for the love of God whom he hath offended, causeth a sinner likewise to take this satisfaction and punishment upon him, assigned by the minister of God, by the virtue of the keys committed to the Church, or sometimes voluntarily taken upon him of his own good will, as S. Paul saith to the Corinthians (2 Cor. vii. 10), that the sorrow which is taken for God's sake, worketh steadfast penance for salvation, and on the other side the sorrow of the world worketh death. For even this sorrow which you have taken for God's sake (saith S. Paul to the Corinthians) how much carefulness hath it wrought in you that ye do not offend again thereafter ? And also it hath wrought such a confession of your fault as ye offer to make satisfaction and amends for the same, and it hath wrought in you anger and indignation against your fault, and fear of the terrible judgment of God for your fault, and desire to be reconciled again to God and the Church, and zeal to be diligent in doing good hereafter, and punishment whereby ye do afflict and punish yourselves for your offence by-past, to the intent ye might escape the correction of God that hangeth over your heads.

All these be the effects of true contrition, which ceaseth not to wash the wounds of sin more and more after forgiveness (as David did, Ps. l. 2), and as natural things be healed by their contraries, so it laboureth to have the wounds of sin fully and perfectly healed, by doing contrary good works to the former sins, that by them the root of sin might be clean grubbed out, and the nest that remaineth, be clearly scoured, and the pride of man's heart pulled down and humbled, and the pronity* and disposition to sin bridled and restrained, which things be done when we do as S. Paul counselleth us—" Like as ye have given the parts and members of your body and

* *i.e.*, Proneness.

soul to serve uncleanness and iniquity to further
iniquity, so give and apply the same parts and members of your body and soul to serve righteousness, for
your satisfaction" (Rom. vi. 19). That is to say,
take as much pains to wash away the dregs and
filthiness of your sins gathered by your naughty
living, as ye took pleasure before to defile and infect
your souls by your said naughty living. And as ye
be now just and sanctified by remission of your sins,
and the presence of God's grace and His Holy Spirit
in your souls ; so labour also to be yet just and
sanctified by purging the sequel, the scars, and the
deformity which remain in your souls after your sins
be remitted, the painful affliction of yourselves, and
by doing the worthy fruits of penance (Matt. iii. 8),
esteeming and pondering the measure of your correction, according to the quantity of your fault.

And whereas penance is two ways taken, the one
to be inward, standing in the contrition of the heart,
the other outward, standing in the affliction of the
flesh, when thou dost condemn and reprove thy sin,
then thou hast penance, and when thou dost by
satisfaction following, punish and correct thy sin,
then thou hast the fruit of penance, and when thy
affliction and pain is no less in correcting of thy sin,
than thy pleasure was in doing of the same, then
thou hast done the worthy fruits of penance, as thus :
if thou hast stolen other men's goods, beside the
ceasing from the sin, and restitution of the same
goods, now begin to give thine own ; if thou hast done
injury to any man in word or deed, make amends
with humble and good words again, and them that

hurt thee, labour to reconcile them with kindness and benefits.

It is not sufficient for a man's health to pull only the dart out of his wound, but also to lay some plaister and medicine to the wound. Recompense thy delicious fare and drunkenness with fasting and drinking of water ; if thou hast seen a woman with an unchaste eye, forbear to see a woman again, and learn after a wound to take more heed.

Thus a sinner's life ought not only to be changed into the better, but also God must be entreated and made merciful, by alms and other painful works, for his sins by-past.

The principal works of satisfaction be fasting, prayer and alms, which be specially commended in the Gospel of Christ (Matt. vi. 1—18). Under fasting be contained all bodily pains and labours, as watching, lying upon the ground, wearing of hair or sackcloth, and other such like. Under alms be contained all the other works of mercy, as well corporal as spiritual, whereof some other time, God willing, ye shall be instructed. And under prayer be contained the prayers of other, as of priests, poor men, and poor scholars, such as by our alms and liberality be procured to pray for us, as it is said in the old law, that the priest shall pray for him and for his sin and it shall be forgiven him (Lev. iv. 20). So that fasting is a medicine to heal perfectly those sins which we have done by concupiscence and desire of the flesh against ourselves and our own bodies. And alms is likewise a medicine to heal perfectly those sins which we committed by concupiscence of the eyes, which is covetousness, deceit, oppression, and unjust dealing against our neighbours. And last of all the pride of life, the contempt of godliness and presumption of mind, which be sins immediately against God, be healed perfectly by instant, humble, and devout prayers.

And the Holy Scriptures do plainly shew how that sinners may here in this life satisfy and content Almighty God for temporal pain with these three works, as the book of Daniel sheweth, where the prophet Daniel exhorteth the King Nebuchadonosor to redeem his sins with alms, that is to say, the seven years of pain which he should suffer for his sins. And old Tobias taught his son that alms delivered from sin (Tobias iv. 11), in which two places by the word (sin) is understood the temporal pain due for sin. For by the merits of our Saviour Christ, which He applied to us in the Sacraments of Baptism and Penance, the guiltiness of our sin and the eternal pains of hell be taken away, and our afflictions whereby we suffer with Christ, and are made like to the image of Christ, taking their virtue of Christ's Passion, and wrought in us by His grace and Holy Spirit, not of their own worthiness but by God's merciful acceptation, are means ordained of God to satisfy Him, and to turn away His anger and displeasure for our sins, and to purchase His further grace. And that fasting and prayer be of the same effect for this purpose that alms is, is plain by the example of the Ninivites, who after the preaching and threatening of Jonas the prophet, being contrite and sorry for their offences, did satisfy and redeem the pain and punishment which they should have had, with fasting in ashes and sackcloth and fervent prayer, and by that means revoked the sentence of God which was spoken by mouth of Jonas (Jonas iii. 7–10). But the Scripture always for the most part joineth these three together, because fasting without mercy to a man's neighbour, and the lifting up of his mind to God, by prayer, is unfruitful and little regarded of God (Isa. lviii. 2–10). And alms joined with surfeiting and the greedy cares of the world, and lacking the fellowship of fasting and prayer, is not meritorious. And the prayer of him that will not bridle the desires of his flesh by abstinence, and shutteth his mercy and compassion from his neighbour that needeth, is not heard of God. But these three joined in a faithful man together, be of great virtue and reach to heaven, and there do turn away the face of God from his sins, and do purchase God's grace for such things as he hath need of, as Tobias saith, Prayer with fasting and alms is good, and better than to store up treasures of gold in his coffers (Tobias xii. 8).

A man may also make satisfaction for his sins with repentance and sorrow for his sin, so that God will forgive him all the temporal pain which he deserved to have had, as God forgave S. Peter the said pain for his great repentance and bitter weeping (Luke xxii. 62), and likewise Mary Magdalene, whose great sorrow is expressed in the Gospel. And because the minister of God knoweth not how much repentance and contrition the sinner hath taken, nor how much he ought to take for due satisfaction, therefore his office is to enjoin the penitent certain works of penance for to make satisfaction, such as the party may easily and shortly do, for avoiding of grudge if it were too hard, and also for avoiding of forgetfulness if it were too long, and then to counsel and exhort the penitent to do more penance and good deeds of his own good will in further satisfaction for his sins already done, and for stopping of the entry of the devil's suggestions to sin to come, and for exercising of himself in virtuous occupations contrary to his sins before.

Wherefore (good people) I beseech you to care and provide for your souls, which Christ hath preferred before His own blood, in that He hath given the one to redeem the other ; fear to fall into the hands of God, and contemn not His judgments ; the certain knowledge of the pains due for our sins, is only reserved to God and to our Lord Jesus Christ, to Whom the Father hath given all judgment ; whereof we may not be curious in searching, but diligent in avoiding by the worthy fruits of penance, which be acceptable to God, for two causes, both for that they be good works of their own nature commended and commanded of God, and also for that they be enjoined us to do by the authority of the keys of the kingdom of heaven given to the Church, and are better accepted of God for our obedience to Him and His Holy Church. Let not the straightness of penance fear us,* nor the conscience of our sins keep us back, for in many good men where sin hath most abounded, there hath grace more abounded.

---

* *i.e.,* Let not the strictness of penance cause us fear.

The sufferings and pains of this time be not equal to that fault which is remitted, to that pain which we have deserved, nor yet to that glory which is reserved for us. As nothing is impossible to them that believe, so nothing is hard or painful to them that love, where devotion driveth them to begin, and grace helpeth them to make an end, both in doing the fruits of penance for their sins past, and also in doing the fruits of virtue for increase of righteousness present, till God deliver us from all pains and dangers of sin, and give unto us the kingdom which He hath prepared for us from the beginning of the world, through Christ our Lord, to Whom with the Father and the Holy Ghost be all honour and glory. Amen.

S

THE TWENTY-FOURTH SERMON.

HOW A MAN SHOULD AFTER PENANCE AVOID SIN AND LIVE WELL.

IT is better (good people) to avoid sin than to amend sin, as it is more wholesome and pleasant for a man with good diet to preserve his health, than after sickness with danger and grief to recover his health. And it is a great deal worse to fall down again after he be fully recovered, than it was to fall first in the beginning. For which cause, after a man be restored again to the health of his soul by the medicine of penance, he ought to be a great deal more careful and vigilant lest he fall again to his old sickness, and by that means come the sooner in danger of eternal death, and he ought evermore to remember the lesson of our Saviour Jesus Christ which He gave to the man sick of the palsy, whom He made whole, which is this : Behold thou art made whole, go thy ways and now sin no more, lest some worse thing chance to thee (John v. 14). To this end how a man should avoid sin and live well, the most part of all the Scripture is written and the most part of all sermons be made, and of no matter may be more said ; but I intend, God willing, at this time only to note unto you three or four general points, which if a man do remember and observe, he shall the better and with more ease avoid sin, and keep himself in grace and good life.

First, I would he should do, as a man doth that hath been sick of a great surfeit and in peril of death, who when he is restored to his health again, he will diligently take heed and refuse those meats that brought him into his sickness, and be forbidden him to eat upon by his physician, and he will remember to feed upon such meats only as the physician prescribeth him and will preserve his health. Even so every man and woman must do and keep like order and diet after their confession, for to keep their souls still in health, they must remember that Christ, our Physician, hath made them whole by the sovereign medicine of penance, and hath forbidden them all manner of sin whereon they surfeited, and therefore they must utterly refuse and forsake, and in no wise eat of that evil meat by willing and consenting to any sin again. Now for the better avoiding of this, a man must do three things : first, consider the naughtiness of sin, and then when any cometh to his mind uncalled for, let him put it away by-and-by, and thirdly, he must keep his five senses well, and fly from the company of evil persons and occasions of sin.

First, let him consider that sin is so vile of itself that every man doth hate and abhor the name of it ; for a man loveth not nor would not be called proud, malicious, covetous, a thief, a lecher or slanderer, and such like. And then, if men did consider the very deeds of sins, they should see that they were much worse, more shameful, more against reason, and so men should hate the deeds of sins more than they do their names. For this is the nature of sin, before it be done it hath some pleasure, but after the deed the pleasure ceaseth, and heaviness cometh in his place, and for the time of the doing of sin, it maketh him no man but a beast, whereby he loseth his honesty, his good name, his riches, his beauty, his health, his strength, his wit, his reason, and is made a fool, a madman, an instrument of the devil, and a very devil for the time. His soul, like a dead carrion, lieth in his body as in a grave, which, when the mouth is open, sendeth forth an evil savour or smell, and infecteth with poisoned words and example the air round about, and all those that have conversation with him, and so is he made odious to himself, in that he defileth his own body, and is the cause of the sickness and corruption of the same, and is also odious to his neighbours, whom he hurteth many ways, and is also most odious to God, Whom he dishonoureth by his naughty living, and diminisheth His glory, and causeth His name to be evil spoken of among the heathen. And thus, when a man lieth impudently in sin, his enemies laugh at him, his friends pity him, all other men abhor him, beside that he loseth God's most gracious favour, in Whose sight he always standeth, and cannot excuse himself by secretness, neither in deed nor in thought. And if he die in this damnable state of deadly sin, his own conscience shall then accuse him before God, and his remembrance shall bear witness against him, and declare how, when, where, and how often he sinned, and shall open his whole vile and beastly life

so plainly before God his Judge, that he shall not be
able to speak for himself one word (Matt. xxii. 12,
13), nor yet to ask mercy, if it were demanded of
him why he did those sinful deeds, but he shall hold
his peace, and see that he is worthy to be damned
and cast into the prison of hell, there to remain in
everlasting pains. If men or women did diligently
consider the naughtiness of these things which God
hath forbidden, and how greatly they be against reason, and then would surely believe that they should
thereby lose God's favour, and set themselves in state
of damnation, and be verily damned to infinite and
everlasting pain if they died so, which is most true,
then, doubtless, they would hate all the ways of iniquity (Ps. cxviii.), and fly from it as from a serpent,
and as the very cause of all these mischiefs that follow, and feed their minds no more with that damnable meat of sin, but refuse it, and forsake it, as a
poison infecting and killing them both in body and
soul.

The second thing to avoid sin is this, when any
sin cometh into a man's mind and remembrance uncalled for, by the suggestion of the devil, or the
motion of his flesh, let him evermore put it away by-
and-by with hatred. And let a man remember this
lesson well, for it is a singular mean and very necessary to defend and keep his soul and will from the
consent and desire to sin. For like as a flesh-fly, if
it be not beaten away as soon as it cometh, will leave
filthy blowings in the flesh, which will be worms, and
destroy it, even so will sin, when it cometh into a
man's mind, cause and make evil thoughts and

desires in man's heart, if it be not put away by-and-by at the first coming. For if a man will think upon sin, and revolve it in his mind, except he do consider it with hatred, then will it engender in his will some pleasure, and it will move him to imagine and think evil, and it will heat him, and set his heart on fire, and blind his reason, and provoke him sore and greatly to consent to do that sin, and at length it will bring his will to agree and to desire and fully determine to do it, and so then it destroyeth and killeth his soul, that is to say, then hath he lost the title which he had to everlasting life, and hath set himself in the terrible and dreadful state of damnation, and hath deserved to have everlasting pains in hell. The more and the longer a man suffereth his mind to be occupied in thinking upon sin, the more desirous shall he be to do it, and the more pain and labour shall he have to put it out of his mind again when he would. Happy is he (saith the prophet) that will hold himself from vice, and will break the heads of the little ones (Ps. cxxxvi. 9), I mean the first motions of sin, upon the stone which is Christ, by withstanding them with faith and prayer. And surely nothing is so evil, so hurtful, and so dangerous to a man's soul, as to suffer his mind and remembrance to be occupied and to think upon sin ; and, therefore, when any sinful thoughts come into his mind, let him make a sharp rod of hatred and abhorring of it, and beat it away by-and-by, and then let him occupy and set his mind upon his other lawful business, or let him do something upon the which he must needs steadfastly think, or let him go to some honest company and commune upon some good matter. But best of all it is to fall to prayer, and with that sword of the Spirit to shift off and drive away the fiery darts of the devil, calling for the aid of the said Holy Spirit to help his infirmity. And thus may a man beat away the flesh-fly of sin, that he shall not rest and leave behind him any filthy blowings of evil thoughts and motions, and so may be kept his soul clean from the worms of deadly and damnable desires and consents.

Moreover, to avoid sin a man must also eschew the outward occasion of it. For if the cause remain, commonly the effect will follow, as thus :—first, let him keep well his five senses, and specially his sight, his hearing, and his feeling from things unlawful and forbidden ; that is to say, let him not behold and cast his eye with inward pleasure upon such things as may lightly and commonly move a man to think upon sin, nor apply and give ear with gladness to hear evil tales, or filthy and dishonest communication ; but when he seeth or heareth such evil, then let him by-and-by take away his sight and hearing from it, with displeasure, and hate the seeing and hearing of it. King David did behold curiously the beauty of his soldier's wife, and suddenly he was smitten in the heart with the dart of adultery (2 Kings xi. 2–4). And if this holy prophet David, that had so much grace of the Holy Spirit, of whom God said He had found a man even as He would wish, if he by the occasion of his eye received poison into his heart, how much shall another man come in danger by the like occasion, that neither hath so much knowledge what he should do, nor yet so much grace to do that he knoweth? And whereas the prophet saith, "Death hath entered in by our windows" (Jer. ix. 21), we may understand by that, that sin entereth into the heart of man by his eyes and ears and other senses, which be as it were the windows of his soul. If the windows be not shut, or else a diligent watch set upon them, surely sin and death will creep in, although the man hath very great knowledge and grace. Like as if a candle be put in the straw the straw will burn, even so our weak and sinful nature is soon set on fire with the burning darts of the devil's temptation, if they be suffered to commence, and their ways and entries be not stopped. Also, besides the diligent keeping of his five senses, a man must flee and forsake the company of evil and lewd persons, and of those that shew evil example or give occasion to vice. For he that toucheth pitch shall soil his hands with the same (Eccles. xiii. 1), and he that keepeth company with a proud man shall begin to be proud. As S. Paul saith, "Do ye not know that a little sour leaven doth make sour the whole batch of dough" (1 Cor. v. 6), even so the vice or evil example of one doth infect a great many, and draweth others that be weak to follow him in the like vice. Depart thou (saith the wise man) from a wicked man, and keep no company with him, and so shall vice and wickedness depart from thee (Ecclus. vii. 2).

The fourth thing for a man to avoid sin is to remember his last end in all his works and deeds, and so he shall not sin for evermore (Ecclus. vii. 40). It is good for a man to think upon the beginning of his life, to consider the middle, and to remember the last end. The beginning bringeth shame, the middle bringeth sorrow, the end bringeth fear. If a man think from whence he came, he shall be ashamed ; if he considers in what case he is, he shall lament; if he remember whither he shall go, he shall be afraid. Man, first of all, when he was in honour, made to the image of God, and to be partaker with angels of the kingdom of heaven, not regarding his dignity, contemning the commandment of God his Maker, and following his own sensual appetite, was compared to unreasonable beasts, and changed the similitude of God with the similitude of beasts, and the honour of his first image being taken away by carnal desires and beastly living, was made like a beast (Ps. xlviii. 13). If a man therefore remember his own nobility, how he was made lord over the works of God, a fellow of angels, a citizen of Paradise, and one of God's household, and being by his own fault cast into inward darkness of error and ignorance, banished from pleasant Paradise, made fellow with brute beasts and a stranger or rather enemy to God, may not he, considering this his beginning, and his great fall into such vile beastliness, be worthily ashamed ? After this, if man consider where and in what state he is, he shall perceive that being in this transitory world, he is in the vale of misery, where nothing is under the sun but vanity, labour, and affliction of spirits (Ecclus. i. 14), where nothing is verily and constantly pleasant, but only by change, by passing from one thing to another, where the remedy of one labour is the beginning of another, where the less evil seemeth

a great good, where the increase of knowledge is the
increase of grief, where man in banishment dwelleth
in wilderness, walketh in darkness, in danger of falling
down the hill, and eating his bread in the sweat of
his face, may not a man, considering whither he is
now brought, be right sorry, and lament that the
time of his travail and dwelling here is prolonged?
But the best remedy to avoid sin, is always to have
in remembrance his last end.

In the last end there be three things, the death of
the body, the judgment of God, and the torments of
hell. What is more horrible than death? What is
more terrible than the judgment of God? And what
is more intolerable than the pains of hell? What
shall a man fear if he tremble not at the remembrance
of these three? Yet if he have lost shame for his vile
beginning, and if he feel no sorrow for his present
misery, at least let him take fear for the dreadful
things to come. For if he now spend his life in the
works of the flesh, in death he shall be divorced and
separated from his body and all the pleasures thereof;
in the judgment he shall be presented before Him,
into Whose hands to fall is most horrible, and be examined of Him to Whom nothing is unknown; in hell,
if he be found guilty, he shall suffer torment without
hope of relief, without measure of quantity, and without end of time. Hath not this man good cause to
live always in fear, and with fear and trembling to
labour about his own salvation? This fear which is
the beginning of wisdom, hath more strength to withstand sin than either shame or sorrow. For shame
is taken away by the multitude of sinners, where the

fellowship of so many evil livers putteth shame out of his heart. And sorrow taketh comfort of the vain pleasures of this present world, and so is weakened and made unable to withstand sin. But fear that proceedeth from a sure and certain faith of things to come, taketh no comfort of the world, seeing that in death he shall carry no worldly good with him, and in judgment he shall neither be able to deceive nor to withstand Christ his Judge, and in hell he shall have no comfort nor redemption but perpetual woe. The fruit of this fear is, that it bringeth before the eyes of our souls sometimes the sins that we have done, to the intent we should be willing and ready to suffer the scourge (as the prophet saith of himself), confessing our iniquity, and thinking for our sin (Ps. xxxvii. 18); sometimes the everlasting pains which we have deserved, to the intent we should think all that we suffer here to be delights and pleasures, in comparison of the torments which we have escaped; sometimes the heavenly rewards for which we labour and hope, to the intent we should esteem the afflictions of this present life not to be equal and worthy the glory that shall be shewed to us; sometimes the Passions which Christ hath suffered for us, that considering what His Majesty hath vouchsafed to suffer for us unprofitable servants, we should be ashamed to draw back and suffer so little for ourselves and our own salvation. And to make an end (as I have declared unto you), he that considereth the naughtiness and vileness of his sin, and endeavoureth himself to put out of mind the first motions of sin which the devil suggesteth, and watcheth diligently the windows of his five senses, and as much as he may, fly the company of evil persons and the occasions of sin, and hath the last end of his life always in his remembrance with fear, being also careful to walk warily and worthily in the sight of God, considering, as occasion shall serve, the sins which he hath done, the eternal pains which he hath deserved, the heavenly rewards which he hopeth for, and the Passions which Christ hath suffered for him, with such intent as I have before rehearsed, no doubt of it, but that man which thus doth, shall avoid sin, shall live well, shall increase in grace, shall continue in righteousness, and by the merciful goodness of God shall attain ever-lasting life, through the merits of our Lord Jesus Christ, to Whom with the Father and the Holy Ghost be all honour and glory, world without end. —Amen.

THE TWENTY-FIFTH SERMON.

OF THE SACRAMENT OF ORDER.

TWO things (good people) be necessary by the salvation of man, both by grace of this world and by glory of the next world—the inward gifts of faith and hope and the outward sacraments of Baptism, penance, and the other like.

God that is our Saviour and the principal cause of our salvation, by giving unto us these inward gifts, doth dispose and prepare the heart of man, and maketh it meet to receive grace and remission of sin ; and also by the receiving of His holy sacraments, He induceth and bringeth into the heart of man the said grace and remission, as it were water through a conduit, or corporal health by a good and profitable medicine. By these two instruments Almighty God doth form and make His Holy Church, and bringeth us to the knowledge of God and His Son Christ, that were before in darkness and the shadow of death, making as of old men and the heirs of hell and damnation to be new men, and the heirs with Christ in the kingdom of heaven. And thus, when we be by these instruments incorporate and made members of Christ's mystical body the Church, He doth also by discipline, rule us His Church, and preserveth us in unity, and multiplieth His manifold graces in us to the attaining of everlasting life.

The inward gifts be wrought in us that be of age, by the preaching of God's Holy Word, for faith cometh by the hearing of the Word of God (Rom. x. 17), which faith being tried by patience in tribulation, worketh hope that never faileth (Rom. v. 3, 4), because the charity of God is poured into our hearts by the Holy Ghost which is given unto us. And how shall men preach God's Word except they be sent (Rom. x. 15). For the office of preaching may not be of any man usurped by presumption, but ought to be faithfully used and practised by God's commission, of them that be for that purpose sent by God and His Church to convert or instruct His people.

For as in the body every part or member is not the mouth, so in the Church every man may not be a preacher. And to the intent that the Gospel of Christ and His Holy Word might be purely set forth without corruption, and that the ministers of the devil, transforming themselves into the Apostles of Christ, as the devil their father is wont oftentimes to do (2 Cor. xi. 13, 14), should not deceive God's people with every wind of untrue doctrine, therefore hath Christ given unto His Church, not every man, but certain men, to be Apostles, prophets and preachers (Eph. iv. 11), who using, as it were, an embassage from Christ, should by His true Word edify His Church, and gather His people in unity of faith.

Likewise the grace that healeth our souls and preserveth them in righteousness, is not ordinarily given but by the outward and sensible ministration of the holy sacraments, which be not always effectual, giving that grace they signify, but when they be in due form ministered of such persons only as have authority from God to do the same, for no man taketh honour to himself, but he that is called of God as Aaron was (Heb. v. 4).

What so excellent as to consecrate the sacraments of God? And what is so pernicious as if he consecrate them that hath received no degree of priesthood, as appeareth by such plagues as lit on Dathan and Core (Num. xvi. 31–33), and also to King Ozias for usurping the office of the priests by their own authority, uncalled of God thereto (2 Par. xxvi. 19). For only their ministration doth God assist, as He hath promised, to whom He hath given power to minister the visible sacraments.

Wherefore as the sacraments be necessary to man's salvation, so it is necessary for certain men to be ordained and authorised of God to minister the same sacraments faithfully and effectually to man's salvation. Likewise when Christ's Church by the ministration of His Holy Word and sacraments, is gathered and collected out of all the profane people of the world into one body, to the intent that all confusion and disorder should be banished out of the Church of God, and that it might be by strait discipline ruled and kept in order, and all disobedience corrected to the edifying of the same Church, as it were a great army set in good array of battle, by order terrible to their enemies (Cant. vi. 3), so that hell-gates shall not prevail against it, therefore hath our Saviour Christ ordained in His Church, certain men to be rulers and judges in all causes which pertain to the salvation of man's soul, to whom all other persons of what state soever they be, owe obedience, subjection, reverence, and temporal relief, as to their spiritual governors and fathers, who take cure and charge of them, and shall make an account to God of their souls.

By this little that I have now said, ye may learn (good people) that the public ministration of the Gospel of Christ standeth in three points: in the preaching of God's Word, in the ministration of the holy sacraments, and in exercising of discipline and jurisdiction; which three shall (by God's promise and the assistance of His Holy Spirit) continually be observed in the Catholic Church to the world's end, for the edifying and building of the same Church in grace and virtue, and for weeding out and banishing of all error and ungodly living.

And also ye may learn, that where * no man may usurp and take upon him of his own authority to intermeddle or to minister that which pertaineth to Christ, without sufficient commission from Him, therefore hath Christ ordained this sacrament of Order, wherein grace or spiritual power is given to certain Christian men, by the outward sign of imposition of the Bishop's hands upon them, to exercise effectually the public ministration of the Church, whereby whatsoever they do in the Church, according to the institution of Christ and the Church, is ratified, accepted, and allowed of Almighty God.

* i.e., Whereas.

Of this grace or power given in the sacrament of Order, writeth S. Paul to Timothy, whom he had ordered and consecrate a priest, saying thus, "Do not neglect the grace which thou hast in thee, which is given to thee through prophecy, or the inspiration of God, by imposition of hands of the order of priesthood" (1 Tim. iv. 14). And also in another place he exhorteth Timothy to stir up the grace of God, which was given to him by the imposition of his hands (2 Tim. i. 6). And because this spiritual power and authority which is given to certain men for the edifying of Christ's Church, is not wholly given to every one of them, but to some more, to other some less by degrees ; whereby one man, as his office and function is greater, so is he exalted in dignity above another ; which diversity in degrees causeth great comeliness and beauty to be in Christ's Church, by reason of such order as every inferior member keepeth to his superior, doing his duty in his own place, and not usurping to do above his calling, therefore this sacrament, whereby such degrees of authority and power be given to men, is called Order, which order of ministers maketh the Church to be builded as a city without confusion (Ps. cxxi. 3), and to be terrible to her enemies as the fore front of an army set in good array (Cant. vi. 3), and is the very knot of the known Catholic Church, containing both good and evil in it, whereby it is preserved without schism, so long as that order is kept without breach, which was institute by Christ, used by His Apostles, and from them brought to us by continual succession.

This visible order, taking his beginning from the

T

authority given to one man, is extended throughout the whole world in the Church, into a great number and multitude of inferior ministrations, as it were many branches proceeding from one tree, or many rivers from one fountain, which altogether take inwardly their increase from the fountain of all grace, and the only supreme Head of our one Church, Jesus Christ our Lord.

For if Christ had not only secretly by inspiration, but also by His sensible commandment and sacrament, sent His Apostles into the world, saying, " As My Father hath sent Me, so I send you" (John xx. 21), giving them authority likewise visibly to send other, the Church of Christ should never have been without schisms and divisions, made by them that, running by their own authority unsent, would have borne men in hand that they were invisibly sent and anointed of God, which was nothing so, and so would have drawn God's people into sects and false doctrine. For which cause S. Paul and Barnabas, being invisibly sent of the Holy Ghost, yet it was the will and pleasure of the same Holy Ghost that they should, by a visible sacrament of imposition of hands, be visibly sent in the authority of Apostles to the ministration of the Church (Acts xiii. 2, 3) ; and such as say themselves they be sent invisibly of God, ought not to be believed or received, except they be as S. Paul and Barnabas were, visibly ordered and anointed by Catholic bishops, such as have their succession from the Apostles. Furthermore, in this Sacrament of Order is given to them that be lawfully ordered the ecclesiastical power of the Church, which is a power given not by the laws of men or of nature, but only by Christ above nature, and after a special sort, to His Apostles and disciples and their lawful successors to the world's end, for the edifying of the Church militant, according to the laws of the Gospel, for the attaining of eternal life. And this power is called in Scripture by the name of the keys of the kingdom of heaven. As a key doth open the door to a man, and bringeth him into the house, so this ecclesiastical power being used with knowledge and discretion by a lawful minister, openeth the door of man's heart to the knowledge of God, and so in process openeth to him the kingdom of heaven.

For it containeth the ministration of all things which be necessary for us sinners to be directed, furthered, and promoted to the attaining of the said kingdom—as to bind and loose, to remit and retain sin, and all other things that be requisite to the preservation of Christ's Church in unity of faith and charity, to the intent it might be partaker of the glory of God.

These keys our Saviour Christ did give to His Church in S. Peter, or rather to S. Peter for the Church, saying to him :—" To thee shall I give the keys of the kingdom of heaven, and whatsoever thou shalt bind upon earth shall be also bounden in the heavens, and whatsoever thou shalt loose upon earth shall be also loosed in the heavens " (Matt. xvi. 19).

And to the other His Apostles and disciples assembled together, He said, " Whose sins you shall remit, be remitted unto them, and whose sins you retain, be retained " (John xx. 23).

And to declare that this power is not invented by man, nor yet given by the authority of any prince or commonalty, our Saviour said, in the giving of it to His disciples, "Take and receive you the Holy Ghost." Whereby we understand that the power to bind or loose, or to remit sin, or finally to govern the Church, is the work only of the Holy Ghost working by His ministers that which is for the salvation of His Church.

And whereas the Blessed Sacrament of the Altar is the highest and greatest sacrament of all other, because whole Christ, both God and man, is contained in it, therefore is priesthood the highest order, wherein is given grace and power over Christ's natural Body and Blood, to consecrate it by the virtue of God assisting His Word, and to make it present in the Blessed Sacrament of the Altar, by the change of the substances of bread and wine, and also to offer it, being the very sacrifice of the New Testament, to God the Father, for the sins and ignorances of His people, and to deliver and minister it to such as by their faith and cleanness of life be worthy to receive it.

So this power over Christ's natural Body our Saviour Himself gave to His disciples in His last Supper, where, after that He had consecrate, offered, and delivered His own Body to His disciples, He said to them, "Do this in remembrance of Me" (1 Cor. xi. 24), by which word He made them priests, and gave them authority and commandment to do as He did then, not once, but continually till His latter coming.

And that the priest may worthily and after due

manner execute this his chief office and function, there be other inferior orders ordained of God and His Holy Church to assist the priest, as deacon and sub-deacon, whose offices be to receive the oblations of the people for the use of the sacrament, to bring them to the Altar, to prepare all things necessary for the consecration, to give consent to the sacrifice made by the priest, besides other things which by Holy Scripture and the universal tradition of the Church they be authorised to do (Acts vi. 3). A priest also hath power given unto him by this Sacrament of Order over Christ's mystical Body the Church, for the instruction, the purgation, and the perfection of the same Church and every member thereof.

And first, concerning the instruction of it, a priest hath authority to preach God's Word, by God's special and visible sending, where our Saviour Christ said to His disciples, " As My Father hath sent Me, so likewise I send you " (John xx. 21). And in another place He said, "Go ye into the whole world, and preach the Gospel to every creature " (Mark xvi. 15)· And also, "Go your ways, and teach all people, baptizing in the name of the Father, and of the Son, and of the Holy Ghost, teaching them to observe all things whatsoever I have commanded you, and I shall be with you all days to the end of the world " (Matt. xxviii. 19, 20).

And as concerning the purgation of God's people, a priest hath authority to remit sin, as a minister in the name and power of the Holy Trinity, both to them that first enter into the Church, by ministering to them the Sacrament of Baptism, and also to them that after baptism have fallen into sin again, by ministering to them the sacrament of Penance, the commandments of God, whereby every priest is authorised to baptize and to remit sins to the penitent sinners, I have heretofore in this sermon sufficiently declared.

And as concerning the perfection of the Church of Christ, and every member thereof, God hath given to priests authority to pray over sick persons (James v. 14), and to anoint them with oil in His name, to the remission of their sins, and the salvation of the sick, according to God's pleasure, and also to join those persons in matrimony, that marry in Christ.

And bishops also, who in the order of priesthood, as the successors of the Apostles, have higher dignity, and distinct offices, and authority, above other inferior priests, for the perfection of the people in Christ's religion, have power to give the Holy Ghost for the confirmation of them that be baptized (Acts viii. 15, 16, and ix. 17), and by imposition of their hands to ordain priests and other ministers of God's Holy Word and sacraments (Titus i. 5 ; Acts vi. 6, and xiv. 22). And further, for purging of Christ's mystical Body, the Church, from all errors, schisms, disobediences, and ungodly living, bishops have power to use spiritual and ordinary jurisdiction, as to call synods for reformation (Acts xv. 6), and good order to be made in the Church, to visit their dioceses, that neither by tyranny, nor by heresy, nor yet by the subtle craft of the devil, the flock of Christ be dispersed or destroyed, to correct by excommunication and other discipline the public crimes of such as be manifestly accused, denounced, or found guilty and obstinate by diligent inquisition, to examine and determine the causes and enormities which arise or may chance in the Church of Christ, and finally to do what shall be thought necessary and expedient for the banishing of vice and error, and the stablishing of virtue, true faith, and godly unity.

For that power which God hath given unto them, is only to build, and not to destroy (2 Cor. x. 8 ; xiii. 10) ; which power is honourable, and to be esteemed and obeyed in all bishops and priests, be they of good living or naughty living. For the life of an evil priest or bishop is no hindrance nor prejudice to the effect and virtue of God's sacraments, which they truly minister, no more than the evil life of a physician hindereth the virtue and operation of a good medicine. Therefore (good people), knowing the necessity and commodity which cometh to us by this sacrament of Order, for our instruction, sanctification, and final salvation, let us give most high thanks to Almighty God, that hath given such power to men, and by the execution of that power, and the distinct degrees and general functions of this sacrament of Order, hath avoided all confusion out of His Church, that it might appear beautiful and glorious in His sight, and let every person take heed that he neither break nor contemn this ordinance of God, and so be occasion of corrupting God's truth, and disturbing His peace and unity, which by this only order is kept and preserved. But in all our prayers let us humbly make supplication, that God of His merciful goodness would preserve His Church continually in this good order without disturbance, and that every minister in his degree might study and labour in the law of God, to be and do as his office requireth, seeking the building of Christ's Church, and not the only increase of his worldly gain, as becometh the servants of God, being bounden to give an account of that is committed to their charge, to the laud and praise of Christ, Who with the Father and the Holy Ghost liveth and reigneth in unity of Godhead for evermore, world without end. Amen.

THE TWENTY-SIXTH SERMON.

IN WHAT ESTIMATION THE PRELATES AND OTHER MINISTERS OF CHRIST'S CHURCH OUGHT TO BE HAD OF THE PEOPLE.

FORASMUCH as the prelates and ministers of Christ's Church (good people) be ordained of God to be judges over His people, in such things as appertain to the salvation of their souls, and also to be their governors and rulers in all true religion, and thirdly to be their ghostly and spiritual fathers, to beget children to God by the Word of Christ and the preaching of the Gospel, therefore, considering that Almighty God doth so honour them, and doth so allow and assist their ministration, in giving to them, being frail and mortal men, such power as no other creature hath at any time received, and all for the building, perfection, and final salvation of His Church, His elect and chosen people, therefore I say, it is commanded to all men and women that be of the flock of Christ, to love and to obey and to honour those ministers of Christ in such sort as the nature and worthiness of their office and ministration doth require. For so S. Paul taught the Thessalonians, saying thus, "We beseech you, brethren, that you would know them that labour among ye" (1 Thess. v. 12) ; that is to say, in knowledging what benefits we have of God by their labour and service, who also be the rulers and governors over you in our Lord, and do admonish you in all goodness, as it were executing Christ's office amongst you, that ye would have them in highest price and estimation by sincere love and charity, more abundantly than other, and that for their work and office' sake, having peace with them, without using any disobedience, contention, or disdain towards them.

By this exhortation of the blessed Apostle S. Paul, may all men and women learn what love they ought to bear towards the ministers of Almighty God, which ought to be in the best sort, not only for the worthiness and virtues of the persons, which is a cause making all men to be loved and favoured the more, but specially for their office and labour sake, and for such benefits as by their service and ministry men receive at God's hand.

For they be not only our neighbours, whom for that respect we ought to love as ourselves, but also they be the causes of our spiritual life, by them we are made Christian men, by them we have the true knowledge of God, remission of our sins, participation with Christ in the unity of His mystical Body the Church, into which Body we are grafted and made living members to bring forth the fruit of holiness and good works ; by them we have given unto us the Holy Ghost, not only to our sanctification, but also to our boldness and strength, whereby we be made able to withstand our adversary the devil, and to overcome all the fiery darts of his crafty temptations ; by them we be nourished and fed, not only with the spiritual food of God's Word, but also with the heavenly and immortal food of Christ's natural Body and Blood, whereby we be sanctified both in body and soul, and receive increase of all God's former gifts and graces, whereby also we be united unto Christ in perfect unity, that is to say, both spiritually in our souls, and also corporally in our bodies, by the worthy receiving of His heavenly and natural flesh into the same, and by that pledge remaining effectually in us, we be assured and rest in resurrection of our bodies to everlasting life.

They be also appointed of Almighty God as ambassadors to reconcile us again to God, when we by trangression of His laws and commandments have offended His Majesty.

By their mouths and ministry God receiveth the vows, requests, and sacrifices of His people, whereby His anger and wrath for the people's offences, is mitigated and taken away. They be anointed of Almighty God to be watchmen and shepherds over the flock of Christ, to give warning when the wolf cometh to devour the sheep, and to reduce and bring home again to the fold, when the flock is dispersed, such as have wandered in error and wicked living. For these benefits and a great number more, which may be easily rehearsed but for tediousness, which all we receive of Almighty God by the labours and service of the prelates and ministers in Christ's Church, we ought to have them in reverence and to esteem them, according to the admonition of S. Paul (1 Cor.

iv. 1), as the ministers of God and the stewards or disposers of God's mysteries, knowing that whoso heareth and obeyeth them, heareth and obeyeth God, and whoso despiseth them, despiseth God (Luke x. 16); for the love and reverence which is given to God's minister, is given to God, and likewise the contempt of him is the contempt of God, as Almighty God said Himself to Samuel, whom the people of Israel refused to rule over them, in these words, " They have not contemned and rejected thee but Me " (1 Kings viii. 7). So that generally the honour or contempt which is used towards God's ministers, tendeth and reboundeth towards God Himself, as appeared by the punishment of such contempt as the Jews used against Moses, which Almighty God reputed as done against Himself (Num. xii. 8).

Furthermore beside love, the people owe to the ministers of Christ's Church obedience, as to their spiritual governors and rulers, to whom Christ our Saviour hath committed the keys of His kingdom, by which is understanded ecclesiastical power to exercise discipline and jurisdiction over God's people, for the edifying and building of them in grace and virtue, and for the correcting and banishing of all error and ungodly living.

This power in the ministers of the Church ought every Christian man and woman to obey under pain of deadly sin. For seeing that all power is of God, he that withstandeth or disobeyeth that power (Rom. xiii. 1, 2), disobeyeth God's ordinance, and so offendeth grievously Almighty God and his own conscience, except it be in such cases where the ministers of

God's Church shall make ordinances, and give commandments contrary to the express commandment of Almighty God, for in such cases men ought rather to obey God than man (Acts v. 29). But all their constitutions, specially such as be universally received throughout the Catholic Church, and be ordained for the conservation and increase of good life and true religion, and for the beauty of good order in the Church and serving of God, and for quietness and discipline uniformly to be kept among the people, all such ordinances and constitutions no man may contemptuously break and disobey without deadly sin, except urgent and evident necessity, or some other greater and more weighty commodity do excuse him. And yet in such necessary and urgent cases where he may be excused for not observing the same, he must beware and take heed that he neither despise nor contemn the authority of the Church, nor yet therein do offend his neighbour by giving him an occasion likewise to disobey, or to judge evil of another.

This obedience to God's ministers S. Paul doth exhort all men unto, writing to the Hebrews (chap. xiii. 17) in this sort, " Be you obedient to your spiritual rulers, and be you subject under their government, because they labour and watch over you as men that shall give an account for your souls."

That thing which God regardeth most, that is to say, the soul of man, for whose cause He took our nature upon Him, and for it did shed His most precious blood, in comparison also whereof He setteth in a manner nothing by all other things within this world, that same hath He committed to the charge of these His ministers, and will of them require a straight account at the last day. Whereby appeareth how much He hath honoured them in committing so precious a jewel to their charge, and also how much all people ought to esteem, obey, and honour them, that, beside the burden of their own proper acts and deeds, will clog and charge their consciences with the cure of other men's souls, which cure to discharge is very hard and difficult unto them, both for that men be masters and lords of their own wills, which be free and subject to no foreign compulsion, and also for that the perfect state of men's souls cannot be known to their curates, except the parties themselves do confess and open the same.

And therefore it is God's will that these, His ministers, shall be of all sorts of men obeyed in the executing of their office committed unto them, both concerning faith and credit to be given to their preachings and exhortations, so long as they sit in the chair of Christ, teaching wholesome and Catholic doctrine, and the imitation of the life of our Saviour, and also concerning the keeping and fulfilling of the ancient and godly constitutions, ordained by the prelates of the universal Church of Christ for good order and conformity of good living, to be kept throughout in the same.

And specially they ought to be obeyed when they shall, by discipline and the censures of the Church, correct the public crimes of any person which, of contumacy contemning the admonitions of his neighbours and the prelates of the Church, refuseth to hear and obey the Church.

For in such cases of contempt, the ministers of Christ may not wink and suffer the people to run headlong without bridle, from one crime to another, to the destruction of themselves and others also, but ought openly to reprove such men, and if that will not serve, then to draw the spiritual sword of excommunication, which is very terrible, and much to be feared of all Christian men, and more than the corporal sword of princes and kings, forsomuch as the death of the soul is more to be feared than the death of the body.

For if a man be justly excommunicate of his own judge having ordinary or lawful jurisdiction over him, he is a member cut away from the body of Christ's Catholic Church, which, so long as he is in that state, is dead, not able to bring forth good fruit, and worthy nothing but to be cast into eternal fire and burnt, as being then a member of the Church malignant (John xv. 6). He is accursed and separate from the company and fellowship, not only of all faithful people in this world, but also of Almighty God and His blessed angels in the kingdom of heaven. He is deprived of the influence of God's grace, and the special protection of Almighty God, secluded from the spiritual communion of Christ's Church, as not partaker of the sacraments and of the prayers, good works, and general suffrages of the same, and is to be taken and esteemed of all good men as an *Ethnick** and publican (Matt. xviii. 17), and is also delivered to Satan the devil. Whereby the devil hath power by permission over him to afflict him with all vexation and

* *i. e.,* Heathen.

affliction corporal, to the intent that, by that means, he perceiving the enormity of his living may yield and be reduced to penance, that his soul may be saved on the day of our Lord (1 Cor. v. 5).

What Christian heart can be so careless of his own salvation, as either by his wilfulness or by his obstinacy to continue in so damnable and dangerous a state of living, which many men wilfully and headlong fall into, by disobeying God's ministers, and that power which is given unto them by Almighty God for the reformation of His people? And although sometimes men may flatter themselves when they be excommunicate, that they need not to fear or regard such excommunication, for that they persuade themselves in their own opinions, either the cause to be unjust, or the process against them to be unlawful, and therefore shall begin not to regard but to contemn the said sentence of excommunication pronounced against them, yet in the name of God I shall advertise you all (good people) to be ware of this point, and not to be your own judges in these cases deceiving yourselves, lest by your so contemning the keys and authority of the Church, ye run in danger of just excommunication otherwise, and shall thereby make that cause to be just in the end, which perchance would have appeared to have been not so weighty in the beginning.

Thus (good people) understanding that the prelates and ministers of Christ's Church be ordained of God to be the physicians and surgeons of your souls, your duty is to love and obey them, not only when they do apply the sweet medicines of God's Word and

His holy sacraments to the diseases of your souls, but also, when as good surgeons they bind the parties that refuse to be cured, and by the censures of the Church and strait discipline do cut and search their desperate and incurable wounds, executing the office of Almighty God, that said by His prophet in this manner, "I shall feed My sheep, and I shall seek and search that is lost; I shall bring home again that is cast away, I shall bind that is broken, I shall save and keep that is fat and strong, and I shall feed them in judgment" (Ezech. xxxiv. 15, 16). And like as I have told you of your duties towards them in loving and obeying them, so ought you also to honour them as the holy Apostle, S. Paul, teacheth, saying, "Those priests that exercise their office, and rule their people well, be worthy double honour, specially those that labour in God's Word and doctrine." For the Scripture sayeth, "Thou shalt not bind up the mouth of the ox that treadeth forth the corn, and he that laboureth is worthy his wages or reward" (1 Tim. v. 17, 18). By which words we understand what is meant by this double honour, not only to think well upon them, to have them in estimation, to love them, to reverence and honour God in them for their work and office' sake, but also to succour and relieve them in their corporal living, to minister unto their necessary sustenance sufficiently with a frank heart and a good will.

For who doth go a warfare upon his own charges? who feedeth a flock and doth not eat of the milk of the same flock (1 Cor. ix. 7)? They that minister unto the people spiritual things, as the Word

U

of God, His holy sacraments and such other, ought likewise to receive again of the people carnal things (Rom. xv. 27). For the scholar which is taught and instructed in the Word of God and the religion of Christ, ought to communicate and to make his master and instructor to be a partner with him in all good things temporal which God hath lent unto him (Gal. vi. 6), for Almighty God hath willed and ordained, that they which serve Him in the preaching and setting forth of His Gospel, should have their living of the Gospel for the setting forth of the same (1 Cor. ix. 13).

By these reasons and sayings which I have here rehearsed unto you (good people) out of the doctrine of the blessed Apostle S. Paul, it appeareth plainly that the payment of tithes, or the tenth part of all manner of fruits, for so much as pertaineth to the substance of them and the sustentation of God's ministers, to the intent they might wholly apply themselves to God's ministry undivided, or without care of the world for their necessary living, is God's ordinance, not only by the instinct of nature, it being most agreeing to natural reason, but also by God's moral law, Who being the Lord, Creator and Giver of all good things, in token of His universal dominion, as it were by a special title and prerogative, hath reserved the tenth part of the fruits of the earth to Himself, and will be honoured with our substance and riches, by the free oblation of those tithes to Him, which He hath willed to be given and converted to the use and sustentation of the ministers of His Church (Prov. iii. 9). For so writeth the wise man, In all thy soul fear thy Lord God and sanctify His priests, with all thy power love Him that made thee, and forsake not His ministers, honour God with all thy soul, and also honour His priests, and purge thyself with the free oblation of that thou hast gotten with the labour of thy hands, give unto them as it is commanded unto thee, their portion of thy chief fruits and tithes (Ecclus. vii. 30-35). Thus (good people) as we are debtors to Almighty God for His infinite and manifold benefits, so by just paying of our tithes to Him we acknowledge our imperfection, His Majesty and universal dominion, our need and misery, His goodness and bountiful liberality, which is according to our duties a giving of thanks for the same, and accepted of Him as a payment of our debts for His benefits, through the merits of His only Son, Jesus Christ our Lord.

And this honour in ministering to the priests of Christ's Church for their living, as I have said before, is not only expressed in the writings of the holy prophets and in the old law of Moses (Mal. iii. 10, Exod. xxii. 29, Num. v. 9, Num. xviii. 11-13, Deut. xiv. 22), which was the figure declaring what might be done in the New Testament, where righteousness doth and ought more to abound than it did in the scribes and Pharisees (Matt. v. 20) ; and yet in this point, concerning the living of the ministers, it was not a bare ceremony shadowing a truth to come, nor yet only judicial, pertaining only to the government of the civil state of that people of the Jews, which is now dissolved, but did instruct men how they should behave themselves in that behalf to God and their neighbour, which ought to take place, and be observed as well now amongst us in the New Testament as amongst them in the Old; but also is declared to be due to be paid of Christian people now in the time of the New Testament by the consent of Christ's universal Church, as well by the testimony of the holy fathers and the universal custom of the said Church, ever since the time that any realm was wholly converted to the faith of Christ, as by the determination of general council; the consent and judgment of whom our Saviour Christ hath taught to be observed in all doubts as a sure argument of the undoubted truth, and a sure pillar for every Christian man to lean unto. And as the withdrawing or not paying of this duty of tithes from God, that hath reserved the same in token of His universal dominion (Deut. xiv. 22), to the intent men should learn to fear Him at all times, is very sacrilege and the contempt of God and His true religion, so is the cause of dearth and famine, and many other plagues which by God's just judgment fall upon the people therefore (Mal. iii. 10). Like as the honouring of God and His ministers in this point, and the true payment of the same, is the cause that God doth bless His people in sending unto them abundance and plenty in all corporal and spiritual benediction.

For which cause I shall most heartily require you to consider what I have said concerning your duty to God and the ministers of His Church, in loving, obeying, and honouring them, which I speak not for their glory or gain worldly, but for your profit, discharging myself in declaring unto you the will and commandment of God in this behalf, to the intent ye might avoid His high displeasure for doing the contrary, and on the other side obtain the abundance of His grace and blessing like obedient servants and thankful children, whom He shall at the last day reward with the fruition of His glory, through the merits and mercy of His only Son Jesus Christ, to Whom with the Father and the Holy Ghost be all honour and glory, world without end. Amen.

THE TWENTY-SEVENTH SERMON.

OF THE SACRAMENT OF MATRIMONY AND WHAT GRACE IS GIVEN IN IT.

AFTER that Almighty God our Lord (good people) had created and made the first man Adam, and had placed him in Paradise (Gen. ii.), He by-and-by coupled and joined unto him in marriage a woman created of his own flesh and bone ; whereby appeareth that matrimony is the elder and more ancient than all the other sacraments, and instituted by God Himself before the fall of man for good and necessary causes—as for the aid and comfort of man, both in their common life together, and also for multiplication of mankind, and the godly bringing up of their children, it being prepared and ordained of Almighty God to be a mean and instrument for lawful generation between them and perpetual con-tinuance of mankind to the world's end.

For which purpose Almighty God, when He had joined them in marriage together, He blessed them with His holy word, saying to them, " Increase you and be you multiplied and full-fill the earth " (Gen. i. 28, ix. 1—7).

Furthermore, Almighty God, to whom nothing is

unknown, but all things, both past, present, and to come, be perfectly before His eyes, foreseeing that man would be deceived by the craft of the devil, and fall from that righteousness which He had created him in, and that as he would by his own free will disobey God his superior, so his flesh and carnal desires should by God's just judgment likewise disobey Him; therefore He ordained matrimony, that as it should be to man and woman before their fall a mean of that generation and multiplying of God's people, so it should be also after their fall a remedy to excuse the unlawful desire of their sinful flesh.

Last of all, Almighty God, foreseeing the bondage and damnation of mankind for his disobedience to God, and of His infinite mercy purposing to redeem mankind again from the said bondage and damnation, by sending His only begotten Son to be made man, and in our flesh to regenerate us, and to restore us to be the loving children of God again; therefore, to teach us this His good will and purpose, that we should by faith continually know His godly counsel concerning our redemption and regeneration, He ordained and instituted this lawful conjunction of man and woman in matrimony, to be a sign or sacrament of the marriage between His only Son, the Lamb of God, our Saviour Christ, and His spouse the Holy Church; whereof S. Paul wrote to the Ephesians (chapter v., verse 31), saying thus, "For this cause a man shall forsake his father and mother and cleave unto his wife, and they shall be two in one flesh. For this sacrament is great, I say in Christ and in the Church." And for the better understanding of this thing, ye may consider that God in the beginning made two marvellous conjunctions in man—one between the soul of man and his flesh, and this conjunction is natural, the other between man and woman in marriage, and this conjunction is voluntary and sacramental. Even so there be two marvellous conjunctions between Christ and the nature of man, the one like to conjunction between man's soul and his flesh, which is when the Word was made flesh, that is to say, when God's Son in His incarnation did join our mortal nature to His godly nature in unity of person. The other is like the conjunction between man and wife, which is made by voluntary love between Christ and His Church, that is to say, that company or congregation of all Christian people, redeemed, sanctified, and nourished by Christ's precious blood, and of this conjunction matrimony is an holy sacrament. For as by the use of matrimony are born and brought forth into the world natural children, so by the virtue of this marriage between Christ and His spouse the Church, are daily begotten to God spiritual children. And as God made unto Adam, our forefather, a wife of a rib taken out of his side when he was cast into a sleep (Gen. ii. 21), even so by the blood and water that ran forth of Christ's side when He slept by death upon the cross, was the Church of Christ married unto Him and made His spouse, to cleave unto Him as one flesh with Him for evermore.

And as Adam spake in the spirit of prophecy, that by matrimony a man should leave his father and mother, and adhere and cleave unto his wife, and that they should be two in one flesh, so our Saviour Christ did so leave His Father, that being in the form of God thought it no robbery to be equal with God, but abased Himself and was made man, and also left the Synagogue, the mother of the Jews, which altogether leaned carnally to the Old Testament, and did adhere unto His wife the Holy Church, to the intent they might be two in one flesh in the peace of the New Testament.

And as a man and his wife have conformity and do agree in one nature of mankind, so Christ did conform Himself to His Church by His humanity. And as at the public celebration of marriage, the friends of the parties so married be called together, and a feast is made among them to declare their common joy and gratulation for the celebrating of this sacrament, even so to the marriage between our Saviour Christ and His spouse, the Holy Church, are called all nations and people, and from every part of the world the friends and servants of God by lively faith do resort thither with unspeakable gladness and joy in the Holy Ghost.

And as there is no worldly love greater than the love between man and wife, who be one heart and one mind, even so the Holy Church loveth Christ, and Christ loveth His spouse the Church, so that He hath given Himself to the death for her, to redeem and wash her from all her spots and wrinkles. And as the wife by duty is subject and obedient to her husband as being her head, so is the Church to Christ her Head and Saviour.

And as the husband adorneth and decketh his wife,

and when case requireth doth also chastise her, to the
intent she might continue in her duty and obedience,
so Christ doth beautify and set forth His wife, the
Church, with spiritual gifts and ornaments, and sometimes by tribulation and adversity doth chastise her,
as well for to exercise her in righteousness as for
correction of her disobedience. Thus ye may perceive (good people) by these comparisons, how matrimony between man and wife is a great sacrament,
resembling unto us and bearing to our remembrance
that heavenly conjunction which is between Christ,
our Saviour, and His spouse the Holy Church, which
is the greatest grace and benefit that God hath given
to man, whereupon man's salvation doth wholly depend.

And as this grace is but only signified by the sacrament of Matrimony, so God doth both signify and
also work effectually other special and singular graces
in them that lawfully in the faith of Christ receive
the same sacrament of Matrimony. Which thing
shall appear, if ye will consider the words of our
Saviour Christ, whereby matrimony as a sacrament
of the New Testament is established and sanctified,
where He saith in the Gospel of S. Matthew after this
sort, " Those persons whom God hath joined, man
may not loose." By which words is declared unto us,
that whosoever be joined in lawful marriage in the
name of God, to the intent to live godly, in the religion of Christ, in that state of life, they be joined
not vainly by contract of man only, but by God
Himself, Who is invisibly present at the making of
that marriage, and doth assist the parties, and is the

author and worker of the knot of matrimony between them. And by the same words also is declared the strength of the knot of matrimony to be such as cannot be broken and dissolved afterward but by the natural death of one of the parties so married. For if God doth so couple and join man and wife together, that no man hath power to separate them asunder afterwards, then is it certain that He giveth to the parties so married His special grace to live together in godly and chaste love in this perpetual bond and knot of matrimony without breach of the same, and so to cherish and love one another as Christ loveth His Church, and shall never be separate and divorced from the same. So that this indissoluble bond of matrimony between the two parties married, which no man can loose and break during the lives of both the parties so married, is that special grace and effect which is wrought by Almighty God in this sacrament, and is also signified by such mutual words of consent, as the two parties did contract matrimony together. Which perpetual bond, although it be made specially for the intent to have children, yet when that cause doth cease by age or barrenness, it may in nowise be broken or dissolved. And also although for fornication of the woman or of the man, there may be made against the will of the party offending, a divorce or separation from bed and board between them, till they be reconciled together again by the penance and submission of the party offending, yet the bond and knot of matrimony which God hath once made, can in nowise be dissolved (1 Cor. vii. 11), and in case the one party, the other being alive, do attempt to marry again, it doth commit fornication.

And this cause or condition of matrimony between husband and wife, is not among the heathen or unchristian people where matrimony is no sacrament of Christ's religion, but only in the city of God which is the Catholic Church. Moreover, beside this inviolable bond which God knitteth by His grace in this sacrament, and by mutual love which He poureth into their hearts, and doth nourish and preserve the same, there is also another singular grace and benefit of God always joined thereunto, whereby (as S. Paul saith) matrimony is made honourable, and in it the bed or carnal copulation may be undefiled and without sin (Heb. xiii. 4). For whereas by God's institution in this sacrament of Matrimony, there is power given to man to use his wife for procreation of children, we must consequently understand that there is also grace given whereby he may do that thing conveniently to the contentation and pleasure of God. For they that worthily in the faith of Christ and in the fear of God, with a right intent, for the end to have fruit of their bodies to serve God, contract matrimony together, to such I say is given the help of God's grace against the unlawful desire and concupiscence of the flesh, that it proceed no further than the honesty of marriage doth require, so that the carnal act and copulation which otherwise were sinful and dishonest, is by the goodness of matrimony lawfully contracted (as I have said before), not only excused and defended from sin, as S. Paul saith, " If thou hast taken a wife, thou hast not sinned, and if a virgin do marry, she sinneth not "

(1 Cor. vii. 28), but also is made honest and meritorious and acceptable to Almighty God, Who also by His special grace doth aid the parties so married, to keep steadfastly that faith and promise which they have made one to another, by which the man hath granted the power and use of his body only to his wife, and likewise the wife to her husband only, and so to avoid adultery and fornication with any other person during their lives natural. Which promise to keep is very hard, or in a manner impossible, without the aid of God's grace given to them in this sacrament. For where the corrupt nature of man's flesh, and his inordinate concupiscence, moveth and inclineth him to desire other women beside his own wife, yet by the grace of matrimony his unlawful desire is restrained, so that he may be content with his own wife alone and avoid fornication. And whereas also man's corrupt nature seeketh rather the satisfying of his carnal lust, than the generation of children, yet in this sacrament of Matrimony he receiveth grace to know his wife, rather for the intent to have children than to fulfil his fleshly desire, and also to communicate with her all that chance to him, good or bad, and to bring up together their children in the religion and fear of God. And likewise, whereas a man by his corrupt nature, after carnal copulation, is wont and disposed to think loathsome, and partly to abhor that woman which he hath known carnally, and so refuseth her and seeketh another, yet in matrimony is given grace and aid, not to disdain the company of his wife, but to remain with her continually without separation or divorce.

All these singular graces and aids, Almighty God ceaseth not of His merciful goodness for His part to give and grant to His faithful people in this sacrament of Matrimony, if they themselves do not wilfully stop at the beginning, or afterwards refuse the same by their ungracious life and wicked intent. For as God is author and giver of all grace and goodness, so He forceth and compelleth no man to be or to continue good against his will.

Therefore (good people) ye may evidently perceive the infinite and unspeakable clemency of Almighty God our Saviour, that by such a sacrament hath so mercifully provided for our carnal concupiscence and desires. He knoweth very well how frail man's flesh is, and how full of corruption and wickedness, and therefore mercifully hath ordained lawful matrimony to restrain man's unlawful desire; for which cause married persons may have boldness and quietness of a good conscience, whereby although they have by the use of matrimony tribulation of the flesh many ways, yet they be certainly assured that their matrimonial life, honestly begun and virtuously continued, hath always the assistance of God's grace, and is blessed of Him, and therefore profitable and meritorious to the salvation of the parties. Whereunto S. Paul beareth witness, writing thus to Timothy (1 Tim. ii. 15), that the wife shall be saved by procreation and bringing forth of children, if the same do continue in faith and love towards God, and in holiness and temperance in their deeds.

Finally, every man and woman ought most steadfastly to believe that marriage is a good thing, and ordained and blessed of Almighty God, and also that it is a better thing to live chastely without marriage, to the intent a man or woman might more fully and freely think upon such things as be godly, and how to please God. And yet to them that have not vowed chastity, either in virginity or widowhood, we ought to believe that it is no sin to marry and to take an husband or wife, and that not only the first marriage is ordained of God, but also that the second and third marriage is granted as lawful for the infirmity of such as cannot otherwise live continently. But to them that have vowed chastity and continent life to Almighty God, we ought to think that (according to the doctrine of S. Paul) it is damnable not only to defile themselves with the deadly sin of fornication, but also to have a will to marry a wife, or to take an husband, because he or she that so doth hath broken and made void his first faith and promise, which by his vow he made to Almighty God.

Therefore, he that shall well consider with himself the goodness of this sacrament, as I have rehearsed, and the singular and manifold graces which God giveth to them that be honestly and for a good intent married in our Saviour Christ, shall both edify his own conscience towards himself, and increase his chaste love towards his wife, and by that laudable state of living highly please Almighty God toward the attaining of his own salvation, which God of His great mercy grant to us by the merits of His dear Son our Saviour Christ, to Whom with the Father and the Holy Ghost be all honour and glory for evermore. Amen.

THE TWENTY-EIGHTH SERMON.

OF THE MANNER HOW TO MINISTER AND CONTRACT MATRIMONY.

IT is to be considered (good people) that although the solemnisation of matrimony, and the benediction of the parties married, is made and given in the face of the Church by a priest—the public minister of the Church, yet the contract of matrimony may be, and is commonly made, by the layman and woman which be married together.* And because for lack of knowledge how such contracts ought to be duly made, and for omitting of such things as be necessary to the same, it chanceth oftentimes that the parties change their minds, and will not keep that promise of marriage which seemed to have passed between them before, whereupon cometh and groweth between such persons and their friends great grudge and hatred, and great suit in the law, therefore I intend at this time, by God's grace, to declare unto you which be the very words whereby this sacrament of Matrimony is contracted, and to open certain cases thereupon depending, to the intent that such contention as commonly is wont to arise upon the ignorance or not observing the same, may the better be avoided,

* See note at end of this sermon.

and the parties so contracting, may without scruple or evil conscience for so much live together in godly and chaste matrimony to the good-will and pleasure of Almighty God.

First, whosoever intendeth to take upon himself this sacrament of Matrimony, his duty is, not headily or rashly and with blind affection, to enter so weighty a matter, but ought, with discretion and deliberation, to choose unto him or her such a make and fellow, with whom he or she shall verily believe and trust to live godly and virtuously, without breach of the bond of matrimony in any case during their natural lives, and to be ware that he enter not marriage with any such person, as the law of God, expressed by the instinct of nature in every man's heart, and the book of Leviticus, and also the holy and ancient Canons of the Church do prohibit and forbid. Which prohibition now extendeth to the fourth degree of consanguinity and affinity, and also taketh place in spiritual kindred, which is between the party that is baptized or confirmed and his godfathers or godmothers, and their children and wife or husband, before such baptism or confirmation, and also between the godfather or godmother and the parents of the child so baptized or confirmed.*

Furthermore, he ought to beware and foresee that he or she be in no error of the person, nor of the con-

---

* A few years after the printing of this sermon, the Council of Trent, in the 24th Session (De. Reform, cap. 2), restricted the impediment of spiritual relationship. It now exists only between the person baptizing and the person baptized, and the father and mother of the baptized ; between the sponsor and the person baptized, and the father and mother thereof ; and similarly in Confirmation.

X

dition and quality of the same person, with whom he or she intendeth to marry. And if any scruple or doubt shall appear unto him or her, concerning the degrees or other impediments which may lawfully stop the contracting of such marriage, then his duty is to resort to know the judgment of his curate. And in case his curate hath not so profound knowledge as to resolve him in all such doubts, then ought he or she further to resort to his ordinary or bishop to be resolved, to whom only the custom of the Church of old time, not without great cause, did specially reserve the hearing and judgment in all causes matrimonial.

And further, ye shall understand (good people) that the manner to administer this sacrament of Matrimony is thus to be used. First, let the man ask the woman if she be content to be his wife, and if she agree thereunto, then let the woman ask the man likewise if he be content to be her husband, and if he say yea, so that the mutual consent of them both be known, without the which no marriage is lawfully made before God, then may the parties proceed to the words which do express this their mutual and voluntary consent, which be the formal words of the sacrament, after this manner :—

Let the man, taking the woman by the right hand, and naming her by her name, as Mary, Jane, or as her name is, say these words : "Jane, here I take thee to my wife," and likewise let the woman take the man by the right hand and name him by his name, as Thomas, or as his name is, saying thus : "Thomas, here I take thee to my husband." Now, when the two parties which marry together have done this and have said these words, then be they insured and justly married together, and be man and wife before God, and they cannot break this marriage in any wise afterward, as the man cannot marry another woman, nor the woman another man, so long as they be both alive. And if the two persons have sufficient record and witness to testify what they have done and said, then be they man and wife in the face of the world, and so both before God and man.

This manner and form of words not only the parties that intend justly to marry together, but also such other as shall be called to be present at the insuring of other, as witnesses of the same, ought diligently to mark and observe, and to see that the parties which shall be insured, say the fore-rehearsed words, for they be the very words which join the man and woman together, and make them husband and wife.

The neglecting or omitting of these formal words or the like in effect and sentence, is oftentimes the cause of great contention, and also may cause that the external judgment of the Church shall vary and disagree from the inward judgment of God. For example, if a man, obtaining in words the woman's consent to marriage, and she his likewise, shall say these words : " Jane, here I give to thee my faith and truth, and I promise thee by it that I will marry thee to my wife ; " and she promiseth and saith to the man the very same, yea, although each party bindeth himself by an oath of a book to perform that promise within two months more or less ; yet for all this, these two persons be not insured and made man and wife by these words, although they have sufficient records to testify the same, because these words be not the formal words of the sacrament of Matrimony, nor make man and woman husband and wife. Yet these persons that make such promise be bounden to marry according unto their promise, under pain of setting themselves in the state of damnation. And yet, notwithstanding, if the man shall marry another woman after this promise, he is then the second woman's husband, and not the first, though the first be still alive.

And the like case is, if the woman marry another man after her promise made before, she is then the second man's wife, and not the first, because the parties at that present time, when the one promised faith and troth to marry the other, did not contract matrimony by the formal words of *the present time*, by which they be kept together in marriage, but said other words signifying promise and time to come, and so afterward change their minds contrary to their promise, whereupon followeth many times grudge, hatred, and suit between the parties and their friends, and sometimes also it followeth that the parties so promising marriage one to another, do live in fornication and deadly sin with the other persons which they married afterwards. And for the further opening of this matter ye shall understand (good people) that if a man and woman do consent in their hearts to be man and wife, and do will and intend so to make themselves by the words which they shall express and say one to another, and then upon this consent and agreement, the man saith unto the woman thus:

" Jane, I promise thee by my faith that I will take
thee to my wife," and the woman saith likewise to
the man, or else some other such words of promise to
marry in time to come, thinking and believing that
by those words they be justly insured and made man
and wife ; now in this case these two persons be man
and wife before God, because they willed and intended
so to be in their hearts, and also intended so to make
themselves in deed by their words.

And yet they be not man and wife before man
and by the judgment of the Church, though they have
sufficient record of what they did and said, because
they did not say the formal words of the present
time, whereby matrimony is contracted ; without
saying of which words (if they can speak) they be not
insured and made husband and wife before man and
by the judgment of the Church, whatsoever they
intended in their hearts ; for the Church must take
the words justly, and judge what they signify after the
common speaking and understanding of them, and
that a man may know, and not after the minds and
intents that persons may speak, for that can no man
know but the speakers themselves.

And therefore in this case, when the words of these
two persons so insuring themselves, be brought before
a judge to be examined, it must be determined that
these two persons be not husband and wife ; and yet, i
either of them do marry, as the man another woman,
or the woman another man, then do they commit
adultery, and live in deadly sin, so long as they be with
those whom they have married. And that is because
they made themselves man and wife before in the

sight of God, Who saw their wills and hearts, and what they intended and did then before Him, and therefore that marriage which they made then they may never break after. And in case the man shall forsake that marriage which he made before God, and shall openly join himself in marriage with another woman afterward, then shall he sin deadly, and continue in the same so long as he is with that woman whom he last openly married, because they be not married before God. Yet doth not the latter woman sin to use the carnal company of that man, because she believeth he is her lawful husband ; nor she is not bound to believe the contrary though he tell her the contrary : and so she may always use him as her husband if he use her as his wife. And the like case is if the woman break from the first insuring and marry another man, then doth not he sin to know her as his wife, but she sinneth, because she knoweth that he is not her husband.

But now what remedy for a man which hath insured and married himself to a woman before God, with a full mind and consent in his heart, and yet forsaketh her afterward, and will not solemnise that marriage, but marrieth another openly, how may he save himself from deadly sin and damnation, seeing his prelate, by the judgment of the Church, will compel him to continue with the second woman whom he married openly, and will not suffer him to forsake her ? Surely the remedy is very painful and dangerous worldly, howbeit, it is better to fall into the hands of man than into the hands of God. And forsomuch as I can learn, the remedy which that man may have is this : he must leave and forsake the second woman, and go if he can, and so think it good, where he may escape the pains of the law. And if he be excommunicate, because he will not be with her, and for going from her, then he must suffer it,* and so he must suffer any other punishment that he shall chance to have therefore, rather than to use carnal company with that woman again, so long as the other- woman is alive, for he knoweth she is not his wife before God, and therefore he should do against God's law, if he should keep her company as her husband, and rather than to do so and offend Almighty God, he must suffer any manner of pain that the law of man may cause him to have. And so must a woman do if she fall into the like case, for this is the remedy, and there is none other that I know.

And forsomuch as I have spoken some part of the prelate's doing hereto, ye shall further know, that if a prelate do, by the judgment and censure of the Church, excommunicate or curse a man or woman for leaving or forsaking the second marriage, he doth it justly and lawfully, because the Church ought to suppose the best and the most likeliest, that is to say, that he which marrieth openly, being a Christian man, would not so have done, if he had married him-

---

* Such an excommunication, though just, *ex parte judicis, i.e.*, in the prelate (as the author immediately explains), and binding *in foro externo*, does not really bind before God. Quia excommunicatio minime incurritur, nisi ob inobedientiam lethalem ; quæ prorsus abest in hoc casu ; et rigidissimum esset asserere eum vere excommunicatum esse, qui Dei timore ductus, Ecclesiæ falsa præsumptione innitenti non obedit.—Sanchez, De Mat. Lii. disp. 39, n. 9.—ED.

self to another woman before God, nor have done so
greatly against his own conscience and God's law.

And also the Church ought to suppose this second
marriage good, because it cannot have a due proof of
the first marriage, which the man saith he made
before God, but ought to judge and determine the
second marriage to be lawful, and may justly excommunicate him that doth forsake it. And moreover, the Church may not believe the man which
saith that he was married before, and that this second
woman is not his wife. For beside, that he granteth
that he hath broken the promise and marriage which
he made before Almighty God, he also confesseth
openly before the Church that he is untrue in his deeds
and words, and not worthy to be trusted and believed,
and, therefore, the Church ought not to allow his saying, nor to believe it as true, concerning the first
marriage, but rather to judge it to be false, and that
he saith so now, because he loveth not this woman,
but hateth her, or else so he saith, for some other evil
purpose.

Wherefore I shall exhort in the name of our
Saviour Christ every man or woman diligently to
look upon themselves and their own consciences,
and discreetly to consider what they will and intend
in their hearts when they make any contract and
promise of marriage openly or secretly. For by
their own consciences and intents they shall be
judged before God, and be condemned if they do
the contrary, although they may with words and
excuses do against it, and defend their so doing
here in the face of the world before man. The

surest way that every man and woman may take in making of these contracts, is to marry always in deed here before man, as they did will to do in their hearts, at the time of their insuring, what words so ever they said then, for so may they always discharge their conscience and put away all doubts, and live justly together husband and wife in the service of Almighty God.

Moreover, the like doubts or ambiguity may chance upon the other side, that is, if a man and woman come together to insure themselves, and do say the very formal words of the sacrament before sufficient record, and yet the man doth not consent in his heart to take that woman to his wife, but saith the words for fear of displeasing his parents or friends, or else for some other naughty purpose, and likewise of the woman. Now these two persons be husband and wife by the judgment of the Church and before man, and if any of them would forsake the other and be married again, they may not so do, though they both grant that they did never consent to be man and wife when they were insured, no, nor though they do both agree to forsake other, and yet they be not husband and wife nor married before God, and that is because they did not will and consent in their hearts so to be when they said the words of matrimony. And therefore, if these two persons do use carnal company together, then the party which did not consent, doth commit fornication and sinneth deadly in so doing the duty of marriage, as long as he continueth in the same will and mind that he had when he was insured, be it the man or the woman. Therefore, let every man and woman take good heed, when they be insured and speak the words of this sacrament, that they think and will then in their hearts the same thing which they do express in their words, or else let them never speak those words neither for father nor friend, or for any other cause. Now, the remedy in this case is easier than in the other before, which is this, that the man must change his mind and consent in his heart to take that woman to his wife as he said before that he did, and the woman likewise. And this done, then they be man and wife before God, and their matrimonial knowledge together is no longer sin but lawful and good afterward. This is the remedy in this case and there is none other.

Many more cases and difficulties in this sacrament of Matrimony I might rehearse, which the Church of God hath fully debated and resolved, but I think these few to be sufficient to the layman for understanding how marriage ought to be ministered and contracted. And notwithstanding that the man and woman consenting to be man and wife, and saying the words of the sacrament, be perfectly married together, yet the marriage of them in the face of the Church afterward, by the ministration of the priest, is not superfluous, but much expedient for sundry causes. First, to the intent that this sacrament should have that solemnity and reverence which is due to so holy a thing instituted by our Saviour Christ Himself, for that conjunction which the priest as God's minister doth us to understand, that matrimony is made by the assistance and working of Almighty God.

Secondly, that the persons which be married may receive and have the fruit of the prayers and suffrages which be said for them in the sacrifice of the Church, and also may be partakers of the blessing of God which is made over them by the priest, whereby we know that the state of living in marriage is blessed of Almighty God.

And thirdly, it is solemnised in the Church that it might have the more record and be more allowed and fortified by the solemnisation, and that all doubts which might be imagined against it, should be put away. Further, I shall not need to allege unto you at this time, but only shall exhort you to have always God and His true religion before your eyes, in entering to this state of life by matrimony, which cannot be dissolved or avoided at the will and affection of man, but must be kept and observed till death depart the same. For as we see by experience how upon naughty and affectionate * beginnings there cometh seldom good success, so if the beginning of these contracts in marriage be used with discretion and godly intent, in such form as I have declared unto you, where the heart and word do join together, and the deed performeth that was promised and said before, then shall these manifold contentions and breach of charity cease, and the parties love one another in chaste love, as Christ loved His Church, and shall labour to bring up their children in the fear of God and knowledge of true

* *i.e.,* Passionate.

religion, which shall be a great help and furtherance to their salvation by the mercy and merits of our Saviour Christ, to Whom with the Father and the Holy Ghost be all honour and praise for evermore. Amen.*

* This sermon shows very clearly the reasons why the Council of Trent established the impediment of clandestinity. It seems to have been quite usual to contract marriage apart from the religious ceremony. The bishop does not even seem to blame those who so acted, provided they afterwards received the nuptial blessing, and renewed their contract before the Church. But the abuses and perplexities which thus arose were innumerable. The records of the spiritual courts in those days are full of them. A specimen may be seen in the Acts of the Chapter of the Collegiate Church of Ripon, published by the Surtees Society in 1875. The Rev. Mr Fowler, the editor, seems to think that these were cases of breach of promise (preface, p. vii.) This is a mistake. The question at issue was whether the marriage contract had been really, though clandestinely, made. When the decree of the Council of Trent was made, England had again fallen into schism, and it was not then, nor has it since been, published in England or Scotland, as it has in Ireland ; and by the will of the Council itself it is not in force where it has not been published.

THE TWENTY-NINTH SERMON.

FOR WHAT INTENT AND WITH WHAT AFFECTION MEN AND WOMEN SHOULD MARRY.

AS in the contracting of marriage (good people), if the right form and laudable manner therein prescribed by the Holy Church be not observed, there chanceth oftentimes much contention and hatred afterward upon the same, as ye have been taught ; even so if the intents of marriage, and the causes that move and provoke men and women to be married, be not godly and honest, the success of those marriages commonly follow thereafter. For which cause I intend, God willing, to declare unto you at this time, which causes be naught and reprovable, and which be honest and godly. For if the intent and cause why men and women do marry be not good and godly, then shall not their life be acceptable to Almighty God, nor yet long pleasant unto themselves, as experience doth many times evidently shew.

A great number of folks do marry for one of these two causes and intents or for both, either to have the lust and uncleanly desire of the flesh fulfilled, or else to get worldly goods and riches thereby. Both these causes, if they be chiefly and principally intended by the parties which marry, be very evil and ungodly.

Many young men and women do use to say in rebuke of other, that they will not marry for riches and goods, but for good love, and yet that good love is most principally for to have their sensual appetite and carnal desire fulfilled, which manner of love doth never long endure between them that so marry, but it decayeth and goeth shortly away. And then such persons begin to mislike one another's conditions, and to wax weary one of another, and after continuance and increase of that weariness, it groweth to be so painful and grievous that the parties wish themselves unmarried again, yea, and many times they wish themselves buried, and no marvel. For an evil tree, such as is carnal concupiscence and fleshly love, can bring forth no good fruit, but such as I have rehearsed.

I need not to shew and judge for what intent goodly young women marry poor and miserable persons when they have done amiss, for they be but a small number. And yet they use more vice under the cloak and cover of marriage, than they durst do before when they were single. Now, against these persons which after such sort and with such intent do enterprise to marry, that they do exclude God from themselves and from their minds (Tobias vi. 17), and do apply and give themselves to satisfy their lusts and pleasure, as horses and mules do, which have no reason or understanding, against all such persons (as the angel Raphael taught the good young Tobias) the devil hath power to prevail.

And although Almighty God of His great mercy,
doth not now suffer the devil to use his malice against
the bodies of such offenders, as he used in the time
of Tobias against the seven wicked husbands of Sarah,
the daughter of Raguel (Tobias vi. 14), yet no doubt
of it their naughty eye doth make dark their whole
body, that is to say, their wicked and lecherous intent
doth corrupt their souls, whereby they come to the
snare of the devil, who spiritually prevaileth against
them.

Moreover, the greater part of the other people doth
marry for the other cause, that is, for goods and
riches. And for this purpose men and women do not
only marry themselves, but they do also study and
labour to marry their children and kinsfolks to glean
and get riches. So that now commonly there is no
other virtuous living, honesty, good conditions, wisdom, stock, lineage, personage, beauty, youth, nor
anything else so greatly regarded and considered as
is worldly goods and possessions. For if the man be
void of virtue and discretion, and let him have deformity, and be without personage and so forth, yet if
he have great land and goods, there shall be no fault
nor lack found in him, but shall have suitors unto
him for their daughters and kinswomen. And on
the other side, if a woman have great substance and
goods and many good lordships and manors, although
she have never one or few good conditions or virtues,
she shall be sure to have suitors to marry with her,
both of great men and other, be she fair or foul,
young or old, beautiful or deformed. But the miserable life and sorrowful pain that such persons many

times have of their marriage, they themselves can tell, and yet they be not able to express with their tongues all that they feel and suffer in their hearts. And then they curse their goods and the day in which they were married. Yea, and moreover, we see daily that great men do sell their children as though they were bonds and slaves, and do nothing study or labour to marry their sons to good wives, nor their daughters to good husbands, but their principal care is to sell them where they have most money. Likewise the buyers do not care for the good conditions of those they buy, but look more upon the lands and rents which those shall have and enjoy, and therefore oftentimes doth the buyers and sellers of such wards and other, marry their children to great misery and endless pain. And thus, for goods and riches they be unkind, unnatural, and cruel fathers unto their children, and cruel friends unto their kinsfolks, in giving and procuring to them so painful and sorrowful a life. And many times they destroy their own families and ancient houses thereby, for that their sons naughtily brought up, or else their sons-in-law evil chosen, for lack of grace, and the rather also for such disagreement as chanceth between them and their wives, married principally for possessions' sake, do waste and consume in small time all that their parents and ancestors, with all their wits, long service, and painful industry and labour, have gotten together in many years before.

And here ye shall understand (good people) that I do not prohibit and forbid men to look for no manner of goods when they will marry. For reason doth grant that both men and women should, before they marry, well consider what craft, occupation, ability, and what goods they have themselves to live withal if they marry. And reason doth admit that they should likewise look what ability and substance they be of with whom they will marry, and weigh and cast how such charges as may grow unto them by children and otherwise, when they be married, may be borne and sustained.

These things men and women which will marry ought well to remember and consider, and therefore I speak not against such considerations and looking for goods. But I say Almighty God and reason doth reprove and condemn all them which do marry most principally for goods and riches. For that intent and purpose is naught and contrary to God's ordinance in that behalf. And it is also evident that goods and money, lordships, rich apparel, delicate fare, and so forth, can do no pleasure or profit unto the hearts of married persons, except they have together faithful love, kindness, and joy, one of another, and godly and comfortable agreement.

Now that I have shewed unto you such causes of marriage as be ungodly, it is likewise requisite to declare the other causes which God Almighty and His Holy Word doth allow, which be the very same wherefore God did institute and ordain this Sacrament of Matrimony, that is to say, the love and desire of children and posterity, by whom God should be more honoured, and the hatred of fornication and unclean life.

The first cause is set forth in the book of Genesis,

Y

where God blessed our first parents, and bade them increase and multiply and ful-fill the earth (Gen. i. 28). Tobias, the younger, shewed that he married only for this first cause, saying unto Almighty God thus, O Lord, Thou knowest that I take this woman to my wife, not for cause of lechery, or to satisfy and fulfil my carnal lust and desire, but I take her only to have posterity and children, to the intent that Thou mayest be always here blessed, lauded, and honoured (Tobias viii. 9) ; and for this intent Christian men should most principally marry, and bring up their children in virtuous living, that they may justly live, laud, and honour Almighty God, and when God sendeth them children, to teach them to do the same. The unchristened and heathen men do marry to have children and to increase their people, but not to have Almighty God lauded and honoured, Whose honour and glory good men should specially seek to set forth and increase both in themselves and in their children.

The other cause is that men and women might by this sacrament have a just and good remedy against the sensual appetite of the flesh, and to avoid the sin of fornication, when they feared that they could not live otherwise chastely ; whereof St. Paul wrote to the Corinthians thus : It is good for a man not to touch his wife, yet for avoiding of fornication, let every man have or use his own wife, and let every wife have or use her own husband, and let the man pay his debt to his wife, and likewise the wife to her husband. For the wife hath not now power of her own body but her husband, and likewise the husband hath not power of his body but the wife. Do not defraud one another, except it be for a time by mutual consent, to the intent ye might give and apply your-selves more freely to prayer, and so forth (1 Cor. vii. 1-5). So that these two intents, that is to say, the love to have children, and the hatred or avoiding of fornication, as they be the principal causes why this sacrament of Matrimony was ordained of God, so they ought to be the principal causes why men and women should marry together. For so shall they receive the graces which God giveth in marriage, and shall beautify His Church, and have great help and furtherance towards their salvation.

And contrary, they that with covetous and leche-rous affections do join themselves in marriage, they lose the grace of the sacrament which they might have had, they dishonour this holy sacrament in making it a cloak and a defence for their naughty and vicious intents, and they bring themselves under the power of the devil, who then is permitted to pre-vail against them.

Moreover, good people, it is expedient when a man will marry for the causes before rehearsed, that he diligently remember and consider the law of matri-mony, that is to say, how he shall bind himself to love his wife as his own body, and better than any other man, woman or child, in such sort as Christ loveth His Church, and did give Himself to the death for it, to make it holy and without spot (Eph. v. 25, 26). And also the man ought not to be bitter and fell against his wife (Col. iii. 19), in using brawlings, chiding or fighting with her. And that he must keep

justly matrimonial chastity, and that he must forsake
to dwell with his father and mother and all other persons, for to be and dwell with his wife, and that he
ought also to cherish, help and comfort her, as he
would do his own person.   For when he marrieth,
he and his wife be made one body.   And this love
and kindness the man must shew his wife, not only
the first day or the first year, or while she is young
and hath health, but he must thus love her, and so
much do for her always so long as he and she live
together, whatsoever sickness or chance cometh to
her, or what conditions soever she have.   For though
a man may for certain causes be from the company
and dwelling with his wife against her will, as if he can
prove that his wife hath given the use of her body
unto another man, and have not kept her matrimonial
chastity, and so forth in some other cases ; yet he can
in no wise break his marriage, nor the bond of it, and
marry another (Matt. xix. 9), nor he cannot be discharged of the obligation and promise which he made
to love his wife, and to do for her as much as for his
own body and person, always when his wife shall
have need.   These considerations and remembrances
ought every Christian man to have when he intendeth
to marry, for what cause soever he marry.   And likewise also when a woman will marry, she must diligently consider after what manner she must live with
her husband, how she shall vow and bind herself
under the pain of damnation, to love her husband
above all men, and to worship him, and meekly and
gladly to obey him, and fulfil that he commandeth
and desireth her to do in all things which pertain to

God's law and the duty of marriage. And she must always have her matrimonial chastity, and help and succour her husband in his need as she would her own person, and she must do all things which she did vow and promise when she was married. For the law of matrimony bindeth the woman to everything touching the duty of a wife, as it doth the man concerning the duty of an husband.

These things well considered on both the parties, shall be a great help and provocation, that they shall study and labour most principally to join and couple themselves unto persons which have abundance of virtues and good conditions, more than for any other sinister affection, seeing nothing can cause or make this matrimonial love and agreement to be kept and continued amongst married persons, so much as honest, equal, and like conditions shall do.

And whereas the Scripture saith that a man may have an house and riches of his parents, but a good and prudent wife is the gift of God (Prov. xix. 14), he ought, before he shall marry, most humbly to beg this good gift of Almighty God with long, devout, and continual prayers, as one special thing whereupon resteth his joy in this world, and by well using of that hope of joy in the next world. And because marriage is an honourable thing, as S. Paul saith (Heb. xiii. 4), let them have no evil affection nor do nothing that might dishonour it. But before they celebrate the same marriage, let them prepare their hearts with fasting and other godly and spiritual exercises, to come worthily to such an honourable sacrament, and to do as becometh the children of holy people, and not like Gentiles and heathen people which know not God (Tobias viii. 5), nor have no godliness before their eyes.

Last of all, I shall exhort and admonish you that be married, to use your marriage in such sort here in this world, as it be no hindrance for you to come to the next world, so to endeavour yourself one to please another, that ye do in nowise displease God your Creator, so to seek and do those things that be temporal, that ye omit not to seek and labour for those things which be eternal, so to be glad of your present prosperity, that ye be not careless without fear of eternal damnation, and so to be sorry for such adversity as chanceth here, that ye be not void of sure and perfect hope of eternal felicity.

Let not the cares of this world so break and cast down your hearts, but that the hope of heavenly and eternal joys may comfort and stay them again. And also let not the flattering face of worldly wealth so inveigle and deceive you, but that the fear of God's eternal judgment may bridle you and keep you in awe. For the minds of godly married persons, although they be not able to forsake the cares of this world, and utterly to contemn worldly things, yet ought they by their desires and godly affections to join themselves to things eternal. These good lessons S. Paul knitteth up in a few words, saying thus, "The time is short, and it remaineth that they which have wives be as having no wives" (1 Cor. vii. 29). As though he should say in longer process, that the end of the world and the last judgment of God draweth near, and so much the more ought every man to be careful how he shall appear and be found at that judgment. And the case of matrimony is not like now to us that be in the end of the world, as it was to the old fathers in the beginning, for amongst them he was accounted and taken as accursed by the sentence of the law, that did not raise up seed in Israel, that died without issue and children ; for that was the time to increase and multiply God's people, by which people it was prophesied that the Prince and Saviour of the world should be born, and for that cause the people of God did as much as they could apply themselves to marriage, whereunto they were kindled and moved not by concupiscence, but by obedience, not for satisfying of their carnal lust, but for religion to obey the law and to have fruit of their bodies. But now since that the fulness of time is come, and the world draweth towards an end, the case is altered. For now, saith our Saviour Christ, in way of exhortation, he that can take the gift of chastity and sole life let him take it (Matt. xix. 12), from which time many that have that gift use it in deed, and he that will not use it may not excuse himself that he hath it not, and in case he be married let him live and be as unmarried, having the same affection to continent life, and the abstinence from the act of matrimony, as Abraham and the old fathers had, who then served not the lusts and desires of their flesh but served the law, the time of increase, and the ordinance of God, being slow and forbearing to require, but sometimes content to pay, their matrimonial debt, and let him so take carnal comfort of his wife that in nowise her love withdraw him from serving of God, seeing he ought to love her in God and for God.   And therefore married persons be bounden, if any displeasant thing chance amongst them, with patience to bear one another's burden (Gal. vi. 2), and so to fulfil the law of Christ, which is charity, seeking to amend that is done amiss between them, rather by discreet and loving admonition, than by furious and unkind correction, which shall be a cause, that either party shall take heed and beware to do anything that might displease the other for very love and for fear of losing the other's favour.

Thus have ye heard (good people) for what cause men and women ought to enter marriage and partly how to live in the same, to the pleasure of Almighty God, according to the example of all holy men and the doctrine of our Saviour Christ, to Whom with the Father and the Holy Ghost be all honour and glory, world without end.   Amen.

THE THIRTIETH SERMON.

OF THE SACRAMENT OF EXTREME UNCTION.

CONSIDERING (good people) that the life of man is but short, and passeth away like a shadow, and that death, as it is certain to come to every man, so it is uncertain what time or what hour it shall come, and also considering that the devil our ghostly enemy, as he ceaseth not all our lifetime, with his crafty temptations, to lay in wait for us to supplant us and to bring us to deadly sin, and so to lose the favours of God our most merciful Father ; so in the time of our infirmity when death approacheth, then I say, is he most busy and fierce to subvert us, and we also at that time least able to withstand him, our mind being then much alienated with the pain of our disease, and the heaviness of our body, which then draweth towards corruption. Therefore our Saviour Christ, our most special helper and comforter in all distresses, hath provided for us a singular and special good medicine, which is the Sacrament of Extreme Unction, the virtue whereof is, at that time of our infirmity, to comfort our souls which be wont to wax heavy for the dissolution of our bodies, and also to strengthen us with the grace of the Holy Ghost, against the violent assaults and temptations of the devil, and also to replenish our heart with gladness against the terror of death, and finally to forgive us our daily trespasses, wherewith we have displeased His Majesty, such I mean as this our transitory life, considering our frailty and weakness, cannot be passed over without, and all this also is done with the assistance of such godly and faithful prayers as the priests of Christ's Catholic Church do make to Almighty God for the sick man, at the ministration of this sacrament of Extreme Unction.

Of which sacrament S. Mark speaketh in his sixth chapter, where it is written that our Saviour Christ did send forth His disciples to preach, prescribing unto them what manner and form they should observe in their progress (Mark vi. 7, &c.), and then it followeth that the disciples going abroad, preached to the people to do penance, and they did cast forth many devils, and they anointed with oil many sick persons, and they were made whole, which thing they did not in their own name and power by presumption but in the power and name of Christ, as He had prescribed and commanded them before to do. And because, in the words of the Evangelist, is set forth plainly the visible sign of oil, and also the invisible effect of grace annexed and following thereupon, therefore the Holy and Universal Church of Christ, as the practice of the same and the consent of the ancient writers do witness, understand and believe this sacrament to be then instituted * of our Saviour

* The theologians who prepared the canons of the 14th Session of the Council of Trent, had indicated that the sacrament of Extreme

Christ. Which thing the holy Apostle S. James, also delivering that to the people which he before had received of Christ, setteth forth more at large, writing thus :—" If any person be sick amongst you, let him call the priests of the Church to be brought in, and let them pray over him, anointing him with oil in the name of our Lord, and the prayer of faith shall save the sick person, and our Lord shall relieve him, and lift him up, and if he be in sins, they shall be forgiven him " (James v. 14, 15). By which words we be assured that God doth assist the ministration of this sacrament, and also we learn how it ought to be used in all points.

First, he telleth to whom it ought to be ministered, that is to say, to Christian men or women such as have received the sacrament of Baptism before, and not to every one of them, but to such as be then visited by the hand of God, with some great sickness of the body, and be in some peril of death by reason of the said sickness, and not by any other outward violence of war or execution ; and not to young infants that have no need of it, nor to such as, either for young age or from frenzy, lack the use of their reason, but to such as have knowledge and have dominion over their own wills, and being in venial sin, do require the same either then or before, as it may be presumed by their former will. So that it is every Christian man's duty to require this sacrament

---

Unction was instituted by our Lord, on the occasion mentioned by S. Mark ; but the fathers of the Council omitted the word *instituted*, and instead of it use the word *insinuated*. The first canon, however, defines that it was instituted by our Lord, without fixing the time.—ED.

with humble request, and with perfect hope to attain the grace and effect which is given by the same.

Secondly, S. James expresseth to whom it appertaineth by office and duty to be minister of this sacrament, in that he willeth the sick man to call for priests of the Church; for only priests be appointed to be the ministers thereof,—not as in their own name and authority, but in the name and authority of our Lord Jesus Christ, so that the priest in that doing doth bear and represent the person of Christ and His Holy Church, who beside his prayers doth minister the outward Sacrament of Aneling, and Christ inwardly worketh the invisible grace of the same in the soul of the party aneled, like as He useth to do in all other sacraments.

Thirdly, S. James expresseth both the matter or outward element of this sacrament, and also the manner how to use it. The matter wherein it is ministered is oil, which is a thing most convenient to declare the effects and graces given by the same. The manner how to use it, is by prayer over the sick person, and by anointing him in such places of his body as were occasions, or as it were windows, whereby sin is chiefly committed, as the places of our five wits or senses. For by the eyes concupiscence, covetousness, and many other vices enter into the soul; by the ears detraction, false reports, and thereupon following anger and envy, and such like infect the soul; by the nose delicious life and much other occasion of sin is ministered; by the mouth, both in tasting and also in speaking, that is against God and his neighbour, a man oftentimes doth offend; by the reins and other parts thereunto adjoining, carnal desires and the concupiscence of the flesh is accustomed to corrupt the soul ; and finally, by the hands and feet is practised much vice, the particulars whereof I need not to rehearse. For these causes the sick person is anointed in the said places, at which time the priest and they that do there assist him, with sure faith and confidence in Almighty God, putting away all mistrust and doubt, make their most humble prayer to His Majesty, that it would please the same, through that unction as a spiritual medicine, and His most merciful goodness, to pardon and remit whatsoever the sick person hath offended by his sight or hearing, or any other part of his body above-mentioned, with many other godly and wholesome prayers thereunto annexed, and used to be said and frequented in the Church of Christ. And thus to pray over the sick person, and to anele him, is not the invention of man, devised by man's wit, but, according to God's ordinance, is done in the name and authority of our Lord, Who is the author of this sacrament, as He is likewise of all the other, by Whose assistance and secret operation this sacrament worketh His spiritual and inward effect ; which effect S. James last of all declareth, saying, " The prayer of faith shall save the sick, and God shall relieve and lift him up, and if he be in sin, they shall be forgiven unto him."

Which effect is double or two ways, the one chief and principal is in purging and making clean the soul from daily and venial sin, which never faileth, if the sick party do not stop the influence of God's grace, which he may do by remaining then in deadly sin, neglecting to procure that to be forgiven unto him before, by the sacrament of Penance, or by mistrusting to receive that grace of God which is signified and promised by that holy unction. Therefore ought every man and woman being sick, first to confess himself and receive the sacrament of Absolution, then to receive the blessed food of immortality in the sacrament of the Altar, for the perfection of God's influence, and the increase of all his former graces, and then afterward with sure faith and confidence in God, require to be aneled of the priests of Christ's Church. And in so doing, beside the perfect purging of his soul, he shall (no doubt of it) feel inwardly great easement against the pains and horror of death, great strength and comfort of the spirit, whereby, like a good warrior and stout champion of Christ, he is then made more able to withstand the violent temptations of the devil, and finally great joy and gladness in himself, great stay and increase of faith and hope towards God, and great desire to be delivered from the miseries of this transitory world, and to be called to the eternal city of God in the kingdom of heaven.

The other effect is the healing of the body from corporal diseases, or at least the mitigation of the same. Which effect is not principal, and doth not always follow : partly for the smallness of faith in the sick person (for great and vehement faith is required to have God's power to work such corporal health in man), partly for that God our most merciful Father, according to His heavenly wisdom, thinketh it best for us otherwise to dispose of us, as He knoweth to be most expedient for the salvation of our souls, or the commodity of His elect people, whose benefit of corporal health, if it had been then bestowed upon us, perchance the malice of our will would have abused it to the offence of God, and the danger of damnation to our souls.

Therefore, in all such indifferent things, as the sickness or health of body, every Christian man ought to commit and refer it to the good will and pleasure of Almighty God, and to think and esteem that to be best, whatsoever God shall work by us, although it seems to be hurtful to us, or to be contrary to our desires and petitions, which in all things (as He taught Himself) ought to be directed and submitted to His will and pleasure, Who always of His godly providence disposeth all things sweetly and mercifully. But, howsoever God shall work concerning our corporal health, we ought surely to trust that God for His part (if there be no stop in us) faileth not to work inwardly in our souls the spiritual effects which I have rehearsed before. And because there be two things which let the soul freely to have recourse to God, and to delight altogether in Him : the one is that weakness and feebleness which is left in the soul of man after the wound of deadly sin, although the guilt of the same be remedied by true penance, the other is, the daily heaping up of many venial sins, into which a man falleth by frailness of nature, by sudden motions, by imperfection or coldness of charity, by vehement agonies of sickness, or by negligence in not taking heed to himself, his acts, and profession. For that cause to remove these two evils, God hath ordained this sacrament of Extreme

Unction to be ministered, whereby the weakness of the soul is strengthened, and all venial sin remitted, if it be well and devoutly received.

And seeing a man must needs once depart hence, and end the journey of this troublesome life, for so-much as the soul is by the flesh loaden, drawn back, infected, disquieted, and weakened, therefore it hath need of a new strength and spiritual medicine, specially at the passage hence by death, that it neither fall, give over, or despair, but that it be relieved, disburdened, pacified, comforted, and made able by the strength of the Holy Ghost to abide with God, and by His aid to pass through the miseries and travails of this life, and to exchange the short and light affections of this time, with the eternal and weighty joys in the kingdom of heaven. All which graces, as I said before, the soul of the sick person receiveth and is endued withal, by the worthy and devout receipt of this holy sacrament ordained of Almighty God for the same purpose.

Thus have ye heard, good people, the meaning and effect of the doctrine of S. James concerning this sacrament, how it ought to be used, what grace and virtue is given to us thereby, which to neglect, and to defraud or deprive ourselves of the benefits thereof wilfully, were great folly. For although it be not absolutely necessary to salvation, as is baptism, without the which no man ordinarily can be saved, yet if it be despised and of contempt not regarded, when it may be had, it is a let and stop to salvation. Wherefore I shall exhort you all in the name of God, that when God by sickness shall visit any of you, ye follow the counsel of the Holy Ghost, uttered and expressed by the writing of this holy Apostle S. James, that ye call for the priests of the Church, I mean the great universal Church of Christ, which is known throughout the world, in the communion whereof, as members of the same Church (to whom only salvation is promised and prepared), see that ye require the said priests or priest (if there be but one) to pray over you, and to anele you in the name of the Blessed Trinity.* And do not defer this till the vehemence of your sickness decay your speech and memory, as it is done amongst many which perversely use the priests of the Church as they use their corporal physicians, never sending for them but in their extremes, when they can do them least good. But seeing S. James willeth the sick person to call or send for the priest, let him do that before his will, his senses, his memory, and understanding do fail him, when he is able to join with the priest in prayer, and to protest the faith and trust he hath in attaining the grace and effect of this sacrament, to the intent he being inwardly armed and strengthened with the same (in token whereof he is then anointed outwardly with the sacrament of oil), might the better withstand the force of the devil and all his deceitful temptations, who is then more busy, as it were, in the extreme conflict to overthrow the soldier of Christ. And then, no doubt of it, Almighty God, Who is true

* When Bishop Watson printed this sermon, Queen Mary was sickly and childless. The preacher seems to have foreseen or dreaded the coming schism under Elizabeth, and that many of his hearers would have to choose between a National Church in schism, perhaps in heresy, and "the great universal Church of Christ."—ED.

and faithful of His promise, will work the effects of grace, whereof S. James here speaketh, in that sick person, as His godly wisdom shall see most expedient for the soul health of that person, specially if he then with humility, meekness, and gladness of heart, with a full hope and confidence in God's mercy, do give and yield up his body and soul, with all the powers of the same, unto his Lord God, his Creator and Redeemer, to be healed and ordered according to His good will by the mean of His holy sacraments, which He hath ordained to be to us as spiritual medicines, whereby the merits of His most blessed death and Passion be ordinarily applied to our commodity.

And he that shall do thus, may cheerfully and with gladness of mind depart this wretched world, with assurance and full trust to attain first the promises of grace, annexed to the worthy and fruitful receiving of His holy sacraments, and in the end to attain the crown of glory and life everlasting, which Christ our Lord hath promised to all them that shall love and long for His coming, which He grant to us all, to Whom with the Father, and the Holy Ghost, three persons and one God, be all glory and honour, world without end. Amen.

APPENDIX.

———•———

ON THE CHILDREN OF HERETICS.

In his fifth sermon Bishop Watson writes :—

"Be you careful and diligent to have your children confirmed in this grace, and to be indued with these excellent gifts of the Holy Ghost, by receiving this Holy Sacrament" (he is speaking of Confirmation) "in the Catholic Church, and specially they whose children were baptized of heretics in the time of any schism, and out of the Catholic Church. For although they did then receive the sacrament of Baptism, which may not be ministered to them again (lest we should show ourselves to crucify Christ again); yet they did not then and there receive the grace of baptism, being out of the Church, but may now receive the grace which they lacked before, and be reconciled to God, and be made members of His holy Catholic Church, and so in time be admitted to receive the blessed Body and Blood of our Lord Jesus Christ."

It is clear that the Bishop is speaking of infants, since no parents then delayed the baptism of their children. As the schism had only been formally ended three years before he wrote, there were many children who had been baptized during the schism too young as yet for confession.

He wished to have these confirmed at once, that through confirmation they might "be reconciled to God."

These opinions are altogether singular; and lest they should derive any weight from the authority of so learned and holy a man as Bishop Watson, it may be well to inquire the source of his error.

Watson refers in the margin to S. Augustin (De Eccl. Dogmat. cap. lii.). In his day this work was commonly attributed to S. Augustin, though it is now given to Gennadius. The author, speaking of the reconciliation of heretics, says: "Si vero parvuli sunt . . . respondeant pro illis qui eos offerunt, juxta morem baptizandi, et sic manus impositione et chrismate communiti, Eucharistiæ mysteriis admittantur." Gennadius, however, does not say that the children had previously been deprived of grace.

On this subject Suarez says (De Sacram. disp. xiii. sect. iv. n. 11): "Minister, quantumvis iniquus vel hæreticus, sicut confert verum sacramentum, ita etiam dabit sacramenti effectum, si suscipiens non ponat obicem. Quod omnes scholastici docent. . . . Et quamvis hoc (de effectu) non sit sub his terminis tam expresse definitum, tamen omnino certum est et necessario sequitur ex principiis fidei. . . .

"Exemplum evidens est in parvulo baptizato ab hæretico; nam si statim moriatur, sine dubio salvabitur; alioqui vel rebaptizandus esset a Catholico priusquam moreretur ne periret, vel maneret omni remedio destitutus; utrumque autem absurdissimum et hæreticum est."

The third course of reconciling the infant by confirmation does not seem even to have occurred to Suarez. Drouvin is as explicit as Suarez: "Quantum ad gratiam spectat, si sacramenta conferuntur infantibus, citra dubium est, gratiam simul cum charactere infundi; quia in qualibet hæresi aut factione schismatis infans baptizetur, cum nullum obicem malæ voluntatis opponat, neque erroris fiat particeps, sacramenti effectu defraudari non potest" (De Re Sacramentaria, tom. i. lib. i. 94, 7).

So also Coustant : " Si de infantibus sermo est, certum est eos ubicunque et a quocunque baptizati fuerint statim consequi gratiam Christi."

Suarez says that this is the teaching of all the Scholastics. It will be enough to quote S. Thomas : " Dicendum quod ille qui ab hæretico baptizatur propter peccatum hæretici non privatur gratia baptismatis, sed quandoque propter peccatum proprium. Unde si sit puer in quem culpa actualis non cadit, si baptizatur in forma Ecclesiæ recipit sacramentum et rem sacramenti " (Dist. vi. qu. i. art 3, questiunc. 3, solut. 3).

So also Scotus (in Lib. iv. Dist. 4, qu. 2, Schol.), who shows that the child is not injured by want of faith in the minister or the sponsors.

It is, however, not difficult to see how Dr Watson fell into his error, for such it surely is. S. Augustin, with whose writings he was more familiar than with the Scholastics, *seems* to deny over and over again, in the most emphatic way, that grace can be conferred by the baptism of heretics. To quote only a few passages out of many :—

" Si baptismi gratiam hoc esse dicis quod est baptismus, est apud hæreticos. Si autem baptismus sacramentum est gratiæ, ipsa vero gratia abolitio peccatorum est, non est apud hæreticos baptismi gratia " (De Bapt. c. Donat.)

Again : "Præter Ecclesiæ societatem aqua baptismi, quamvis eadem sit, non solum non valet ad salutem, sed valet potius ad perniciem " (C. Faust. l.xii. cap. 17).

But that S. Augustin did not intend to include infants in these propositions seems clear from the reasons he elsewhere gives for the uselessness of heretical baptism.

" Sacramenta hæreticis insunt sed non prosunt, quia cum illa recta sunt, ipsi perversi sunt " (C. Donat. Ep. cap. 22), which cannot be said of infants. And again : " Nec nos abnuimus eum, qui apud hæreticos vel in aliquo schismate extra communionem Ecclesiæ baptizatur, non ei prodesse, in quantum hæreticorum et schismaticorum perversitati consentit " (C. Donat. lib. iii. cap. 10).

Hence he makes an exception for a Catechumen holding the Catholic faith, and in no way consenting to schism or heresy, who in danger of death would receive baptism from the hands of a heretic, when no Catholic could be found (C. Donat. lib. vi. cap. 5, l.vii. cap. 52).

I doubt not that he would have made the same exception for infants, for the same reason, though I do not find a passage where he has said this explicitly. Nor have I found the question of infants who are baptized by heretics anywhere discussed by other fathers, Latin or Greek. S. Asterius Amassenus indeed says : " On account of the heterodox father the child is baptized yet not baptized, but rather drowned in heresy. It has scarcely begun the voyage of life, and already it has made shipwreck " (Hom. 20 in Psal. 6). But when the context is examined his meaning becomes clear. The danger was that the child would be educated in the sect in which it had been baptized, and was therefore entangled by its baptism in its parents' heresy.

EDITOR.

PRINTED BY BALLANTYNE, HANSON AND CO.
EDINBURGH AND LONDON

A

Select Catalogue of Books

LATELY PUBLISHED BY

BURNS AND OATES,

17, 18 PORTMAN STREET

AND

68 PATERNOSTER ROW.

LONDON:
ROBSON AND SONS, PRINTERS, PANCRAS ROAD, N.W.

𝔅ooks lately published

BY

BURNS AND OATES,

17, 18 PORTMAN STREET, W., & 63 PATERNOSTER ROW, E.C.

————◦————

Sin and its Consequences. By His Eminence
the CARDINAL ARCHBISHOP OF WESTMINSTER. Second
edition. 6*s.*

> CONTENTS : I. The Nature of Sin. II. Mortal Sin.
> III. Venial Sin. IV. Sins of Omission. V. The Grace
> and Works of Penance. VI. Temptation. VII. The Dere-
> liction on the Cross. VIII. The Joys of the Resurrection.

'We know few better books than this for spiritual reading. These lectures
are prepared with great care, and are worthy to rank with the old volumes
of sermons which are now standard works of the English tongue.'—*Weekly
Register.*

'We have had many volumes from his Grace's pen of this kind, but perhaps none more practical or more searching than the volume before us.
These discourses are the clearest and simplest exposition of the theology of
the subjects they treat of that could be desired. The intellect is addressed
as well as the conscience. Both are strengthened and satisfied.'—*Tablet.*

'Of the deepest value, and of great theological and literary excellence.
More clear and lucid expositions of dogmatic and moral theology could not
be found. No one can read these very forcible, searching, and practical
sermons without being deeply stirred and greatly edified.'· -*Church Herald.*

'His Grace has added to Catholic literature such a brilliant disquisition
as can hardly be equalled.'—*Catholic Times.*

'As powerful, searching, and deep as any that we have ever read. In
construction, as well as in theology and in rhetoric, they are more than remarkable, and are amongst the best from his Grace's pen.'—*Union Review.*

The Prophet of Carmel: a Series of Practical Considerations upon the History of Elias in the Old Testament; with a Supplementary Dissertation. By the Rev. CHARLES B. GARSIDE, M.A. Dedicated to the Very Rev. JOHN HENRY NEWMAN, D.D. 5s.

'There is not a page in these sermons but commands our respect. They are Corban in the best sense : they belong to the sanctuary, and are marked as divine property by a special cachet. They are simple without being trite, and poetical without being pretentious.'—*Westminster Gazette.*

'Full of spiritual wisdom uttered in pure and engaging language.'—The *Universe.*

'We see in these pages the learning of the divine, the elegance of the scholar, and the piety of the priest. Every point in the sacred narrative bearing upon the subject of his book is seized upon by the author with the greatest keenness of perception, and set forth with singular force and clearness.'—*Weekly Register.*

'Under his master-hand the marvellous career of the Prophet of Carmel displays its majestic proportions. His strong, nervous, incisive style has a beauty and a grace, a delicacy and a sensitiveness, that seizes hold of the heart and captivates the imagination. He has attained to the highest art of writing, which consists in selecting the words which express one's meaning with the greatest clearness in the least possible space.'—*Tablet.*

'The intellectual penetration, the rich imagination, the nervous eloquence which we meet with throughout the whole work, all combine to give it at once a very high place among the highest productions of our English Catholic literature.'—*Dublin Review.*

'Is at once powerful and engaging, and calculated to furnish ideas innumerable to the Christian preacher.'—*Church Review.*

'The thoughts are expressed in plain and vigorous English. The sermons are good specimens of the way in which Old Testament subjects should be treated for the instruction of a Christian congregation.'—*Church Times.*

Mary magnifying God: May Sermons. By the Rev. Fr. HUMPHREY, O.S.C. Cloth, 2s. 6d.

'Each sermon is a complete thesis, eminent for the strength of its logic, the soundness of its theology, and the lucidness of its expression. With equal force and beauty of language the author has provided matter for the most sublime meditations.'—*Tablet.*

'Dogmatic teaching of the utmost importance is placed before us so clearly, simply, and unaffectedly, that we find ourselves acquiring invaluable lessons of theology in every page.'—*Weekly Register.*

By the same,

The Divine Teacher. Second edition. 2s. 6d.

'The most excellent treatise we have ever read. It could not be clearer, and, while really deep, it is perfectly intelligible to any person of the most ordinary education.'—*Tablet.*

'We cannot speak in terms too high of the matter contained in this excellent and able pamphlet.'—*Westminster Gazette.*

Sermons by Fathers of the Society of Jesus.

Third edition. 7s.

CONTENTS : The Latter Days : Four Sermons by the Rev. H. J. Coleridge. The Temptations of our Lord : Four Sermons by the Rev. Father Hathaway. The Angelus Bell : Five Lectures on the Remedies against Desolation by the Very Rev. Father Gallwey, Provincial of the Society. The Mysteries of the Holy Infancy : Seven Sermons by Fathers Parkinson, Coleridge, and Harper.

Also, printed separately from above,

The Angelus Bell : Five Lectures on the

Remedies against Desolation. By the Very Rev. Father GALLWEY, Provincial of the Society of Jesus. 1s. 6d.

Also Vol. II. in same series,

Discourses by the Rev. Fr. Harper, S.J. 6s.

Also, just published, Vol. III. 6s.

CONTENTS : Sermons by the Rev. George R. Kingdon : I. What the Passion of Christ teaches us ; II. Our Lord's Agony in the Garden ; III. The Choice between Jesus and Barabbas ; IV. Easter Sunday (I.) ; V. Easter Sunday (II.) ; VI. Corpus Christi. Sermons by the Rev. Edward I. Purbrick : VII. Grandeur and Beauty of the Holy Eucharist ; VIII. Our Lady of Victories ; IX. The Feast of All Saints (I.) ; X. The Feast of All Saints (II.) ; XI. The Feast of the Immaculate Conception ; XII. The Feast of St. Joseph. Sermons by the Rev. Henry J. Coleridge : XIII. Fruits of Holy Communion (I.) ; XIV. Fruits of Holy Communion (II.) ; XV. Fruits of Holy Communion (III.) ; XVI. Fruits of Holy Communion (IV.). Sermons by the Rev. Alfred Weld : XVII. On the Charity of Christ ; XVIII. On the Blessed Sacrament. Sermons by the Rev. William II. Anderdon : XIX. The Corner-Stone a Rock of Offence ; XX. The Word of God heard or rejected by Men.

WORKS WRITTEN AND EDITED BY LADY GEORGIANA FULLERTON.

The Straw-cutter's Daughter, and the Portrait in my Uncle's Dining-room. Two Stories. Translated from the French. 2s. 6d.

Life of Luisa de Carvajal.   6s.

Seven Stories.   3s. 6d.

CONTENTS: I. Rosemary: a Tale of the Fire of London. II. Reparation : a Story of the Reign of Louis XIV. III. The Blacksmith of Antwerp. IV. The Beggar of the Steps of St. Roch: a True Story. V. Trouvaille, or the Soldier's Adopted Child: a True Story. VI. Earth without Heaven : a Reminiscence. VII. Ad Majorem Dei Gloriam.

' Will well repay perusal.'—*Weekly Register.*
' Each story in this series has its own charm.'—*Tablet.*
' In this collection may be found stories sound in doctrine and intensely interesting as any which have come from the same pen.'—*Catholic Opinion.*
' As admirable for their art as they are estimable for their sound teaching.'—*Cork Examiner.*

A Sketch of the Life of the late Father Henry Young, of Dublin.   2s. 6d.

Life of Mère Marie de la Providence, Foundress of the Order of the ' Helpers of the Holy Souls.'

The materials of this Biography have been drawn from the ' Notice sur la Révérende Mère Marie de la Providence,' published in Paris in 1872 ; the work of the Rev. Père Blôt, ' Les Auxiliatrices des Ames du Purgatoire ;' and some additional documents furnished to the authoress by the Religious of the Rue de la Barouillière.   2s.

Laurentia : a Tale of Japan.   Second edition.   3s. 6d.

' Has very considerable literary merit, and possesses an interest entirely its own. The dialogue is easy and natural, and the incidents are admirably grouped.'—*Weekly Register.*
' Full of romantic records of the heroism of the early Christians of Japan in the sixteenth century. Looking at its literary merits alone, it must be pronounced a really beautiful story. —*Catholic Times.*

Life of St. Frances of Rome.   2s. 6d.; cheap edition, 1s. 8d.

Rose Leblanc : a Tale of great interest.   3s.

Grantley Manor : the well-known and favourite Novel.   Cloth, 3s. 6d.; cheap edition, 2s. 6d.

Germaine Cousin : a Drama.   6d.

Fire of London : a Drama.   6d.

OUR LADY'S BOOKS.
Uniformly printed in foolscap 8vo, limp cloth.

No. 1.

Memoir of the Hon. Henry E. Dormer.   2s.

No. 2.

Life of Mary Fitzgerald, a Child of the Sacred Heart.   2s.; cheap edition, 1s.

Meditations for every Day in the Year, and
for the Principal Feasts. By the Ven. Fr. NICHOLAS LAN-
CICIUS, of the Society of Jesus. With Preface by the Rev.
GEORGE PORTER, S.J.   6s. 6d.

'Most valuable, not only to religious, for whom they were originally
intended, but to all those who desire to consecrate their daily life by regu-
larly express and systematic meditation; while Father Porter's excellent
little Preface contains many valuable hints on the method of meditation.'—
Dublin Review.

'Full of Scripture, short and suggestive. The editor gives a very clear
explanation of the Ignatian method of meditation. The book is a very useful
one.'—*Tablet.*

'Short and simple, and dwell almost entirely on the life of our Blessed
Lord, as related in the Gospels. Well suited to the wants of Catholics
living in the world.'—*Weekly Register.*

'A book of singular spirituality and great depth of piety. Nothing could
be more beautiful or edifying than the thoughts set forth for reflection,
clothed as they are in excellent and vigorous English.'—*Union Review.*

Meditations for the Use of the Clergy, for
every Day in the Year, on the Gospels for the Sundays.
From the Italian of Mgr. SCOTTI, Archbishop of Thessa-
lonica. Revised and edited by the Oblates of St. Charles.
With a Preface by his Grace the ARCHBISHOP OF WEST-
MINSTER.

Vol. I. From the First Sunday in Advent to the Sixth
Saturday after the Epiphany.   4s.

Vol. II. From Septuagesima Sunday to the Fourth Sunday
after Easter.   4s.

Vol. III. From the Fifth Sunday after Easter to the Eleventh
Sunday after Pentecost.   4s.

Vol. IV., completing the work.   4s.

'This admirable little book will be much valued by all, but especially by
the clergy, for whose use it is more immediately intended. The Archbishop

states in his Preface that it is held in high esteem in Rome, and that he has himself found, by the experience of many years, its singular excellence, its practical piety, its abundance of Scripture, of the Fathers, and of ecclesiastical writers.'—*Tablet.*

'It is a sufficient recommendation to this book of meditations that our Archbishop has given them his own warm approval. . . . They are full of the language of the Scriptures, and are rich with unction of their Divine sense.'—*Weekly Register.*

'A manual of meditations for priests, to which we have seen nothing comparable.'—*Catholic World.*

'There is great beauty in the thoughts, the illustrations are striking, the learning shown in patristic quotation considerable, and the special applications to priests are very powerful. It is entirely a priest's book.'—*Church Review.*

The Question of Anglican Ordinations discussed. By the Very Rev. Canon ESTCOURT, M.A., F.A.S. With an Appendix of Original Documents and Photographic Facsimiles. One vol. 8vo, 14s.

'A valuable contribution to the theology of the Sacrament of Order. He treats a leading question, from a practical point of view, with great erudition, and with abundance of illustrations from the rites of various ages and countries.'—*Month.*

'Will henceforth be an indispensable portion of every priest's library, inasmuch as it contains all the information that has been collected in previous works, sifted and corrected, together with a well-digested mass of important matter which has never before been given to the public.'—*Tablet.*

'Marks a very important epoch in the history of that question, and virtually disposes of it.'—*Messenger.*

'Canon Estcourt has added valuable documents that have never appeared before, or never at full length. The result is a work of very great value.'—*Catholic Opinion.*

'Indicates conscientious and painstaking research, and will be indispensable to any student who would examine the question on which it treats.'—*Bookseller.*

'Superior, both in literary method, tone, and mode of reasoning, to the usual controversial books on this subject.'—*Church Herald.*

May Papers; or Thoughts on the Litanies of Loreto. By EDWARD IGNATIUS PURBRICK, Priest of the Society of Jesus. 3s. 6d.

'There is a brightness and vivacity in them which will make them interesting to all, old and young alike, and adds to their intrinsic value.'—*Dublin Review.*

'We very gladly welcome this volume as a valuable addition to the now happily numerous manuals of devout exercises for the month.'—*Month.*

'Written in the pure, simple, unaffected language which becomes the subject.'—*Tablet.*

'We cannot easily conceive a book more calculated to aid the cause of true religion amongst young persons of every class.'—*Weekly Register.*

'They are admirable, and expressed in chaste and beautiful language. Although compiled in the first place for boys at school, they are adapted for the spiritual reading of Catholics of every age and condition of life.'—*Catholic Opinion.*

WORKS OF THE REV. FATHER RAWES, O.S.C.

Homeward: a Tale of Redemption. Second edition. 3*s*. 6*d*.

'A series of beautiful word pictures.'—*Catholic Opinion.*
'A casket well worth the opening; full to the brim of gems of thought as beautiful as they are valuable.'—*Catholic Times.*
'Full of holy thoughts and exquisite poetry, and just such a book as can be taken up with advantage and relief in hours of sadness and depression.'—*Dublin Review.*
'Is really beautiful, and will be read with profit.'—*Church Times.*

God in His Works: a Course of Five Sermons. 2*s*. 6*d*.

SUBJECTS: I. God in Creation. II. God in the Incarnation. III. God in the Holy See. IV. God in the Heart. V. God in the Resurrection.

'Full of striking imagery, and the beauty of the language cannot fail to make the book valuable for spiritual reading.'—*Catholic Times.*
'He has so applied science as to bring before the reader an unbroken course of thought and argument.'—*Tablet.*

The Beloved Disciple; or St. John the Evangelist. 3*s*. 6*d*.

'Full of research, and of tender and loving devotion.'—*Tablet.*
'This is altogether a charming book for spiritual reading.'—*Catholic Times.*
'Through this book runs a vein of true, humble, fervent piety, which gives a singular charm.'—*Weekly Register.*
'St. John, in his varied character, is beautifully and attractively presented to our pious contemplation.'—*Catholic Opinion.*

Septem: Seven Ways of hearing Mass. Fifth edition. 1*s*. and 2*s*.; red edges, 2*s*. 6*d*.; calf, 4*s*.; French Translation, 1*s*. 6*d*.

'A great assistance to hearing Mass with devotion. Besides its devotional advantages it possesses a Preface, in clear and beautiful language, well worth reading.'—*Tablet.*

Great Truths in Little Words. Third edition. Neat cloth, 3*s*. 6*d*.

'A most valuable little work. All may learn very much about the Faith rom it.'—*Tablet.*
'At once practical in its tendency, and elegant; oftentimes poetical in its diction.'—*Weekly Register.*
'Cannot fail to be most valuable to every Catholic; and we feel certain, when known and appreciated, it will be a standard work in Catholic households.'—*Catholic Times.*

Hymns, Original, &c.   Neat cloth,   1s. ;
cheap edition, 6d.

*The Eucharistic Month.   From the Latin of
Father LERCARI, S.J.   6d. ; cloth, 1s.

*Twelve Visits to our Lady and the Heavenly
City of God.   Second edition.   8d.

*Nine Visits to the Blessed Sacrament.   Chiefly
from the Canticle of Canticles.   Second edition.   6d.

*Devotions for the Souls in Purgatory.   Second edition.   8d.
                    * Or in one vol.,
Visits and Devotions.   Neat cloth, 3s.

WORKS BY FATHER ANDERDON, S.J.

Christian Æsop.   3s. 6d. and 4s.

In the Snow : Tales of Mount St. Bernard.
Sixth edition.   Cloth, 1s. 6d.

Afternoons with the Saints.   Eighth edition,
enlarged.   5s.

Catholic Crusoe.   Seventh edition.   Cloth gilt,
3s. 6d.

Confession to a Priest.   1d.

What is the Bible ? Is yours the right Book ?
New edition.   1d.

Also, edited by Father Anderdon,
What do Catholics really believe ?   2d.

Cherubini : Memorials illustrative of his Life.
With Portrait and Catalogue of his Works.   By EDWARD
BELLASIS, Barrister-at-Law.   One vol., 429 pp.   10s. 6d.

Louise Lateau of Bois d'Haine: her Life,
her Ecstasies, and her Stigmata : a Medical Study. By Dr. F. LEFEBVRE, Professor of General Pathology and Therapeutics in the Catholic University of Louvain, &c. Translated from the French. Edited by Rev. J. SPENCER NORTHCOTE, D.D. Full and complete edition. 3*s.* 6*d.*

'The name of Dr. Lefebvre is sufficient guarantee of the importance of any work coming from his pen. The reader will find much valuable information.'—*Tablet.*

'The whole case thoroughly entered into and fully considered. The Appendix contains many medical notes of interest.'—*Weekly Register.*

'A full and complete answer.'—*Catholic Times.*

Twelve New Tales. By Mrs. PARSONS.
1. Bertha's Three Fingers. 2. Take Care of Yourself. 3. Don't Go In. 4. The Story of an Arm-chair. 5. Yes and No. 6. The Red Apples under the Tree. 7. Constance and the Water Lilies. 8. The Pair of Gold Spectacles. 9. Clara's New Shawl. 10. The Little Lodgers. 11. The Pride and the Fall. 12. This Once.

3*d.* each ; in a Packet complete, 3*s.* ; or in cloth neat, 3*s.* 6*d.*

'Sound Catholic theology and a truly religious spirit breathes from every page, and it may be safely commended to schools and convents.'—*Tablet.*

'Full of sound instruction given in a pointed and amusing manner.'—*Weekly Register.*

'Very pretty, pleasantly told, attractive to little folks, and of such a nature that from each some moral good is inculcated. The tales are cheerful, sound, and sweet, and should have a large sale.'—*Catholic Times.*

'A very good collection of simple tales. The teaching is Catholic throughout.'—*Catholic Opinion.*

Marie and Paul: a Fragment. By 'Our
Little Woman.' 3*s.* 6*d.* ; gilt edges, 4*s.*

'We heartily recommend this touching little tale, especially as a present for children and for schools, feeling sure that none can rise from its perusal without being touched, both at the beauty of the tale itself and by the tone of earnest piety which runs through the whole, leaving none but holy thoughts and pleasant impressions on the minds of both old and young.'—*Tablet.*

'Well adapted to the innocent minds it is intended for. The little book would be a suitable present for a little friend.'—*Catholic Opinion.*

'A charming tale for young and old.'—*Cork Examiner.*

'To all who read it the book will suggest thoughts for which they will be the better, while its graceful and affecting, because simple, pictures of home and family life will excite emotions of which none need be ashamed.'—*Month.*

'Told effectively and touchingly, with all that tenderness and pathos in which gifted women so much excel.'—*Weekly Register.*

'A very pretty and pathetic tale.'—*Catholic World.*

'A very charming story, and may be read by both young and old.'—*Brownson's Review.*

'Presents us with some deeply-touching incidents of family love and devotion.'—*Catholic Times.*

Dame Dolores, or the Wise Nun of Eastonmere; and other Stories. By the Author of 'Tyborne,' &c. 4s.

CONTENTS: I. The Wise Nun of Eastonmere. II. Known Too Late. III. True to the End. IV. Olive's Rescue.

'We have read the volume with considerable pleasure, and we trust no small profit. The tales are decidedly clever, well worked out, and written with a flowing and cheerful pen.'—*Catholic Times.*

'The author of *Tyborne* is too well known to need any fresh recommendation to the readers of Catholic fiction. We need only say that her present will be as welcome to her many friends as any of her former works.'—*Month.*

'An attractive volume; and we know of few tales that we can more safely or more thoroughly recommend to our young readers.'—*Weekly Register.*

Maggie's Rosary, and other Tales. By the Author of 'Marian Howard.' Cloth extra, 3s.; cheap edition, 2s.

'We strongly recommend these stories. They are especially suited to little girls.'—*Tablet.*

'The very thing for a gift-book for a child; but at the same time so interesting and full of incident that it will not be contemned by children of a larger growth.'—*Weekly Register.*

'We have seldom seen tales better adapted for children's reading.'—*Catholic Times.*

'The writer possesses in an eminent degree the art of making stories for children.'—*Catholic Opinion,*

'A charming little book, which we can heartily recommend.'—*Rosarian.*

Scenes and Incidents at Sea. A new Selection. 1s. 4d.

CONTENTS: I. Adventure on a Rock. II. A Heroic Act of Rescue. III. Inaccessible Islands. IV. The Shipwreck of the Czar Alexander. V. Captain James's Adventures in the North Seas. VI. Destruction of Admiral Graves's Fleet. VII. The Wreck of the Forfarshire, and Grace Darling. VIII. The Loss of the Royal George. IX. The Irish Sailor Boy. X. Gallant Conduct of a French Privateer. XI. The Harpooner. XII. The Cruise of the Agamemnon. XIII. A Nova Scotia Fog. XIV. The Mate's Story. XV. The Shipwreck of the Æneas Transport. XVI. A Scene in the Shrouds. XVII. A Skirmish off Bermuda. XVIII. Charles Wager. XIX. A Man Overboard. XX. A Loss and a Rescue. XXI. A Melancholy Adventure on the American Seas. XXII. Dolphins and Flying Fish.

History of England, for Family Use and the Upper Classes of Schools. By the Author of 'Christian Schools and Scholars.' Second edition. With Preface by the Very Rev. Dr. NORTHCOTE. 6*s.*

Tales from the Diary of a Sister of Mercy. By C. M. BRAME. New edition. Cloth extra, 4*s.*

CONTENTS : The Double Marriage. The Cross and the Crown. The Novice. The Fatal Accident. The Priest's Death. The Gambler's Wife. The Apostate. The Besetting Sin.

'Written in a chaste, simple, and touching style.'—*Tablet.*
'This book is a casket, and those who open it will find the gem within.'—*Register.*
'They are well and cleverly told, and the volume is neatly got up.'—*Month.*
'Very well told : all full of religious allusions and expressions.'—*Star.*
'Very well written, and life-like ; many very pathetic.'—*Catholic Opinion*

By the same,

Angels' Visits : a Series of Tales. With Frontispiece and Vignette. 3*s.* 6*d.*

'The tone of the book is excellent, and it will certainly make itself a great favourite with the young.'—*Month.*
'Beautiful collection of Angel Stories.'—*Weekly Register.*
'One of the prettiest books for children we have seen.'—*Tablet.*
'A book which excites more than ordinary praise.'—*Northern Press.*
'Touchingly written, and evidently the emanation of a refined and pious mind.'—*Church Times.*
'A charming little book, full of beautiful stories of the family of angels.'—*Church Opinion.*

ST. JOSEPH'S THEOLOGICAL LIBRARY.
Edited by Fathers of the Society of Jesus.

Vol. I.

On some Popular Errors concerning Politics and Religion. By the Right Honourable Lord ROBERT MONTAGU, M.P. 6*s.*

CONTENTS : Introduction. I. The Basis of Political Science. II. Religion. III. The Church. IV. Religious Orders. V. Christian Law. VI. The Mass. VII. The Principles of 1789. VIII. Liberty. IX. Fraternity. X. Equality. XI. Nationality, Non-intervention, and the Accomplished Fact. XII. Capital Punishment. XIII. Liberal Catholics.

XIV. Civil Marriage.   XV. Secularisation of Education.
XVI. Conclusion.   Additional Notes.

This book has been taken from the 'Risposte popolari alle obiezioni piu diffuse contro la Religione; opera del P. Secondo Franco.   Torino, 1868.'   It is not a translation of that excellent Italian work, for much has been ómitted, and even the forms of expression have not been retained ; nor yet is it an abstract, for other matter has been added throughout.   The aim of the editor has been merely to follow out the intention of P. Franco, and adapt his thoughts to the circumstances and mind of England.

Considerations for a Three Days' Preparation for Communion.   Taken chiefly from the French of SAINT JURE, S.J.   By CECILIE MARY CADDELL.   8d.

' In every respect a most excellent manual.'—*Catholic Times.*
' A simple and easy method for a devout preparation for that solemn duty.'—*Weekly Register.*
' A beautiful compilation carefully prepared.'—*Universe.*

The Spiritual Conflict and Conquest.   By Dom J. CASTANIZA, O.S.B.   Edited, with Preface and Notes, by Canon VAUGHAN, English Monk of the Order of St. Benedict.   Second edition.   Reprinted from the old English Translation of 1652.   With fine Original Frontispiece reproduced in Autotype.   8s. 6d.

The Letter-Books of Sir Amias Poulet, Keeper of Mary Queen of Scots.   Edited by JOHN MORRIS, Priest of the Society of Jesus.   Demy 8vo, 10s. 6d.

Sir Amias Poulet had charge of the Queen of Scots from April 1585 to the time of her death, February 8, 1587. His correspondence with Lord-Treasurer Burghley and Sir Francis Walsingham enters into the details of her life in captivity at Tutbury, Chartley, and Fotheringay.   Many of the letters now published are entirely unknown, being printed from a recently-discovered manuscript.   The others have been taken from the originals at the Public Record Office and the British Museum.   The letters are strung together by a running commentary, in the course of which several of Mr. Froude's statements are examined, and the question of Mary's complicity in the plot against Elizabeth's life is discussed.

Sœur Eugenic: the Life and Letters of a

Sister of Charity. By the Author of 'A Sketch of the Life of St. Paula.' Second edition, enlarged. On toned paper, cloth gilt, 4s. 6d.; plain paper, cloth plain, 3s.

'It is impossible to read it without bearing away in one's heart some of the "odour of sweetness" which breathes forth from almost every page.'—*Tablet.*

'The most charming piece of religious biography that has appeared since the *Récits d'une Sœur.'*—*Catholic Opinion.*

'We have seldom read a more touching tale of youthful holiness.'—*Weekly Register.*

'The picture of a life of hidden piety and grace, and of active charity, which it presents is extremely beautiful.'—*Nation.*

'We strongly recommend this devout and interesting life to the careful perusal of all our readers.'—*Westminster Gazette.*

Count de Montalembert's Letters to a School-

fellow, 1827-1830. Qualis ab incepto. Translated from the French by C. F. AUDLEY. With Portrait. 5s.

'Simple, easy, and unaffected in a degree, these letters form a really charming volume. The observations are simply wonderful, considering that when he wrote them he was only seventeen or eighteen years of age.'—*Weekly Register.*

'A new treasure is now presented for the first time in an English casket—the letters he wrote when a schoolboy. The loftiness of the aspirations they breathe is supported by the intellectual power of which they give evidence.'—*Cork Examiner.*

'Reveal in the future ecclesiastical champion and historian a depth of feeling and insight into forthcoming events hardly to be expected from a mere schoolboy.'—*Building News.*

'Display vigour of thought and real intellectual power.'—*Church Herald.*

Ecclesiastical Antiquities of London and its

Suburbs. By ALEXANDER WOOD, M.A. Oxon., of the Somerset Archæological Society. 5s.

'O, who the ruine sees, whom wonder doth not fill
With our great fathers' pompe, devotion, and their skill?'

'Will prove a most useful manual to many of our readers. Stores of Catholic memories still hang about the streets of this great metropolis. For the ancient and religious associations of such places the Catholic reader can want no better cicerone than Mr. Wood.'—*Weekly Register.*

'We have indeed to thank Mr. Wood for this excellent little book.'—*Catholic Opinion.*

'Very seldom have we read a book devoted entirely to the metropolis with such pleasure.'—*Liverpool Catholic Times.*

'A very pleasing and readable book.'—*Builder.*

'Gives a plain, sensible, but learned and interesting account of the chief church antiquities of London and its suburbs. It is written by a very able and competent author—one who thoroughly appreciates his subject, and who treats it with the discrimination of a critic and the sound common sense of a practised writer.'—*Church Herald.*

LIBRARY OF RELIGIOUS BIOGRAPHY.

Edited by EDWARD HEALY THOMPSON.

Vol. I.

The Life of St. Aloysius Gonzaga, S.J.

Second edition.   5s.

'Contains numberless traces of a thoughtful and tender devotion to the Saint. It shows a loving penetration into his spirit, and an appreciation of the secret motives of his action, which can only be the result of a deeply affectionate study of his life and character.'—*Month.*

Vol. II.

The Life of Marie Eustelle Harpain; or

the Angel of the Eucharist.   Second edition.   5s.

'Possesses a special value and interest apart from its extraordinay natural and supernatural beauty, from the fact that to her example and to the effect of her writings is attributed in great measure the wonderful revival of devotion to the Blessed Sacrament in France, and consequently throughout Western Christendom.'—*Dublin Review.*

'A more complete instance of that life of purity and close union with God in the world of which we have just been speaking is to be found in the history of Marie Eustelle Harpain, the sempstress of Saint-Pallais. The writer of the present volume has had the advantage of very copious materials in the French works on which his own work is founded: and Mr. Thompson has discharged his office as editor with his usual diligence and accuracy.'—*Month.*

Vol. III.

The Life of St. Stanislas Kostka.   5s.

'We strongly recommend this biography to our readers.'—*Tablet.*

'There has been no adequate biography of St. Stanislas. In rectifying this want Mr. Thompson has earned a title to the gratitude of English-speaking Catholics. The engaging Saint of Poland will now be better known among us, and we need not fear that, better known, he will not be better loved.'—*Weekly Register.*

Vol. IV.

The Life of the Baron de Renty; or Per-

fection in the World exemplified.   6s.

'An excellent book. The style is throughout perfectly fresh and buoyant.'—*Dublin Review.*

'This beautiful work is a compilation, not of biographical incidents, but of holy thoughts and spiritual aspirations, which we may feed on and make our own.'—*Tablet.*

'Gives full particulars of his marvellous virtue in an agreeable form.'—*Catholic Times.*

'A good book for our Catholic young men, teaching how they can sanctify the secular state.'—*Catholic Opinion.*

'Edifying and instructive, a beacon and guide to those whose walks are in the ways of the world, who toil and strive to win Christian perfection.'—*Ulster Examiner.*

Vol. V.

The Life of the Venerable Anna Maria

Taigi, the Roman Matron (1769-1837). Third edition. With Portrait. 6s.

This Biography has been written after a careful collation of previous Lives of the Servant of God with each other, and with the *Analecta Juris Pontificii*, which contain large extracts from the Processes. Various prophecies attributed to her and other holy persons have been collected in an Appendix.

'Of all the series of deeply-interesting biographies which the untiring zeal and piety of Mr. Healy Thompson has given of late years to English Catholics, none, we think, is to be compared in interest with the one before us, both from the absorbing nature of the life itself and the spiritual lessons it conveys.'—*Tablet.*

'A complete biography of the Venerable Matron in the composition of which the greatest care has been taken and the best authorities consulted. We can safely recommend the volume for the discrimination with which it has been written, and for the careful labour and completeness by which it has been distinguished.'—*Catholic Opinion.*

'We recommend this excellent and carefully-compiled biography to all our readers. The evident care exercised by the editor in collating the various lives of Anna Maria gives great value to the volume, and we hope it will meet with the support it so justly merits.'—*Westminster Gazette.*

'We thank Mr. Healy Thompson for this volume. The direct purpose of his biographies is always spiritual edification.'—*Dublin Review.*

'Contains much that is capable of nourishing pious sentiments.'—*Nation.*

'Has evidently been a labour of love.'—*Month.*

The Hidden Life of Jesus: a Lesson and

Model to Christians. Translated from the French of BOUDON, by EDWARD HEALY THOMPSON, M.A. Cloth, 3s.

'This profound and valuable work has been very carefully and ably translated by Mr. Thompson.'—*Register.*

'The more we have of such works as the *Hidden Life of Jesus* the better.'—*Westminster Gazette.*

'A book of searching power.'—*Church Review.*

'We have often regretted that this writer's works are not better known.'—*Universe.*

'We earnestly recommend its study and practice to all readers.'—*Tablet.*

'We have to thank Mr. Thompson for this translation of a valuable work which has long been popular in France.'—*Dublin Review.*

'A good translation.'—*Month.*

Also, by the same Author and Translator,

Devotion to the Nine Choirs of Holy Angels,
and especially to the Angel Guardians.   3s.

'We congratulate Mr. Thompson on the way in which he has accomplished his task, and we earnestly hope that an increased devotion to the Holy Angels may be the reward of his labour of love.'—*Tablet.*

'A beautiful translation.'—*Month.*

'The translation is extremely well done.'—*Weekly Register.*

New Meditations for each Day in the Year,
on the Life of our Lord Jesus Christ. By a Father of the Society of Jesus.   With the imprimatur of the Cardinal Archbishop of Westminster.   New and improved edition. Two vols.   Cloth, 9s.; also in calf, 16s.; morocco, 17s.

'We can heartily recommend this book for its style and substance: it bears with it several strong recommendations. . . . It is solid and practical.' —*Westminster Gazette.*

'A work of great practical utility, and we give it our earnest recommendation.'—*Weekly Register.*

The Day Sanctified; being Meditations and
Spiritual Readings for Daily Use. Selected from the Works of Saints and approved Writers of the Catholic Church. Fcp. cloth, 3s. 6d.; red edges, 4s.

'Of the many volumes of meditations on sacred subjects which have appeared in the last few years, none has seemed to us so well adapted to its object as the one before us.'—*Tablet.*

Deserves to be specially mentioned.'—*Month.*

'Admirable in every sense.'—*Church Times.*

'Many of the meditations are of great beauty. . . . They form, in fact, excellent little sermons, and we have no doubt will be largely used as such.' —*Literary Churchman.*

Reflections   and   Prayers   for   Holy Com-
munion. Translated from the French. With Preface by the CARDINAL ARCHBISHOP OF WESTMINSTER. Fcp. 8vo, cloth, 4s. 6d.; bound, red edges, 5s.; calf, 9s.; morocco, 10s.

'The Archbishop has marked his approval of the work by writing a preface for it, and describes it as "a valuable addition to our books of devotion."'—*Register.*

'A book rich with the choicest and most profound Catholic devotions.'— *Church Review.*

Lallemant's Doctrine of the Spiritual Life.
Edited by the late Father FABER. New edition. Cloth, 4*s.* 6*d.*

'This excellent work has a twofold value, being both a biography and a volume of meditations. It contains an elaborate analysis of the wants, dangers, trials, and aspirations of the inner man, and supplies to the thoughtful and devout reader the most valuable instructions for the attainment of heavenly wisdom, grace, and strength.'—*Catholic Times.*

'A treatise of the very highest value.'—*Month.*

'The treatise is preceded by a short account of the writer's life, and has had the wonderful advantage of being edited by the late Father Faber.'—*Weekly Register.*

The Rivers of Damascus and Jordan : a
Causerie. By a Tertiary of the Order of St. Dominic. 4*s.*

'Good solid reading.'—*Month.*

'Well done and in a truly charitable spirit.'—*Catholic Opinion.*

'It treats the subject in so novel and forcible a light that we are fascinated in spite of ourselves, and irresistibly led on to follow its arguments and rejoice at its conclusions.'-- *Tablet.*

Legends of our Lady and the Saints ; or
our Children's Book of Stories in Verse. Written for the Recitations of the Pupils of the Schools of the Holy Child Jesus, St. Leonard's-on-Sea. 2*s.* 6*d.*

'It is a beautiful religious idea that is realised in the *Legends of our Lady and the Saints.* The book forms a charming present for pious children.'—*Tablet.*

'The "Legends" are so beautiful that they ought to be read by all lovers of poetry.'—*Bookseller.*

'Graceful poems.'—*Month.*

The New Testament Narrative, in the Words
of the Sacred Writers. With Notes, Chronological Tables, and Maps. Cloth, 2*s.*

'The compilers deserve great praise for the manner in which they have performed their task. We commend this little volume as well and carefully printed, and as furnishing its readers, moreover, with a great amount of useful information in the tables inserted at the end.'—*Month.*

'It is at once clear, complete, and beautiful.'—*Catholic Opinion.*

QUARTERLY SERIES.

Conducted by the Managers of the 'Month.'

———•———

VOLUMES PUBLISHED.

The Life and Letters of St. Francis Xavier.
By the Rev. H. J. COLERIDGE. Sec. edit. Two vols. 18s.

'We cordially thank Father Coleridge for a most valuable biography. . . . He has spared no pains to insure our having in good classical English a translation of all the letters which are extant. . . . A complete priest's manual might be compiled from them, entering as they do into all the details of a missioner's public and private life. . . . We trust we have stimulated our readers to examine them for themselves, and we are satisfied that they will return again and again to them as to a never-exhausted source of interest and edification.'—*Tablet.*

'A noble addition to our literature. . . . We offer our warmest thanks to Father Coleridge for this most valuable work. The letters, we need hardly say, will be found of great spiritual use, especially for missionaries and priests.'—*Dublin Review.*

'One of the most fascinating books we have met with for a long time.'—*Catholic Opinion.*

'Would that we had many more lives of saints like this! Father Coleridge has done great service to this branch of Catholic literature, not simply by writing a charming book, but especially by setting others an example of how a saint's life should be written.'—*Westminster Gazette.*

'This valuable book is destined, we feel assured, to take a high place among what we may term our English Catholic classics. . . . The great charm lies in the letters, for in them we have, in a far more forcible manner than any biographer could give them, the feelings, experiences, and aspirations of St. Francis Xavier as pictured by his own pen.'—*Catholic Times.*

'Father Coleridge does his own part admirably, and we shall not be surprised to find his book soon take its place as the standard Life of the saintly and illustrious Francis.'—*Nation.*

'Not only an interesting but a scholarly sketch of a life remarkable alike in itself and in its attendant circumstances. We hope the author will continue to labour in a department of literature for which he has here shown his aptitude. To find a saint's life which is at once moderate, historical, and appreciative is not a common thing.'—*Saturday Review.*

'Should be studied by all missionaries, and is worthy of a place in every Christian library.'—*Church Herald.*

The Life of St. Jane Frances Fremyot de

Chantal. By EMILY BOWLES. With Preface by the Rev. H. J. COLERIDGE. Second edition. 5*s.* 6*d.*

'We venture to promise great pleasure and profit to the reader of this charming biography. It gives a complete and faithful portrait of one of the most attractive saints of the generation which followed the completion of the Council of Trent.'—*Month.*

'Sketched in a life-like manner, worthy of her well-earned reputation as a Catholic writer.'—*Weekly Register.*

'We have read it on and on with the fascination of a novel, and yet it is the life of a saint, described with a rare delicacy of touch and feeling such as is seldom met with.'—*Tablet.*

'A very readable and interesting compilation. . . . The author has done her work faithfully and conscientiously.'—*Athenæum.*

'Full of incident, and told in a style so graceful and felicitous that it wins upon the reader with every page.'—*Nation.*

'Miss Bowles has done her work in a manner which we cannot better commend than by expressing a desire that she may find many imitators. She has endued her materials with life, and clothed them with a language and a style of which we do not know what to admire most—the purity, the grace, the refinement, or the elegance. If our readers wish to know the value and the beauty of this book, they can do no better than get it and read it.'—*Westminster Gazette.*

'One of the most charming and delightfu volumes which has issued from the press for many years. Miss Bowles has accomplished her task faithfully and happily, with simple grace and unpretentious language, and a winning manner which, independently of her subject, irresistibly carries us along.'—*Ulster Examiner.*

The History of the Sacred Passion. From

the Spanish of Father LUIS DE LA PALMA, of the Society of Jesus. The Translation revised and edited by the Rev. H. J. COLERIDGE. Third edition. 7*s.* 6*d.*

'A work long held in great and just repute in Spain. It opens a mine of wealth to one's soul. Though there are many works on the Passion in English, probably none will be found so generally useful both for spiritual reading and meditation. We desire to see it widely circulated.'—*Tablet.*

'A sterling work of the utmost value. proceeding from the pen of a great theologian, whose piety was as simple and tender as his learning and culture were profound and exquisite. It is a rich storehouse for contemplation on the great mystery of our Redemption, and one of those books which every Catholic ought to read for himself.'—*Weekly Register.*

'The most wonderful work upon the Passion that we have ever read. To us the charm lies in this, that it is entirely theological. It is made use of largely by those who give the Exercises of St. Ignatius; it is, as it were, the flesh upon the skeleton of the Exercises. Never has the Passion been meditated upon so before. . . . If any one wishes to understand the Passion of our Lord in its fulness, let him procure this book.'—*Dublin Review.*

'We have not read a more thoughtful work on our Blessed Lord's Passion.

It is a complete storehouse of matter for meditation, and for sermons on that divine mystery.'—*Catholic Opinion.*

'The book is—speaking comparatively of human offerings—a magnificent offering to the Crucified, and to those who wish to make a real study of the Cross will be a most precious guide.'—*Church Review.*

Ierne of Armorica : a Tale of the Time of Chlovis. By J. C. BATEMAN. 6s. 6d.

'We know of few tales of the kind that can be ranked higher than the beautiful story before us. The author has hit on the golden mean between an over-display of antiquarianism and an indolent transfer of modern modes of action and thought to a distant time. The descriptions are masterly, the characters distinct, the interest unflagging. We may add that the period is one of those which may be said to be comparatively unworked.'—*Month.*

'A volume of very great interest and very great utility. As a story it is sure to give much delight, while, as a story founded on historical fact, it will benefit all by its very able reproduction of very momentous scenes. . . . The book is excellent. If we are to have a literature of fiction at all, we hope it will include many like volumes.'—*Dublin Review.*

'Although a work of fiction, it is historically correct, and the author portrays with great skill the manners and customs of the times of which he professes to give a description. In reading this charming tale we seem to be taken by the hand by the writer, and made to assist at the scenes which he describes.'— *Tablet.*

'The author of this most interesting tale has hit the happy medium between a display of antiquarian knowledge and a mere reproduction in distant ages of commonplace modern habits of thought. The descriptions are excellent, the characters well drawn, and the subject itself is very attractive, besides having the advantage of not having been written threadbare.'—*Westminster Gazette.*

'The tale is excessively interesting, the language appropriate to the time and rank of the characters, the style flowing and easy, and the narrative leads one on and on until it becomes a very difficult matter to lay the book down until it is finished. . . . It is a valuable addition to Catholic fictional literature.'—*Catholic Times.*

'A very pretty historico-ecclesiastical novel of the times of Chlovis. It is full of incident, and is very pleasant reading.'—*Literary Churchman.*

The Life of Dona Luisa de Carvajal. By Lady GEORGIANA FULLERTON. 6s. (See p. 6.)

The Life of the Blessed John Berchmans. By the Rev. FRANCIS GOLDIE, S.J. 6s.

'A complete and life-like picture, and we are glad to be able to congratulate Father Goldie on his success.'—*Tablet.*

'Drawn up with a vigour and freedom which show great power of biographical writing.'—*Dublin Review.*

'One of the most interesting of all.'—*Weekly Register.*

'Unhesitatingly we say that it is the very best Life of Blessed John

Berchmans, and as such it will take rank with religious biographies of the highest merit.'—*Catholic Times.*

'Is of great literary merit, the style being marked by elegance and a complete absence of redundancy.'—*Cork Examiner.*

'This delightful and edifying volume is of the deepest interest. The perusal will afford both pleasure and profit.'—*Church Herald.*

The Life of the Blessed Peter Favre, of the
Society of Jesus, First Companion of St. Ignatius Loyola. From the Italian of Father GIUSEPPE BOERO, of the same Society. With Preface by the Rev. H. J. COLERIDGE. 6s. 6d.

This Life has been written on the occasion of the beatification of the Ven. Peter Favre, and contains the *Memoriale* or record of his private thoughts and meditations, written by himself.

'At once a book of spiritual reading, and also an interesting historical narrative. The *Memoriale, or Spiritual Diary*, is here translated at full length, and is the most precious portion of one of the most valuable biographies we know.'—*Tablet.*

'A perfect picture drawn from the life, admirably and succinctly told. The *Memoriale* will be found one of the most admirable epitomes of sound devotional reading.'—*Weekly Register.*

'The *Memoriale* is hardly excelled in interest by anything of the kind now extant.'—*Catholic Times.*

'Full of interest, instruction, and example.'—*Cork Examiner.*

'One of the most interesting to the general reader of the entire series up to this time.'—*Nation.*

'This wonderful diary, the *Memoriale*, has never been published before, and we are much mistaken if it does not become a cherished possession to thoughtful Catholics.'—*Month.*

The Dialogues of St. Gregory the Great.
An old English version. Edited, with Preface, by the Rev. H. J. COLERIDGE. 6s.

'The Catholic world must feel grateful to Father Coleridge for this excellent and compendious edition. The subjects treated of possess at this moment a special interest. . . . The Preface by Father Coleridge is interesting and well written, and we cordially recommend the book to the perusal of all.'—*Tablet.*

'This is a most interesting book. . . . Father Coleridge gives a very useful preface summarising the contents.'—*Weekly Register.*

'We have seldom taken up a book in which we have become at once so deeply interested. It will suit any one; it will teach all; it will confirm any who require that process; and it will last and be read when other works are quite forgotten.'—*Catholic Times.*

'Edited and published with the utmost care and the most perfect literary taste, this volume adds one more gem to the treasury of English Catholic literature.'—*New York Catholic World.*

The Life of Sister Anne Catherine Emme-rich. Edited, with Preface, by the Rev. H. J. COLERIDGE. 5*s.*

St. Winefride; or Holywell and its Pil-grims. By the Author of 'Tyborne.' Third edition. 1*s.*

Summer Talks about Lourdes. By Miss CADDELL. Cloth, 1*s.* 6*d.*

Blessed Margaret Mary Alacoque: a brief and popular Account of her Life; to which are added Selections from some of her Sayings, and the Decree of her Beatification. By the Rev. CHARLES B. GARSIDE, M.A. 1*s.*

A Comparison between the History of the Church and the Prophecies of the Apocalypse. Translated from the German by EDWIN DE LISLE. 2*s.*

CATHOLIC-TRUTH TRACTS.

NEW ISSUES.

Manchester Dialogues. First Series. By the Rev. Fr. HARPER, S.J.

No. I. The Pilgrimage.
 II. Are Miracles going on still?
 III. Popish Miracles tested by the Bible.
 IV. Popish Miracles.
 V. Liquefaction of the Blood of St. Januarius.
 VI. 'Bleeding Nuns' and 'Winking Madonnas.'
 VII. Are Miracles physically possible?
 VIII. Are Miracles morally possible?

Price of each 3*s.* per 100, 25 for 1*s.*; also 25 of the above assorted for 1*s.* Also the whole Series complete in neat Wrapper, 6*d.*

Specimen Packet of General Series, containing 100 assorted, 1*s.* 6*d.*

Check Out More Titles From HardPress Classics Series In this collection we are offering thousands of classic and hard to find books. This series spans a vast array of subjects — so you are bound to find something of interest to enjoy reading and learning about.

Subjects:
Architecture
Art
Biography & Autobiography
Body, Mind &Spirit
Children & Young Adult
Dramas
Education
Fiction
History
Language Arts & Disciplines
Law
Literary Collections
Music
Poetry
Psychology
Science
…and many more.

Visit us at www.hardpress.net

Im The Story
personalised classic books

JANE
IN
WONDERLAND

LEWIS
CARROLL

"Beautiful gift, lovely finish.
My Niece loves it, so precious"

Helen R Brunfeldon

⭐⭐⭐⭐⭐

UNIQUE
GIFT

FOR KIDS, PARTNERS
AND FRIENDS

Timeless books such as:

Kids

Alice in Wonderland · The Jungle Book · The Wonderful Wizard of Oz
Peter and Wendy · Robin Hood · The Prince and The Pauper
The Railway Children · Treasure Island · A Christmas Carol

Adults

Romeo and Juliet · Dracula

Highly Customizable **Change** Books Title **Replace** Characters Names with yours **Upload** Photo (for inside page) **Add** Inscriptions

Visit
Im The Story .com
and order yours today!

CPSIA information can be obtained
at www.ICGtesting.com
Printed in the USA
BVHW081616120819

555665BV00014B/1186/P